CHOPIN'S LETTERS

CHOPIN'S LETTERS

Collected by HENRYK OPIEŃSKI
Translated from the original Polish and French
with a Preface and Editorial notes by
E. L. VOYNICH

VIENNA HOUSE
New York

Originally published by Alfred A. Knopf,
New York, 1931, and reprinted by arrangement
with the original publishers

First VIENNA HOUSE edition published 1971

International Standard Book Number:
0-8443-0020-9

Library of Congress Catalogue Card Number: 79-163798

Manufactured in the United States of America

CHOPIN'S LETTERS

PREFACE

These letters, which I believe have not before appeared in English as a complete collection, are of great interest from several points of view.

They throw light on the genesis of some of Chopin's compositions; on his character, personality and mental habits; on his teachers, colleagues and pupils; on the environment which moulded his childhood, and the inhibitions which throughout life hampered him, both as a musician and as a man. We see here the conflicting influences of Bach and of Italian opera; of Polish folk-song and of pianistic virtuosity; his tragic devotion to George Sand and his utter inability to understand her; the crystalline clarity of his artistic instinct, and the imperfect thinking which enabled him, after living for years among French intellectuals, to retain almost unmodified the provincial prejudices of his youth.

We see his delightful relations with the family at home; his affectionate loyalty to old friends, and perpetual unconscious exploitation of them; his irritable temper and warm heart; his Rabelaisian jokes and essential conventionality; his protecting tenderness to Solange Clésinger; his naïve contempt for Jews and English, for publishers, Portuguese and similar inferior creatures; his charming modesty and regal pride; and his acceptance, at their own valuation, of the crowd of rich amateurs and brainless royalties, in whose palaces his genius permitted to him the status, now of a tame prodigy, now of a " poor relation."

Editing has proved no easy task. I feel that these letters would lose much of their value and interest for English-speaking readers without some knowledge of the persons and events constantly referred to in them. There are so many of these that even had it been possible to trace them all, any adequate mention would have overweighted the book with footnotes. Where I have used Dr. Opieński's admirable notes or quoted from other authors, I have appended an acknowledgment: Op. = Opieński; Karł. = Karłowicz; Hoes. = Hoesick; Leicht. = Leichtentritt. Where no such acknowledgment is made, the note is my own.

In the case of a few very famous or widely known names, as: George Sand, Mickiewicz, Humboldt, Arago, Jenny Lind, it has appeared to me sufficient to put just the dates of birth and death, without any biographical details.

It has sometimes been hard to decide which reference is relevant and illuminating, and which superfluous. How much space should be allotted, for example, to the frequently mentioned public affairs of Poland? It depends on the place they held in Chopin's affections; and just what that place was I do not know, and doubt whether he did. His love for his native land: for its speech, its proverbs, its humour, its songs, its folkways, is beyond question; nor can any serious reader doubt the sincerity of his sympathy with its desperate struggle against alien oppression. Yet that sympathy had strange bedfellows. That he took no part in the struggle need not surprise us; the wind bloweth where it listeth, and a creative artist, however keen his sympathies, must live under the compulsion of his art. But it is a little startling to find a Polish patriot not merely keeping but proudly treasuring a diamond ring given him by the Tzar, and, even after 1831, accepting favours from the Grand Duke Constantine.

Scarcely less puzzling is the fragment of a diary (pp. 148–50) said, on the authority of the late Count Stanislaw Tarnowski, a Polish university professor who published it in 1871, to have been written in Stuttgart in 1831, on the receipt of the news that Warsaw had been taken and sacked by Russian troops. What Chopin must have suffered while waiting to learn the fate of his relatives and friends, we can guess from the music composed during those terrible days; it is easy to believe that his imagination was haunted, as well it might be, by nightmare images of his mother murdered and his young sisters struggling in the grasp of drunken soldiers; but that such a diary as this, and such music, could come from the same hand, in the same week, is surely somewhat strange.

As others also seem to have been puzzled by this riddle, I asked Dr. Opieński his opinion as to the authenticity and accuracy of the fragment, and quote from his prompt and courteous reply. Count Tarnowski had the MS. (the original? or a copy?) from Chopin's friend, Princess Marcellina Czartoryska. The original was later accidentally destroyed; but Dr. Opieński assures me that " no Polish biographer has ever doubted " the Tarnowski version; and mentions, as a psychological corroboration which should set my doubts at rest, that very coincidence with the music which first aroused them.

In deference to his conviction, I include the fragment. Since the diary no longer exists and all the persons connected with it are dead, each reader must decide for himself whether he can reconcile this kind of thing, either with the raging passion of the D minor Prelude and C minor Etude or with the stifled agony of the E minor Prelude. The human mind is a queer jumble, and it is possible that Chopin really did write like that. But, remembering how easily — and how innocently — platitudes and appropriate sentiments find their way into the defenceless mouths of the dead; how much apocryphal stuff was circulated about Chopin even during his life, how short a time he had been underground when Turgeniev failed to discover a fashionable watering-place without at least one titled lady " in whose arms this composer breathed his last "; it seems only fair to give him the benefit of the doubt.

Another difficulty was the problem of attributions. Where Chopin seems to have really used a Polish folk-tune, I have tried to give the actual tune in the best version I could find. Where responsible authors appear to believe that a composition may have been inspired by a poem, I have given a reference to the poem; but it seems to me that fanciful and probably groundless

[1] See Huneker, p. 31; also Leichtentritt.

interpretations of or names for particular Mazurkas or Preludes are best ignored.

The case of the four " Ballades " is a special one. Whether there is any authentic evidence of their supposed connection with Mickiewicz's wonderful ballads, I do not know. But that Chopin and Mickiewicz were personal friends; that the composer was much under the poet's influence; that he knew and was deeply impressed by the ballads, we know; and I have therefore felt justified in devoting a little space to them.

According to M. Cortot, the G minor Ballade is based on the epic poem: " Konrad Wallenrod " ; and the other three on ballads, written by Mickiewicz on the legends which he had learned in Lithuania from the local peasantry; the F major on that called " Świteź " ; the A flat major on " Świtezianka " ; and the F minor on " Trzech Budrysów."

" Konrad Wallenrod" is a story of pagan Lithuania. The Knights of the Teutonic Order have invaded the country, enslaved the inhabitants and forcibly converted them to Christianity. A Lithuanian, carried off by them in childhood from the house of his murdered parents, baptized and brought up as a German, conceives a scheme of vengeance for the wrongs of his people. He feigns German sympathies and Christian beliefs, distinguishes himself in the Spanish war against the Moors, returns to Lithuania as a devout and militant Christian, is elected Magister of the Order and then deliberately involves it in ruin and disgrace. The only part of the poem which is in ballad form is the magnificent " Alpuhara": a tale of a Moorish chieftain, who issues from his besieged city to tender his submission to the Spaniards, declares himself converted to Christianity, insists on embracing the leaders of the Spanish army, and only then shows his face and announces that he has brought them a present of the plague: — " Watch me, and see how you are going to die."

The next two ballads refer to the haunted Świteź lake, on which no one might launch a boat, for fear of the anger of the water-lilies. That called by the name of the lake tells how the Russians of Novgorod attacked a Lithuanian castle whose owner had left his young daughter in charge during his absence. The girl, unable to resist the invaders, prayed to her gods to save her and her fellow maidens from dishonour by striking them dead. The water engulfed the city, and the maidens became water-lilies. Whoever attempts to interfere with the solitude of the lake is stricken with disease and dies.

" Świtezianka (The Świteź Woman) " is an Undine story. A hunter meets a maiden in the wood; she accepts his love, exacting a promise of faithfulness. Then she leaves him and he walks homewards beside the lake. Seeing, as he supposes, another girl at the water's edge, the fickle lover makes his way to her through the marsh. It is the same maiden, the nymph of the lake. She reproaches him bitterly for his unfaithfulness, drags him down and drowns him. She can be seen dancing in the water, while his miserable ghost wails under the larch-trees of the shore.

" Trzech Budrysów " is in a lighter vein. The three sons of Budrys, a patriarch of pagan Lithuania, are sent out by their father to seek their fortunes. He tells them that they will find war and loot in three directions: One is to follow the chieftain who is attacking the Russians, and to bring back sables and cloth of silver; one is to join the expedition against the German Knights of the Cross, from whom he can take amber and Christian ecclesiastical vestments; and one is to ride to Poland and bring back a Polish wife, since the wealth of that country consists of the beauty of its women. All three young men go, and each in turn comes back bringing a Polish bride.

Even the comparatively simple work of translation has had its share of difficulty. Some letters are written in a mixture of Polish and French, with the idioms of the two languages tangled together; others, originally French, have been at some time translated into Polish, and now from Polish into English; some of the early ones are written in a schoolboy jargon of French, German, Latin, and in one case Italian phrases transliterated into Polish; and so on. Also, they are full of proverbs and local allusions, and in some cases contain words not to be found in any Polish dictionary which I have been able to consult. Notwithstanding his hearty scorn for foreigners who misspell Polish names, Chopin seems to have been totally indifferent to the spelling of any non-Polish name. His usual method, apparently, was to make a rough guess at the sound of it, and then put that guess, approximately, into a Polish transliteration. Thus: Daily News *becomes* Deliniuz; *etc. — But he did not trouble himself to remember, even from day to day, just how he had done this; so sometimes in the same letter we get Soliva and Soliwa, Hasslinger and Haslinger, Mendelson, Mendelssohn, Mendelsson, etc.*

I have done my best to thread my way through this jungle, preserving the erratic spelling and occasionally inserting either [sic] *or the correct spelling in square brackets, to help the reader out. This last has not always been easy to find. For example, when a French name, in transliteration, comes out with a final o, the real termination may be au, aux, ault, aulx, aud, auld, aut, etc.*

Another puzzle has been what to do with Polish place-names. The partition of the country for generations between three foreign powers, all of which tried to destroy the national speech, one by Russifying, the other two by Germanizing, has resulted in such confusion that no satisfactory method can be found. After consultation with Mr. Knopf's editor I have reluctantly adopted the somewhat clumsy method of giving the two capital names, Warsaw and Cracow, in English; names of secondary cities in Polish with an English translation in square brackets, as: Wrocław [Breslau] Poznań [Posen]; and those of smaller places in Polish alone.

For this, as for all other defects in the performing of a delightful but not very easy task, I must beg the reader's indulgence.

E. L. VOYNICH
New York; June 1931.

CHOPIN'S LETTERS

CHOPIN'S LETTERS

1.

To his father, on his name-day. [In verse]

When the world declares the festivity of your name-day,
my Papa, it brings joy to me also, with these wishes;
that you may live happily, may not know grievous cares,
that God may always favour you with the fate you desire,
these wishes I express for your sake.

F. CHOPIN
6 December 1816.

2.

To his mother, on her name-day. [In verse]

I congratulate you, Mummy, on your name-day!
May the heavens fulfil what I feel in my heart:
That you should always be well and happy, and
have the longest and most satisfactory life.

F. CHOPIN
16 June 1817.

3.

To his father, on his name-day. [In verse]

How great a joy I feel in my heart.
That a day so pleasant, so dear and glorious
Begins, a day that I greet with the wish

That long years may pass in happiness,
In health and vigour, peacefully, successfully.
May the gifts of heaven fall richly upon you.

F. Chopin
6 December 1817.

4.

To his father on his name-day.

Dear Papa!

I could express my feelings more easily if they could be put into notes of music, but as the very best concert would not cover my affection for you, dear Daddy, I must use the simple words of my heart, to lay before you my utmost gratitude and filial affection.

F. Chopin

6 December 1818.

5.

To Eustachy Marylski in Pecice.
[*Warsaw, September 1823.*]

Dear Marylski!

I went myself to Pan Zubelewicz to find out when the lectures for beginners, not the examinations, begin; he told me that they begin either the 16th or the 17th of this month, the Commission not having yet decided whether the public session of the Academy shall be the 15th or the 16th. He also told me that the lectures are to be in the morning and the examinations in the afternoon, and that after the 15th he will not put anyone down. Excuse my writing so badly, I am in a hurry. Please tell Weltz what I have told you, and remember me kindly to him and Tytus. Białobłocki came to Warsaw on Saturday; he will enter his name on Tuesday, leave on Wednesday and return for the term. Mamma and Papa send greetings to your parents and Ludwika to your sister; and I embrace you and your brothers heartily.

F. Chopin

Messrs. Kulikowski, Karwowski [Karnowski?], Wilczyński, and Krzywicki are retired, and that professor from Kalisz has got Kulikowski's place. Pan Dobronoki [?] sends you greetings. Goodbye. Don't show this letter to anyone, because everybody would say that I can't write and don't know anything about politics.

6.

To Wilhelm Kolberg.
Szafarnia, 19 August 1824.

Dear Wilus'!

Thanks for remembering me; but on the other hand I am annoyed with you, that you are such a mean and horrid etcetera and only write such a scrap to me. Were you short of paper or pens, or did you grudge the ink? Perhaps you had no time to do more than put in a scrawl? Eh, eh, that's it; you go horseback riding, enjoying yourself, and forget about me — Well, well; give me a kiss and I'll forgive you.

I'm glad you're well and jolly, because that's what is wanted in the country. I'm so glad I can write to you. I also am enjoying myself; and you're not the only one that rides, for I can stick on too. Don't ask how well; but I can, enough for the horse to go slowly wherever he prefers, while I sit fearfully on his back; like a monkey on a bear. Till now I haven't had any falls because the horse hasn't thrown me off; but — if ever he should want me to tumble off, I may do it some day.

I won't bother you with my affairs, because I know they won't interest you. The flies often alight on my lofty nose, but that's unimportant, because it's rather a custom of these importunate beasties. The gnats bite me; but that doesn't matter, because it's not on the nose. I run about the garden, and sometimes walk. I walk in the woods, and sometimes ride, not on horseback but in a carriage, or trap, or coach; but with such honour that I always sit at the back, never in front. Perhaps I've bored you already, but what can I do? If not, then write by the first post, and I will continue my epistles at once.

I end my letter therefore without compliments, but amicably. Keep well, dear Wilus', and please do write to me. We shall meet in 4 weeks. I embrace you heartily. Your sincere friend.

F. CHOPIN

My respects to your Mamma and Papa, and I embrace your brothers.

7.

To JAN BIAŁOBŁOCKI IN SOKOŁOWO.
[*Sokołowo, end of summer 1824 or 1825.*]

DEAR, BELOVED JALEK!

We start very early tomorrow. I promised to come to you yesterday, but I couldn't get to Sokołowo [1] till today. I'm very sorry that I shan't see you again on these holidays; I must just say goodbye to you on this bit of paper and give you a letter for Panna Kostancja,[2] which Ludwika [3] has sent by post, in a letter to me. I wish you the best of health, and that your leg should get quite well. Kiss your Papa for me and thank him for the decoction, to which I am much indebted. Tell him that I will never forget about it. So, dear Jasia, we have to part without any real goodbye. I kiss you heartily. Remember me, as I remember you.

F. F. CHOPIN

[1] The Białobłockis' country home near Szafarnia, where he was spending a summer holiday with the Dziewanowskis. [Op.]
[2] Kostancja Białobłocka.
[3] Chopin's sister Ludwika.

Greetings to Panna Florentina. I should like to follow you to Radomin, but I can't. I should like to wait; I can't; for Panna Ludwika [1]— oh that Panna Ludwika! — is waiting for me. I shall come back quickly, because I want to pack my things at once. Give me a kiss! You would not believe how sorry I am! — I don't want to go away. Why have I jolted all this way in a carriage to find nobody at home! But at least you will know that I did come. I came to say an affectionate goodbye to you and your Papa.

I don't myself know what I've written; I have never before been in such a situation.

8.

To the Same.
[Warsaw] Friday, 8 July 1825.

DEAR JASIA!

It's lucky that there is such a good opportunity to write to you. I have to report to you that we are all pretty well; secondly, that the examination is close upon us, just under my nose (in old Poland they used to say: " in my belt "; but as I don't wear a belt, only a big nose, you have an excellent reason why I should tell you it is under my nose). Don't expect me to write much to you; I am very busy, and the gentleman who brought the note from Panna Kostancja came this evening and leaves tomorrow. Kresner and Signora Bianchi [2] give a concert on Monday, not in the theatre, but in Elert's Hall in the German hotel. It's a concert *à la* Krogólski [3] by private subscription; Kresner gave me 12 tickets, but I sold only 3, as the price is 6 złotys.[4]

I'm sorry you are not here; I have had some very good times with Your Benevolence, gossiping, joking, singing, crying, laughing, fisticuffing, and so on.

[1] Ludwika Dziewanowska.
[2] Musicians in one of whose concerts he had taken part.
[3] A local musician.
[4] 1 złoty = about 11 cents.

In my next letter I will let you know rather more fully, by post, when we shall meet, for we hear that the examination is to be on the 26th of this month. I'm writing after dark; tomorrow I have to get up early, and tonight to sit up and sit up, sit up, still sit up, and perhaps even sit up all night.

Amice, vale! I can't tell you anything, except that I haven't yet had a letter from you from Sochaczew. If you haven't written, a bad wigging awaits you in my next letter.

I must add one thing more to this; that is: that you are to tell me whether your leg is better, and whether you arrived all right.

This letter is like a field where peas and cabbages are mixed up together. There's no logic, je sais qu'il manque logique; mais que faire, on se hâte, car on n'a pas le temps pour écrire honnêtement. Si c'est comme ça,[1] forgive me; I'll send a longer and better letter by post; now I just embrace you heartily.

F. F. CHOPIN

Żywny[2] and Pani Dekert are well; they don't know I am writing to you, or would send messages. My respects to your Papa.

9.

To the Same.

[*Warsaw, 27 November 1825.*]

MON CHER!

La lettre que vous m'avez écrite, rejoiced me, although, comme je vois, it contains sad news. Votre jambe vous fait mal; I grieve for that; not que vous êtes assez gai, as I see from the letter, ça m'a donné de la sauce,[3] and leaves me in the best of humours.

[1] I know that it lacks logic; but what can one do; one hurries because one has not the time to write properly. If that's the way, [The French phrases in this and in the following letters to Białobłocki are written with Polish spelling.]

[2] Wojciech Żywny (1756–1840), a Bohemian, Chopin's first music teacher, much beloved by him and a close friend of the family. [Op.]

[3] The letter which you have written to me . . . as I see . . . Your leg hurts you . . . that you are fairly gay . . . that has given me pep . . .

Demain nous finissons notre examination. Je ne prendrai pas de prix, car les lavements le prennent — When I come to you, I will explain this riddle — est-ce possible qu'on donne un prix à un lavement? [1] It would need a long explanation to make this clear in a letter; but one spoken word will show you all the finesse of this expression.

On Monday, as Panna Ludwika has decided, we leave here, and arrive in Szafarnia on Wednesday. Si vous voulez me voir, venez le premier, car autrement [2] my good Guardian Lady will not allow me to go to you.

Tomorrow at this hour quel bonheur quel plaisir; [3] when I go to bed, I shan't get up so early on Friday. I have new breeches with [undecipherable] well cut (though this last is not true); a new muffler on my neck — you can call it by some other name, as perhaps you don't understand that one, — a tie for je ne me souviens plus,[4] how many złotys, je le paie avec l'argent et la main de ma chère soeur Louise.[5]

Ecoutez, ecoutez, ma'mzelle Dorothée
Adolf Szydłowski [6] in the servant's part.

Ecoutez, here I begin the end of my letter, we shall soon meet; you know that I don't like to scribble much (except with 4 hands); so forgive me for stopping now. We are all well, I have had 3 letters from you; examination tomorrow; Panna Leszczyńska sends you greetings; Pan Domowicz has been in Warsaw; Żywny is still wearing the old wig; Pani Dekert shakes your hand; Barciński embraces you; I'll bring you a book for Okunie. All the household sends love to you; same to your Papa. Give your muzzle! I love you.

F. F. Chopin

[1] Tomorrow we finish our examination. I shan't take a prize, for the enemas take it. . . . Is it possible that a prize should be given to an enema? . . .

[2] If you want to see me, come first, for otherwise . . .

[3] what joy what pleasure.

[4] I don't remember.

[5] I pay it with the money and the hand of my dear sister Ludwika.

[6] Listen, listen, Miss Dorothea . . . Listen. Probably a reference to some amateur theatricals, of which the Chopins were very fond. [Op.]

Oh, I can smell Sokołowo!
A Monsieur Monsieur Jean Białobłocki à Sokołowo — par bonté.

10.

To his parents in Warsaw.
Kowałowo, Friday [*1825*].

My dearest Parents; and you my dear Sisters!

Since my health is as good as a faithful dog, and Pan Zboiński's yellow eyes are lowered [?],[1] and as we are starting for Płock, it would be funny of me if I didn't write to tell you so.

Today, then, to Płock, tomorrow to Rościszew, the day after to Kikol, two or three days in Turznia, two or three in Kozłow, a moment in Gdańsk [Danzig], and home. Perhaps somebody will say: — " He's in a hurry to get home, since he talks about it." No, not a bit; your Honours, or your Nobilities, are entirely mistaken; I wrote it only to arouse a pleasurable emotion, such as greetings usually produce. Who could be homesick? Not I at all; perhaps somebody else, but not I — All the same, there isn't any letter from Warsaw; when we get to Płock today I shall turn the whole postbag over to see if there's something for me. How are things in that new room? How are they grilling themselves for the examination? Is Tytus sighing for the country? Is Pruszak just the same? How did Pan Skarbek get on with that dinner, the 3rd one, that I was to have gone to the country for with him? I'm as inquisitive about everything as an old woman. But what can I do? If you give a dog no meat, the dog has to fast, and what else can it do except run here and there looking for food? So I'm going to Płock in the hope of meat; I suppose you didn't know that in summer the last post — Now I shall have to expect to be for a long time again without letters, so I shan't worry; it's hard to know where to catch me, but I shall write regularly at every step, and let you

[1] Phrase ungrammatical.

know what address to put. But, according to Pan Zboiński, you can write by Toruń [Thorn], Schwetz, to Kozłow, and we shall find the letter on arriving. That's a good idea; I hope it will be adopted (for Izabela).[1]

I wanted to send my bundle to you, Sisters, but I have no time to write, we're just starting; it's 8 in the morning, and we never get up before 7; the air is fine, the sun is shining beautifully, the birds are twittering; there isn't any brook or it would murmur, but there is a pond and the frogs are piping delightfully! But the very best of all is a blackbird that is performing all kinds of virtuosity under our windows; and, after the blackbird, the Zboiński's youngest child Kamilka, who is not 2 years old yet. She has taken a fancy to me, and lisps: "Kagila loves oo." And I loves oo a billion times, Papa, Mamma, Mamma and Papa, just as she loves me; and I kiss your hands.

Affectionately,
F. Chopin

For my sisters: kisses, kisses, kisses.
Greetings to Tytus, Prus, Bartoch, everybody.

11.

To Jan Matuszyński in Warsaw.
[*Szafarnia, 1825.*]

Dear Beloved Jasia!

Oh, Mme de Sévigné would not have been able to describe to you my delight on receiving your letter so unexpectedly; I should sooner have looked for death than for such a surprise. It would never have entered my head to suppose that such an inveterate paper-smudger, a philologist who keeps his nose in his Schiller, would take up his pen to write a letter to a poor booby as slack as grandfather's horsewhip;[2] To a person who

[1] His sister Izabela Chopin.
[2] Polish proverb: as slack as a wet string.

has scarcely read a page of Latin yet; to a pigling who, fattening on hogwash, hopes to arrive at, anyway, the tenth part of your beefiness.

It really is a great favour; a great Hon-our from my John; and if anybody can ever rate it too highly, it's I, just now; and I should not apply it to myself, were I not deigning to take my pen in my hand to insult the beefiness of your Nobility.

All this is only an *exordium;* now I come to the real matter; and if you wanted to frighten me with your Puławy and your hare, I intend to take down such an inexperienced sportsman with my Toruń, and my hare (which was certainly bigger than yours), and my four partridges, which I brought in the day before yesterday. What did you see in Puławy? What? You saw only a tiny part of what my eyes rested on in full. Did you see at Sybillie a brick taken from the house of Copernicus, from his birth-place? I have seen the whole house, the whole place, certainly a little profaned at present. Imagine, Jasio, in that corner, in that very room, where that famous astronomer received the gift of life, stands now the bed of some German, who probably, after eating too many potatoes, often emits many zephyrs; and on those bricks, of which one was sent with great ceremony to Puławy, crawl many bed-bugs. Yes, Brother! The German does not care who lived in that house; he treats the whole wall as Princess Czartoryska would not treat a single brick.

But never mind Copernicus; let us come to the Toruń cakes. In order that you may know them well, perhaps better than you know Copernicus, I have to announce to you a fact of importance with regard to them, which may surprise such a mere paper-smudger as you; that fact is as follows. According to the custom of the pastry-cooks here, the cake-shops are booths, provided with cupboards, well locked up, in which the various kinds of cakes rest, assembled in dozens. You doubtless will not find this in the *Adagiorum Hiliades;* but I, knowing your interest in such important matters, inform you, in order that when translating Horace, you may be able to help yourself out in passages of dubious significance. That is all that I am in a position to write to you about Toruń; perhaps I can tell you personally; now all I can say in writing is that of everything there the cakes make the strongest impression. It is true that I saw the entire fortifications on all sides of the town, with all details; I saw a wonderful machine for transporting sand from place to place, a perfectly simple and most interesting thing, called by the Germans Sandmaschine; I also saw Gothic churches, founded by the Knights of the Cross, one of them dating from 1231. I saw a leaning tower, a fine town hall, fine inside and out; its special feature is that it has as many windows as there are days in the year, as many halls as there are months, as many rooms as the weeks, and the whole building is magnificent, in the Gothic style. But all that does not outshine the cakes; oh the cakes! I sent one to Warsaw. But what do I see? I have only just sat down, and here is the last sheet before me! It seems to me that I have but just begun to write, just started to talk with you, and now I've got to stop! Dear beloved Jasia, all I can do is to embrace you heartily. It's 10 o'clock, everybody's going to bed and I must go too. In Warsaw, on the 22nd. I shan't be there earlier — I will finish this letter orally and will embrace you heartily, dear Jasia. Now, from 20 miles away I press you to my lips and say goodbye till we meet.

Your sincerest and most affectionate friend

F. CHOPIN

How I want to see you; I would go 2 weeks without playing to see you really, because mentally I see you every day. Don't show this letter, because I'm ashamed of it. I don't know whether there's any sense in it, because I haven't read it through.

12.

To JAN BIAŁOBŁOCKI.

[*Warsaw*] *Thursday,* [*8*] *September* [*1825*].

DEAR AND BELOVED JASIA!

Extro, extra, extrissime I am delighted with your letter; reading it I at once remembered Sokołowo, that Sunday, the pantaleons,[1] the apples and other joyful past moments. But extro, extra, extrissime I am sorry to think that you have been wondering over my long silence; that you never had the letter sent to Szafarnia by the returning coach. Don't be surprised; remember at what time I begin to write letters! Also how many shelves, and boxes, and cupboards there are, how many hundreds of pieces of music all in disorder on the piano, like peas and cabbage — even not counting the Hummels, and Rieses and Kalkbrenners (to whom fate has doubtless allotted a place, in so large a community, with Pleyel, Hemerleyn and Hoffmeister): — all lying waiting for me! And what say Maciejowski, Jasiński, Matuszewski, Końcewicz, Dziekoński! That future *Maturitas!* I hope I have accounted to you for my time during this last fortnight, by just reminding you of a few things; I hope no wigging awaits me in a letter from Sokołowo! — So, having now thrown off the heaviest burden; and it's a double burden, because I've not only made my excuses but also started my letter, which is always a difficulty for me (pardon my slipping a little into macaronism), I can go on to my real, literary, alias epistolary correspondence, and inform you, Firstly: that we are all well. Secondly, that we have a new "skubent,"[2] a son of Tekla Czachowska's brother, and our nephew: Juliusz Czachowski, who keeps the house in fits of laughing by constantly addressing my sisters as "Aunt Zuzia, Aunt Ludwisia, Aunt Izabelka, Aunt Emilka, and me as Uncle Fryc. Thirdly, that the exhibitions are opening in Warsaw, both in the Town Hall and in the University. I don't tell you what is where, because as yet there's nothing to see and I haven't seen anything; but very soon my goggles will behold jolis tableaux, jolis portraits, jolies machines, bons pianos, bons draps, in short quelque chose d'excellent;[3] my paw shall describe them for you and the Dobrzynie messenger shall bring the description. As for

[1] The name properly belongs to a particular kind of 18th-century piano, but was frequently used for any kind of horizontal piano with hammers striking downwards.

[2] Probably the servant's pronunciation of "student." Chopin's father took in pupils.

[3] pretty pictures, pretty portraits, pretty machines, good pianos, good cloth . . . something excellent.

musical news, all we hear is that a certain noble gentleman named Gordon, the son of a woman who keeps a shop for mineral waters in Warsaw, and a pupil of Prague conservatorium, is to come to Warsaw, and that his playing is as interesting as Eve's apple; about that I'll tell you later. That's the end of my news, and it's also got to be the end of my letter; otherwise there'd be an end of Thursday's letter-writing, for it's 4 o'clock already. Herewith I throw myself upon the favour of your Noble Excellency my Benefactor, and remain, as I was and even one better than I was, because longer.

F. F. CHOPIN

13.

To the Same.
Warsaw, [Sunday] 30 October 1825.

DEAR JASIA!

Dear Jalko, — once more, dear Jasko!

I suppose you're wondering why I haven't written to you for so long; don't be surprised; first read my last letter, and then the following:

The day before yesterday, sitting at the table with a pen in my hand, I had just written " Dear Jasia " and the first sentence of a letter, which, as it was about music, I was reading with the utmost pomp to Żywny, as he sat over Górski, who was falling asleep at the piano. Żywny beating time, wiping his nose, twisting his handkerchief into a roll, poking it into the pocket of his clumsily made green coat, begins, adjusting his peruke, to ask: — " *And to whom do you write that letter?* " I answered: — " To Białobłocki." — " *Huh, huh, to Mr. Białobłocki?* " — " Yes to Białobłocki." — " *Where to?* " — " To Sokołowo, as usual." — " *And how is Mr. Białobłocki, — do you know?* " — " All right; his leg is better."— " *What! better, huh, huh, — that's good; and has he written to you, Pan Fridrich?* " [*sic*] — " Yes," I answer, " but a long time ago." — " *How long?* " — " Why do you ask? " — " *He, he, he, he, he, he!*" giggles Żywny. I ask in surprise: — "Have you any news of him?" — "*He, he, he, he, he, he*" (he giggles harder, wagging his head). — "Has he written to you?" I ask. — "*Yes,*" answers Żywny; and makes us miserable with the news that your leg is no better and that you have gone to Old Prussia for treatment. — "But where?" — "To Bischoffswerter." I never heard of the place before, and though such a name would have set me laughing at any other time, I just hated it this time, especially as you hadn't let me know anything about it; and anyhow it was your turn to write to me. So I stopped my correspondence there and then; and not knowing what to write, or how to write, or where to write to, was so late with my letter that it never reached the post.

You see the casual way in which such important news has got round to me. I hope you'll forgive me for not having written by the last post. I should like to tell you some news, as it might amuse you; but except for the following, I have none to tell. The Barber of Seville[1] (Le Barbier de Seville) was played on Saturday in the theatre, which is now under the direction of Dmuszewski, Kudlicz and Zdanowicz; I liked it very much. Zdanowicz, Szczurowski and Polkowski played well; also Aszpergerowa and two other women: one sniggering and with a cold in the head; the other tearful, thin, in slippers and dressing-gown, always yawning in time to the music. Besides that, a certain Mr. Rembieliński, a nephew of the President,[2] has come to Warsaw from Paris. He has been there 6 years, and plays the piano as I have never yet heard it played. You can imagine what a joy that is for us, who never hear anything of real excellence here. He is not appearing as an Artist, but as an Amateur. I won't go into details about his quick, smooth, rounded playing; I will only tell you that his left hand is as strong as the right, which is an unusual thing to find in one person. There would not be space on a whole sheet to describe his exquisite talent adequately. Pani Dekert is rather feeble; the rest of us are all well. Adieu, my life; I must leave off; a job for Macek

[1] *Il Barbiere di Siviglia,* Rossini. 1st performance 1816.

[2] Of the local educational commission. Alexander Rembieliński was a gifted pianist, who died young. [Op.]

is waiting for me. Write to me, my life; I wish our letters could fly, like syncopations.

Give me a kiss; I hug you heartily.

F. F. CHOPIN
(*your loving friend*)

Buniamin [Benjamin?] asked after you, and was surprised that you have not written to him. Respects from all of us to your Papa.

The whole household sends you a hug, and the children wish you better health. Mamma and Papa expect a letter telling them how you are, and embrace you heartily.

N.B. When we asked Żywny why he had not told us about you, and he told us that he had said nothing because in the letter to him you had sent no message to us, he got a bad wigging from Mamma.

Greetings from Pani Dekert and Cerzyńska.

14.

To the Same.
Warsaw [*November 1825*].

DEAR JASIA!

Kostusia is in Warsaw, so I can't refrain from scribbling just a few lines to you. Though I have not managed to collect much news for you, I must give you what little there is, beginning with the following: I was badly upset on learning that you were worse; but am very happy to know that I shall soon see you quite well again. I do not envy you your hot treatments, but if I knew that it would get you well sooner, I myself, yes I myself, like you, would not shave for nearly two months. Apparently you never got that letter; it's of no consequence; but you will get it; I couldn't write to you at your Bischoffswerter, because I had not the address. But Kostusia will kindly send on this letter together with the other, if it has not already gone.

As for how things go, that you know from my last letter that the Barber has been praised everywhere on the stage, and Freischütz, which has been expected so long, is to be given. I have done a new polonaise on the Barber, which is fairly well liked; I think of sending it to be lithographed tomorrow. Ludwika has done a splendid mazurka, such as Warsaw has not danced for a long time. It's her *non plus ultra*, but really, it is also a *non plus ultra* of its type. It's springy, charming, in one word it's danceable; without boasting, it's exceptionally good. When you come, I'll play it for you. I am appointed organist to the Lyceum. So you see, my wife and all my children will have double cause to respect me. Aha, Noble Sir, what a head I've got! The most important person in the whole Lyceum, after his reverence the priest!

Every Sunday I play the organ for the Wizytki [1] and the others sing. My life, it's hard for me to write any more to you this time, because I've got to fly to the Czetwertyński's, and besides that Kostusia is going away. I'll write more by post; and now, only that we all embrace you, especially I, your sin(cerest) fr(iend)

F. F. Chopin

Pani Dekert, Żywny, Bardz., Leszczyń, all send you kisses.
[A postscript from Żywny, in German, is written on the back of this letter.]

15.

To the Same.
[*Żelazowa Wola,*[2] *Saturday, 24 December 1825.*]

Dear Jasia!

You would never guess where this letter comes from! Do you suppose it's from the back door of the Pavilion of the Kazimir Palace? No. But perhaps it's — um, um — Don't guess, it's no use; I'm writing from Żelazowa Wola. That's one riddle, solved,

[1] Nuns of the order of the Visitation.
[2] The Skarbek estate, where Chopin was born.

but can you guess when I'm writing, when? And that you can't guess, so I must tell you: I'm writing, after getting out of a carriage and just sitting down to New Year's Eve supper. Fate decreed, and though Mamma didn't a bit want to allow me to go, it was all no use, and Ludwika and I are at Żelazowa Wola. New Year is coming, so I ought to send you good wishes, but for what? You have everything, so I will wish you nothing except health, which you must now try for. This year — that is 1826 — I hope we shall meet. I don't write to you much, because I've nothing to write about. I'm well, we're all well, I've had your letter, was pleased to get it, ask for more. You already know when I'm writing, so don't be surprised if it's short and dry, because I'm too hungry to write anything fat: non est plenus venter, itaque non scribit libenter, nisi ad te, cujus litteras quotidie expecto.[1] There's a proof that I haven't yet forgotten my Latin. But, but, if it hadn't been for that lunch at the Jaworek's I should have finished this letter before now. Papa and I were invited there the day before yesterday to a "lax" (not laxans). On receiving Jaworek's invitation, I at first thought he had been seized by diarrhoea and was offering me the same; but later, when the *lax* was brought out to show how big it was and how many persons could eat it, I found that it was a salmon (in German Lachs) which had been sent to him from Danzig. There were a lot of persons there; among others a noble gentleman called Czapek, a Czech pianist who had come from Vienna with Pani Rzewuska, and of whose playing I can't say much, and a certain Pan Żak (which means a Czech *żak*,[2] not a Polish one), from the Prague Conservatorium, who played the clarinet as I have never before heard it played. It will be enough if I tell you that he gets two notes at once with a single breath.

Give me a kiss, My Life. I wish nothing for you but recovery. I hope you'll be better with every day; the wish of all our family, and especially of

Me

Your sincerest friend

[1] The belly is not full, therefore one does not write with pleasure, except to you, whose letters I daily expect.

[2] schoolboy.

The whole household would send you greetings if they knew I was writing. I expect a letter.
N.B. I'll be in Warsaw on Thursday.

16.

To the Same.
Warsaw, [Sunday] 12 February 1826.

DEAR JASIA!

I'm badly worried to have had no news of you for so long. It was still 1825 when I wrote to you, and this is 1826 and I have no letter! Only Panna Konstancja (alias Kostusia) in her letters to Ludwika — which, it is true, are more frequent than ours — sometimes drops a word about your health, of which, as you know, all our house wants to hear. Every Briefträger [1] (nota bene, not Pani Wyszyńska) raises our hopes when he comes into that blue courtyard; but how he grieves us when we don't hear his boots on the stairs, or when the red postmark on the letter is not Dobrzyń but Radom or Lublin or something else. But really it is not the fault of the Briefträger, but of the Briefschreiber,[2] who probably doesn't write only because he doesn't want to tire the poor fat man that has, all the same, to climb so high. But you don't need to be so considerate: it's pretty cold weather, nobody is grumbling at the heat; one only hears people complaining of the cold; so it really won't do any harm, dear Jasia, if you make him stir his stumps even twice before Easter. After this observation I expect that I have ensured an answer to this letter. I would like to have answers both to this and to my last letter; but that I leave to your graciousness; knowing the generosity of the King (once upon a time [3]) I don't doubt the result of my petition.

[1] letter-carrier, postman.
[2] letter-writer.
[3] Possibly a reference to Białobłocki's part in amateur theatricals. [Op.]

I don't write about Staszyc,[1] because I know that the papers have given you all sorts of details about his richly poor funeral. I will only mention that the Academicians carried him from Holy Cross, all the way to Bielany, where he had wished to be buried; that Skarbek made a speech by the grave, that his coffin was stripped through love and enthusiasm, that I have for a keepsake a bit of the pall with which the bier was covered, and that 20,000 persons accompanied the corpse. On the way there were several fisticuffing encounters, both with the shopkeepers, who wanted to insist on carrying the remains of the Honoured Man, and with other citizens who also were determined to take the corpse away from the Academicians. I can't remember whether I told you of the death of Dybek; it is said that Niemcewicz is failing. Everybody's falling ill, and I too. You maybe suppose that all this scribbling is being done at a table; you're wrong, it's from under my quilt, and comes out of a head that's tied up in a nightcap because it's been aching, I don't know why, for the last four days. They have put leeches on my throat because the glands have swelled, and our Roemer says it's a catarrhal affection. It's true that from Saturday to Thursday I was out every evening, till 2 in the night; but it's not that, because I always slept it off in the morning. I should bore you if I wrote any more about such an illness to you who are so much more ill, therefore I will fill up the remainder of this paper with something else. Your Papa has been in Warsaw, came to us and to Bruner [*sic*], and ordered a choraleon [2] for the church. I wanted to send you a letter by him, but he had gone, and our letters were left in Warsaw. Adieu, dear Jasia, and please write to your sincere friend

F. F. CHOPIN

Mamma and Papa, all the children and Zuzia wish you a quick recovery.

1 Stanislaw Staszyc: Polish statesman, philanthropist and man of science: 1755–1826. The Hrubiesz several times referred to is the estate which he bought in order to free the 4,000 peasant inhabitants from serfdom and set them up as small holders.

2 Choraleon, or eolimelodikon; invented by a Polish professor, J. F. Hoffmann. Brunner was the maker of the instruments for Hoffmann. [Hoes.]

Father Benjamin has been to see me; he sent greetings to you. He will begin teaching on Wednesday.

Żywny, Pani Dekert, Bardziński, Pan Leszczyński and all: N.B. Bardziński has left us; his Magister examination comes off soon, and he would have no quiet to write his thesis; but we have another Academicus from Lublin, a worthy successor to the good Antoś!

In answer to your greeting, Papa sends you a thousand wishes for good health, that it may come soon.

Marylski brought the letter long ago, but is going only today. [*Last three words difficult to read*]

17.

To the Same.
[*Warsaw*] *2nd day of Whitsuntide.*
[*Monday, 15 May 1826.*]

Dear, Beloved Jasio!

I am really ashamed to have been so long in answering your letter; but various circumstances which have steadily pursued me (I think you can understand my condition this year, because you yourself have had to go through it) just didn't allow me to do as I wished to do. Your commission is partly executed; I've bought the music for you; as far as I can judge by my own taste, it should give you pleasure in the house. As for Glücksberg, Papa himself went to him. But he told Papa that he takes subscriptions only by the month, that he has no catalogue yet and can't supply more than a few works. It might still come off, but he demands a thaler a month; the worst is that one doesn't know which few works to choose, until the catalogue comes. Though I have bought the music, I have not yet given it to Wysocki. It's all Euterpe: — that is, a collection of airs and other pieces by Rossini, arranged, very well, for the piano at Diabelli's in Vienna (this work answers to " Philomel " for singing), and a Polonaise of Kaczkowski, very good, beautiful, that you can listen to and rejoice in (and also exercise your fingers, which have doubtless gone stiff, if I may say so); in addition, as you wished, some of my own scrawls. All these will be at Wysocki's this week without fail.

You wouldn't believe, how joyful I am that you have taken flight from your Bishopric.[1] I say, joyful — that is, in one way; but in another way it has grieved me. It appears, Most Noble Mr. Jan, that you have imbibed a lot of German virtue; a long time ago you invited me and now you advise me not to leave here! See what that confounded miserliness leads to! I wish, since you learned it, that you had never gone to Bischoffswerter; my intentions, my best plans and projects have now gone to pieces; and the person that I thought I could count on, begins to think in this economical and miserly way. It's true, I'm in no condition to slang you as you deserve; but what is put off is not put away. If not now, then later, I shall claim satisfaction: *nota bene*, not with a bullet; you would win on that, because I've given mine to Rogoziński, who seems able to paint something. Rogoziński makes me think of Podbielski, of whose misfortune I must tell you. About 3 months ago, when he was here . . .[2] the wind caught him, and paralysis set in. He can use neither hand nor foot, though Zabiello is doing his utmost for him; but there is some hope of recovery, as he is already a little better; electricity has helped him a good deal. I fairly often see that Rembielinski of whom I wrote to you; you would not believe how beautifully he plays; he came to see me lately, to my great delight. As for the news of Warsaw, you have the Courier. For personal news I can tell you only that Col. Gutkowski, at whose house I hurt my foot, is dead; that Zubelewicz has a daughter; that Jarocki has got married in Podolia and brought his wife here straight from the wedding; that on Sunday, a week ago today, I went to the Zamoyskis', where nearly the whole evening was spent in admiring Długosz's Eolipantaleon; [3] Długosz has sold it to a certain Mniewski (who

[1] Bischoffswerter.

[2] Margin of letter injured; a word unreadable.

[3] A musical instrument, combination of pianoforte and choraleon; invented by Długosz, a skilled artisan, and made by Brunner. On the inventor's invitation, Chopin improvised publicly on this instrument in 1825, with great success. [Op.]

used to go to Pani Pruska's in a beige coat, and who is now getting married); that Kosiński has died, that Woelke has a daughter, that Domowicz lately came to Warsaw and sent greetings to you; that Zakrzewski is in Warsaw; that I have a little cupboard for my music; finally that my boots are in holes and I have to wear shoes. Would anybody suppose that I should start off for Bielany in the manner of our watchman, who has just come to ask Mamma for permission [. . .] that Bielany [. . .][1] lots of people this year. My Botanical Garden, the old one, alias behind the palace, has been beautifully done up by the Commission. There are no more carrots that used to be so nice to eat beside the spring; nor sandwiches, nor arbours, nor salads, nor cabbages, nor bad smells; only flower-beds à la manière anglaise.[2] I have now written down everything that could come into my head in a quarter of an hour, so nothing is left to me but to assure you that towards you I am always I and shall always be I as long as I live.

Mamma and Papa and I send our respects to your Papa, and greetings to you, because you have no claim to respect as yet. Kiss Panna Konstancja's face from all the children, and her hands from me.

Pani Dekert, Żywny, Bardz. — etc., etc. — send greetings.

Perhaps you can't read this, as you haven't read a letter from me for a long time; but forgive me; I am hurrying to catch the post and have no time to read it over.

F. F. Chopin

18.

To the Same.

[*Warsaw, June 1826.*]

Dear Jasia!

Don't expect to find this letter the usual name-day compliments: all those showy feelings, exclamations, apostrophes,

[1] Margin injured, words unreadable. [Op.]

[2] In the English style.

pathetic bits and similar rubbish, nonsense, stuff, and piffle. They are good enough for heads that can find trivial phrases in the absence of friendship; but when people have a tie of eleven years of friendship, when they have counted the months together 132 times, have begun 468 weeks, 3960 days, 95,040 hours, 5,702,400 minutes, 342,144,000 seconds together, they don't need reminders, or complimentary letters, because they'll never write what they want to write.

Starting therefore, *ad rem,* I begin with the matter in hand; and first I want to get out the thing I can't digest; which is that your Nobility has not written to me for several months. Why? What for? *Cur?* Warum? Pourquoi? It *annoys* me very much, and if I don't see an improvement there'll be trouble. That I can't write very often counts for nothing; you know that I am swatting for a diploma, but that sausage isn't for this dog; we hear a good deal about one-year students.[1]

Operam et oleum perdidi,[2] if you remember Tyrocinium.[3] But apparently it's no use, to spoil my paper; I might as well write you good news instead of bad. Ecce homo! A person turned up in the world yesterday; Linde, Linde has got a successor. We're all pleased, and I hope you will share our joy. We often hear news in our barracks,[4] as you know well from my last letter.

There's a lot said about Freischütz[5] being given in two or three weeks; it seems to me that it will make quite a noise in Warsaw. Apparently there will be many performances, and that is right. It certainly is much if our opera can manage to give Weber's splendid work. But considering the aim towards which Weber was striving in the Freischütz, his German origin, that strange romanticism and the extremely subtle harmony, peculiarly suited to German taste; one may gather that the Warsaw public, accustomed to Rossini's light airs, is likely at

[1] Chopin was one of the "one-year students," for whom the normal two years in Class 6 was reduced to one. He did not, however, take the examination but went to Reinertz, for his health, before the date. [Op.]

[2] I have lost labour and oil.

[3] A Latin primer used in the school. [Op.]

[4] The Casimir Palace in Warsaw, commonly known as "The Cadets' Barracks," having once been used as a school for cadets. [Op.]

[5] Weber: *Der Freischütz.* 1st performance 1819.

first to praise it not from conviction but just in accordance with expert opinion, because Weber is praised everywhere [. . .] [1]

Ecce femina, non homo; [2] the rector has a daughter. Although it was yesterday declared to be a son, and only today a daughter, it is the latter statement that is correct. Yesterday we had a visit from an important man, Pan Kozicki, who applied leeches to one of the boys and talked a lot about the alimentary and laryngeal canals and the Adam's apple, because it was on the throat that he did the operation. He was in coloured stockings, dirty boots, etc. — with, as usual, a poor shirt and a new, or rather renovated hat. Please do let me know whether you received the music. I have not sent you any of my scrawls, but instead of that the waltzes of Aleksander Rembieliński, which I think you will like; and if any of them should at first appear to you too difficult, just get to work hard with your stiff fingers (because I suppose you didn't play at Bischoffsweder) [*sic*] and you will see that they are worthy of you, that is, as beautiful as you. Don't think that I have written the last comma in the spirit of Pliny; habit counts for a lot, and a dog sometimes appears beautiful to his master. — Ha, ha, ha! — what a metamorphosis; the master is the dog and the dog the master! That's only for a moment; no dog is more faithful than I. Podbielski is better, though he has twice had a bad scare since his attack. About a month ago, walking in the street, I saw a carriage overturn at the corner of Kozie St. I ran up and found Podbielski on the ground; it was the first time he had ventured out for air. Luckily someone was with him in the carriage and got him, with difficulty, into another one.

If you knew what changes there are in our Botanical Garden, you'd hold your head (in astonishment) — They have put such flower-beds, paths, plantations, shrubs and so on, that it's a pleasure to go in, especially as we have a key. If this letter seems to you rather wild, don't be surprised, because I'm not well. If you find nothing about the holidays, don't be surprised, because I'll write about that in my next letter. If I don't send you my clavi-cembalo rubbish, don't be surprised, because

[1] Word illegible.
[2] Behold a woman, not a man.

that's me. If you expect any messages from home, read the following. Both Mamma and Papa, both my sisters and our friends, tell me to send their sincere good wishes. Only from Ludwika there's no message, because she has been in the country at Pani Skarbek's for the last two weeks. We expect her today or tomorrow. Domowicz was in Warsaw the day before yesterday. Żywny is all right; Pani Dekert is not well. Bardziński sends special greetings. Live happily, my dear, beloved Jasia; I expect a letter, I embrace you heartily.

F. F. Chopin

Respects to your Papa from the whole House. Kisses on the face to Panna Konstancja from the children, and on the hand from me.

If you see Szafarnia, Plone, Gulbiny, Radomin, Ornowka, remember my name, look at the potatoes and say mournfully: "Here once he entered bravely with a horse, here the . . . [? word doubtful] came to his aid."

19.

To Wilhelm Kolberg in Warsaw.
Reinertz, 18 August [1826].

Dear Wilus'!

After passing through Błonie, Sochaczew, Lowicz, Kutno, Kłodawa, Koło, Turka, Kalisz, Ostrów, Międzyborz, Oleśnica, Wrocław [Breslau], Nimsch, Frankenstein, Warta and Glatz, we reached Reinertz, where we are staying. I have been drinking whey and the local waters for two weeks, and they say that I am looking a little better, but I am said to be getting fat, and am as lazy as ever, to which you can ascribe the long lethargy of my pen. But believe me, when you learn about my mode of life, you will agree that it is difficult to find a moment for sitting at home. In the morning, at 6 o'clock at the latest, all the patients are at the wells; then there's an atrocious band of wind players:

a dozen caricatures of various types collected together; the head one, a thin bassoonist with a snuffy, spectacled nose, frightens all the ladies that are afraid of horses by playing to the freely perambulating Kur-Gäste. Then there's a sort of rout, or rather masquerade; not everybody in masks, those are only a small proportion, besides those who " get hanged for company." [1] This promenade, along the beautiful avenues that connect the Establishment with the town, usually lasts till 8, or according to the number of glasses that people have to drink in the morning. Then everyone goes home to breakfast. After breakfast people usually go for a walk. I walk till 12; then one has to eat dinner, because after dinner one has to go back to Brunn. After dinner there's usually a bigger masquerade than in the morning, because everyone is dressed up, all in different clothes from those of the morning. Again there's vile music, and so it goes till evening. As I have to drink only two glasses of Lau-Brunn after dinner I get home to supper fairly early. After supper I go to bed. So when can I write letters?

There you have my days, as they go, one after another. They go so fast that I have been here a long time and have not seen everything yet.

It's true I walk on the hills that surround Reinertz; often I am so delighted with the view of these valleys that I hate to come down, which I sometimes do on all fours. But I have not yet been for the excursions that everybody takes, because it's forbidden to me. Near Reinertz there is a mountain with rocks known as Heu-Scheuer, from which there is a wonderful view; but the air at the very top is not good for everybody, and unluckily I am one of those patients to whom it is not allowed. But never mind that. I have already been on the mountain called Einsiedelei, where there is a hermitage. You go to the top of one of the highest hills near here, and climb up about 150 steps in a straight line, cut out of the stone almost vertically, to the hermitage, from which there is a splendid view all over Reinertz. We expect to go up a certain Hohemenze, a hill said to be in beautiful surroundings; I hope it will come off.

But it's useless to bore you with these descriptions, from

[1] A Polish and Russian proverb: "and the Jew hanged himself for company."

which you can't get much idea of the thing, because not everything lends itself to description. As for the ways of the place, I am already so used to them that nothing now worries me. At first it seemed strange to me that in Silesia the women work more than the men; but as I don't do anything myself, it's easy for me to acquiesce in that.

There have been plenty of Poles in Reinertz, but now the company is thinning; nearly all there were are acquaintances of mine. A good deal of social gaiety goes on between the families; even the most important German names join in the drawing-room amusements. In the house where we lodge there is a certain lady from Wrocław; her children, lively and intelligent youngsters, talk a little French. They want to talk Polish, so one of them, a friend of mine, begins to me: — " Zien dobry." [1] I answered: " Dobry dzień," and as I liked the boy, I told him how to say: " Dobry Wieczór." [2] By the next day he was so muddled that instead of " Dobry Dzień," he said: " Zien Wiesior." I didn't know how he got it to that, and had quite a job to explain to him that it's not " Zien Wieczór," but " dobry wieczór."

I've taken up too much of your time; perhaps you'd rather be doing something else. But I'm just finishing. I'm going to the Brunn for two glasses of water and a gingerbread, whereby I remain for always

The same as always
FR. CHOPIN

Dziewanowski has written to me; I think of answering tomorrow. He says he has written to you too. He's a good fellow not to have forgotten. Alfred Kurnatowski has been here with his parents and sisters; I think Fontana knows him; tell him he left the day before yesterday.

My respects to your papa and mamma.

I really don't know what I've written to you; I know it's a lot, but I don't want to read it over.

[1] *Dzień dobry:* good day.
[2] good evening.

20.

[In French]

To JOZEF ELSNER IN WARSAW.
Reinertz, August [*1826*].

DEAR SIR,

Since our arrival in Reinertz, I have been promising myself the pleasure of writing to you; but, as my time is entirely taken up by the cure, it has been impossible for me to do so till now, and it is only today that I have managed to steal away for a moment and give myself up to the pleasure of conversing with you, and at the same time to render you an account of what I have done with the commissions which you were so kind as to give me. I have tried to do my best about them; I have delivered the letter addressed to Herr Latzel, with which he was much pleased; as for Herr Schnabel and Herr Breuer, they will not receive your letters till I return by way of Breslau. Your kindness and the keen interest which you have taken in me, make me believe that it will not be indifferent to you if I tell you what is the state of my health. The fresh air and the whey which I take very conscientiously have set me up so well that I am quite different from what I was in Warsaw. The magnificent views offered by beautiful Silesia enchant and charm me; but one thing is lacking, for which not all the beauties of Reinertz can compensate me: a good instrument.

Imagine, Sir, that there is not one good piano, and all that I have seen are instruments which cause me more distress than pleasure; fortunately this martyrdom will not last much longer, the moment of our farewells at Reinertz approaches, and we expect to start back on the 11th of next month. But, before I have the pleasure of seeing you, allow me, Sir, to assure you of my highest respect.

F. F. CHOPIN

Mamma sends her respects to you.
Please also remember me to Madame your wife.

21.

To Jan Białobłocki.
Warsaw [*Saturday*], *2 November* [*1826*].

Dear Jasia!

I never noticed how these 3 months were flying; it doesn't seem long since I sent you a letter, yet there it is; I admit the fault myself; I confess that a quarter of a year has grown old since then. It is a most merciful action on your part to be pleased to pardon me; your graciousness reaches to the clouds! — But as for mine, that's quite another story. I proclaim my wrath, wrath to be assuaged by nothing, except one scrap of paper, for which like a fool, I wait to this day. Glory be to God, a scribble on the 20th from Sokołowo; nothing more, and today's the 2nd. Don't you know what interests me more than all your grain and potatoes and horses? Pause! Repent! Turn to the blessed means indicated above, and: *petenti veniam dabo.*[1]

As for Brunner, the following fact explains the verses: As the choraleon has been quite finished for a month, and he had no news from your Papa, he took it to pieces, and is now putting it together again, as I told him that I should like to see it. He says that he thinks your Papa will be pleased; that it has remained here all this time because he has invented certain improvements (of which he talked a lot to me), which he has added to it. I have not yet seen it, so I can't describe it to you in detail; but I shall soon see it, and will let you know by post. About the money due to him, he will give his view himself, in the letter to your Papa which is now in the post (unless he has received it; written the 20th). Well, what of it? This of it, that you see the commission, or trust, has been excellently fulfilled. Now ask since when I've had such *activitas?* A short answer: Since Sokołowo, for really I got so fat, so lazy, that, in one word, I don't want to do anything, anything at all. Learn, my life, by these presents. That I don't go to the Lyceum. Really

[1] I will give pardon to the penitent.

it would be stupid to sit perforce for 6 hours a day, when both German and German-Polish doctors have told me to walk as much as possible; it would be stupid to listen to the same things twice over when one can be learning something new during this year. Meanwhile I go to Elsner for strict counterpoint, 6 hours a week; I hear Brodziński, Bentkowski and others, on subjects connected in any way with music. I go to bed at 9. All teas, evenings and balls are off. I drink an emetic water by Malcz's orders, and feed myself only on oatmeal *quasi* a horse. But the air here is not so good for me as at Reinertz. They make up a tale that perhaps next year I may have to repeat the lau Brunn,[1] anyway as a formality! But it's a far cry to that; and probably Paris would be better for me than the Bohemian frontier. Bardziński is leaving before this year is out, and I — perhaps in 50 years' time.

As God sends. Give a kiss, dear Jasia; more by post.

F. F. CHOPIN

The paper I am writing to you on is from Reinertz.
Żywny, Pani Dekert, in a word, all our friends greet you.
Our respects to the Papa, and I thank him for his kind postscript.
PP. To the Dziewanowskis, Białobł., Cissow. etc.

I will write by post to Panna Konstancja from Ludwika and all of them.

[Postmark:] Warsaw, 2 October,

A Monsieur, M. Jean Białobłocki
à Sokołowo.

22.

To the Same.
Warsaw, [Monday] 8 [January 1827].

RESPECTED PAN JAN!

You are not worthy, you scoundrel! Forgive me for being compelled to use in my indignation a title so justly belonging

[1] The medicinal spring.

to you — You are not worthy that I should extend to you a hand with a pen in it! This is your gratitude for the bloody sweat of the brow of my excellence, for the fatigue and toil I have endured in buying Mickiewicz, or those tickets? This your response to my New Year wishes? Yes, pause; and confess that I am right in saying you are not worthy that I should extend a hand to you! The only motive which impels me to write to you today is to acquit myself of the suspicion or judgment which might fall on me on account of the money left with me. Perhaps you think that I spent it during the carnival at some friend's little ball, or that I have converted the rites of Bach [us] [1] into something worthy of a son of Apollo? Mistaken notion! Low thoughts! Bosh! I have bought you (for nothing) two airs from Freischütz, with which you ought to be pleased. It is true that they are for a female voice; they are sung by Kupińska and Aszpergerowa; but as I know, or at least can imagine, how squeakily you must sing, my dear life, when your leg hurts you (I don't know anything about it) — they are just the thing for you. Transpose the voice part an octave lower, and it will be for a tenor voice, like yours if I remember rightly. The two together cost 2 złotys, so how much have I left? I must do an arithmetical calculation (imagine Tarczyński at an examination of the elementary class). For instance: Somebody had 3 złotys, spent 2, how much has he left? eh? 2 from 3 leaves 1, so there remains 1 złoty, or 30 gr., or 90 szelągi. I should like to spend it on something interesting for you; it will probably be from the Italian,[2] so that you shall have something fashionable. So far nothing has been engraved; but as I have not been to Brzezyna's [3] for 4 days, I may get something tomorrow, and if so will try whether Dziewanowski can still take it with him. Excellent intention! The result of it will appear when you open the score; you ought to be as much interested, in the past now, as I am today in the future! I also send you my mazurka, of which you have heard; later perhaps you'll get another; it would be too many pleasures at once. They are

[1] Possibly this may be a pun on Bach and Bacchus?

[2] Probably a reference to Rossini's opera: *L'Italiana in Algeria*, which had been performed in Warsaw with great success in Dec. 1826. [Op.]

[3] A music-shop frequented by Chopin. [Op.]

already published; meanwhile I am leaving my Rondo, that I wanted to have lithographed, stifling among my papers, though it is earlier and therefore has more right to travel. It's having the same luck as I!

The sledging is fairly good; they have been running about Warsaw with little bells for 4 days; there have even been a few accidents, such as usually accompany these moments. For instance: a shaft hit some lady on the head and killed her, horses have bolted, sledges have been smashed, and so on. The masked ball on New Year's Eve is said to have been fine. I have never yet attended one of these entertainments, so I have the desire and hope to go this year with Bardziński. Pani Szymanowska gives a concert this week. It is to be on Friday, and the prices are raised; they say the parterre is to be half a ducat, the stalls a ducat, and so on. I shall be there for sure, and will tell you about her reception and playing.

Write to me! Give me a kiss, Dear Life.

F. F. CHOPIN

Mamma is not well; she has been in bed for 4 days; she suffers much from rheumatism. She is a little better now, and we hope that God will give her complete recovery.

Respects to your Papa from us.

23.

To the Same.
Warsaw. Monday, 14 March [*1827*].

BELOVED JASIA!

Are you alive? Or not? Glory be to God; it's more than 3 months since you wrote a word to me. My worthy name-day has gone by and I haven't had a letter. All this appears to confirm the tale that is told about you in Warsaw with mourning and tears. And do you know what they say? They say that you're dead! We had all blubbered (for nothing), Jędrzejewicz [1] had written a panegyric for the Courier, and suddenly came the thunderclap, that you're alive! Yes, actually alive! As pleasant news penetrates more easily into hearts desiring consolation, we decided that the last thing people were saying was likely to be the right one. So, having dried my tear-swollen eyelids, I take up my pen to inquire of you, are you alive or did you die? If you are dead, please let me know, and I will tell the cook, for ever since she heard about it she has been saying her prayers. It may be a case of Cupid's dart; for, though she is an aged dame, our Józefowa,[2] all the same, when you were in Warsaw you impressed her so that (on hearing of your death) she kept on repeating for a long while: — " What a young gentleman that was! Handsomer than all the other young gentlemen that come here! Neither Pan Wojciechowski, nor Pan Jędrzejewicz is so handsome, none of them, none! Lord! how he once ate up a whole cabbage from the market, just for naughtiness! " — Aha, aha! A wonderful Threnody! It's a pity Mickiewicz [3] isn't here; he would have written a Ballad called " The Cook." Well now, leaving all that aside, I'll come to the point: We have illness in the house. Emilja has been in bed for 4 weeks; she has got a cough and has begun to spit blood and Mamma is frightened. Malcz ordered bloodletting. They bled her once, twice; leeches without end, vesicators, sinapisms, wolfsbane [?]; horrors, horrors! — All this time she has been eating nothing; she has grown so thin that you wouldn't know her, and is only now beginning to come to herself a little — You can imagine what it has been like in the house. You'll have to imagine it, because I can't describe it for you. Now about other subjects.

The Carnival is over, which is sad. Old Benik is dead; you can guess what that has meant for Papa! His daughter Klementyna, who married Dolbyszew, has also died, before she had lived with her husband for nine months. In a word, the most miserable things have happened, to sadden our house. The last

[1] Kalasanty Jędrzejewicz, later Chopin's brother-in-law.
[2] Wife of Joseph.
[3] Adam Mickiewicz 1798(9?)–1855.

straw was the story from hell, or at least I don't know where else it came from — about your death. That one cost me not only tears, but money as well. Naturally, on learning of it (imagine, if you were to hear of my death) — (N.B. I am alive) — I wept so much that I got a headache; and as it was 8 in the morning and my Italian comes at 11, I couldn't have my lesson. That's several złotys (Wojciechowski and Weltz were quite upset); the next day, to cheer me up, they made me go to the theatre. Again several złotys! So you might let me know whether you really are dead. I await a letter, for I can't write any more; it's 4 o'clock.

Give me a kiss, beloved Jal.

F. F. Chopin

Brunner thinks of sending the Choraleon shortly by the Vistula; write if you want him not to do it, or anything; this German doesn't know what he's doing. The best thing would be for your Papa to write to him.

We all embrace you after your resurrection.

My respects to the Papa.

24.

To Jan Matuszyński in Warsaw.

Warsaw [*1827*].

Dear Jasia!

What has happened that we haven't met for so long? I expect you every day, and find that you don't come; just because I want to speak to you about this: As the weather is so bad now, I should like to make a fair copy of the piano part of the variations, and I can't do it without your copy. Would you please bring it to me tomorrow, and the day afterwards you shall have both.

Your
F. F. Chopin

25.

To Tytus Wojciechowski in Potruzyń.
From Warsaw, 9 September 1828.

Dear Tytus!

You can't believe how I have been longing for news of you and your Mother; so you can imagine how pleased I was to get your letter. I got it at the Pruszak's in Sanniki; I have been there all summer. I won't write about my visit, because you have been in Sanniki yourself. I couldn't answer at once because we were expecting to start for home every day. I'm writing now in a half crazy state, because I really don't know what's happening to me. I am starting today for Berlin; it's for an opera of Spontini; I'm going, by diligence, to test my strength. The cause of all this is a set of monkeys from all the Cabinets of Europe. In imitation of the congresses in the Swiss Cantons, and later in Munich, the King of Prussia has empowered his University to invite the leading learned men of Europe for a session of naturalists, with the famous Humboldt for president. Jarocki, as a former pupil of the Berlin Academy, whose doctorate he now holds, has been invited as a zoologist. Lodgings have been taken in Berlin for 200 naturalists; they are to have board in common, etc. German arrangements of course; also invitations printed on vellum paper, very important; and Spontini is to give either Cortez or Olimpia.[1] A certain Lichtenstein, friend and teacher of Jarocki, and secretary of the conference, was an intimate friend of Weber, is a member of the Sing-Akademie, and according to Ernemann, is in good relations with Zelter, who directs the music department. Good friends in Berlin tell me that, knowing Lichtenstein, I shall meet the most important musicians of Berlin, with the exception of Spontini, with whom he apparently does not associate. I wish I could meet the Poznań [Posen] Radziwiłł there (of that there seems to be a doubt); he's hand in glove with Spontini. I shall

[1] Spontini (G. L. P.) 1774–1851. His operas had a great vogue at that time. *Fernand Cortez* was first produced in 1809; *Olimpia* in 1819.

be there only two weeks, with Jarocki; but it's good to hear first-class opera even once; it gives one a conception of fine technique. Arnold, Mendelson [*sic*] and Hank are the pianists there; the last is a pupil of Hummel. When I get back, I'll tell you what I've seen; but now, at your request, I will write you Warsaw news. Firstly: Colli and Mme Tusaint appeared in "The Barber" a few weeks ago. It happened that I came to Warsaw from Sanniki for a few days just then with Kostuś. I was extremely anxious to see that one act (they played only the first) in Italian; I rubbed my hands for joy all day long. But in the evening, if it hadn't been for Tusa, I should have murdered Colli. He was such an *Arlechino* [*sic*] *italiano*, and so out of tune, that it was abominable. It's enough to say that in one exit he went head over heels. Imagine Colli, in short breeches, with a guitar, in a round white hat, on the floor, Oh, shame! "The Barber" went disgracefully. Zdanowicz sang the best, in this slander. A new opera, Telemachus, has been, or was to be played. I didn't see it; I know there have been rehearsals, but I didn't attend, so I can't tell you anything. I think you have not yet seen Othello; and you have praised Polkowski, who is at his best in that opera. Mme Meyer is singing as usual. Mme Zimmermann is already playing and apparently beginning to study. But that's enough of theatricals; now about the University. Oborski, who gave me a scare over your departure: — he burst into the room where we were all assembled for the rehearsal of the Corpus Domini choruses, and in a rather wild manner told me that you wanted him to say goodbye to me as you had had to leave in the night: — Oborski seems to be in Baden. So Gąsie told me; I was with him yesterday, on the Luther tower of the church, to watch the review on the Wola. Gąsie has been in Cracow, and has a lot to tell about it; he was robbed on the journey; he tells the adventure most pathetically. Today I met Obniski; he is well, asked a lot about you, where you are, when you're coming back; and sent messages to you. Pruszak, who brought me back on Thursday, went home again on Saturday, to start for Gdańsk [Danzig] on Sunday. Pani Pruszak started the day before. Kostuś and I have been at your lodging, but I didn't try the piano, for Kostuś didn't know where to find the key of it; from its appearance I don't think anything has gone wrong with it; it looked quite healthy. About your things, whether they have been moved or not, and so on, you will hear from Kostuś, who will no doubt write to you. At Sanniki I re-wrote the *C-major Rondo* the last one, if you remember, for 2 pianofortes;[1] Ernemann and I tried it today at Bucholtz's and it went fairly well. We think of playing it some day at the Resource.[2]

About my new compositions; I have nothing but a *G-minor Trio*[3] begun shortly after you left and not yet quite finished. I tried the first *Allegro* with the accompaniment, before I went to Sanniki; now that I'm back I think of trying the rest. I expect this *Trio* to have the same luck as my *Sonata* and *Variations.* They are already at Leipzig; the first, as you know, is dedicated to Elsner; on the second — perhaps too boldly — I have put your name. My heart asked for it and our friendship permitted it, so don't be angry. Skarbek has not come back yet. Jędrzejewicz is going to stay a year in Paris. He has got to know Sowiński; that pianist who has written a few words to me, saying that before he comes to Warsaw, he would like to know me in advance by correspondence; that, as he is on the editorial staff of the Parisian periodical: *Revue Musicale, publiée par M. Fetis,* he would be glad to have some information about the state of music in Poland, about what prominent polish musicians there are, about their lives, etc. I'm not going to mix up with it. I shall write to him from Berlin that I don't undertake such things, especially as Kurpiński has begun to occupy himself to some extent with it. Besides, I have not yet judgment enough for a leading Parisian paper, which must publish only the truth; I have heard opera neither well nor badly done. I should hurt many people's feelings! Kurpiński is now in Cracow; Zyliński is conducting the opera; it is said that Freischütz was abominably given yesterday. The choir singers were a beat behind each other. Father says I shall lose my high opinion of foreign lands; I will tell you that for certain in a

[1] Op. 73; posthumous; edited by Fontana. [Op.]
[2] A concert hall.
[3] Op. 73; posthumous; edited by Fontana. [Op.]

month's time; I shall be leaving Berlin at the end of this month. Five days in a diligence! If I fall ill I shall come home by extra post. And I'll let you know. I forgot one bit of important news: Albrecht is dead. With us all goes on as usual; the good Żywny is the life of everything. This year I was to have gone to Vienna by diligence with Papa; and perhaps it would have come off, but the mother of little Niezabytowski asked us to wait for her and then never came. Papa spent all his vacation at home. A long time ago, that is, two or three months ago, I hated to pass Rezler's stone house; but yesterday, going to Brzezina, I went in at Lafor's door instead of by the front entrance. I only yesterday met the Castels. She seems to me to resemble him, and all Warsaw has the same impression. I am very sorry that the time you spend with your Mamma is not so free as it was last year. We are all grieved at your dear Mamma's indisposition, and all wish for her recovery. Your ears must often have burned,[1] for there has been no day that we have not spoken of you.

I must stop, for my bundle of Hartman's work has already gone to the post, and I am going to where Geysmer and Lauber are sitting; I'll give them greetings from you if you like. Now give me a kiss.

Your devoted
F. CHOPIN

Kiss your Mamma's hands and feet for me. My parents and family send their respects and best wishes for recovery, and so do all our friends: — Żywny, Zoch, Górski, etc. — These few names will remind you of our house. I kiss you again, again. But do be decent and sometimes write a word, or half a word, or one letter; I shall be pleased with even that.

Forgive me if I have written any rubbish; I haven't time to read it through — Once more, *adieu.*

[1] Literally: "you must often have had the hiccups"; a Polish idiom.

26.

To his Family.
Berlin, Tuesday, 16 September 1828.

MY DEAREST PARENTS AND SISTERS!

On Sunday about 3 in the afternoon we diligence-jogged into this much-too-big town. From the post house they brought us straight to the Kronprinz inn, where we still remain. We are comfortable and content here. On the day of our arrival Jarocki took me at once to Lichtenstein's, where I saw Humboldt.[1] Lichtenstein promised to introduce me to the principal masters of my art; he is sorry that we did not arrive a day earlier, as that very morning his daughter played with the orchestra. Not much loss, I thought privately. Was I right? I don't know yet, because I have not seen or heard her. On Sunday, the day we arrived; Winter's *Das unterbrochene Opferfest*[2] was played. I could not get to it because of the visit to Lichtenstein. Yesterday was a general banquet of all those learned caricatures, whom I have divided here into three classes; not presided over by Humboldt, who manages things very well, but under the presidency of some other Master of Spigots, whose name I can't remember at this moment, but I have it written under a portrait of him that I made. The dinner went on so long that I could not get to the concert of the nine-year-old violinist Birnbach, who is rather highly spoken of here. Today I am going to " Ferdinand Cortez," Spontini's famous opera; so, in order not to be made late again by the caricatures, I asked Jarocki to let me dine alone. That done, I am writing this letter, and then I go to the opera. There is a rumour that Paganini, the famous violinist, is coming here; perhaps it will come true. Radziwiłł is expected about the 20th of this month; it would be good if he came.

Until now I have seen nothing but the zoological congress; but I already know a good deal of the town, as for two days I have poked about and gaped at the handsomest streets and bridges.

[1] Humboldt (Fr. Wilh. v.): 1767–1835.
[2] *The Interrupted Sacrifice:* opera by Winter. 1st performance: Vienna, 1795.

I won't bother to go into details of the principal buildings, I will tell all that when I come back; but my general impression of Berlin is that it's too widely built: that double the amount of population could fit into it easily.

At first we were to have lodged in the *Französische Strasse,* but the arrangement was changed, much to my joy, as it is a very dismal street; you scarcely see half a dozen persons in it. Probably that is because of its width; it's as wide as our Leszno. Today I shall see for the first time what Berlin is like in my sense of the phrase.

I should prefer to sit at Schlesinger's in the morning, rather than to wander about the 13 rooms of the zoological congress. It's true they are fine; but the above-mentioned music-shop would be far more useful to me. But you can't have too much of a good thing;[1] I'll go to both. This morning I looked over two piano-factories. Kisling is at the end of the *Friedrichstrasse:* he had not a single finished one, so my trouble was for nothing. It's fortunate that the landlord of this house has a piano and that I can play on it. Our innkeeper admires me every day when I go to visit him, or rather his instrument.

The journey was not so bad as it looked at first; or else I have managed to acquire much energy in the licensed Prussian diligences; they certainly seem to have agreed with me, for I am well, and very well.

Our travelling companions were a German jurisconsult living in Poznań and distinguished for heavy facetiousness, and a fat agronomist who has travelled so much that diligences have been his education. That was all the company we had till the last stop before Frankfort, when there joined us a sort of German Corinne, full of *ach's* and *ja's* and *na's:* in a word, a real romantic doll. But it was quite amusing, especially as all the way she was furious with her neighbour the jurisconsult.

The environs of Berlin on this side are not particularly beautiful, but impress one through their neatness, cleanliness, selection of things; that is, by a certain circumspectness that catches the eye at every touch and turn. I have not been on the other side of the town, and can't go today; perhaps tomorrow. The

[1] Literally: "From increase the head does not ache:" a Polish proverb.

day after tomorrow begin the sessions, for which Lichtenstein has promised to give me a pass. On the same day there is to be a reception for the naturalists at Humboldt's. Pan Jarocki wanted to try if he could get me invited; but I asked him not to do so; it would not be of much use to me, and then, the other foreign guests might look askance on the presence of an outsider among them. As it is, I think one table neighbour has already cast sour glances at me. That was a professor of botany from Hamburg, Herr Lehmann. I envied him his fingers. I broke my roll with two hands; he crushed his into a wafer with one. Zabka also had paws like a bear's. He talked across me to Jarocki, and got so excited in conversation that he waved his fingers over my plate and strewed it with crumbs. He must be really learned, because he had a large and clumsy nose as well. I sat on thorns while he messed up my plate, and afterwards had to wipe it with my table-napkin.

Marylski hasn't a farthing's worth of taste if he says the Berlin women are beautiful. They dress, that's true; but it's pitiful to see the gorgeous rumpled muslins on such dowdy images.

Your sincerely affectionate

FRYDERYK

27.

To his Family.

Berlin, 20 September 1828.

I am well, and since Tuesday they give something new in the theatre every day, as if on purpose for me. Still better, I have already heard one *Oratorio* in the *Singakademie, Cortez,* Cimarosa's: *Il Matrimonio Segreto,*[1] and enjoyed listening to Onslow's: *Colporteur.*[2] But Handel's *Oratorio: Cäcilienfest,* is nearer to the ideal that I have formed of great music. There is no celebrated female singer here just now, except Fräul. Tibaldi

[1] 1st performance 1792.

[2] 1st performance 1827.

(alto), and the 17-year-old von Schätzel girl, whom I heard first at the *Singakademie* and then in the theatre, in the *Colporteur.* I liked her better in the *Oratorio;* perhaps I was in a better mood for listening. But even then there was a *but;* let's hope that won't be so in Paris.

I have not been again at Lichtenstein's, as he is so busy with the affairs of the session that Pan Jarocki could scarcely get a few words with him. In spite of that, he took the trouble to get me a ticket for the sessions. I had a splendid place, saw and heard everything and even had a good look at the kronprinz. I have seen Spontini, Zelter, and Mendelsohn, but did not speak with any of them as I felt shy about introducing myself. Prince Radziwiłł is expected today; after lunch I shall go and inquire. I saw Princess Lignicka in the *Singakademie,* and observing someone in a livery talking to her, asked my neighbour whether that is the King's *kammerdiener.* — "*Ei, das ist ja Exzellenz von Humboldt,*" [1] said he. The ministerial uniform changed his appearance so much, that though the features of this great *pedestrian* (you know, he has climbed Cimborasso), are printed on my memory, I did not recognize him. Yesterday he was at the *Colporteur,* or as they call it here: *Hausirer* (in Polish I suppose it should be *Kramarz* [2]). He was in Prince Karl's royal box.

The day before yesterday we visited the library. It is huge, but has very few musical works. I saw there an autograph letter of Kościuszko, which Falkenstein, the biographer of our hero, had copied out, by the shape of the letters. Finding that we were Poles and could easily read the document that he had been obliged to draw laboriously, letter by letter, he asked Pan Jarocki to translate the text into German, and wrote it down from dictation in his pocketbook. He is still a rather young man, and holds the post of secretary of the Dresden library. I also met the editor of the Berlin musical Gazette and exchanged a few words with him.

Tomorrow Freischütz! — That is what I want. I shall be able to compare with our singers. Today I received a ticket for the *Exercirhaus* dinner.

I have some more caricatures now.

[1] Why, that's his Excellency von Humboldt.
[2] pedlar.

28.

To his Family.
Berlin, 27 inst. [1828].

I am well, and have seen all there was to see. I am coming back to you. On Monday, that is a week from the day after tomorrow, I shall embrace you. My holiday is doing me good. I do nothing but go to the theatre. Yesterday was: *Das unterbrochene Opferfest;* in which one chromatic scale emitted by Miss Schätzel, took me back to your arms. " Your "[1] reminds me of a Berlin caricature. The drawing is of a Napoleonic soldier on sentinel duty, with a carbine, standing and asking: " Qui vive? "[2] and a fat German woman answering: "La vache."[3] She means to say:—"Die Wäscherin;[4] but desiring to be more elegant and better understood by the French soldier, she Gallicized her dignity!

Among the more important scenes of my trip I can count my second dinner with the naturalists. On Tuesday, the eve of our departure, we had a banquet with songs suitable to the occasion. Every living creature sang, and everyone that sat at the table drank and clinked glasses in time to the music. Zelter conducted; in front of him, on a crimson pedestal, stood a large gilded goblet, a mark of the highest musical status. We ate more than usual, for the following reason:

The naturalists, and particularly the zoologists, have occupied themselves chiefly with the improvement of meat, sauces, broth, and such things; so during the few days of the sessions they made great progress in eating. At the *Königstheater* there has been a skit on the scientific guests; in some comedy, which I did not see but was told about, men are drinking beer, and one asks another:—" Why is the beer in Berlin so good now? "—" Because the naturalists have come," is the answer.

But it's time for bed; I must be at the post house early

[1] A pun: *Wasze:* your, in Polish; *Wäsche:* laundry, in German.
[2] Who goes there?
[3] The cow.
[4] The laundress.

tomorrow. We shall stay two days in Poznań, *in gratiam* for a dinner to which Archbishop Wolicki has invited us.

When we meet, we'll talk enough!

Goodbye, etc.

29.

To Tytus Wojciechowski in Poturzyń
Warsaw, 27 December 1828.

Dearest Tytus!

I have put off writing till the moment when the sense of friendship conquered the habit of laziness.

As I want this letter to be in your house for the 1st and 4th of January, I take up my pen, sleepy as I am. I won't fill up this paper with a lot of compliments, affected good wishes and the usual silly phrases, because I know you and you know me; there you have the reason of my silence. Max gave me the news about you and about your Mamma's health, the morning after he arrived in Warsaw. On his way to the University he ran in to see me and very enthusiastically talked to me about Hrubiesz. Some of his descriptions were admirable: for instance, about your neighbour who has come back from Paris. When I asked: — "Does he curl his hair?" he answered gravely and succinctly: — "Pani Pruszak is going to give another comedy; I have the role of Pedro, in *Les projets de mariage*, par Duval." After the new year they are going away to two weddings; one is that of Panna Skarzyńska from Cracow and Luszczewski; the other that of Panna Skarzyńska from Studzieniec, — by the way, the eldest one, and I don't know with whom. I know you will shake your head and say: "What rubbish that Fryc [*sic*] does put down"; but I've written it and I'm not going to scratch it out, for I've no time to copy this. From another village we hear that Jędrzejewicz has been made a member of some society in Paris, probably the geographical. But what will amuse you most is that I, poor I, have got to give lessons. Here is the cause of it. *Noli " a fatto infelice la signorina governante della Casa, nella strada Marszałkowska. La signorina governante a un bambino nell' ventre, e la Contessa sive la padrona non vuole vedere di piu il seduttore." Il migliore evento e, che credevano avanti, che tutto e apparito, ch' il seducente son io perque io ch'era piud'un messo a Saniki,*[1] *e sempre andava colla governante camminar nell' giardino. Ma andara camminar e niente di piu. Ella non e incantante.* Poor me, *non li o avuto alcuno apetito* for such good fortune for myself.[2] *Madama* Pruszak so persuaded Papa and Mamma that I am to give the lessons. *Oleum et operam perdidi.* But let it be as they like.

The score of the *Rondo à la Krakowiak* is finished. The introduction is original; more so than I myself even in a beige suit. But the Trio is not yet finished. There's a room upstairs which is to be at my service; steps have been made to it from the wardrobe room. I am to have an old piano there, and an old bureau, and it's to be my den. The orphaned *Rondo* for two pantaleons has found a step-father in the person of *Fontana;* [3] perhaps you have met him at our house; he goes to the university. He has been over a month learning it, but he has learned it, and the other day, at Bucholtz's we tried what effect it *might* produce. Might, because, as the pantaleons were not quite in tune, the emotion didn't always come off; and you know what a difference all those details make to a thing. For the last week I have written nothing either for men or for God. I fly about from Anasz to Kaifasz; [4] today I go to Pani Wincengerode's to an evening party; from there to another at Panna Kicka's. You know how nice it is, when you're sleepy and they ask you to improvise. Try to please everybody! I very seldom get an idea like the one that came to my fingers so easily one morning on your pantaleon. Wherever you go there are Leszczyński's bad instruments; I

[1] Sanniki, the estate of the Pruszak family.

[2] In incorrect Italian mixed with Polish "Noli has brought unhappiness upon the governess of the House, in the Marszałkowska Street. The governess has a baby in her inside, and the Countess, or lady of the house, does not wish to see the seducer again. The best part of it is that they thought at first that it is I that must be the seducer, because I was more than a month at Sanniki, and always walked in the garden with the governess. But I walked, and that's all. She is not attractive. Poor me, I had no appetite for such good fortune for myself.

[3] Juljan Fontane, 1810–70: Polish musician; Chopin's fellow student and life-long friend. After the Polish insurrection of 1830 he settled in Paris, and after Chopin's death edited many of his unpublished MSS.

[4] From Ananias to Caiaphas: Peter to Paul.

haven't seen one that has a tone approaching that of your sister's pantaleon, or of either of ours. Yesterday the Polish theatre opened with *Preziosa* [1] and the French one with *Rataplan.*[2] Today *Geldhab,*[3] tomorrow the *Locksmith.*[4] Tomorrow and Sunday I dine at Pruszak's. Kostuś told me that you have written to him; don't think I'm cross because you haven't written to me. I know your soul, so it doesn't matter about paper; if I have written such a lot of nonsense to you, it's only to remind you that you are as much in my heart as ever and that I'm the same Fryc as before.

F. CHOPIN

You don't like to be kissed. But let me do it today. Best wishes for your Mamma's health from the whole household. Embrace your brother for me. Żywny sends you greetings.

On the 9th of September at the Pruszaks' I re-wrote the C-Major Rondo for 2 pianofortes. The G-minor Trio is not quite finished.

27th of December. The score of the Rondo *à la Krakowiak* is finished. The Trio is not finished yet.

30.

To his Family.
Vienna, 1 August 1829.

MY DEAREST PARENTS AND SISTERS!

We reached Vienna yesterday; safe, gay, healthy, all right, almost comfortable. From Cracow we travelled with less discomfort in a *Separatwagen* than we should have done in a private carriage. Beautiful scenery in Galicia till Bielsk, and afterwards in Upper Silesia and Moravia, made it a very pleasant

[1] A play by Wolf (from Cervantes); incidental music by Weber. 1st performance 1821.

[2] Probably: *Rataplan, der Kleine Tambour,* opera by Pillurtz, 1831.

[3] *Pan Geldhab:* a Polish comedy by Alexander Fredro (1793–1876), who had a considerable vogue in Warsaw, both as a writer of comedies and as a translator of Goethe into Polish.

[4] Auber's opera: *Miller and Locksmith* (*Le Maçon*). 1st performance 1825.

journey; all the more so as showers, which sometimes fell only at night, saved us from the discomfort of the dust.

Before I begin to describe Vienna I must tell you what happened at Ojców. After dinner on Sunday, we engaged a peasant's cart of the 4-horse Cracow type and started off in the finest style. After leaving the city and beautiful environs of Cracow, we told our driver to go straight to Ojców where we expected to find Pan Indyk, the man who usually puts everyone up for the night; Panna Tańska has slept there. As ill luck would have it, Indyk lives a whole mile from Ojców, and our driver, not knowing the way, drove into the Pradnik, a little river, or rather, a clear stream, and no other way could be found, as there were rocks to the right and left. About 9 in the evening, when we were wandering about and not knowing what to do, we met two strangers, who took pity on us and undertook to guide us to Indyk. We have to go on foot for a good half mile,[1] in the dew, among a mass of rocks and sharp stones, and to keep crossing the stream on round logs; and all this in the dark night. At last, after many efforts, bumps and grumbles, we crawled out at Pan Indyk's house.

He was not expecting guests so late. He gave us a little room under the cliff, in a hut built specially for tourists. Izabela! It was there that Panna Tańska slept! So all my companions undressed and dried their clothes by the fire which the kind Pani Indyk had made. I alone, sitting in the corner, wet to the knees, shall I undress and get dry, or not? Suddenly I see Pani Indyk going into the nearest cupboard to fetch bedding. Struck by a happy thought I follow her, and see a lot of the Cracow woollen caps. These caps are double, like nightcaps. Being desperate, I buy one for a złoty, tear it in two, take off my boots, wrap up my feet, tie the strings well round and save myself from a quite certain chill. I then drank some wine by the fire and had a good laugh with my kind companions; meanwhile Pani Indyk made up beds for us on the floor, and we slept beautifully.

[The remainder of this letter is known only from an abridged account of it given by Karasowski.]

[1] Equivalent to about $2\frac{1}{2}$ English miles.

31.

To his Family.
Vienna, 8 August 1829.

I am well and happy. I don't know why, but I appear to astonish the Germans, and I am astonished at their finding anything to be astonished at. Thanks to Elsner's letter, Haslinger doesn't know what to do with me. He told his son to play to me, showed me everything of musical interest that he has, and apologized for not introducing me to his wife as she is not at home. With all that, he has not yet printed my things. I did not ask him about them; but, while showing me his finest editions, he informed me that my *Variations* will probably appear in a week's time in the *Odéon*. I didn't expect that.

He wants me to play in public. They tell me here that it would be a great loss for Vienna if I were to leave without being heard. All this is incomprehensible for me. Schuppanzigh, to whom I also had introductions, told me that, though he is not giving winter quartets any more, he would try to arrange one during my visit to Vienna.

I have been once to the Hussarzewskis'; the old man was enthusiastic about my playing and asked me to dinner. At the dinner there were a lot of Viennese folk, and, as if he had arranged it with them, they all told me to play in public. Stein wanted at once to send one of his instruments to my lodging, and then to the concert, if I give one. Graff, who, by the way, makes better instruments, made the same offer. Würfel declares that if I want to show something new and to make a sensation, I must play in public without fail. Blahetka, a journalist here, whom I met at Haslinger's, also advises me to play in public. They are awfully pleased with the *Variations*.

I also met Count Gallenberg there; he is director of the theatre, where I have already heard several bad concerts. Haslinger insists that the best chance for my compositions will be for Vienna to hear them; that the papers will praise them, everybody assures me of that. In a word, whoever hears me tells me to play in public, and Würfel also adds that, as I am now in Vienna and my things are to appear at once, I certainly must play, because otherwise I should only have to come back specially. They assure me that now is the most favourable time, because the Viennese are hungry for new music. A young artist should not throw away such an opportunity. Moreover, if I were to appear only as an executant, it would count for less; but as I bring out my own compositions, I can safely venture; etc.—He wants me to play first the *Variations*, then the *Krakowiak Rondo*, as a striking novelty, and finally to improvise. Will it come to that? I don't know yet.

Stein is very friendly and polite to me, but I could not play on his instrument; I'd rather have a Graff. Haslinger, Blahetka and Würfel agree with that. I shall decide today.

Wherever I turn, everybody clacks my head off about playing in public. I now know plenty of musicians; only Czerny I have not seen yet, but Haslinger promises to introduce me to him.

I have seen three operas: *The White Lady*,[1] *Kosciuszko*, and Meyerbeer's *Knight of the Cross*.[2] The orchestra and choir are splendid. Today *Joseph in Egypt*.[3] In the Academy of Music I have heard *Mayseder* play solos twice. I like the town, which is fine to look at; they want me to stay for the winter.

Würfel has just come in; I am going with him to Haslinger.

P.S. I have decided. Blahetka says that I shall cause a *furore*, that I'm a virtuoso of the first rank, that I count with Moscheles, Herz and Kalkbrenner. Würfel today introduced me to Count Gallenberg, Kapellmeister Seyfried and everyone else he encountered, as a young man whom he was persuading to give a concert (*nota bene* without any pay), which greatly pleased Count Gallenberg, as it is a question of his pocket. The journalists all stare at me with round eyes; the members of the orchestra bow deeply, because the director of the Italian opera, which no longer exists, walks arm in arm with me. Würfel really is making everything easy for me; he will come to the

1 *La Dame Blanche:* comic opera by Boïeldieu. 1st performance 1825.

2 *Il Crociato in Egitto;* one of Meyerbeer's Italian operas (early work). 1st performance 1824.

3 Is this an error for Rossini's *Mose in Egitto* (1818)?

rehearsal himself and is genuinely taking trouble over my début. He was kind to me in Warsaw too; he spoke very nicely of Elsner.

They are all surprised that Kessler, Ernemann and Czapek can get on in Warsaw when I am there. But I explain to them that I play *bloss aus Musikliebe* [1] and don't give lessons. I have chosen one of Graff's instruments for the concert; I'm afraid Stein will take offence, but I will thank him warmly for his kindness.

I hope the Lord will help me. — Don't worry!

32.

To his Family.
[*Vienna*] *Wednesday, 12 August 1829.*

You know from my last letter, dearest Parents, that I have been persuaded to give a concert. So yesterday, that is, Tuesday evening at 7, in the Imperial-and-Royal opera-house, I made my entry into the world!

Here they are speaking of this appearance in the theatre as: "*Eine musikalische Akademie.*" [2] As I got nothing for it, and didn't try to get anything, Count Gallenberg hurried on the concert, arranging the programme as follows:

A Beethoven *Overture* [3]
My *Variations* [4]
Singing (Miss Veltheim)
My *Rondo.* [5]

Then more singing, then a short ballet to fill out the evening. At rehearsal the orchestra accompanied so badly, that I substituted *Freie Phantasie* for the *Rondo*. As soon as I appeared on

[1] only for love of music.
[2] A musical Academy.
[3] Prometheus.
[4] On "La Ci Darem La Mano."
[5] Op. 5. *Rondo à la Mazur.* [Op.]

the stage, the bravos began; after each variation the applause was so loud that I couldn't hear the orchestra's *tutti.* When I finished, they clapped so much that I had to come out and bow a second time. The *Freie Phantasie* didn't go off quite so well, but there was a lot of clapping and bravos, and I had to come out again. That was easier to do, because the Germans appreciate that sort of thing. The whole notion was suggested only on Saturday, and on Tuesday Würfel carried it out; I owe him a great deal. On Saturday I met Gyrowetz, Lachner, Kreutzer and Seyfried; I had a long talk with Mayseder. Standing in front of the theatre, I saw Count Gallenberg; he came up to me and proposed that I should play on Tuesday; so I consented, and I didn't get hissed! When I come home, I'll tell you more about it than I can write; but you need have no anxiety for me and my reputation.

The journalists have taken a fancy to me; perhaps they'll stick a patch on me,[1] but that's necessary to underline the praise. Gallenberg likes my compositions. The stage manager of the theatre, Demar, is very kind and amiable to me. He was so encouraging with his assurances before I went on to the stage, and kept my thoughts off it so well that I was not very nervous, especially as the hall was not full.

My friends and colleagues spread themselves over the hall to listen for opinions and criticisms. Celiński can tell you how little fault-finding there was; only Hube overheard more. Some lady said: "*Schade um den Jungen dass er so wenig Tournüre hat.*" [2] If that is all the fault anybody found — and otherwise they assure me that they heard only praises, and that they never started the bravos themselves — then I don't need to worry!

I improvised on a theme from the *White Lady.* At the request of the stage manager, who liked my Rondo so much at rehearsal that yesterday, after the concert, he squeezed my hand and said: — "*Ja, das Rondo muss hier gespielt werden*"; [3] — at his request that I should also take a Polish theme, I chose

[1] To speak against a person; Polish idiom.
[2] A pity the boy has so little style.
[3] Yes the Rondo must be played here.

Chmiel,[1] which electrified the public, as they are not used here to such songs. My spies in the stalls assure me that people even jumped on the seats.

Wertheim, who happened to arrive yesterday from Carlsbad with his wife, went straight to the theatre, but did not find out that it was I who was playing; he called on me today to congratulate me. He saw Hummel in Carlsbad, and says that Hummel mentioned me, and that he is writing to him today about my début.

Haslinger is printing; the poster of the concert is being preserved.

All the same it is being said everywhere that I played too softly, or rather, too delicately for people used to the piano-pounding of the artists here. I expect to find this reproach in the paper, especially as the editor's daughter thumps frightfully. It doesn't matter, there has always got to be a *but* somewhere, and I should rather it were that one than have people say I played too loud. Yesterday Count Dietrichstein, a personage in touch with the emperor, came on to the stage; he talked a lot with me in French, complimenting me and asking me to stay longer in Vienna. The orchestra cursed at my badly written score and grumbled, right up to the improvisation, after which they added their bravos to the clapping and yells of the whole audience. I see that I have them for me; about other artists I don't know yet; but they ought not to be hostile, seeing that

[1] An orgiastic drinking-song, very popular at peasant weddings. Chmiel is the hop-vine. The use of the third mode in a song of this gay and riotous character is sufficiently unusual to explain to some extent the startling effect of the tune. In Gloger's collection it is given as follows:

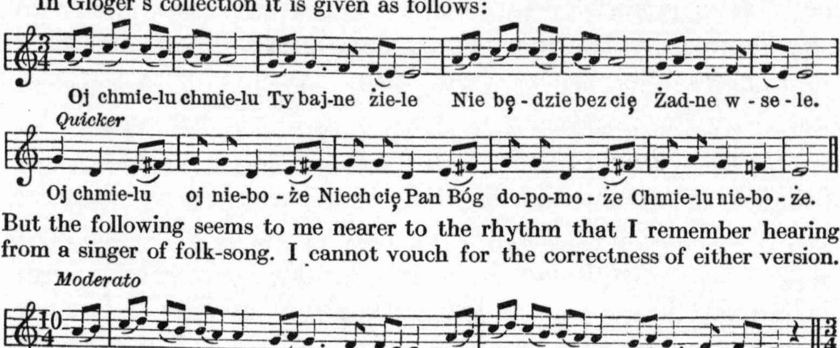

But the following seems to me nearer to the rhythm that I remember hearing from a singer of folk-song. I cannot vouch for the correctness of either version.

Moderato

Oj chmie-lu chmie-lu Ty baj-ne żie-le Nie bę- dzie bez cię Żad-ne we - se-le.

Quickly *accell.* *rall.*

Oj chmie-lu, oj nie-bo - że, Niech cię Pan Bóg do-po - mo - że Chmie-lu nie-bo - że.

I did not play for material gain. Thus, my first appearance has been as fortunate as it was unexpected. Hube says that no one ever attains anything by ordinary methods and according to any prearranged plan; that one must leave something to luck. And it was just trusting to luck that I let myself be persuaded to give the concert. I decided that if the papers should so smash me that I could not again appear before the world I would take to interior housepainting; it's easy to smear a brush across paper, and one is still a son of Apollo.

I wonder what Pan Elsner will say to all this; perhaps he won't like my having played? But they made such a dead set at me that I could not refuse, and after all I think it did no harm. Nidecki in particular showed me great friendliness yesterday; he looked through and corrected the orchestral parts, and was genuinely pleased at the applause.

I played on a Graff instrument.

Today I am wiser and more experienced by about 4 years.

Ah! You must have been surprised that my last letter was sealed with:—" Madeira." I was so distracted that I took the seal nearest to my hand, which was the waiter's, and sealed my letter in a hurry.

33.

To his Family.

[*Vienna*] *Thursday, 13. 8* [*1829*].

If I ever wanted to be with you, it's now. Today I met Count Lichnowski, who couldn't praise me enough; Würfel took me to him. It's the same who was Beethoven's greatest friend. It's said everywhere here that the local nobility likes me. The Schwartzenbergs, the Wobrzes, etc. all speak in high terms of the delicacy and elegance of my playing; Count Dietrichstein, who came on to the stage, is an example. Countess Lichnowska and her daughter, with whom I had tea today, are greatly delighted that I am to give a second concert next Tuesday. She told me, if I go to Paris by way of Vienna, not to forget to call on them, and they will give me a letter to some *comtesse*, Lichnowski's sister. They are very kind.

Czerny has paid me a lot of compliments; Schuppanzigh and Gyrowetz also. Today in the *Antiken* Kabinet some German caught sight of me; directly I spoke, he asked Celiński: — " Is that Chopin? " and rushed up to me with big jumps, delighted to have the pleasure of meeting such a *Künstler:*[1] " *Sie haben mich vorgestern wahrhaft entzückt und begeistert.*"[2] It was the man who sat beside Maciejowski and was so overjoyed with *Chmiel.*

I shan't give a third concert, and would not even give a second but that they insist on it; besides, it occurred to me that people might say in Warsaw: — " What is it? He only gave one concert and went away; perhaps it was a failure." They promise me good reviews; today I called on a journalist; luckily he likes me.

I don't write about how kind Würfel is to me, because I can't describe it.

This time too I shall play for nothing; but that is to please the count, whose pocket is emaciated; but this is a secret. I am to play the *Rondo* and to improvise.

For the rest, I am healthy and happy; eat and drink well. I like Vienna and the Poles here fairly well. In the ballet there is one who on the evening of the concert took such care of me that he brought me water with sugar, cheered me up, and so on.

Please tell Pan Elsner all this, and make my excuses to him for not writing; I'm so confused that I don't know where the hours go to.

My thanks to Pan Skarbek, who first advised me to give concerts: it is a start in life.

34.

To his Family.

[Vienna] 19 August 1829.

If I was well received the first time, it was still better yesterday. The moment I appeared on the stage there were bravos, re-

[1] artist.

[2] Yesterday you really delighted and enchanted me.

peated three times; and there was a larger audience. Baron—I don't know what his name is: the financier of the theatre, thanked me for the *receipts,* saying that:—"If such a crowd has come it is surely not for the ballet, which everybody knows well." All the professional musicians are captivated with my *Rondo.* Beginning with Kapellmeister Lachner and ending with the pianoforte-tuner, they are surprised at the beauty of the composition. I know that both ladies and artists liked me. Gyrowetz, standing by Celiński, clapped and shouted "Bravo!" I only don't know whether I pleased the stony Germans. Yesterday one of them returned from the theatre, and I was sitting at supper; the others asked him how he had enjoyed himself.—"A good ballet," he answered. "But the Academy?" I saw that he had recognized me, though my back was turned to him, because he began to talk of something else. I felt I ought not to hamper him in expressing his feelings, so I went to bed, saying to myself:

"There is not a mother's son
Can be liked by everyone."

I have played twice, and the second success was better than the first; it goes *crescendo;* that's what I like.

As I leave at 9 this evening, I must return some calls this morning. Schappanzigh reminded me yesterday that, as I am leaving Vienna so soon, I must also come back soon. I replied that I shall come to learn; to which the baron retorted:—"In that case you have nothing to come for." Only compliments, but pleasant ones. No one here wants to take me as a pupil. Blahetka said nothing surprised him so much as my having learned all that in Warsaw. I answered that under Żywny and Elsner the greatest donkey could learn. I am sorry that I still have not had any notices in the press; I know that one is lying already written in the office of the paper to which I have subscribed, and which the editor, Mr. Bäuerle, will send to Warsaw. I don't know, perhaps they are waiting for the second concert. It comes out twice a week, on Tuesdays and Saturdays; perhaps you will soon read something good or bad about me.

I have captured both the learned and the emotional folk. They will have something to talk about.

I wanted to write about other things, but yesterday sticks in my head, and I can't collect my thoughts. . . .

My finances are all right so far. I have just been to Schuppanzigh and Czerny to say goodbye. Czerny is more sensitive than any of his compositions.

I have packed my bag; now I have only got to go to Hasslinger, and then to the café opposite the theatre, where I shall find Gyrowetz, Lachner, Kreutzer and Seyfried.

In two nights and one day we shall be in Prague; at 9 in the evening we shall start in the *Eilwagen;* it will be a fine journey and a fine company.

35.

To his Family.
Prague, Saturday, 22 August 1829.

After tender farewells in Vienna, — really tender; Panna Blahetka gave me her compositions with an autograph inscription for a keepsake and her father told me to embrace my Papa and Mamma and congratulate them on such a son. Young Stein wept; Schuppanzigh, Gyrowetz, in a word all the artists took leave of me most affectionately.

After all scenes, and promises to come back, we got into the *Eilwagen.* Nidecki and two other Poles, who were starting half an hour later for Trieste, saw us off. They stayed some days in Vienna, and we saw a good deal of them. One of them is called Niegolewski; he is from Great Poland, a young fellow, travelling with his tutor, or rather companion, Kopytowski, who is a member of the Warsaw Academy. Pani Hussarzewska, on whom I called to say goodbye, — they are both very decent people — wanted to keep me to dinner; but I had no time, I had to rush to Hasslinger. He also, after affectionately begging me to come back and *seriously* promising to issue my Variations within five weeks, to impress the world with them, sends his respects and greetings to Papa, although he has not the pleasure of knowing him.

We got into the *Eilwagen,* and a young German with us. As we were going to sit together for two nights and a day, we introduced ourselves. He is a merchant from Gdańsk, and knows the Pruszaks, Sierakowski of Waplew, Jawurek, Ernemann, the Grossers, and so on. Two years ago he was in Warsaw; his name is Normann. He turned out an excellent travelling companion; he was on his way back from Paris. We have put up at the same hotel, and have decided, after seeing Prague, to make an excursion together to Teplitz and Dresden. It would be childish to miss the opportunity to see Dresden, especially as our finances allow it and travelling four together it will be cheap and comfortable.

After many bumps and jolts in the *Eilwagen* we reached Prague yesterday at noon, and went straight to the *table d'hôte.* After dinner we called on Hauke, to whom Hube had given Maciejowski a letter of introduction. I was sorry I had not thought of writing to Skarbek and asking for a letter to this famous scholar. As we had lingered in the cathedral church in [*sic*] the castle, we did not find Hauke at home. The town is beautiful on the whole, when one sees it from the castle hill; large, ancient and once opulent. Just before leaving Vienna, I was given six letters: five from Würfel, one from Blahetka to Pixis, asking him to show me the Conservatorium. They wanted me to play here too, but I am staying only three days; besides, I don't want to spoil what I gained in Vienna; here, even Paganini was grilled; [1] so I shall leave it alone. The five letters from Würfel are to the director and kapellmeister of the theatre and to the leading musical lights of the place. I shall present them, as he specially asked me to do so, but I have no intention of playing. The good Würfel has also given me a letter to Klengel in Dresden.

I must stop writing, for it is time to go to Hauke; I shall introduce myself as Skarbek's godson, and hope that I shall not need any letter.

[1] Literally: whetted (as on a grindstone); a Polish idiom.

36.

To his Family.
Dresden, 26 August 1829.

I am well and very cheerful. A week ago today, in Vienna, I did not know that I should come to Dresden. We saw Prague at lightning speed, but not in vain. Hauke was pleased to have news of Pan Skarbek. We had to write our names in his book, which is devoted to those who visit the Prague Museum, and particularly in connection with him. Brodziński, Morawski, etc. — are already there. So each of us had to think of something to say; one in verse, the other in prose. Szwejkowski wrote a long speech. What was a musician to do here? Luckily Maciejowski hit on the idea of writing a four-verse mazurka,[1] so I added the music and inscribed myself together with my poet, as originally as possible. Hauke was pleased; it was a *Mazur* for him, celebrating his services to the Slavonic world. He gave me a complete set of views of Prague for Pan Skarbek.

I won't go into details about where he conducted us, to what beautiful views; I have no space to describe the magnificent cathedral church with the silver St. John Nepomuk, the lovely chapel of Wacław decorated with amethysts and other precious stones — I'll tell you when I come.

The letters of Blahetka and Würfel to Pixis procured for me the kindest reception. Pixis stopped his lesson, made me stay and asked about a lot of things. Looking at the bureau, I see Klengel's visiting-card; I ask whether some namesake of the famous Dresden man is in Prague. He replied that Klengel himself has just arrived, and, not finding him at home, has left this card.

I was pleased, because I had a letter to him from Vienna; I mentioned this to Pixis, and he asked me to come to him after dinner, as that was the hour of the appointment that Klengel had made with him. So it happened that we met on the stairs, going to Pixis. I listened to his playing of his *Fugues* for two hours. I

[1] These old national dances have words.

did not play, because they did not ask me to do so. He plays well, but I should have liked him to play better (hush). Klengel gave me a letter: — "*All Ornatissimo Signor Cavaliere Morlacchi, primo maestro della Capella Reale,*" in which, as he told me, he asks him to show me the whole musical *Wesen*[1] of Dresden, and to present me to Miss Pechwell, his pupil, whom he regards as the best pianist there. He was very amiable; before he left I spent two hours in his rooms. He is on his way to Vienna and Italy, so we had something to talk about.

It is an excellent acquaintance, and I value it more than I do that of poor Czerny. (Hush!)

In Prague we stayed only three days. The time flew so fast that there was no catching it. I was busy all the time; with the result that, the day before leaving, I left the room half-dressed, blundered into a strange bedroom, and had got inside before some cheerful traveller greeted me with an astonished: — "*Guten Morgen!*" — "*Bitte um Verzeihung!*"[2] and I fled. The rooms are just alike. We left Dresden by *Separatwagen* at midday, and reached Teplitz in the evening.

The next morning I found in the *Badeliste*[3] the name of Ludwik Lempicki, so I went at once to say good day to him; he was pleased. He told me there are many Poles here, among others old Pruszak, Joseph Kochler and Kretkowsky from Kamionnia. They eat together *im deutschen Saale*,[4] but he would not be at dinner that day, as he was invited to the castle, to Prince Clary's. It is a great, almost sovereign family, owning the whole town of Teplitz, and extremely kind. Princess Clary is a sister of Chotek, the Bohemian viceroy. Lempicki asked me to give him the pleasure of bringing me to them for the evening, as he is at home in the castle, and would mention me at dinner. As we were giving up the day to seeing the place, I agreed.

We went everywhere, including Wallenstein's palace at Dux. There is a fragment of the great soldier's skull, and the halberd with which he was killed, and many other relics. In the evening, instead of going to the theatre, I dressed, put on the white gloves

1 affairs.
2 Good morning!—Please excuse!
3 Visitor's list at a bathing-resort.
4 In the German Hall.

of my second Viennese concert, and at half past eight went with Lempicki to the prince's.

We enter: — "Kleine aber honette Compagnie." [1] Some Austrian prince, some general, whose names I have forgotten, an English sea-captain, several young men of fashion, probably also Austrian princes, and a Saxon general called Leiser, covered with orders and with a scar on his face.

After tea, before which I had had a long talk with Prince Clary himself, his mother asked me to "be pleased to" sit down to the pianoforte; a good one, by Graff. I was "pleased," but on my side asked them to "be pleased to" give me a theme for improvisation. Immediately among the female company that was sitting round a big table, lace-making, knitting and embroidering, began cries of: — "*Un thème, un thème.*" Three of these young princesses agreed that one of them should call Herr Fritsche, apparently young Clary's tutor; and he, by general consent, gave me a theme from Rossini's *Moses.*

I improvised; and it went off so well that General Leiser had a long talk with me afterwards, and hearing that I was going to Dresden, at once wrote this letter to Baron von Friesen:

"*M. Frédéric Chopin est recommandé de la part du Général Leiser à Monsieur le Baron de Friesen, Maître de Cérémonie de S. M. le Roi de Saxe, pour lui être utile pendant son séjour à Dresde, et de lui procurer la connaissance de plusieurs de nos premiers artistes.*" Underneath, in German: "*Herr Chopin ist selbst einer der vorzüglichsten Pianospieler, die ich bis jetzt kenne.*" [2] This is a literal copy of General Leiser's letter, written in pencil and not sealed.

I played four times that evening, and the princesses asked me to stay in Teplitz and come to dinner with them the next day. Lempicki even offered to take me to Warsaw with him, to enable me to wait. But I did not want to abandon my travelling companions, so I declined with many thanks.

Yesterday at 5 in the morning, having engaged a hackney

[1] A small but choice gathering.

[2] General Leiser recommends Mr. Frederick Chopin to Baron von Friesen, Master of Ceremonies to the King of Saxony, asking him to be helpful to him during his visit to Dresden and acquaint him with some of our leading artists.— Mr. Chopin is himself one of the finest pianists that I have yet heard."

coach for two thalers, we left Teplitz, arrived at Dresden at 4 in the afternoon and at once met Lewiński and the Labęckis.

This journey is a very lucky one for me; today Goethe's *Faust*, and on Saturday, Klengel tells me, an Italian opera.

I began this letter yesterday evening, and am finishing this morning.

I must dress; I am going to Baron Frieser and Morlacchi, as I have no time to waste. We expect to leave here in a week, but before that, if the weather is fine, we want to see Saxon Switzerland. Then we shall stay a few days in Wrocław [Breslau] before coming home. I am in such a hurry to get back to you, dearest Parents, that I should rather not stop at the Wiesołowskis'. I'll tell you the story afterwards; quite an adventure, but fine, fine.

[P.S.] *Maître de Cérémonie* Baron de Friesen received me courteously, asked where I am staying; told me he regrets that the Chamberlain, who directs the music, is out of town just now, but that he will find out who is replacing him; and that, though my visit here is short, he will do his best to be of service to me in some way. Plenty of bows and ceremonies. I'll keep the rest for next letter, which I will write from Wrocław in a week or ten days.

I have seen the picture gallery here, an exhibition of produce, the principal gardens; I have returned some calls, and am now going to the theatre; I hope that's enough for one day!

[2nd P.S.] My letter has lain here till late at night; I have just come back from *Faust*. I had to stand outside the theatre from half past 4; the show lasted from 6 to 11. Devrient, whom I saw in Berlin, played Faust. Today is Goethe's eightieth anniversary. It's terrible phantasy, but a great one. Between the acts they played selections from Spohr's opera of the same name. — I am going to bed — . Tomorrow morning I expect Morlacchi; I am to go with him to Miss Pechwell. He comes to me, not I to him! Ha, ha, ha! — Good night!

Your FRYDERYK

37.

To TYTUS WOJCIECHOWSKI IN POTURZYŃ.
Warsaw, 12 September 1829.

You wouldn't have had any news of me but for Winc. Skarzyński. I met him, and he told me you will not come to Warsaw till the end of this month, though Kostuś told me in Dresden that you were to come to your Sister on the 15th.

I mean to tell you personally of my *big* journey; which would give me the more pleasure because I really should like to have a chat with you; but know, my dear fellow, that I have been in Cracow, Vienna, Prague, Dresden and Wrocław. The first week was spent in Cracow on nothing but going about and looking at the environs. Ojców is really pretty; but I won't write much about it; because you know where and what it is from Panna Tańska's very truthful description. I went on to Vienna in a gay but rather unfamiliar company; and if Cracow so occupied my attention that I could give few moments to home or to you, Vienna so overwhelmed, stupefied and hallucinated me that, receiving no news from home for more than two weeks, I never worried about it. Imagine, in so short a time I had to play in public twice in the Imp.-Royal Theatre. This is how it happened. Haslinger, my publisher, told me it would be better for my compositions if I gave concerts in Vienna; that no one knows my name, that the compositions are difficult and recondite. I, however, not having intended to come out yet, and also not having practised for some weeks, refused, saying that I was not capable of doing myself justice before so famous an audience; so we left it at that. Meanwhile Count Gallenberg, the head of the Vienna theatre, who writes the beautiful ballets, came in, and Haslinger represented me to him as a coward who is afraid to appear. The count was kind enough to offer the use of his theatre; but I, being convinced of my own view, declined with thanks. The next morning someone knocks at my door, and in comes Würfel to implore me, and say that I shall disgrace my parents, Elsner and my own self, if, having the chance, I refuse to be heard in Vienna. They hammered at me till I consented; Würfel at once arranged everything and the posters were out the next day. It was difficult to back out; but I still did not know whether to play or not. Three *piano-manufacturers* offered to send their pantaleons to my room. I declined, because the room was too tiny; besides those few hours of practising would not have helped me much, as I had to appear in two days. So, in one day, I made acquaintance with Meyseder, Gyrowetz, Lachner, Kreutzer, Schupanzig [*sic*], with Mertz, with Levi; in a word with all the big musicians of Vienna. Nevertheless the orchestra was sulky at rehearsal; chiefly, I think, because I had just arrived from nowhere and was already playing my own compositions. So I started the rehearsal with the *Variations* dedicated to you, which were to have been preceded by the *Krakowiak Rondo*. They went well, but I began the Rondo several times and the orchestra muddled it frightfully and complained of the bad script. All the confusion was caused by pauses written differently at the top and bottom of the score, although I explained that only the top numbers count. It was partly my own fault; but I had thought they would understand. But they were annoyed at the inaccuracy, and besides, they are all *virtuosi* and composers too; anyhow they played so many tricks that I was just ready to fall ill for the evening. But Baron Demmar, the stage manager, seeing that it was a little want of goodwill on the part of the orchestra — all the more so because Würfel wanted to conduct, and they don't like him, I don't know why — proposed that instead of playing the *Rondo* I should improvise. At that suggestion the orchestra opened big eyes. I was so annoyed that in desperation I consented; and who knows whether the risk and my bad temper were not just the goad that stirred me up to do my best in the evening. Somehow or other the sight of the Viennese public did not frighten me; so, as it is not the custom there for the orchestral players to mount the stage — they stay in their seats — I sat down (pale, with a rouged-up partner to turn the leaves, who boasted to me that he had turned over for Moscheles, Hummel, Herz, etc. — when they came to Vienna) — to a magnificent instrument of Graff; perhaps the finest one in Vienna. You may believe me that I played from desperation. The Variations produced such an effect that, apart from the clapping after each one, I was obliged to come back to the stage after finishing. The Intermezzo was sung by Fräulein Weltheim, one of the King of Saxony's court singers. Then came the time for improvising. I don't know how it happened, but it went in such a way that the orchestra started to clap, and I again had to return after leaving the stage. That finished the first concert. The Viennese papers praised me enthusiastically — I don't count the Courier — then I played a second time during the week, as they begged me to; I was glad, because no one could say I had played once and run away. Besides, that second time I insisted on playing the Krakowiak Rondo, which ravished — forgive my saying it — Gyrowetz, Lachner, all the local celebrities and even the orchestra. I was recalled, not once, but twice. At that concert I was also obliged to repeat the Variations, as they were tremendously admired by the ladies, and also by Haslinger. They are to appear in the Odéon; I hope that is honour enough. Lichnowski, Beethoven's protector, wanted to give me his pianoforte for the concert — that is a great deal to offer. He thought mine was too weak in tone; but that is my way of playing, which, again, delights the ladies, and especially Blahetka's daughter, who is the first pianist of Vienna. She must like me (*nota bene* she is not 20 yet; living at home; a clever and even pretty girl); she gave me her own compositions with an autograph inscription, for a keepsake, when I left. About the second concert a Viennese newspaper wrote: — "This is a young man who goes his own road, on which he knows how to please, and which differs widely from all other concert forms" etc., etc. — I hope that is enough. It ends: "Today again Mr. Chopin gave universal satisfaction." Forgive my having to write to you these opinions about myself; but I am writing it to you, and that gives me more pleasure than any newspaper. I have made close friends with Czerny; we often played together on two pianofortes at his house. He's a good fellow, but nothing more. Of all my pianist acquaintances I am most glad of Klengel, whom I met at Pixis's house in Prague. He played me his fugues; one can say they are a continuation of Bach's; there are 48 of them, and as many canons.

One sees how different from Czerny. Klengel gave me a letter to Morlacchi in Dresden. Morlacchi, the head Kapellmeister of the King of Saxony, received me very courteously, called on me, and took me to Miss Pechwell, a pupil of Klengel, who is regarded as the leading woman pianist there. She plays well. We visited the Saxon Switzerland, which has many beauties. The Gallery is wonderful. Only the Italian opera was taken away from under my nose. I left the very day that they played *Crociato in Egitto;* the only consolation was that I had seen it in Vienna. Pani Pruszak, Olesia and Kostuś are in Dresden; I saw them at the moment of departure: "how delightful, how delightful, Pan frycek, Pan frycek!" I was so pleased that, if I had been alone, I should probably have stayed on. Pruszak himself is in Teplitz, where I saw him. Teplitz is lovely; I was there one day, and spent the evening at Princess Clary's. Sorry I must stop, but I have scribbled enough to you. I expect your arrival, sir; I often pass near the Sto Jurska St. going to Brandt, and want to write to you when I see it. I kiss you heartily, right on the lips; may I?

F. Chop.

I met Max today. He told me he is really cured, and staying *à l'hotel garni.* In a green coat; he was so kind as to promise me a call. He asked after you, but sent no message, as he did not know I was writing; I didn't know it myself this morning. If you think of it, dash off a few words on paper for me. Did you know that Panna Filipina, a cousin of Linde, who was with Berger? She is dead. On my way home I attended the wedding of Panna Bronikowska Melasi: a beautiful child; she has married Kurnatowski. She often spoke of you, and sent greetings. Her cousin, of the same age, was married a few days before her: a still prettier child; it was as nice as a wedding should be. I've written such a lot that I don't want to get up. Give me a kiss. My love to Pan Karol.

F. Ch. —Papa and Mamma send you greetings and good wishes; the children the same.

38.

To the Same.
Warsaw, 3 October 1829.

Dear Tytus!

I have this moment received a letter from you, just as I was starting to write to you again, thinking either that my first letter had not reached you, or that I must have written something frightfully stupid. I am glad that you are well, as I conclude from your letter; I shall learn more about that from Karol. You write that I am to explain to you more clearly, what is happening to me and to the persons that I know about. Kostuś sent me a letter by his father, who returned from Teplitz to the Łowicz fair on St. Matthew's day;[1] he says he thinks of going to Dresden for Christmas, where they will be gay; as in all probability Pani Sokołowska will spend the winter there. Also he says that Panna Wanda has been so ill with inflammation of the kidneys that there was a time when the doctors gave little hope; she fell ill at Marienbad, and is now convalescent at Dresden. I have not written yet to Kostuś — I don't need to explain to you why — you know how lazy I am; I could scarcely manage to scrawl a few words to Würfel. You write that you read about my concerts in two newspapers. If they were Polish papers, you could not get much satisfaction. Not only were they of course in translation, but they purposely muddled up the Viennese reports in a damaging way; I can tell you better about that by word of mouth. Hube, who came back last week, after visiting Trieste and Venice, brought me some cuttings from the Viennese periodical Zeitschrift für Litteratur, in which my playing and compositions are discussed at length and highly praised, — forgive me for telling you this, — at the end they speak of me as a "*Selbstkräftiger Virtuoz,*"[2] and also as richly endowed by nature; if such cuttings should fall into your hands, I need not be ashamed. If you want to know what I intend to do with myself

[1] September 21st.
[2] Virtuoso of independent powers.

this winter, learn that I shall not stay in Warsaw; but where circumstances will lead me, I don't know. It is true that Prince Radziwiłł, or rather she, who is very amiable, has invited me to Berlin, even offering me quarters in their own palace; but what of that, when I must go on where I have begun, especially as I promised to return to Vienna. Besides, it says in one of the newspapers there that a longer stay in Vienna would be a useful *Anschlag*[1] for my entry into public life. I am sure you will see that I must go back to Vienna; but it is not for Panna Blahetka, of whom I think I wrote to you. She is young, pretty and a pianist; but I, perhaps unfortunately, already have my own ideal, which I have served faithfully, though silently, for half a year; of which I dream, to thoughts of which the *adagio* of my concerto belongs, and which this morning inspired the little waltz I am sending you. Attention to one point here: No one knows about this but you. How I should like to play the waltz to you, dearest Tytus. In the *Trio* the bass melody should dominate till the high E flat of the violin in the 5th measure;[2] but I need not write you that, because you will feel it. No musical news except that there is music at Kessler's every Friday. Yesterday, among other things, they played Spohr's Octet; lovely, exquisite. There was an evening at Sowan's, but not very good. I met Bianchi there; he travels with the Chiavinis; he plays the violin well, but altogether he seems to me a coxcomb. Soliwa[3] [*sic*] asked politely after you. I met Oborski yesterday. He asked whether I have any news of you, and told me about himself. It seems he has got a job in the Bank; he is *dans la correspondance;* for the last two days he has been going through enormous piles of letters from various foreign bankers. He looks well. Jelski gave him this post and the former one, just as he was. He is still *à l'hotel garni*, so you can understand on whom he will call. I have not yet seen Kopciuszek[4] here; today is The Wife Exchange.[5] The French theatre opens on Monday. Barański sends

[1] stroke.

[2] I cannot identify this waltz; it may not have been published.

[3] Carlo Soliva, 1792–1851; Italian composer; professor of singing at Warsaw Conservatorium.

[4] *Cenerentola:* an opera of Rossini.

[5] Apparently *Le Marché des femmes:* an opera of Bierey. 1st performance about 1805.

you greetings; he is in Switzerland now; Jędrzejewicz was to leave Geneva for Italy; Wojcicki has returned from London, is teaching in the Lyceum. When you come back next month, you will find portraits of all our family, including Żywny (who often speaks of you); he has had himself painted as a surprise for me, and Miroszesio has got him wonderfully lifelike. Before I received your letter I went to Miodowa street; I usually look up at the Chodkiewiczs' windows, but the shutters of your room were just as yesterday and the day before. And you must know that Vincent Skarzyński raised my hopes for nothing by telling me that you were certainly coming back soon.

I go to Brzezina every day. There's nothing new except a concerto by Pixis, for which I don't care much. You wouldn't believe how dreary I find Warsaw now; if it weren't for the family making it a little more cheerful, I shouldn't stay. But how dismal it is to have no one to go to in the morning to share one's griefs and joys; how hateful when something weighs on you and there's nowhere to lay it down. You know to what I refer. I often tell to my pianoforte what I want to tell to you. Kostuś will be pleased when I tell him you have written and are coming, or at least promising to come. You must carry out your intention of coming, I should be beside myself with joy if I could travel with you; but I have to travel differently from you; I shall go from Vienna to Italy to study, and next winter I expect to be with Hube in Paris, unless everything changes; which may be the case, as Papa would like to send me to Berlin, which I don't wish. *A propos* of Berlin, old Pruszak is going to Gdańsk. Paulin Łączyński, whom I met lately, declares that Pruszak won't hold out for the winter without his wife. However that may be, Pani Pruszak is determined to stay at Dresden till Christmas. If I go to Vienna, perhaps I could go to Dresden and Prague on the way, to see Klengel, the Prague Conservatorium, etc., again. In that case, how glad I should be to see Kostuś. Obniski asks to be remembered to you. I met Geysmer the day before yesterday. I hope I shall see you before leaving Warsaw; I may have to go in November, but not till the end of the month. We never said goodbye; your last words were: "Then I'll send you my bag." Imagine, my hold-all was lost on the way back from

Panna Bronikowska's wedding! That's enough; I may bore you with these banalities, and I would hate to do anything you dislike. If you can, write me two words, and you'll make me happy for several weeks. Forgive me for sending you the waltz; perhaps it will make you angry with me, but really I did it to give you pleasure, for I do love you desperately.

F. CHOPIN

39.

To the Same.
Warsaw, 20 October 1829.

DEAREST TYTUS!

You will perhaps wonder how I got such a mania for letter-writing; this is the third to you in such a short time. I start at 7 this evening by diligence for the Wiesołowskis' in the province of Poznań [Posen] and am writing first, because I don't know how long I shall be there. My passport is taken only for a month, as I expect to get back in two weeks. The reason of my journey is that Radziwiłł will be on his estate beyond Kalisz. You see, there were all sorts of beautiful offers about my going to Berlin and living in his palace; very amusing; but I don't see any advantage in it, even if it could come off, which I doubt. It is not the first gracious favour on a piebald horse [1] that I have seen. But Papa wont believe that it was only *des belles paroles*,[2] and that is why I have to go, as I think I have already told you. You see how kind I am; I'm ready to tell you the same thing ten times over, and always as news.

Pani Pruska came yesterday, and told me that Panna Wanda has recovered, and that Kostuś is bored in Dresden, which I can scarcely believe. Mme Soliwa and the children went last week to Italy, to her mother-in-law. I heard it from Ernemann, whom I met at Kessler's quartet evening.

You must know that Kessler gives little musical evenings on

[1] A Polish proverb.
[2] Fine phrases.

Fridays. They all meet and play; no pre-arranged programme; everybody plays what falls under his hand. So, last Friday week we had Ries's C sharp minor concerto, in quartet; Hummel's E major Trio; Beethoven's last Quartet — I haven't heard anything so great for a long time; Beethoven snaps his fingers at the whole world — then a Quatuor of Prince Ferdinand of Prussia, alias Dussek; [1] and finally some singing; or rather, not singing, but a parody of singing, which was really extraordinary. You must learn that Zimmermann, who plays the flute, possesses a peculiarly funny voice, which he produces with the help of cheeks and hand. It's something like a cat, and something like a calf. Nowakowski also can make a queer voice, like a small, out-of-tune toy whistle; he does it somehow by squeezing his lips flat. Filip, taking advantage of this, has written a duet for Zimmermann and Nowakowski, with a choir; it's sheer absurdity, but very well done, and so comic that there was no leaving off. It came after the Beethoven Trio, but did not erase the tremendous impression which that work had made on me, all the more as it was very well played. Serwaczyński accompanied, and he is an excellent accompanist. He is to give a concert this week. In my opinion that is a pity; but people explain it by his wanting to stay here, which would be nice; he wants to teach, and thinks this the best way to get pupils. When I come back and you are in Warsaw, we will play the Trio two or three times; he has promised me this. Bielaski needs such a lot of coaxing, and there is not much difference; he really accompanies very well.

Elsner likes the adagio of the concerto; he says it is new. About the Rondo I don't want anyone's opinion just yet, because I am not yet quite satisfied with it myself. I wonder whether I shall get it quite finished when I come back, or not. I heard yesterday that some girl has arrived here from Petersburg; I don't remember her name. She is said to be very young and to play the fiddle astonishingly. Next Sunday they are to give a revival of Kurpiński's old opera: The Palace of Lucifer.[2] I

[1] Joh. L. Dussek (Duschek), 1761–1812, Bohemian composer, was a close friend of Prince Ludw. Ferd. of Prussia, who was also a musician, and for whose death in battle he wrote his Harmonic Elegy.

[2] *Pałac Lucypera*, opera. First performance, 1811; by K. Kurpiński, 1785–1857; Polish composer and conductor.

meet Oborski; Obniski is *Magister,* with a tip-top degree, Masłowski ditto. Barciński writes from Geneva, sends greetings to you, has been to Schaffhausen with Jędrzejewicz. Barciński goes back to France, and the other to Munich.

Many thanks for the note, written by your brother; I was pleased to have it. You are fortunate that, when you wish it, you can make people happy and gay; you don't know how cross I was in the morning and how sweet-tempered after dinner, when the letter had come. I must stop now, as I have several things to see to before the journey. I embrace you heartily; people usually end their letters that way without thinking what they write; but believe me that I do mean what I write, because I love you.

F. CH.

I have done a big *Exercise en forme* in a way of my own; I will show it to you when we meet.

40.

To the Same.
Warsaw, 14 November 1829.

DEAREST TYTUS!

I received your last letter, in which you send me a kiss, at Antonin, at the Radziwiłłs'. I was there a week; you can't think how I enjoyed it. I came back by the last post; and even then I was scarcely allowed to leave. So far as my temporary personal pleasure went, I would have stopped there till they turned me out; but my affairs, and particularly my unfinished concerto, which is waiting impatiently for the completion of its finale, spurred me on to abandon that paradise. There were two Eves in it: — young princesses, very kind and friendly, musical, sensitive creatures. The old princess, too, knows that it is not birth which makes a person, and her behaviour so draws one to her that it is impossible not to love her. You know how fond of music he is; he showed me his *Faust,* and I found in it many things showing so much ingenuity, even genius, that I would never have expected it from a viceroy. Among others, there is one scene, where Mephistopheles tempts Gretchen, playing on the guitar and singing before her house, and at the same time you hear choral singing from the neighbouring church. In performance this contrast would produce a great effect; on paper you can see the skilfully constructed song, or rather diabolical accompaniment, against a very solemn chorale. This will give you a notion of his way of regarding music;— in addition, he is a whole-hearted Gluckist. Theatre music, for him, is of value in so far as it paints the situations and emotions; therefore his overture has no finale, is only an introduction; and the orchestra is kept all the time off the stage, so that no movement of bows, no blowing nor exertion shall be visible. I wrote while there an Alla Polacca with a violoncello.[1] There is nothing in it but glitter; a *salon* piece, for ladies; you see, I wanted Princess Wanda to learn it. I have been giving her lessons. She is quite young: 17, and pretty; really it was a joy to guide her little fingers. But joking apart, she has a lot of real musical feeling; one did not have to say: *crescendo* here, *piano* there; now quicker, now slower, and so on. I could not refuse to send them my polonaise in F minor, which captivated Princess Eliza; so please send it to me by the first post; I don't want them to think me discourteous, and I don't want to write it out from memory, my Dear, because perhaps I might get it down wrong. It will give you a notion of the character of this princess, that I had to play her this polonaise, and nothing pleased her so much as the A flat Trio. They are all excellent folk. On the way home I went to an evening party at Kalisz; Pani Łączyńska and Panna Biernacka were there. She insisted on my dancing, so I had to dance the Mazur, with a girl who is even prettier than she, or anyhow quite as pretty: Panna Paulina Nieszkowska, who will not marry General Mycielski, who is paying his addresses to her. Panna Biernacka talked a lot to me about you and your brother, and one could see what tender feelings that winter spent in Warsaw had aroused in her. I talked the whole evening with her, or rather asked and answered questions; I never liked her

[1] Op. 3. [Op.]

so much as that evening, especially when she spoke of the lovable character of Pan Karol. I am not joking. I told her that you would hear all about the evening, that I should complain to you of her having made me dance; but she was not afraid of you. I met her father, his Sulisławice is near Antonin. One of the fine things to see at that party was the dancing of Jaxa Marcinkowski; he capered in muddy boots, till he nearly fell down. I was only one day in Kalisz. Kostuś has written to me, but I have not answered yet. Princess Radziwiłł wants me to go to Berlin in May, so there is nothing to prevent my spending the winter in Vienna. I don't think I shall leave here till December. Papa's name-day is the 6th, so probably I shall go towards the end of the month, therefore I hope to see you first, and am making no plans. If I should go before you come, which probably will not be the case, I would write to you; there is nothing I more desire than to see you — especially abroad. You can't think how much I feel that something is missing in Warsaw now; I have no one I can speak two words to, no one to turn to with confidence. You want my portrait; if I could steal one from Princess Eliza, I would send it to you; she has drawn me twice in her album and, I am told, has got a good likeness. Mieroszewski has no time now; my life, you are too kind; and believe me, I am nearly always with you; I will never desert you, I shall be till death your most affectionate

F. CH.

I remind you again of the F minor Polonaise; please, my Life, send it to me by the first post.

I have written a few Exercises; I could play them well to you. Papa, Mamma, the children and Żywny all greet you. Jędrzejewicz has written from Vienna; he is coming home. Kurpiński's " Palace of Lucifer " was given, but was not a success.

Last Saturday, at the Resource, Kessler played Hummel's E major concerto. Serwaczyński also played. Perhaps I shall play next Saturday; if so I shall play your [1] Variations. Mme Bourgeois Schiroli, a beautiful contralto, sang twice at musical evenings at Soliwa's, Teichmann tells me. Panna Wołków is in

[1] his by dedication.

mourning for her mother, and Panna Gładkowska has a bandaged eye. Żyliński has even sung with Mme Schiroli; but he says he felt like a rat beside her. That is all the news I have. I have not seen Max for a long time, but he is probably well. Gaszyński has written a little comedy in verse for the Theatre of Varieties to which everybody is rushing now. The title is: The Doctor's Waiting-room. Gąsie is well; Rinaldi asks after you every time he meets me. Next Sunday will be played: The Millionaire (*Bauer als Millionär*); a little comic opera by Dechseler. I don't know why they play this German rubbish here; I suppose for the stage decorations and various ludicrous metamorphoses which amuse children. They will rush for it. Sachetti was to do the scene painting. That is all that comes to my pen. I am not writing to tell news; just to be in your company. Once more let me embrace you.

F. Ch.

41.

To the Same.

[*Warsaw*] *Saturday, 27 March 1830.*

My dearest Life!

I have never missed you as I do now; I have no one to pour things out to, I have not you. One look from you after each concert would be more to me than all the praises of the journalists, of the Elsners, the Kurpińskis, Soliwas, and so on. Directly after receiving your letter, I wanted to give you an account of my first concert; but I was so distracted, and so busy with preparations for the second one, which I gave on Monday, that when I sat down I could not collect my thoughts. I am still in the same condition today; but, as the post is going I will not wait for a moment of mental quiet: so rare a moment with me. About the first concert: the hall was full, and both boxes and stalls were sold out three days beforehand, but it did not produce on the mass of the audience the impression I expected. The first *Allegro* is accessible only to the few; there were some bravos, but

I think only because they were puzzled: — What is this? and had to pose as connoisseurs! The Adagio and Rondo had more effect; one heard some spontaneous shouts; but as for the Potpourri on Polish themes,[1] in my opinion it failed to come off. They applauded, in the spirit of: let him go away knowing we were not bored. Kurpiński found new beauties in my concerto that evening; but Wiman still admitted that he can't see what people find in my Allegro. Ernemann was quite satisfied; Elsner complained that my pantaleon was dull, and that he couldn't hear the bass passages. That evening the " gods " and the people sitting in the orchestra were quite content; on the other hand, the pit complained that I played too softly; they would have preferred to be at Kopciuszek's [2] to hear the discussions which apparently centred round my person. Therefore, Mochnacki, praising me to the skies in the Polish Courier, — especially for the Adagio, ended by counselling *more energy*. I guessed where this energy lies, so at the next concert I played on a Viennese piano instead of on my own. Diakow, the Russian general, was kind enough to lend me his own instrument, which is better than Hummel's; and consequently the audience, an even larger one than before, was pleased. Clapping, exclamations that I had played better the second time than the first, that every note was like a pearl, and so on; calling me back, yelling for a third concert. The Krakowiak Rondo produced a tremendous effect, the applause bursting out again four times. Kurpiński regretted that I did not play the Fantasia on the Viennese piano, as did Grzymała the next morning in the Polish Courier. Elsner says it's only after this second concert that people can judge of me; although I sincerely prefer to play on my own piano. However, the universal verdict is that the other instrument is better suited to the place. You know the programme of the first concert; the second began with Nowakowski's symphony (*par complaisance*); [3] then the first Allegro from the concerto. Bielawski played Beriot's Variations; then the Adagio and Rondo. The second part started with the Krakowiak Rondo; then Pani Majer sang, better than ever, Soliwa's air from Henela and Malwina.

[1] Op. 13.
[2] A café frequented by artistic and literary persons. [Op.]
[3] by courtesy.

Finally I improvised, which greatly pleased the first tier boxes. If I am to tell you the truth, I did not improvise as I should have wished to do; it would have been not for that public. Nevertheless I am surprised that the Adagio was so generally admired; wherever I turn, I hear only about the Adagio. Doubtless you have all the newspapers, or at least the principal ones; so you will see that they were pleased. Moriolówna [Mlle de Moriolles] sent me a laurel wreath, and today I received somebody's verses. Orłowski has written some mazurkas and waltzes on the themes of my concerto. Sennewald, Brzezina's accompanist, asked me for my portrait, but I could not allow that, as it would be too much at once, and I don't want anyone to wrap up butter in me, as happened with Lelewel's portrait.

I will send it to you, as soon as possible; if you want it you shall have it; but no one else except you shall have my portrait. There is only one other person to whom I would give it, and even then to you first, for you are my dearest. No one but myself has read your letter. As always, I carry your letters about with me. What joy it will be, in May, when I get outside the walls of the town, to think of my approaching journey, and get out your letter and really convince myself that you care for me, or at least to look at the handwriting and signature of the person I love so much! Last week they wanted me to give one more concert; but I won't. You can't think what misery are the last three days before a concert. For the rest, I shall finish the opening Allegro of the 2nd Concerto before the holidays, and then wait with my third concert till after the holidays; although I know that I might have a larger audience now, because the whole fashionable world wants to hear me again. Among the voices from the stalls at the last concert, calling for a third one, somebody cried out: — "Town Hall" so loud that I heard it from the stage; but I don't think I shall obey; if I do give another it will be in the theatre. It is not a question of money, for the theatre did not bring in much, as everything was handed to the cashier and he did as he liked. From both concerts, after covering the cost, I had less than 5,000, though Dmuszewski said they had never had so large an audience for a pianoforte concert as for the first one, and the second was still bigger. But the point is that at the Town Hall, with just as much trouble, there would be little more result: I should still be playing not for everybody, but either for the highest class, or for the crowd. I feel, more than ever before, that the man has not been born who can please everyone. Dobrzyński is annoyed with me because I did not take his symphony; Pani Wodzińska is angry because I did not reserve a box for her; and so on. *A propos* of Wodzińska, whom I met two days ago at the Pruszak's at Marjan's name-day party, it reminds me that I also met your brother there; he still has his good moments, and sent greetings to you. Shortly before the name-day, — I think on St. Joseph's day, — they celebrated the 25-year jubilee of their marriage, *alias* silver wedding. Naturally the dinner could not go off without milk foods and various rustic dainties; no, that's not for me. Yesterday I dined at Moriol's [1] and went on a party at Diakow's, where I saw Soliwa. He sent greetings to you and promised to give me some letter for you one day. Kaczyński and I played Hummel's *La Rubinelle*, and there was some fairly good music. I don't want to stop writing, all the more because I believe I have not put down what I wanted, to amuse you. I kept everything back for the dessert, and now there is no other dessert than a hearty embrace, for I have no one but you.

F. CHOPIN

Papa, Mamma and the children all send you best greetings. Żywny. I see Max, and have been to the theatre at Potocki's and to a musical evening at Pani Nakwaska's. I saw Łączyński lately in a hackney coach.

[1] Count M. de Moriolles; tutor to the son of the Grand Duke Constantine of Russia. Chopin was on terms of friendship with de Moriolles' daughter (referred to as "Moriolka") and had played before the Grand Duke at the palace in Warsaw.

42.

To the Same.

Warsaw, 10 April, 1830. Saturday; the anniversary of Emilja's death![1]

MY DEAREST LIFE!

I wanted to write to you last week, but it went so fast that I don't know where it's gone. You must know that our world has gone music crazy, has not slacked off even for Holy Week; and last Monday there was a big evening at Filipino's, where Mme *Sauvan* sang the duet from Semiramide[2] beautifully, and I had to accompany the buffo duet from the Turk,[3] which was sung by repeated request, by Soliwa and Gresser. I won't write you any more details except that Pani Gładkowska asked after you.

Everything is ready for the coming evening at the Lewicki's, when among other numbers Prince Galitzin will play Rode's Quartet; there will be Hummel's *La Sentinelle*,[4] and at the end my Polonaise with the violoncello, to which I have added an *Adagio* introduction, specially for Kaczyński. We have tried it, and it is all right. There is my drawing-room musical news; now I come to press news about music, which is less important for me than the other, especially as there are fairly gracious criticisms of me; I should like to send them to you. In one half-sheet long article in the Warsaw Gazette there must be a good deal of sneering at Elsner, for Soliwa told me at Moriol's dinner that if he were not afraid to give provocation, having lady pupils to bring out, he should have answered it himself. He also told me that you had written to him; I hope that if he answers you he will not miss the opportunity. It is difficult to give you an idea of all this in a few words; if I could I would send you the news-

[1] His youngest sister.

[2] Opera by Rossini. 1st performance 1823.

[3] *Il Turco in Italia:* opera by Rossini. 1st performance 1814.

[4] Apparently a mistake; I can find no trace of such an opera by Hummel. It may be: *La Sentinelle;* Devint (?), 1798 (?), or: *La Sentinella Notturna;* Agnelli, 1817.

papers, so that you could understand the thing properly. But as a word to the wise is enough, I will just sketch what has happened. After my concerts there was a flood of press notices, particularly in the Polish Courier; though their praises were somewhat exaggerated, they were still possible. The Official Bulletin also devoted some pages to panegyrics, but with the best intentions, it included in one number such preposterous remarks that I felt desperate when I read an answer in the Polish Gazette, which quite justly deprived me of the exaggerated attributes given me by the other. You must know that in that article the Official Bulletin declared that the Poles should be as proud of me as the Germans are of Mozart; obvious nonsense. But in the same article the writer says that if I had fallen into the hands of some pedant or Rossinist — which is a stupid term — I should not have been what I am. I am nothing, but he is right in saying that, if I had not been taught by Elsner, who imbued me with convictions, I should doubtless have accomplished still less than I now have. This sneer against Rossinists and indirect praise of Elsner infuriated you *know* whom to such an extent that the Warsaw Gazette, beginning with Fredro's " Friends "[1] and finishing with " Count Ory,"[2] bursts out in the middle with: Why are we to be grateful to Elsner, who is not going to shake pupils out of his sleeves; —then, if you please, it points out that, besides me, there was Nowakowski's symphony at my concert, and " even the devil can't make a whip out of sand."[3] 35 years ago Elsner wrote a quartet, which bears on the title-page: " *dans le meilleur goût polonais* ";[4] the words were doubtless added by the publisher on account of the Polish minuet. The article jeers at this quartet without mentioning the composer. Soliwa says, he could jeer at Cecilia[5] in the same words; moreover, this article, always referring to me in the most delicate and loving way, several times makes a long nose at me, and advises me to study Rossini, *but not to copy him*. This advice is in consequence of the other article, which spoke of me as original; this the

[1] A comedy by Fredro.
[2] Opera by Rossini: *Le Comte Ory*. 1st performance 1828.
[3] You can't make a silk purse out of a sow's ear.
[4] "In the best Polish style."
[5] St. Cecilia?

Warsaw Gazette will not admit. I am invited to the Easter meal [1] at Minasowicz's the day after tomorrow; Kurpiński will be there. I wonder what he will say to me. You don't know how affectionately he always greets me. I saw him at Leszkiewicz's concert on Wednesday week. Young Leszkiewicz plays very well, but still chiefly from the elbow. All the same, I believe he will turn out a better player than Krogulski. I have not yet ventured to express this opinion, although people have several times tried to pump me. But enough of this music; now I start to write not to Sir Music-Lover, but to Tytus Wojciechowski, landowner.

Yesterday was Good Friday; all Warsaw went to visit graves; and I drove from one end of the city to the other with Kostuś, who returned from Sanniki the day before yesterday. Kot sends you greetings, and à propos informs you of the following: — "When I sat down to lunch with Panna Alexandra after the morning lesson, a conversation started; Pani Sowinska was told of Panna Alexandra's engagement to Pan Mleczko. I say that I had not heard of it; then I am told that, as they know my good will to the household, they inform me that Pan Mleczko has made a declaration after a scene of great emotion. Pani Pruszak says she never had so dreadful a moment as when he threw himself at her feet in tears, etc. — Wishing to know what came of it, I wait to hear the result of the declaration; and am told that although Pan M. is getting on, Panna A. is still too young, so they are to wait a year — i.e. till Panna A's next birthday, when she will herself be able to decide whether to accept or refuse the offer. All the same, Pan M. visited graves with them yesterday. Obniski sends you greetings; Geysmer sends you greetings. I met Łączyński the day before yesterday; he has grown terribly thin — and I saw brother Karol, who looks as healthy as a flower-bud. Aha, the Briefträger! [2] and a letter — from you! Oh, my dearest, how good you are! That I think of you, that is not surprising! — I see from your letter that you have read only the Warsaw Courier; read the Polish Couriers and the 91st No. of the Warsaw Gazette. Your advice about evening parties is sound,

[1] *Swięcony* (consecrated): a ceremonial lunch on Easter day, with special cakes, Easter eggs, etc. . . . The food is blessed by a priest.

[2] postman.

and I have declined several invitations to them, as if I had a presentiment of your view; you don't know how my thoughts turn to you before every action. I don't know whether it is because it was with you that I learned to feel, but whenever I write anything, I want to know whether you like it, and I think my second Concerto in E minor will have no value in my judgment till you have heard it. Bromirski called today to invite me for Thursday, and I assure you that you can see him going away with a refusal. As for Gąsie, I met him two days ago, and we talked of you; he is melancholy, and complains that circumstances are unfavourable to the arts. When I see him, I hope today, I will tell him that you have written. I have no nonsense at hand to send you; and it's not worth while. As for the 3rd concert, which people here are expecting, I shan't give it, because I should have to give another just before leaving. That new one is not yet finished; I should play the Polish Fantasia, by request, and your Variations, for which only I am waiting. As the Leipsic fair has begun, Brzezina too can get conveyed there. That Frenchman from Petersburg, that people take for another Field—the man that wanted to treat me to champagne at the 2nd concert,—he is a pupil of the Paris Conservatoire, and is called *Dunst.* He called on Soliwa, and told him he would call on me, but I have not seen him yet. He has given a concert in Petersburg and had a success, so he must play well. You are doubtless surprised that a Frenchman from Petersburg should have a German name. Kocio has just arrived with Walery Skarzyński, and the Gendre [1] is travelling with them. The carriages roll, the ladies' hats blaze from the distance; a beautiful time. Here comes Celiński, who disposes of my promenades; he is a good fellow, he looks after my health. I'll go out with him; perhaps I may see someone who will remind me of you; you are the only person I love.

F. CHOPIN

My Parents and sisters send you their best compliments. And Pan Żywny; he would scold me otherwise.

A propos, here is some comic news: Orłowski has made my

[1] son-in-law.

themes into mazurkas and gallops; however, I have asked him not to print them.

" Count Ory " is good, especially the orchestration and choruses. The finale of the first act is beautiful.

43.

To the Same.

Warsaw, 17 April 1830 Father's name-day.

My dearest Life!

What a relief in my intolerable boredom when I get a letter from you; just today I needed it, I was more bored than ever. I wish I could throw off the thoughts that poison my happiness, and yet I love to indulge in them; don't know myself what is wrong with me; perhaps I shall be more tranquil after this letter; you know how I love writing to you. You say you have become a guardian, which made me laugh. You tell me about some *cotillon,* and I guess that it must have been Walery's work. You say that perhaps you are going to come; that rejoiced me, for I too shall stay over for the Sejm.[1] You doubtless know from the papers, which, luckily for me, you keep, that it opens on May the 28th, so our hope will last for a whole month, especially as the Courier announces Fräulein Sontag. Dmuszewski is the same as ever; tells lies, invents various queer things. I met him yesterday, and he told me the absurd news that he is bringing out, in the Courier, a sonnet to me. " For the Lord's sake," said I — " don't do such silly things." — " It's already in print," said he, with the smile of one doing a kindness, apparently supposing that I ought to be glad to have met with such an honour. A poor sort of kindness! Everyone that has anything against me will again have a chance to jeer. As for the mazurkas on my themes, the commercial love of gain has conquered. I don't want to read anything more that people write about me, or to hear anything they say.

[1] Parliament; Diet; suppressed after the insurrection.

On Sunday I should have liked just to hear what Kurpiński had to say about the Warsaw Gazette article; but as luck would have it I did not find him among all the notabilities at Minasowicz's Easter feast. He was not there; Ernemann was the only musician present. As I wanted to see how he would receive me, I called on him with Easter wishes, but missed him both times. Today I saw Soliwa. Perhaps he's a tricky Italian; but he showed me what he has written in reply to that article; *nota bene* in French, and for himself, not for publication in any paper; it was excellent; he justly rebukes them on Elsner's account, without mentioning any names. He is affectionate to my face, but it's worthless; and I am polite, but don't go near him when I can possibly help it, in spite of his invitations. Ernemann called on me; he thinks the opening *Allo*[1] better in the new concerto; he came yesterday, just as Kostuś was leaving. I was there today; the journey to Dresden is put off on account of the Sejm; the last new project is that Kostuś and Hube, the same univ. prof. with whom I travelled last year, should make a little trip through France and Italy. Hube, as he told me two days ago, intended to go straight to Paris, stay a while, and go on to Italy for the winter, spending January in Naples, where I was to meet him. Kostuś went to him this morning, to get a better idea of him and of his plans. If they go, it won't be till June, even the end of the month. Magnus went to Vienna a week ago; he is to come back the end of this month. I hope not with empty hands. Tomorrow is the Magic Flute, and the day after is a concert of a blind flutist, Grünberg, about whom I wrote to you. He wanted me to play at his concert. I had a good excuse: That I had already refused someone else, and that it would not do to discriminate. Malsdorf will play the violoncello for him. That's a great favour from the Baron; Szabkiewicz will play the clarinet, and yesterday I went to Zyliński's again and he promised to sing for him. He wanted me to go to Pani Majer with him; I know that she would consent to sing, for me, but she would resent it inside; so I preferred not to ask her, and undertook only to sell a few tickets. Pani Pruszak took ten. *A propos*, at the lesson today, just in the middle of Kramer's *Etude*, I learned from her

[1] Allegro.

that you have sent your wheat to Gdańsk and that perhaps you are coming. The news about the wheat comes from M. Charles. I answered that you had not written to me, as I am ignorant of the subject. It seems to me somewhat queer that you should be occupied with wheat; but I believed it because I know how you like to work at any thing you have undertaken. The children want to read your letters, but they will never be allowed to; I keep them for myself alone and read them in my heart every day; so Ludwika is cross, all the more because I told her that you had sent no message for her. Tomorrow is the Russian Easter, but I shall not go to anyone's Easter meal. I have never eaten so little at Easter before; even at Pruszak's *swięcony* on Monday or Sunday, I forget which, when there was a crowd of people, with ham and *babas*,[1] etc., I didn't even stop to dinner. They were going to have a big banquet, Chatelain Lewiński, Alfons, the Mleczkows, Dziewanowski, who seemed to me detestable, — everybody. N. has asked me to hold his baby boy at the christening; I could not refuse, all the more as it is the wish of the unhappy woman who is leaving for Gdańsk. Pani Pruszak is to be my fellow godparent. This is to be a secret from my family, who do not know about it. Do you know, I was preparing to go to you last week; but it came to nothing; partly because I have urgent work; I've got to write like fury. If you come to Warsaw while the Sejm is sitting, you will certainly be here for my concert, — I have a sort of presentiment — I shall believe in it implicitly, however it turns out, for I often dream of you. How often I take night for day, and day for night; how often I live in my dreams, and sleep in the daytime; — worse than sleep, because I feel just the same; and instead of recuperating during that state of numbness, as one does in sleep, I get weaker and more tired than ever; — love me, please.

F. CHOPIN

My parents send you best greetings,[2] — and the children, and Żywny.

[1] traditional Easter foods.
[2] word doubtful.

44.

To the Same.
Warsaw, 15 May 1830. Saturday.

MY DEAREST LIFE!

You are probably surprised that Fryc did not answer your letter at once, but I did not know the thing you asked me about in that letter, so I had to wait. So now learn, my little Soul, that Fräulein Sonntag will certainly be here in June and perhaps by the end of May. Also that the ladies G. and W.,[1] in obedience to an order issued by His Excellency the Minister Mostowski, are to appear, one in Paer's *Agnes*,[2] the other — i.e. W. — in *The Turk*. What do you think of such a choice of operas? Yesterday I was at an evening at Soliwa's; there was scarcely anyone there but the Sauvans and the Gressers. G. sang an aria, specially written into the opera for her by Soliwa, which is to be her show piece. It really has quite good bits, and suits her voice in places. W. is to sing in *The Turk*, also an air inserted to show off her voice; it's by Rossini, written for one of the best singers, who appeared in that opera. She sings it well; you will agree when you come. I suppose you will not miss the opportunity to hear Sonntag. How grateful I am to that Sonntag! She is said to be in Gdańsk already, and then comes on to us. But altogether we're going to have plenty of music. Woerlitzer, pianist to His Majesty the King of Prussia, has been here for two weeks. He plays excellently. He's a little Jew, very intelligent by nature, and has played us several things which he has learned very thoroughly. He has called on me. He's really only a child still, 16. His *forte* is the Moscheles Variations on Alexander's march. He plays them splendidly; I think there is nothing lacking. He has been heard twice in public, and both times he has played these Variations. When you hear him, you will be pleased with his playing; although, between ourselves, he is not up to the title that he bears. There is also a Frenchman here, a M. Standt.

[1] Two opera singers: Gładkowska and Wołkow.
[2] *Agnese:* opera by Ferdinand Paer. 1st performance 1819.

He thought of giving a concert, came to me, reconsidered the matter, and gave it up. But one queer bit of musical gossip is that Pan Blahetka, the father of that pianist girl, has written to me from Vienna, that she will come, if I advise it, during the Sejm sessions. A delicate situation. The German gentleman wants money, and if by chance it should turn out a failure, he would be annoyed with me. So I answered at once: — That I had long been wondering whether he would not undertake this trip, and that many persons are anxious to hear her, especially the whole musical world; — but, I delicately inserted: Sonntag is coming, Lipiński is coming, there's only one theatre, which costs over 100 thalers; there will be balls, Whitsuntide is approaching, there will be many excursions, etc., etc. So that I should have nothing to reproach myself with. Perhaps she will come; I should be glad, and on my side would do all I could for her, even if it came to playing on two pantaleons, for you have no idea how kind that German was to me in Vienna. Kostuś is at Częstochowo with his mother; they come back next week, and on June 1st they go with Hube, by way of Berlin, to Paris, where they will stay 2½ to 3½ months, and then go on through Switzerland to Italy. As for my journey, I now don't know what will happen. I think that instead of going abroad this year I shall wait till I get a fever, and that will be the end. I shall stay through June, through July; I shan't even want to get away, on account of — well, you already know, on account of nothing, unless it's the heat. The Italian opera in Vienna starts only in September, so *Henneberg* told me yesterday, so there's no hurry, especially as the Rondo of the new concerto is not finished, and for that one must be in the mood. I am not even hurrying with it, because, once I've got the opening Allegro, I don't worry about the rest. I can give another concert, for I haven't played my Variations yet, and Blahetka writes to me that they came out lately and that Haslinger has taken them to the Easter fair at Leipsic. I hope that Magnus will bring them to me when he returns from Vienna; he went to Galicia on his own business, and was to go on from there to Vienna. The *Adagio* of the new concerto is in E major. It is not meant to be loud, it's more of a romance, quiet, melancholy; it should give the impression of gazing tenderly at a place which brings to the mind a thousand dear memories. It is a sort of meditation in beautiful spring weather, but by moonlight. That is why I have *muted* the accompaniment. Mutes are little combs which fiddlers put across their strings to deaden them and which give them a sort of nasal, silvery tone. Perhaps that's bad, but why should one be ashamed of writing badly in spite of knowing better — it's results that show errors. Here you doubtless observe my tendency to do wrong against my will. As something has involuntarily crept into my head through my eyes, I love to indulge it, even though it may be all wrong. I know you understand. Pani Pruszak and I held N.'s adopted boy for the christening; you have no idea what a lovely child. Mlle Dupont was married at 7 this morning to Pan Cechowski, Pana Skrodska's brother. Dr. Bixel, that old doctor of 63, has married his dead wife's niece, a girl of 17. The whole church was full of sightseers, and the bride could not understand why people pitied her; I know that from the bridesmaid, Moriolles's daughter. As soon as I have posted this letter, I shall go and call, as they have sent to me. You know what favourites of mine they are; I willingly admit it; but one must be docile and respect the disguises of hidden feelings. You know, I should never have believed that I could be so secretive as I am when I have not the heart to tell you what is distressing me. Today I go to the theatre. Pan Smochowski, a new tragedian from Lwow [Lemberg], is to play the part of Werowski in Teresa, the Orphan of Geneva.[1] I don't expect much of his acting, but I'll see what it's like. They say that Pasta is coming, but I doubt it. There is more likelihood of the famous though rather *passée* singer Frau Milder Hauptmann. Romberg also is expected. Let them come; I rely on you and hope that this time you will be here for my concerto. I think I shall try the opening *allegro,* in the house, at the end of May; that is, in two weeks. I shall play it early in June, so as to be done with it before the general entertainments announced by the Courier. So write to me, when you are sure to be in Warsaw; I should be more disappointed than the first time if I had to do my show act without you. No, you don't know how much I love you, I can't show it to you in any

[1] A play.

way, and I have wished for so long that you could know. Ah, what would I not give, just to press your hand, you can't guess — half of my wretched life.

F. CHOPIN

I don't tell you the concert programme, for I don't know it yet. I shall try to get Teichmann. He was to have sung the duet from Armida with Pani Majer at my second concert, as he was nervous about singing alone; but unfortunately it had been sung the week before by Pani Cymmermann and Polkowski, so Kurpiński did not want it repeated, as it would suggest an intention of showing that they can sing it better. I have written such a lot, and still I should like to go on. I meant to send you a new waltz to amuse you, but you shall have it next week.

The parents and children send you best greetings. Żywny also ioins.

45.

To the Same.
Warsaw, 5 June 1830.

MY DEAREST LIFE!

You have missed 5 of Fräulein Sonntag's concerts! But don't grieve, for you will still hear her if you really come on the 13th. I think that date will be a Sunday, and you will arrive just when I shall have the first home rehearsal of the *Allegro* of the 2nd Concerto, taking advantage of the absence of Sonntag, who told me yesterday with her own charming lips that she is going to Fischbach at the request of the King of Prussia. You can't think how delightful it was to meet her more intimately, just in the house, on a sofa. You know, we think of nothing but this messenger of God, as some enthusiasts here have named her. Prince Radziwiłł introduced me to her in the best possible way; I am most grateful to him. During the week that she has been here, I have not profited much by the acquaintance, as I saw that she was worn out by incredibly dull visitors: governors of fortresses, generals, voyevodas,[1] senators and adjutants, who just sat there gaping at her and talking about the weather. She receives them all most courteously; she is too kind-hearted for anything else, but yesterday, before she could go to the theatre for rehearsal, she was forced to lock her door in order to put on her hat; the manservant in the vestibule is overwhelmed by the callers. I have not called on her once, but she has asked me about a song which Radziwiłł arranged for her and gave to me to copy. It's a set of Variations on an Ukraïnian Dumka.[2] The theme and cadence are lovely, but I don't like the middle, nor does Sonntag. I have altered it a little, but it's still not good. I'm glad she is going away after today's concert; it will relieve me of this worry, and meanwhile perhaps Radziwiłł will come for the end of the Sejm, and withdraw his variations. Sonntag is not beautiful, but extraordinarily pretty. She charms everyone with her voice, which is not very big, and we usually hear a range of only:

but it is very highly cultivated; her diminuendi are non plus ultra, her portamenti lovely, and especially her ascending chromatic scales are exquisite. She sang us Mercadante's air very, very, very beautifully, Rode's Variations; the last one with the roulades was particularly good; the variations on Swiss themes were so much admired that, when recalled, instead of bowing to express her thanks, she sang them over again! She is incredibly good-natured. Yesterday the same thing happened with Rode's variations. She sang us the Cavatina from the Barber, the famous one, and from the Magpie;[3] you can imagine what a difference from everything that you have ever heard. She also sang that

[1] Wojewoda: An old Polish military title.

[2] Elegiac folk-song: The Ukraïna is exceptionally rich in folk-tunes; many of the *Dumki*, especially, are of quite extraordinary beauty.

[3] *La Gazza Ladra:* opera by Rossini. First performance 1817.

air from the Freischütz that you know, marvellously. I called on her once, and met Soliwa and the girls there: I heard them sing that duet of his, what's it called? — *barbara sorte* at the end; in the major, you know. Sonntag told them that their voices are strained; that their method is good but that they must produce their voices differently if they don't want to lose them altogether in two years. In my presence she told Panna Wołkow that she has a great deal of facility and many graces of manner, but une voie [*sic*] trop aigue. She asked them to come to her often, and she would do her best to show them her way. It is a supernatural amiability; it is coquetry, carried to such a point that it becomes natural; it is impossible to suppose that anyone could be like that by nature, without knowing the resources of coquetry. She is a million times prettier and more attractive in morning dress than in evening and gala costume, although those who have not seen her in the morning also fall in love with her. On her return, she will give concerts till the 22nd, after which, as I hear from her own lips, she goes to St. Petersburg; so hurry, come, and don't lose more than those five concerts. Everyone says Pasta is coming too, and they are to sing together. There is also a certain Mlle Bellevile [*sic*] here, a Frenchwoman, who plays the piano very well; most lightly and elegantly, ten times better than Voerlitzer; she gives a concert on Wednesday. She was at court on that famous musical evening when Sonntag was there, and the two ladies distinguished themselves. Voerlitzer also was there, but was not so much liked; that I have from Kurpiński, who accompanied Sonntag at court. People have expressed surprise that I was not there, but I am not surprised. Kocio Pruszak starts at 4 this afternoon with Hube. Pani Pruszak, Oleś and the others escort them as far as Łowicz; from there they go with their own horses to Kalisz, and from there on by extra post. But a little more about Sonntag. She uses a few embroideries of a quite new type, which produce an immense effect, though less than those of Paganini; perhaps because the type is slighter. It seems as if she breathed some perfume of the freshest flowers into the hall; she caresses, she strokes, she enraptures, but she seldom moves to tears. Though Radziwiłł told me she so acts and sings Desdemona's last scene with Othello that no one can refrain from weeping. I mentioned that to her, asking whether she would not sing that scene for us in costume; she is said to be a splendid actress as well. She answered that really she had often seen tears in the spectators' eyes, but that acting tires her, and she had made a vow to appear as seldom as possible in dramatic parts. So come without fail, and forget your rustic fatigues in the lap of pleasure; Sonntag will sing for you and you will renew your strength for your work. What a pity that I can't post myself to you instead of this letter. Perhaps you would object; but I want you, and I expect you clean-shaven.

F. Chopin

Today Sonntag sings something from Semiramide. Her concerts are short: usually she sings 4 times, and no one plays between except the orchestra. And really her singing is so exciting that one needs a rest after it. The girls from the Conservatorium will not appear this month.

Mlle Belleville has played my printed Variations in Vienna, and knows one of them even by heart. It's a pity that I have nothing more to write about; I don't want to get up from this letter to part from you —. And do you love me, too?

This paper blots so much that I shall have to make an envelope.

Father, Mother, the children, Żywny and all.

Gąsie says, when you come, he will tell you what he meant to write about.

46.

To the Same.
Warsaw, Saturday, 21 August 1830.

Disgusting Hypocrite!

This is the second letter I am writing you. You won't believe that; you'll say: Fryc is lying; but this time it's the truth. After returning here happily with the Baron I wrote to you at once; but as my parents were at Żelazowa Wola, it was very natural that I did not stay long in Warsaw, but left a letter to you, which was to have been posted. When I came back with my parents on Tuesday, I found the letter in the place where I had left it, by the tea-cups. Karol, who came to the house during my absence, told me he saw it, lying on the cups. It's an ill wind that blows nobody good. Perhaps in this letter I shan't abuse you as much as I did in the first one when your Poturzyń affairs were fresh in my memory. I sincerely assure you that I love to think of all that; I feel a sort of homesickness for your fields; I can't forget that birch tree under the windows. That cross-bow,— it's so romantic! I remember how you wore me out over that cross-bow for my sins. But I must account to you for my time, I must tell you definitely when I am leaving and I must write you various important matters. Of all Warsaw I have been most occupied with Aniela.[1] I've been to the performance. Gładkowska does not lack much; better on the stage than in a hall. Quite apart from the tragic acting — splendid, nothing to be said about that,— the singing itself, if it weren't for the F sharp, and G, sometimes in the high register one could not ask for anything better of its kind. As for her phrasing, it would delight you; she shades gorgeously, and though on first entering her voice shook a little, afterwards she sang very bravely. The opera was cut down; perhaps that is why I did not feel any longwindedness or boredom. Soliwa's air is immensely effective in the second act; I knew it might produce an effect, but did not expect such a huge one. When she sings a romance to the harp in the second act, Ernemann, behind the scenes, plays for her on a piano, without spoiling the illusion; the last time she sang it very well. I was pleased. At the end Aniela was recalled and showered with applause. A week from today will be the first appearance of Fiovilla in the Turk. Wołków is better liked. You must know that Aniela has a terrible number of opponents, who don't know themselves why they criticize the music. I don't deny that this Italian could have chosen something better for Gładkowska. The Vestal[2] might possibly have brought her better luck, but even this is good, and

[1] I can find no mention of an opera with this title; but the reference is probably to Paër's *Agnese*.

[2] *La Vestale:* opera by Spontini; 1st performance 1805.

has many rare beauties and difficulties, which she handles remarkably for a beginner. Szczurowski is dreadful; scraps of Talma, Kemble, Devrient and Żółkowski in turn; you can't make anything of it, he's perfectly cracked. Zdanowicz, according to Soliwa, is non plus ultra! Salomonowicz is unfortunate: Nawrocka drawls continually and Zyliński digests his dinner on the stage. Yesterday, at the rehearsal of the Turk, he infuriated me with his cold-bloodedness; he counted the Turks as if they were sticks. Wołków sang well and acts very well; it's the right part for her and she has really got it. Perhaps her eyes do more with the public than her throat. She several times took the high D cleanly and easily. I have no doubt she will be more liked than Gładkowska. The quintet went splendidly. The general was delighted. Kostuś is in Frankfort with Kinzel; they will come back by Milan, Trieste and Vienna. Hube is still there and won't reach Rome till the 15th of next month. What shall I do? I leave here the 10th of next month, but I must rehearse my Concerto first, as the Rondo is finished. Kaczyński and Bielawski come to me tomorrow. My Polonaise with the Violoncello, and the Trio, are to be rehearsed incognito at 10 in the morning, before Elsner, Ernemann, Żywny and Linowski. We shall play till we drop. That is why I have invited no one except these and Matuszyński, who has always been decent to me; not like a certain false Hypocrite, Scoundrel, Wretch, and you can guess who! Kostuś sent me greetings by Panna Palczewska. Pani Pruszak is in Marienbad, and Mleczko too; they have gone there to drink the waters. My dear Pietruś Dziew [1] has stopped at Reinertz on his way and is taking the whey cure. I saw Oborski at the Varieties; he was friendly. Walery is swaggering about the streets with diamond studs and the air of a banker. Wincenty is always kind; irreproachable, just as he was a good official. I saw Łączyński (who probably is still staying with you, as I should do in his place) the day after he came to Warsaw; no doubt he told you. The baron is sitting through the assizes; he is at Conti's, and I have seen him only once since he came back; he tells me his mother is still very ill. I saw the Governor yesterday and spoke to him of you. Karol must have left; he had to get back to the estate.

[1] Dziewanowski.

Today they give Hamlet and I am going. Yesterday Panna *Riwoli* [*sic*], now Pani *Krowa,* appeared in Olesia Pruszak's role, les premiers amours, in Gąszyński's translation. Niviński plays your part well, Jasiński plays Kot's part better than Kot did, Szymanowski takes mine scarcely as well as I, a long way behind Heroch; and Kratzer — I never in my life saw a better means for getting rid of rats. Kucharski, on the other hand: c'est du Cherubini. I must hurry to take this letter to the post, or the poor thing will be left at home like its brother. Next week I shan't be able to refrain from abusing you for the thing I ought to have written about today, and that will be enough. I don't want anything from you, not even a handshake; I'm disgusted with you for ever. You're a Hellish Monster. I embrace you.

F. Chopin

If there are any letters for me, send them *retro.* Forgive the way I write; I'm stupider than ever today. Papa and Mamma and my sisters send you best greetings.

47.

To the Same.
Still in Warsaw; Tuesday, 31 August 1830.

Dearest Tytus!

I did need your letter; I got rid of my cold when it came. If only my two letters might have the blessed result of curing you of falseness and hypocrisy when you read them, how happy I should be! But I am sure this letter will do nothing of the sort; indeed it will probably lead to worse things; it will rouse anger in your lion heart, and it's lucky that I'm 40 miles away, otherwise the whole weight of your wrath would instantly fall on me. My guilt is great, but dear to the heart of the guilty one; I am still in Warsaw, and — as I love you —

nothing tempts me to go abroad. You may believe me that next week I really shall go; that is in September, for tomorrow is the first; but I go to satisfy my vocation and my reason, which last must be very small, since it has not strength enough to destroy everything else in my head. The journey is getting near, and in this week I have a whole concerto to rehearse in quartet, to get the quartet into agreement with me, to get a bit familiar with it, for Elsner says that without that the rehearsal with the orchestra won't go right. Linowski is copying it against time; has started on the Rondo. Last Sunday I tried the Trio; I don't know, perhaps it's because I had not heard it for a long time, but I was rather *pleased with myself* (lucky person). Only one notion came into my head; instead of violins to use violas, because on the violin it's the fifth that has most resonance, and here it is not much used. The viola will be more powerful against the violoncello, which is in its own register; — and then to print. That's enough for me. Now about other musicians. You will say that here too I have kept the rules of egoism which you gave me. Soliwa screwed up Panna Wołków for last Saturday; what with her coquetry, her good acting and her very pretty eyes and teeth, she charmed both stalls and pit. We have no other actress so pretty; but in the first act I could not recognize her voice. She came out luxuriously dressed, for a stroll on the sea beach, — with a lorgnette in her hand; flashed her eyes, turned round so captivatingly that no one would believe it was a beginner. But in spite of tremendous clapping and bravos, she was so nervous that I did not recognize her till the air in the second act, though even that she did not sing as well as at the second performance, two days ago, when the first act also went better. As for her singing, Gładkowska is incomparably superior, and, seeing Wołków on the stage, it is even a greater difference than I expected. Ernemann and I agreed that there won't be a second Gładkowska, as regards purity and intonation and higher emotions, as they are understood on the stage. Wołków sometimes gets out of tune; whereas I have twice heard the other also in Aniela, and she did not take one doubtful note. Meeting her the day before yesterday, I delivered your compliments, for which she sends you many thanks.

Wołków's reception, according to Celiński, was finer than that of the other; which must concern the Italian, because he told me yesterday that he did not wish her to be more popular than the other, but saw that it would be so. But that, of course, must be put down to the Turk, or rather to Rossini, who makes more impression on our public, especially when it is also charmed by the garments of a young girl and by what is under the garments, than all the complaints of an unhappy daughter or the most beautiful exaltations of Paër. Gładkowska is to appear shortly in the Magpie; " shortly " probably means after I am beyond the frontier. Perhaps you will be in Warsaw then; if so you can tell me your opinion. Her third role is to be in the Vestal. I don't know what Wołków will play.

The day before yesterday I went for the second time to General Szembek's camp. You must know that he is still at the consistory at Sochaczew, and asked Michal to bring me to him. As, however, it did not come off, he sent Czaykowski, his adjutant, the brother of that Panna Czaykowska who plays and who faints, to fetch me to him. Szembek is very musical, plays the fiddle well, has studied under Rode, is a thorough-paced Paganinist, and therefore belongs in a good category musically. He ordered his band to perform; they had been practising all the morning, and I heard some remarkable things. It's all on trumpets: a kind called Bugle; you would not believe that they can do chromatic scales, extremely fast, and *diminuendo* ascending. I had to praise the soloist; poor chap, he doubtless won't serve for long, he looks consumptive, and still young. I was greatly impressed when I heard the Cavatina from The Dumb Girl [1] played on these trumpets with the utmost accuracy and delicate shading. He has a piano in the camp; and I don't know how it happened, but he really understood me, he was not pretending. He was most impressed by the *Adagio:* wouldn't let me go. I was even late for the Turk. A propos, in a certain Berlin paper there is a very stupid article about music in Warsaw. First they speak about Aniela,[2] praising her very justly, both for singing, for feeling and for her acting; then

1 *La Muette de Portici:* opera by Auber, 1782–1871. 1st performance 1828.

2 This appears to refer to Gładkowska in the part.

it goes on: "This young artist comes from an institution founded under leadership of MM. Elsner, and Soliwa. The first is a professor of composition, and has trained several pupils, among others MM. Orłowski, Chopin, etc., who may, in time, become etc., etc." May the devil carry away such a fellow. "*On vous a joliment collé,*"[1] said Bouquet to me, blinking his red eyes; and Ernemann added that I ought to think myself lucky to be put into the second place. The article says no more about these pupils, and just ends with: "As for appraising the work of MM. Elsner, Soliwa and Kurpiński, we will leave that till later." Idiotic rubbish by some smart Warsaw fellow. I was going to forget about Rinaldi; for heaven's sake do send me the book, either by Łączyński or somehow; the Italian gives me no peace: why the devil did I forget to bring that book back from the Poturzyń people. Kostuś is to be in Vienna with Kimmel next month, so old Pruszak tells me; then he joins his mother in Dresden and returns to Warsaw; Hube meanwhile will range over Italy. My head aches when I think of Italy; I believe that . . .

Enough of this nonsense; forgive me, dear; as always, I've written I don't know what to you. But you get enough profit from your buckwheat to pay for this letter, even if there were nothing in it but a bit of paper from my hand and my signature, with which signature I am always ready to appoint an infernal . . .[2] for you. Yesterday I had a long time with Winc. Skarzyński. He asked a lot about you; he's fond of you. Everyone talks to me of Oleś, and no one of somebody. I am glad that the secret is buried in my heart, and that what begins with you ends with me. And you can be glad that in me you have an abyss into which you can safely fling everything, as if into a second self, for your own soul has long lain at the bottom of it. I keep your letters, as if they were ribbons from a beloved one. I have the ribbon; write to me, and in a week I will enjoy myself chattering to you again.

Yours for always

F. CHOPIN

[1] They've done you nicely.

[2] word doubtful.

Best greetings from my parents and sisters. Ludwika thanks you for your message, which I read to her. Żywny embraces you and the acquaintances; Max, Soliwa and so on send compliments.

I still don't want to leave this paper. Imagine, Panna F. wants to insist that I should attend to her, teach her to play the piano and so on. . . . Her father comes to me, not for this; he has several times tried to push me towards her, but she does not tempt my appetite. The poor girl has to play in public and knows nothing. I sent her to Ernemann, and Ernemann doesn't want her and suggested Dobrzyński; says she is from Lithuania and he too, so they ought to get on. It's absurd.

48.

To the Same.

[*Warsaw*] *Saturday, probably 4 September 1830.*

DEAREST TYCIA!

I tell you, Hypocrite, that I am more crazy than usual. I am still here; I have not the strength to decide on my date; I think I shall go away to forget my home for ever; I think I shall go away to die; and how dismal it must be to die anywhere else except where one has lived! How horrible it will be to see beside my death-bed some cold-blooded doctor or servant instead of my own family. Believe me, I am sometimes ready to go to Chodkiewicz's to find tranquillity with you; then, when I leave the house, I walk the streets, get melancholy, and come home again, what for? — Just to mope. I have not rehearsed the concerto yet; somehow or other I must leave all my treasures before Michaelmas and get to Vienna, condemned to perpetual sighing. What stuff! You, who know so much of human powers, explain to me why man supposes that today is only going to be tomorrow. Don't be silly, is the only answer that I can give to myself; if you know another one, send it to me.

Orłowski is in Paris; Norblin has promised to obtain for

him by new year a post at the *Variétés* theatre. Le Sueur received him well and has promised to remember his musical education. That fellow can do well if he wants to. My plans for the winter are: 2 months in Vienna, and then to Italy, and perhaps to spend the winter in Milan. I shall have letters. Moriolles's daughter came back from the waters two days ago. Ludwik Rembieliński is in Warsaw; I saw him at Lours's, where I got into a dispute with Ernemann about the Turk and Agniesz,[1] the Italian and the Pole. Soliwa is still conducting those operas in which his girls have appeared; you will see, he will gradually harness Kurpiński. Already he has one foot in the stirrup, and a certain bewhiskered cavalry man [2] will support him. He has Osiński also on his side. Palstet saw Rastawiecka a few days before her death; he says, she knew what her condition was. Pani Palstet wishes me to say that she is annoyed with you for not coming straight to Telatyn. That's her joke; the sort of old woman's joke that is peculiarly irritating to people who like to joke with only one person.

Today we had the Alpine singers in the theatre: something on the lines of those Tyroleans who came two years ago; no doubt you remember. Gresser told me they are worse, and the Warsaw Courier says they are better than those. I shan't go to them today; I'd rather go on Wednesday to hear them in the Resource in the Mniszek palace. There's to be a big evening there, and they are to sing in the garden. Win. Skarzyński tells me his side has lost in the lawsuit between the two legs of the Resource (i.e. between Zejdler Zakrzewski & Co. and Steinkeler [*sic*], Zelazowski & Co.); but they are to appeal. They are called Honey because they live in the Miodowa [3] St. and the Steinkeler gang call themselves the Mniszkovs.[4] This explanation is in order to tell you that Honey has lost, but unjustly. Bucholtz is finishing his instrument à la Streicher, he plays well on it; it is better than his Viennese one, but far less good than the Vienna Viennese one. Today my letter ends with nothing, even less than nothing, just with what I've written; that is because it's 11:30 and

[1] *Agnese.*
[2] Probably a reference to General Rozwiecki. [Op.]
[3] *Miód:* honey.
[4] Inhabitants of the Mniszek palace, where the Resource hall was.

I'm not yet dressed and sit writing while Moriolka[1] waits for me; then to Celiński to dinner, then I promised to go to Magnuszewski, so there won't be time to come back before four and finish out this sheet, for whose emptiness I grieve and suffer, but can't help it. Anyhow I'm writing you something, and it seems to me that's good of me. I can't let myself go in this letter, for if I did Moriolka would not see me today, and I like to give pleasure to decent folk when I believe in their goodwill. I have not been there since I came back, and I confess that sometimes I attribute the cause of my grief to her; and I think that is what people believe, and I am composed on the outside. Her father laughs, and perhaps would rather weep; and I laugh too, but also on the outside.

Let us go to Italy, dear; from today you will get no letter from me for a month, neither from Warsaw nor perhaps from elsewhere; so till we meet, you will have no news of me. Stuff and nonsense is all I can manage; but to get away, — and you too. You'll keep me waiting for you. I shall receive letters: " I must just finish the mill, and start the distillery, and see to the wool, and the lambs, and then it will be next sowing time "; and it will be neither mill, nor distillery, nor wool that will keep you, but — something else. A man can't always be happy; perhaps joy comes for only a few moments in life; so why tear oneself away from illusions that can't last long anyhow. Just as on the one hand, I regard the tie of comradeship as the holiest of things, so on the other hand, I maintain that it is an infernal invention, and that it would be better if human beings knew neither money, nor porridge, nor boots, nor hats, nor beefsteaks, nor pancakes, etc. — better than as it is. To my mind, the saddest part of it is that you too think the same way, and would perfer to know nothing of them. I am going to wash now; don't kiss me, I'm not washed yet. You? If I were smeared with the oils of Byzantium, you would not kiss me unless I forced you to it by magnetism. There's some kind of power in nature. Today you will dream of kissing me! I have got to pay you out for the horrible dream you gave me last night.

F. CHOPIN

[1] Mlle de Moriolles.

— for ever a lover of the personification of Hypocrisy. *A propos:* Write to me, and don't forget about Rinaldi; that's all. Mamma and Papa send you best greetings. The children came downstairs to remind me to send messages from them; and please tell them that I forgot. Żwyny always sends greetings. The Italian, Soliwa, asked me when you are coming to Warsaw, and sends best compliments. Pani Linde is in Gdańsk. I have not seen your sister in Warsaw. Pani Plater has come back.

49.

To the Same.
Warsaw, 18 September 1830.

My Dearest Life!

Beastly hypocrite! Disgusting, loathsome Count Ory! Abélard, etc.

I don't know why, but I feel happy, and Father and Mother are pleased about it. Pawlowski brought me the letter and book; you did well to send it back, for the Italian was worrying my life out if I met him in the street. Last Wednesday I rehearsed my Concerto with the quartet. I was pleased, but not altogether; people say the finale is the best part of it, because the most comprehensible. Next week I will write you how it goes with the orchestra; we shall try it on Wednesday; tomorrow I want to go through it again with the quartet. When we have rehearsed it, I shall go; but where, when I don't want to go anywhere? All the same, I don't mean to stay in Warsaw; and if you suspect any love-affair, as many persons in Warsaw do, drop it, and believe that, where my ego is concerned, I can rise above all that, and if I were in love, I would manage to conceal the impotent and miserable *passion* for another few years. Think what you like; anyhow, a letter brought by the count, whom I met two days ago in the Cellar (and who promised to honour our threshold with his podgy person before leaving), will explain things better. I don't want to travel with you. I'm not making it up; indeed as I love you, it would spoil that moment, worth a thousand monotonous days, when we embrace each other abroad for the first time. I could not now await you, receive you, talk to you, as I could do then, when joy will shut out all cold conventional phrases and let one heart talk to the other in some divine tongue. Divine *tongue,* — what an unfortunate expression; like divine navel, or liver; — horridly material. But to come back to the moment when I meet you there. — Then, perhaps, I could let myself go; could tell you what I always dream of, what is everywhere before my eyes; what I constantly hear, what causes me more joy and more sorrow than all else on earth. But don't think that I'm in love; — not I; I have put off that till later.

I have begun a Polonaise with the orchestra; but so far it's just rudiments; it's only a beginning of a beginning. I have now changed the opinion of Kamieński that I held in the country. You will learn more about that from Pawlowski. Today I am writing *anticipando,* to set my mind at rest, as I shall not start before Michaelmas. That is quite positive. I can see you crumpling up my letter and turning crimson with rage. Brother, it's not as we would, but as we can. Don't think it's my pocket that is delaying me. There's no very important reason, but by the grace of God there are as many little bothers as one needs to make the difference. It's unlikely that I can escape my deserts according to the Berlin newspaper; luckily the Vienna one has taken a different tone about my Variations. The reviewer says they are short, but so vigorous, so high, so deep, and so philosophic as well, that he can't describe them. He ends by saying that, apart from their surface elegance, these Variations have an inner quality which will last. This German has paid me a compliment for which I must thank him when we meet. But there is no exaggeration, and that is as I would have it, for he does grant me independence. To anyone but you I would not chatter about myself this way; but as you count for me and I should like to count for you, I sing my own praises the way dealers do with their wares. To be second fiddle to Orłowski is for me neither too much nor too little. Today his new ballet is to be given, on Lesbenier's huge scale. A great fuss is expected. Yesterday I was at Cichocki's — that fat man — for his name-day. I played Spohr's Quintetto for piano, clar., fag., valtorn [*sic*] [1] and flute. Beautiful, but dreadfully unpianistic. Everything he tried to write to display the piano is insufferably difficult, and often you can't find your fingers. It was to have been played at 7, and we began at 11. Aren't you surprised I didn't go to sleep? But there was such a pretty girl there; she reminded me of my ideal. Imagine, we stayed till 3. The Quintet was so late because the ballet rehearsal lasted till 11. That gives you a notion, what a huge ballet. Today they are kicking up their heels.

Yesterday I wrote to Bartek, to London. Antoś Wodziński is back from Vienna. I am certainly going there, but can't specify the date. I was to have started this day week, by the Cracow diligence, but gave it up. I know you think me completely dissuaded from it. But please believe me, as I love you, that I do think of my own good, and dedicate to it everything that I do for people. For people! That is, for people to see, so that repute, which means so much here, may not be unfavourable to me; it's only superficial, nothing inside. You see, people often call such things as a ragged coat or an old hat disaster. When I have nothing to eat, you'll have to take me in at Poturzyń as a clerk; I will live over the stable, just as this year in the courtyard, and be so comfortable with you. If only my health lasts, I hope to work all my life. Sometimes I wonder whether I really am lazy; whether I ought to work more, when my physical strength allows it. Joking apart, I have convinced myself that I really am not such a hopeless vagabond, and that when necessity compels me I can do twice as much work as I do now. You will admit that I can't arraign myself better before you than by acquitting myself. It's no use, I know that I love you and want you to love me always more and more, and that's why I scribble all this. Often trying to make oneself out better only makes one out worse. But I think that with you I don't need to appear either better or worse. The sympathy that I feel towards you forces your heart, in some supernatural way, to

[1] Waldhorn.

feel the same sympathy. You are not the master of your thoughts; but I am, and I won't be thrown over, any more than trees will give up the foliage that brings them life, and joy, and character. Even in winter it shall be green in my heart. My head is green, but heaven knows there's warmth in my heart, so don't be astonished at such vegetation. Enough! Just give me a kiss; for ever your

F. CHOPIN

I've only just realized what a lot of nonsense I have scribbled to you; clearly my imagination dates from yesterday; I've had no sleep, so forgive my fatigue; I danced the Mazurka. Mamma and Papa embrace you warmly. The children too. Ludwika is not quite well, we hope she will soon be better.

I met the President; he was glad of the count's arrival and wants to send you letters or parcels or something from Gdańsk by him. Walery is always Walery. His neighbour, Panna Kolubakin, has died. Wincenty is well, splendid. Kostuś is probably in Dresden with the others.

Sokołowska has arrived; still unwell. Your letters are still on my heart and on the ribbon — for though they don't know, they feel, these dead things, that they both came from familiar hands.

50.

To the Same.
Warsaw, Wednesday morning, 22 September 1830.

MY DEAREST LIFE!

I have an opportunity to explain to you why I am still here. My father did not wish me to travel, a few weeks ago, on account of the disturbances which are starting all over Germany. Not counting the Rhine provinces, the Saxons, who already have another King, Brunswick, Cassel, Darmstadt, etc., we heard that in Vienna too some thousands of persons had begun to be sulky about the flour. What was wrong with the flour I don't know, but I know there was something. In the

Tyrol also there have been rows. The Italians do nothing but boil over; and at any moment, Moriolles told me, they expect some news of this kind. I have not yet tried for my passport, but people tell me that I can get one only to Austria and Prussia; no use to think of Italy and France. And I know that several persons have been refused passports altogether; but that would doubtless not happen to me. So I shall probably go within the next few weeks through Cracow to Vienna, for people there have now refreshed their memory of me and I must take advantage of that. Don't be surprised either at me or at my parents; that is the whole romance. Yesterday Pawlowski came to me; he leaves very early tomorrow; so, as I am rehearsing the second Concerto today, with full orchestra, except trumpets and kettledrums, I invited him, to please you; he can tell you about it. I know that the tiniest details of this sort interest you. I am sorry you are not here, for I shall have to judge of the Concerto by Ernemann's opinion. Kurpiński will be there also, and Soliwa, and all the best of the musical world; but, with the exception of Elsner, I have not much faith in these gentlemen. I wonder how the Italian will look at the Kapellmeister, and Czapek at Kessler, Filip at Dobrzyński, Molsdorf at Kaczyński, Le Doux at Sołtyk, and Pawlowski at all of you. There has been no instance of all these gentlemen ever having been seen together before. I am succeeding in accomplishing it, and I do it for the raritas.

The latest diplomatic news is that M. Durand, the former French consul who protested against Filip [1] and wanted to enter the Russian service, has been recalled to France, and in his place there arrived yesterday a new tricolour consul, whose name even diplomatists do not yet know. There is also a new bass singer, Pan Bondasiewicz, who has already had the misfortune to make a fool of himself twice, in the Turk and in the Barber, in Szczurowski's place. Unless one counts a not too bad supson [2] of a voice, he has not one quality. He sings fairly well in tune, which seems the only reason why the Kapellmeister should have permitted him to appear in the first Polish theatre.

[1] Louis Philippe.
[2] *soupçon.*

You must know that this Pan Bondasiewicz, whom our public has already converted into Brind-, Band- and Bombasiewicz, at one time delighted provincial audiences. He is so bad here that we have to slow down all the *tempi* because he can't keep up. Perhaps he can still train, he is not old. Szczurowski was ill, so this man replaced him. Luckily he has recovered and perhaps will appear on Sunday in the Magpie, when Panna Gładkowska will sing Anusia or somebody, under Kurpiński's direction. This will not prevent the Italian from getting the job of Kapellmeister in two or three years, for Kurpiński is trying for a post in Petersburg, as he confided to me secretly. After Panna Gładkowska's appearance in the Magpie, Panna Wołków will appear in the Barber, which I doubtless shall not see. Did you know Woycicki—, no you didn't, so I won't write about him.

I have just finished the second Concerto and am still as hebes as before I first began to learn my notes. It's a pity I have started to write on such a day, when I can't put two thoughts together. When I begin to consider my own case, I am sorry for myself, that I am often quite absent-minded. If I have something before my eyes that interests me, horses could trample over me and I shouldn't see them; the day before yesterday that nearly happened to me in the street. On Sunday, being struck by an unexpected glance in church, I blundered out in a state of delightful torpor, and for a quarter of an hour didn't know what I was doing; meeting Dr. Parys, I didn't know how to explain my confusion, and had to make up a tale of a dog running under my feet and getting trodden on. I'm such a crazy person sometimes that it's dreadful. I should like to send you a few silly things of mine, but I shan't have time to copy them today. The Italian, Rinaldi, is pleased, and thanks you for sending him the books. He tells me that Bezobrazov is taking lessons from him, but learns nothing, only pays. I'll swear that's a first step to Panna Wołków. Orłowski's new ballet, so far as the music goes, is really very good, and has many fine bits. The machinery of it is enormous, and therefore it does not always come off. The first time was the worst, the second better; the third I don't know, but the prince was there, so it must have gone better. The last decoration is the best. They hop about too much. It's dreadfully long; ends at half-past 10. I apologize for today's letter, but you can't have any other; today is my holiday. Also the university opens today, and I must fly, to make sure of Elsner, Bielaski, the desks, and the sordini which I forgot all about yesterday. Without them the Adagio would go to pieces, and I don't believe it can have much success, as it is. The *Rondo* is *effective*, the *Allegro powerful.* Oh, accursed self-love! But if I owe self-conceit to anyone, it is to you, Egoist; whom one frequents, such one is.[1] There's one thing in which I don't imitate you, that is, in taking sudden decisions; but I have a sincere desire to decide secretly, without a word, to leave here on Saturday week, without *pardon,* in spite of all laments, tears, reproaches and falling at my feet. My music in my bundle, the string on my knapsack, the knapsack on my shoulder, and to the diligence. Tears will be showered like peas on every hand, the length and breadth, from Copernicus to Zdroje, from Brank [?] to King Zygmunt; and I, cold and dry as a stone, laughing at my poor children's tender farewells. I use too many auxiliary words; but that's today, for indeed, if — if you were not so far, so far away, somewhere or other beyond Hrubiesz, I should tell you to come, and I know you would like, if only as a penance for your other enormous sins, to give comfort to other people, even if you detest them. If I could do anything to comfort you, I would do it; but believe me, there is no cure for all that, till Vienna. You live, you feel, you are lived and felt by others; therefore you are unhappily happy. I understand you, I enter into your mood; and — let us embrace each other, for there's nothing more to say.

F. CHOPIN

My parents press your hand. Sisters and brothers embrace you. Kiss me again. This has not taken well; [2] I must put it in an envelope. Forgive my being such a pig, *entre nous soit dit,* — but indeed I ask pardon. Only don't be cross. Today I learned that there are new riots in Berlin.

[1] A proverb.
[2] Apparently the seal. [Op.]

51.

To the Same.
[*Warsaw*] *5 October* [*1830*].

MY DEAREST LIFE!

I needed your letter to calm me down; you can't imagine how bored I am with this accursed but natural confusion. After the orchestral rehearsal of the second Concerto, it was decided to give it in public, and next Monday, i.e. the 11th of this month, I bring it out. On one hand I am sorry; on the other, I am curious to see the general effect. I think the Rondo will impress everyone. About that Rondo Soliwa said to me: "*Il vous fait beaucoup d'honneur.*" Kurpiński spoke of its originality, Elsner of its rhythm. But in order to arrange what you can call a good evening, I have to avoid those wretched clarinets or bassoons between the piano numbers; so Gładkowska will sing in the first part, and Wołków in the second. For the overture I shall give neither of the usual Leszkas and Lodoiskas,[1] but Wilhelm Tell.[2] Poor me, you don't know what I went through when the two ladies asked permission to sing. The Italian was quite willing to consent; but I had to go higher, to Mostowski himself; but, being quite indifferent, he graciously consented. What they will sing I don't yet know; all the Italian told me is that one air must have a chorus. There have been only 2 performances of the Magpie. The first time, Gładkowska was a little nervous, and did not sing the first Cavatina so well as the second time. It is admirable when she sings this:

She does not take it off short, like Mayer, but sings:

[1] *Lodoiska:* opera by Cherubini. 1st performance 1791.
[2] Rossini. 1st performance 1829.

so that it is not a quick *gruppeto*, but eight clearly sung notes. In the last act the prayer from Rossini's "Mahomet" [1] has been added, or rather inserted, after the funeral march, as better fitted for her voice, that in the "Magpie" being too high. That's enough about the opera. Wołków is now studying the "Barber," and then an Italian opera [2] (on tour), in which they are to sing a duet; that is why Soliwa did not wish them to sing one at my concert. I shall play on that instrument which Belleville formerly did not want to give me. At the latest I shall be out of Warsaw a week after the concert. My travelling trunk is bought, my whole outfit is ready; my scores are corrected, my pocket handkerchiefs are hemmed, my trousers are made. Only to say goodbye, and that's the worst. Your somebody will experience that trouble. My parents and the children too; they are good chicks; nothing has so delighted them for a long time as your fraternal greeting, which I gave them from your letter. I must write shortly today, for I have to go to Ernemann this morning and for the chorus voices for Kratzer, if he will teach them for me; but I know he detests me. News: Old Gorski, *tiego, tiego,*[3] has married Panna Pągowska; but none of the family knew anything about it. Imagine, his son was with him when he started for Bielany, to the wedding; and asked to be taken with him for the drive, having no idea that his father was getting into the carriage *en qualité* of a bridegroom. The father got rid of him by giving him a stall ticket for "Preziosa," and meanwhile went off hunting. The next morning, Władzio went to him with Wincenty Skarzyński with name-day wishes: they were puzzled to find the father so embarrassed and looking at the window every moment; but as old Pągowski was in the room, and Gorski was just starting in the carriage, the son supposed that it was Pągowski who was going to a hotel, and was not astonished when, on the way out, he met Panna Pągowska (now his stepmother) and her mother entering the room. So, after saying goodbye to his father, who took leave of him hastily and showing embarrassment, he went to Dziekoński, who

[1] *Maometto II.* 1st performance 1820.
[2] by Fioravanti. [Op.]
[3] Probably for *tego* (of that); he may have stuttered.

had arrived in the night. On entering he greets the stepfather, who starts by complaining of want of sleep. — Why? — " But confound it, your father took away all the mattresses for the wedding." — " How do you mean? " — " Well, — haven't you just come from him? " — " But it's impossible, that he would not have told me." — " Ask the servant, who stayed with the carriage." The son went home very sad, to find that " tiego, tiego " had played such a dirty trick. Pani Dziekońska knows nothing about it. You know that Panna Pągowska; you met her at the Pruszak's: small, not bad-looking; she used to be persecuted about young Gorski, and probably the father got married for his son. Father Dekert (whom you know) married them. Hube is going to Italy. Nowakowski is in Białystok to sniff round at what is going on there; he has found a job there; I hope he won't come back. Nowakowski the actor has an engagement in Cracow. It's a pity. But Dmuszewski told me they can't keep him, because he demands fearful conditions. The first is that his wife should act, and she doesn't know how. I am going now to old Pruszak, even before Ern[emann]; — I have important business with him, concerning only them. I can't tell you about it, but it's a peculiar matter, and not a milky one; rather a pursy one. I know he will receive me kindly. Give me a kiss, dearest belovéd; I know that you still care for me, but I'm always so afraid of you, — as if you were some sort of tyrant over me; I don't know why I'm afraid of you. God knows it's only you that have power over me, you and — no one else. Perhaps this is the last letter I shall write to you.

Till death, Your

F. CHOPIN

Parents, children, Żywny —

Skarzyński always asks me about you. *A propos, les demoiselles du Conservatoire* sent you greetings a long while ago. Gład. and Wołków are to remain another year under Soliwa, — and have confessed to me that they are bored.

Tuesday, 5 October.

52.

To the Same.
[*Warsaw*] *Tuesday, 12 October 1830.*

MY DEAREST LIFE!

Yesterday's concert was a success; I haste to let you know. I inform your Lordship that I was not a bit, not a bit nervous, and played the way I play when I'm alone, and it went well. Full hall. First Goerner's Symphony. Then my noble self's Allegro E minor, which I just reeled off; one can do that on the Streycher piano. Furious applause. Soliwa was delighted; he conducted on account of his aria with chorus, sung beautifully by Panna Wołków, who was dressed like a cherub, in sky blue. After the aria came the Adagio and Rondo; then the pause between the 1st and 2nd parts. When they returned from the buffet and left the stage, which they had mounted to produce an effect favourable to me, the 2nd part began with the Overture to Wilhelm Tell. Soliwa conducted well and it made a great impression. Really, the Italian has shown me so much kindness this time that it is difficult to thank him enough. He then conducted the air for Panna Gładkowska (dressed just right for her face, in white, with roses on her head) — she sang the Cavatina from *La Donna del Lago,*[1] with the recitative, as she has sung nothing yet, except the aria in Agnes. You know: — "*Oh quante lagrime per te versai.*" She took: "*tutto detesto,*" down on the low B, in such a way that Zieliński said that B was worth a thousand ducats. You must know that the aria was transposed for her voice, which profited greatly by the change. After Panna Gładkowska had been escorted from the stage we started the Potpourri on The Moon that Set,[2] etc. This time I was all right and the orchestra was all right, and the pit understood. This time the last mazurka elicited big applause, after which — the usual farce — I was called up. No one hissed, and I had to bow 4

[1] Opera by Rossini, 1819.

[2] A well-known song: "The moon had set, the dogs were asleep," the tune of which Chopin used in his Fantasia on Polish Themes: Op. 13. [Op.]

times; but properly now, because Brandt has taught me how to do it. I don't know how things would have gone yesterday if Soliwa had not taken my scores home with him, read them and conducted so that I could not rush as if I would break my neck. But he managed so well to hold us all that, I assure you, I never succeeded in playing so comfortably with the orchestra. The piano, apparently, was much liked; Panna Wołków still more; she shows up well on the stage. She is now to appear in the Barber; it is to be on Saturday if not on Thursday. I am thinking of nothing now but packing; either on Saturday or on Wednesday I start, going by Cracow. Yesterday I learned that Wincenty may be going to Cracow, I must find out. Perhaps we could travel together, if he is not going too late. I saw Karol in Warsaw the other day, well and cheerful; and he earnestly wanted to know when you are to meet in Lublin. He hopes to find letters from you on his return home. As for Kostuś, his father told me that he has been at Buda for the coronation with Seweryn and Kinel, and therefore is not yet in Paris; but he intends to return there, and is probably now on the way. I must stop, my Life; Pan Lasocki is waiting for me to go to Ernemann with him for the purpose of engaging him to give his daughter lessons. Afterwards porridge, now a kiss to you.

Your most affectionate

F. Chopin

The children, Mamma, Papa, everyone, Żywny, all embrace you warmly.

53.

To his Family.

Wrocław [Breslau], Tuesday, 9 November 1830.

My dearest Parents and Sisters!

We arrived very comfortably and in the best weather, at 6 on Saturday evening, and put up *Zur Goldenen Gans.*[1] We at once

[1] The Golden Goose.

went to the theatre, where they gave The King of the Alps,[1] which is to be put on at home. The pit admired the new decorations, but we found nothing to make a fuss about. The artists played fairly well. The day before yesterday they gave Auber's *Miller and Locksmith,* — badly. Today is Winter's Interrupted Sacrifice,[2] I am curious to see how it goes. They have no very good singers; but the theatre is very cheap; a stall seat costs 2 zls. I like Wrocław better this time.

I delivered the letter to Sowiński; I have barely seen him once; he called on us yesterday, but we were out. We had gone to the local Resource, where Schnabel, the Kapellmeister, asked me to be present at rehearsal for this evening's concert. They give three such concerts a week. I found the orchestra, small, as usual, assembled for rehearsal, a piano and, as umpire, some amateur, named Hellwig, who is preparing to play the Moscheles E flat major concerto. Before he sat down to the instrument, Schnabel, who had not heard me for four years, asked me to try the piano. It was difficult to refuse, so I sat down and played a few variations. Schnabel was immoderately pleased, began begging me to play in the evening. Schnabel especially pressed me so earnestly that I could not refuse the old man. He is a great friend of Elsner; but I told him I am doing it only for him, as I have not played for some weeks. I have no desire to distinguish myself in Wrocław. To that the old man replied that he knows all that, and that, seeing me in the church yesterday, he wanted to ask me to play but did not dare to. I then went with his son to fetch the music, and played them the Romance and Rondo of the 2nd Concerto. At the rehearsal the Germans admired my playing: — "*Was für ein leichtes Spiel hat er,*" [3] said they; but nothing about the compositions. Tytus even heard one say: " he can play, but not compose." *Nota bene,* at *table d'hôte* the day before yesterday, some gentleman of very attractive appearance was sitting opposite to us. On entering into conversation, I found that he knows Schultz of Warsaw, and is a friend of the people to whom Schultz gave me a letter. He is a merchant

[1] *Der Alpenkönig:* opera by Rosek von Reiter, 1779–1830.
[2] *Das unterbrochene Opferfest.* 1st performance 1795.
[3] How light his playing is.

named Scharff; very amiable; he took us all over Wrocław; engaged a *fiacre* himself and showed us the prettiest drives. The next day he put our names down at the Bourse, got us *Fremdenkarten* [1] for yesterday's concert and sent them to us before the rehearsal. How surprised must he and the gentlemen who arranged about the tickets have been, when the Fremder [2] turned out the chief musical figure of the evening. Besides the *Rondo* I improvised, for connoisseurs, on themes from The Dumb Girl of Portici. Then they finished up with an Overture, and then dancing began. Schnabel wanted to give me supper, but I took only broth.

Of course I have met the *Oberorganist* here, Herr Köhler; he promised to show me the organ today. I also met a certain baron, or the devil knows what, called Nesse or Neisse; a pupil of Spohr, who is said to be a fine violinist. Another local expert and musician, named Hesse, who has travelled all over Germany, also paid me compliments; but, except Schnabel, whom one could see to be genuinely delighted, and who kept taking me under the chin and caressing me every moment, none of the Germans knew what to do. Tytus enjoyed watching them. As I have no established reputation as yet, they admired and feared to admire; could not make out whether the compositions were good, or whether they only thought they were. One of the local connoisseurs came up to me and praised the novelty of the form; saying that he had never before heard anything in that form. I don't know who he was, but he was perhaps the one who understood me best. Schnabel is full of the utmost amiabilities, even offered a carriage; but we left after 9, when they began to dance.

I am glad to have given pleasure to the old man.

Some lady to whom the director introduced me after the concert, calling her the best local pianist, thanked me profusely for the delightful surprise, and regretted that I am not to be heard in public. The umpire consoled himself by singing Figaro's air from the Barber, but — wretchedly.

Yesterday they talked a lot about Elsner, and praised some

[1] Guest tickets.

[2] Guest.

Variations of his for orchestra, with an Echo; I said, that if they could hear his Coronation Mass, they would be able to judge what a composer he is. The Germans here are awful, at least yesterday's company; our Herr Scharff is an exception.

Tomorrow at 2 we leave for Dresden. Kisses! Kisses! Kisses!

Kindest greetings to Żywny, Elsner, Matuszyński, Kolberg, Marylski, and Witwicki.

54.

To the Same.
Dresden, 14 November 1830.

I can scarcely find a moment for a few words to give you news of me. I am just back from a Polish dinner: that is, where only Poles were present. I left them there and came back to write; the post goes at 7, and I should like to hear The Dumb Girl of Portici again today.

We didn't like leaving Wrocław; a closer acquaintance with the people to whom Scholz gave me letters made the town very pleasant for us. My first call here was on Fräulein Pechwell. She played on Friday at the local Resource, and got me admitted. The same evening the Dumb Girl was played in the theatre; it was hard to choose, but I really had to attend the lady's evening, so I went there. Another important reason for going was that I was told I should hear there the best local woman singer: an Italian by birth, called Plazzesi. So I put on my best clothes and sent for a sedan-chair; got into this queer box and asked to be taken to Kreissig's house, where the evening was to be held. I laughed at myself on the way, being carried by these bearers in livery; I was greatly tempted to stamp out the bottom, but restrained myself. This vehicle took me right up the steps. I got out and sent in my name to Fräulein Pechwell; the master of the house came out with bows and scrapes and many compliments, and conducted me into the hall, where I found, at the two sides, eight enormous tables, at which sat a crowd of ladies. Their adornments, consisting less of diamonds than of wires,[1] flashed in my eyes. Joking apart, the number of ladies and wires was so great that one could have feared some revolt against men, which only baldness and spectacles could combat; there was a great deal of glass, and a good deal of bare skin.

The rattling of these wires, and also of tea-cups, was suddenly interrupted by music from the other end of the room. First they played the Overture from Fra Diavolo,[2] then the Italian lady sang; not bad. I got into conversation with her, and also met her accompanist Sig. Rastrelli, the sub-director of the opera here, and Sig. Rubini, the brother of the famous singer whom I hope to meet in Milan. This polite Italian promised me a letter to his brother; it's all I need. He was kind enough to take me yesterday to the rehearsal of the " Vespers " composed by Morlacchi, the court Kapellmeister here. I took the opportunity to recall myself to his memory; he at once put me to sit beside him and talked a lot with me.

The Vespers were sung today by the famous Neapolitan male sopranos Sassaroli and Tarquinio; Rolla, a well-known concert-master here, to whom I had a card from Soliwa, played the violin *obligato* [*sic*]. I made acquaintance with him, and he promised me a letter to his father, the director of the Milan opera. But let us return to the evening.

Fräulein Pechwell played the piano, and I, after talking with one and another, went off to the Dumb Girl. I can't judge of it because I didn't hear it all. Only after this evening shall I be able to tell you anything positive.

Going to Klengel in the morning, I met him outside the house; he recognized me at once, and was so friendly that he even pressed me to his heart. I respect him greatly. He invited me to come to him tomorrow morning, but asked first where I am staying. He tried to persuade me to appear in public, but about that I am deaf. I have no time to lose, and Dresden will give me neither fame nor money.

General Kniaziewicz, whom I saw at Pani Pruszak's, also spoke of a concert, but declared that it would not lead to much.

[1] knitting-needles.
[2] Comic opera by Auber. 1st performance 1829.

Yesterday I was at the Italian opera, but it was badly done; but for Rolli's *solo* and the singing of Fräulein Hähnel from the Vienna theatre, who made her début yesterday as Tancredi,[1] there would have been nothing to hear. The King, surrounded by the whole court, was in the theatre, and also in church at the high Mass today. They sang a Mass by Baron Miltitz, one of the local nobles, under the direction of Morlacchi. I liked the voices of Sassaroli, Muschetti, Balwig and Zezi best. The composition itself is nothing much. Dotzauer and Kummer, famous local violoncellists, had several soli, which they played well; otherwise nothing special. Except my Klengel, before whom I shall doubtless have to distinguish myself tomorrow, there is nothing here worth noticing. I like to talk with him, because one can really learn something from him.

Except the picture galleries, I have not looked again at anything in Dresden; it is enough to see *grüne Gewölbe* [2] once.

55.

To the Same.
Prague, 21 November 1830.

The week in Dresden went so fast that I could not keep track of it. I would start out in the morning and not get back till night. Klengel, when I got to know him better, that is, when I played him my concerto, said that it reminded him of Field's playing, that I have a rare touch, that though he had heard much about me, he had never expected to find me such a virtuoso. It was not idle compliment; he told me that he hates to flatter anyone or force himself to praise them. So, the moment I had left — and I sat with him the whole morning, till 12 — he went to Morlacchi and to Lüttichau, the *general director* of the theatre, to find out whether I could be persuaded to be heard during the four more

[1] *Tancredi:* opera by Rossini, on a play by Voltaire. 1st performance 1813. This opera was afterwards very popular in Paris.

[2] The room in Dresden Castle where the crown jewels were kept.

days that I am to remain in this town. He told me afterwards that he did this for Dresden, not for me, and that he would like to compel me to give a concert, if getting it up would not demand too much time. The next morning he came to me, and informed me that till Sunday — and this was on Wednesday — there was not one free evening; on Friday was to be the first performance of Fra Diavolo, and on Saturday, that is: yesterday, Rossini's *La Donna del Lago* in Italian. I received Klengel as I would receive few persons in my life; definitely, I love him as if I had known him for thirty years. He also shows much sympathy with me. He asked for the scores of my concertos, and took me to Pani Wiesołowska for the evening. On the same day there was a reception at Pani Szczerbinin's, but I stayed so long at the Niesołowskis' that all the guests had gone when Klengel took me to Pani Szczerbinin. But I had to dine there the next day. I was caught everywhere, like a dog. I went the same day to Pani Dobrzycka, who invited me for her birthday, the next day. There I met the Saxon princesses, the daughters of the former king: that is, the sister and the brother's wife of the reigning monarch. I played in their presence; they promised me letters to Italy, but I have not got all yet; one sent me two letters to my hotel just before I left; the rest I expect to receive in Vienna, through Pani Dobrzycka, who knows where to find me there. The letters are addressed to the queen of the two Sicilies, in Naples, and to a princess Ulasino, of the Saxon royal house, in Rome. I am also promised letters to the reigning princess of Lucca and to the wife of the viceroy of Milan. The letters are to be forwarded by Kraszewski, to whom I am writing specially about it today. In Dresden I also dined at the Komars'. Klengel gave me a letter to Vienna, where I shall also go later; he drank my health in champagne at Pani Niesołowska's; she also made much of me, didn't know where to put me to sit, and insisted on calling me Chopski.

Rolla is the first violin; the rest from Vienna, where we arrive at 9 on Tuesday morning.

General Kniaziewicz took a great fancy to me; he told me that no pianist had ever made so pleasant an impression on him.

56.

To JAN MATUSZYŃSKI IN WARSAW.
Vienna, 22 November [1830].

DEAR JASIO!

Let me know your house number. You know what is happening to me, how glad I am that I am in Vienna, that I am making so many interesting and useful acquaintances, that I may be going to fall in love. I don't think about any of you. Only I sometimes look at the hair ring that Ludwika made, which I love the more, the farther away from them I go. I love you too, more now than in Warsaw. But do you all love me? Esculapius, if you have not written to me, may the devil carry you off, may a thunderbolt strike you in Radom, may it tear the button off your cap! I left a message in Prague that all letters should be sent on to Vienna, and so far, there is nothing. Did the rain upset you? I have a presentiment that you are ill. For heaven's sake don't take risks; you know how many times I have come to grief. My clay will not melt with the rain this time; the inside of it is at 90 degrees Réaumur. Perhaps, — ah no, it won't happen, only a little house for a kitten can be made from my clay! Ah, you scoundrel! You have been to the theatre! You have used your opera glass, you have ogled others! You have darted your eyes at shoulder knots — [?] If it's so, may the lightning strike you, you are not worthy of my affection. Tytus knows, and is glad; he always respected [her] and expected it; if I write to you, I do it for myself, for you are not worth it. Fräulein Heinefetter was lovely yesterday in Othello,[1] and sang beautifully. Later I will write you everything, but I want your number. Give me a kiss, embrace Father Alfons for me, I have written to Marcel. Kisses to all my colleagues, kisses.

F. CHOPIN

[1] Opera by Rossini. 1st performance 1816.

This pen is like a ladle; and besides, it is tumbling from my hand. Don't be surprised at this scrawl. I would write more, but I am afraid to; I can't collect my thoughts.

[Overleaf.] You are requested to keep off the grass. You are ordered not to be inquisitive old women. Herewith I send a packet of kisses—a baker's dozen—to my honoured colleagues.

And to My Court Physician Jan Matuszyński,[1] the order of St. John of the 1st class with pies, in his palace, when I come to you.

By the courier: Ludwika, Izabella or Zuzia.

57.

To his Family.
Vienna, 1 December 1830.

My small heart giggled for joy at your letter, the first that has come in the four weeks since I parted from you. It made me eat a better dinner, and the Wild Man—that's the name of the excellent inn where I eat—has charged me for a large appetite for strudeln,[2] a whole bottle of Rhenish and several Kreutzers. The joy was general, because Tytus also had letters from home. Thank Celiński for the enclosed note; it took me back to your arms. I imagined I was sitting at the pianoforte; Celiński standing opposite and looking at Żywny taking snuff with Linowski. Only Matuszyński was missing; I think he must still be feverish—But enough of romancing; my turn for holidays will come one day, there are plenty of pretty German girls;—but when will it come, when!—

Just imagine, Fräulein Blahetka is in Stuttgart with her parents; perhaps they will return for the winter. I heard the news from Haslinger, who received me most amiably, but has not yet printed either the Sonata or the second Variations, for all that.

[1] Matuszyński was a medical student.
[2] pancakes.

He'll get some pepper [1] the moment Tytus and I are settled in our lodging. We have engaged one in the principal street, the Kohlmarkt; three rooms, on the third floor, it's true, but delightful, splendid, elegantly furnished, by the month, for a small rent. My share is 25 florins. Some chief admiral, an Englishman, is still occupying them, but he moves out today or tomorrow. An admiral! And I shall be Admiration, so the rooms won't lose anything; [Footnote:] *Don't read this letter to everyone; people might think I had got my head turned.* [Letter continues:] especially as the landlady, or rather owner of this lodging, is a baroness, a widow, pretty, fairly young; who told us that she has lived long in Poland, and had heard of me in Warsaw. She knows the Skarzyński's, has been in high society; asked Tytus whether he knows the young and pretty Pani Rembielińska, etc. So, if there were nothing more, such a respectable lady is worth 25 florins, especially as she likes Poles, does not care for Austrians, is herself Prussian and a very sensible woman.

As soon as we move in, Graff, the piano-manufacturer, will send us an instrument. Würfel began to talk about giving a concert the moment he saw me. He is very unwell, and does not go out, only gives lessons at home; he has had lung hæmorrhage, which has weakened him badly. But he continues to bombard me about a concert, saying that the local papers have written a lot about my *F minor* concerto; as to which I do not know and have had no curiosity to find out.

I will give a concert; but when, where, what, I don't know.

My swollen nose has not allowed me to present myself as yet at the embassy, or to call on Pani Rzewuska, to whom everybody goes. She lives near to Hussarzewski, to whom I have already boldly gone several times, in spite of my nose. He, like Würfel, advises me not to play for nothing. Malfatti received me most amiably, most heartily, as if I were his cousin. As soon as he read my name, he embraced me, and said he would do all he could to serve me; had already written about that to Władysław Ostrowski. He added that he will mention me to Pani Tatyszczew,[2]

[1] get a wigging.
[2] This is the Russian name Tatishchev, in Polish spelling.

will give me all necessary introductions, and will even try at court; though he doubts whether anything will come of that, as the court is now in mourning for the king of Naples. He also promised to introduce me to Baron Dunoi, the chief of the local music *Verein;* that should be an excellent acquaintance.

Another one which may also be useful is with Herr Mittag; through Klengel's letter. This is a man who sees things the right way, and I think will be the most helpful to me of all the musicians. Czerny, on whom I have already called (humbly as always and with everybody), asked me what I "*hat fleissig studiert.*"[1] He has again arranged some overture for 8 pianos and 16 players, and is quite pleased. Otherwise I have not yet seen a single pianist here.

I have been twice to Frau Weyberheim, Frau Wolf's sister, and am invited there for tomorrow evening; — "*un petit cercle des amateurs.*"[2] From there I go to call on Rozalja Rzewska, who receives between 9 and 10, and who has been notified of my arrival by Hussarzewski. There I am to meet that famous Signora Cibini, for whom Moscheles wrote the 4-hand Sonata.

The day before yesterday I went to Stametz, to the *Comptoir*. They received me, with my letters, just as they would receive everyone who comes for money; gave me a card to the police, so that I could get my residence permit, and — that is all. But perhaps it will be different later. I also went that day to Herr Geymüller, with whom Tytus placed his six thousand. Herr Geymüller, after looking at my name, remarked, without reading the rest, that he was: "very glad to meet such a *Künstler*[3] as I, but cannot advise me to get myself heard, for there are so many good pianists here that one needs a great reputation to gain anything." He ended by adding that he "cannot do anything for me, as times are difficult," etc. I had to gape at him, and swallow all that. When he finished his tirade, not before, I told him that I really do not know whether it is worth my while to be heard, as I have not yet called on any of the notabilities here, even on the ambassador, to whom I have an intro-

[1] had studied industriously.
[2] A little group of amateurs.
[3] artist.

duction from Warsaw from the Grand Duke,[1] etc. That made him open his eyes; and I then took my leave, with apologies for interrupting his business. Wait a bit, you h—— [*hycel:* dog-hanger] [2] Jews!

I have not yet been to Lachner, the conductor of the orchestra, for I don't know where I can receive callers. From the *Stadt London,* where everything was too salt, we moved to the Lamm in the Leopoldstadt, and here we are camping for the moment, till the thin, sickly, whiskered and greenish-yellow-and-mauve English sailor moves from the baroness's house. In that " lodging in the grand style " — the phrase belongs to Tytus, who insists on regarding me as a conceited person — it will be time to play and to think about concerts; but not unpaid concerts. Well, we shall see.

I have not been either to Pani Rarzak, or to Pani Elkan, or to Rothschild, or to the Voigts, or to lots of other people. Today I go to the embassy; there is one baron Meindorf, whom Hussarzewski told me to ask how best to get to Tatyszczew. I have not yet touched the money which I got two days ago at the bank. I hope I shall treat it with respect. All the same, I should be glad if I could have a little at the end of this month, for the journey to Italy, if my concerts do not bring in anything.

The theatre costs me more than anything; but I don't regret it, because Fräulein Heinefetter and Herr Wild nearly always sing. During this week I have heard three entirely new operas. Yesterday they gave Fra Diavolo; the Dumb Girl is better; before that was Mozart's Titus,[3] and today Wilhelm Tell. I don't envy Orłowski, who accompanies Lafont; perhaps there may come a time when Lafont will accompany me. Is that rather too bold? Well, really, it may come. Nidecki thinks of staying here all the winter. All this week has been taken up with my nose, the theatre and Graff, to whom I go every day after dinner, to play, and exercise my stiff fingers a little after the journey. Yesterday I introduced Nidecki to Graff.

[1] Constantine of Russia.

[2] *Hycel:* a flayer of hides and destroyer of stray dogs and cats; a trade formerly practised in Poland by a very poor class of Ghetto Jews. The word is also employed as a general term of abuse.

[3] *La Clemenza di Tito.*

I really don't know how this week has gone; we have not looked round, nor have I yet taken any definite steps towards a concert. *Questia?* Which Concerto shall I play: F or E? Würfel declares the one in F is better than the A flat Hummel, which Hasslinger has just brought out. Haslinger is shrewd; he wants to put me off, courteously but lightly, so that I may give him my compositions for nothing. Klengel is surprised that he did not pay me for the Variations. Perhaps he thinks that if he appears to have slight regard for my things I shall take it seriously, and give them to him for nothing? " For nothing " is finished; now *bezahl,*[1] beast!

Graff advises me to appear in the *Landständischen Saal,* where the Spiritual Concerts are held; that is: in the best and finest place. For that I shall need permission from Dietrichstein, but that will not be difficult to get, through Malfatti.

People say I have grown fat —

All is well with me. I trust in God and in Malfatti — the magnificent Malfatti — that it will be still better.

58.

To the Same.
Vienna, Wednesday before Christmas.

I have no calendar, so I don't know the date.

Yesterday it was seven weeks since I left you. Why? — Well, it has happened. Just yesterday! On Tuesday, at the same hour when I went off to Wola, I was at a dance at the Weiberrheims. The place was full of young, good-looking people, not at all old-fashioned. They wanted me to dance, insisted on choosing me for the *cotillon;* I did a few turns, and then went home. The hostess and her tactful daughters had asked a lot of musical personages for that evening; but I did not play, as I did not feel in the mood. She introduced Herr Likt, whom Ludwika knows; a kind courteous, honest German; he regarded me as something

[1] pay.

great, so I did not want to disconcert him with my playing. I also met there the son-in-law of Lampi, whom Papa knows; a charming and handsome boy, who paints beautifully. *A propos* of painting: yesterday morning Hummel came to me with his son; he is finishing my portrait; it's so like that it couldn't be better. I am sitting on a stool, in a dressing-gown, with an inspired expression of I don't know what. Pencil, or rather chalk, looks like an engraving; size for a folder. Old Hummel is kindness itself. As he is friendly with Duport, formerly a famous dancer and now the entrepreneur of the Kärthnerthor theatre, he introduced me to him yesterday. M. Duport is said to be niggardly; he received me most graciously, perhaps in the hope that I will play for him for nothing; but he is mistaken. We exchanged casual *avant propos* — would I call to play; but when, what or how, not a word. If he offers too little, I shall give my concert in the big redoubt hall.

Würfel is better; last week, at his house, I met Slawik, a fine violinist, though still quite young; 26 at the most. I liked him very much. As we walked back together, he asked me: — was I going straight home? — Yes, I answered. — " Then better come with me to your countrywoman, Pani Bayer." As it happened, Kraszewski had sent me a letter to her from Dresden, together with the one to the wife of the viceroy of Milan. I could not use the letter at once, as I had not the address, and there are thousands of Bayers in Vienna. — " All right," I told Slawik, — " only I will fetch the letter first." It was the same lady. Her husband is a Pole from Odessa, a neighbour of Chomentowski. The wife, who apparently had heard a lot about me, invited us to dinner the next day; that was Sunday, and Slawik played; I liked him, after Paganini, better than anyone. He also took a fancy to my noble self, and we agreed to write a piano and violin duet together: an idea which had occurred to me in Warsaw. He is a great violinist, of real genius. As soon as I meet Merk[1] we can undertake a trio, and I may meet him any day at Mechetti's. Yesterday Czerny and I went together to Diabelli, who has invited me to an evening party for musicians alone, next Monday. On Sunday an evening at Likt's where all the great

[1] A famous Austrian cellist (1795–1852).

musical world will be, and an overture for eight hands; and on Saturday there is to be some old church music at the house of Hofrath Kiesewetter, author of a work on music.

You must know that I am now on the fourth floor. Some English people, hearing from my predecessor of my delightful lodging, wanted to have one of the rooms; but, coming ostensibly to look at one, they examined all three, and like them so much that they at once offered me 80 florins a month to give them up, to my unmeasured delight. Baroness Lachmanowicz, Pani Uszak's sister-in-law and now my kind young landlady, had on the fourth floor a similar lodging; she showed it to me, I accepted, and am now housed for 10 florins a month, as if I were paying 70. You doubtless think: the poor fellow is in an attic! Not at all; there is the fifth floor above me, and only then the roof; and 60 florins in your pocket are in your pocket. People call on me, and Pan Hussarzewski has to climb all those stairs. But the street is priceless: in the middle of the town, close to everything. A beautiful walk below, Artaria on my left, Mechetti and Haslinger on my right, the theatre behind me; what more can I want? . . .

Malfatti has scolded me, because, having promised to dine at Pani Schaschek's at 2, I came at 4; I am to go there again, with him, to dinner on Saturday. If I am late, Malfatti threatens to perform a very painful operation on me; I won't write what, for it's ugly. I see that Papa is annoyed at my rattlepatedness and unbecoming behaviour to people; but it will all come right, for Malfatti likes me, I am glad to say.

Nidecki comes to me every morning to play. When I write a 2-piano concerto, we will play it in public together; first, though, I must appear solo. Haslinger continues to be polite, but quiet.

I don't know whether to go to Italy now, or what. Please write to me about it. Mamma is glad I have gone away, but I am not glad. It has happened — Embrace Tytus for me, and ask him to write, for the love of God. — No, you can't conceive how joyful I am when I get a letter from you. Why is the post so slow! Well, you won't be angry with me for worrying about you. —

I have met here a very nice boy called Leibenfrost, a friend of Kessler; he often comes to me, though I have only once called on him. When I am not asked to dinner anywhere, I eat in town with him. He knows all Vienna, and whenever there is anything special to see, he takes me there at once. Yesterday, for instance, was a beautiful excursion to *Bastei,* archdukes in their aristocratic frock-coats — in a word, all Vienna. I met Slawik there, and arranged to meet today and choose a Beethoven theme for variations. In one way I am glad to be here, but in the other! —

How nice it is in this room. A roof opposite me, and pigmies down below. I am higher than they! The best moment is when, having finished playing on Graff's dull piano, I go to bed with your letters in my hand. Then, even in sleep, I see only you.

Yesterday at the Bayer's we danced the mazurka. Slawik lay on the floor, to represent a sheep, and some old German *Contessa* with a big nose and a pockmarked face, did some kind of queer waltz step with long thin legs, holding her skirts gracefully with two fingertips in the ancient manner, and keeping her head turned stiffly towards her partner, so that her neck bones stuck out here and there. But she is a fine person, serious, cultured; talks fluently and has the *usage du monde.*

Among the numerous pleasures of Vienna the hotel evenings are famous. During supper Strauss or Lanner play waltzes; they are the local Swieszewscy. After every waltz they get huge applause; and if they play a *Quodlibet,* or jumble of opera, song and dance, the hearers are so overjoyed that they don't know what to do with themselves. It shows the corrupt taste of the Viennese public.

I wanted to send you a waltz that I have composed, but it is late now; you shall have it afterwards. I don't send the mazurkas because they are not copied yet; they are not for dancing.

I don't want to say goodbye to you, I should like to keep on writing. If you see Fontana, tell him I am going to write to him. Matuszyński will get a huge letter, if not today, then by the next post.

59.

To Jan Matuszyński in Warsaw.

Vienna. Christmas Day, Sunday morning. Last year at this hour I was with the Bernadines. Today I am sitting alone, in a dressing-gown, gnawing my ring and writing.
[*26 December 1830.*]

Dearest Jasio!

I am just back from Slawik's — a famous violinst with whom I have made friends — Since Paganini I have heard nothing like him; he can take 96 notes staccato on one bow, and so on; incredible; there I started getting homesick for the piano, and came back with the notion of weeping out the Adagio of the variations on a Beethoven theme, which we are writing together. But one step to the post office, which I never pass without going in, gave a fresh turn to my feelings. The tears, that should have fallen on the keys, bedewed your paper; I was starving for a letter.

My letters are nothing to you, for you are at home; but I read and re-read your letter without end. Freyer has been to see me several times — though I have not once managed to get to him; he heard from Schuch that I am in Vienna. He is living with Rostkowski; I think that is the name of the young man sent by the government; the one that had a lawsuit with Roliński. He told me a lot of interesting details of the latest news, and enjoyed your letter, part of which I gave him to read. The other part has grieved me deeply. Is there really even a little change? Did she[1] not fall ill? I could easily believe some such thing about so sensitive a creature. Don't you think so? Is it perhaps the terror of the 29th?[2] May God forbid its being because of me! Calm her, say that, so long as my strength lasts — that till death — that even after death my ashes will strew themselves under her feet. But that's all nothing, whatever you can say — I will write. I would have written long ago, would not have fretted

[1] "She" appears to be Konstancja Gładkowska, the singer, with whom he was in love.

[2] The insurrection of 1830 broke out on November 29th.

over it so long; but people! —If by any chance it should fall into strange hands, it might injure her reputation; so it is better you should be my interpreter; speak for me, "et j'en conviendrai." Your phrases in French just finished me; a German who was walking with me in the street while I was reading your letter could scarcely hold me up by the arm, and could not make out what had happened to me. I wanted to seize hold of all the passers-by and kiss them; I felt as I have never felt before, because it was the first letter from you! I bore you, Jasio, with my stupid passion; but it's difficult to wake up and write casual things to you. Yesterday I dined with a Polish lady called Beyer, whose Christian name is Constance. I love to go there for the reminiscence; all the music, the pocket handkerchiefs and table-napkins have her name on them. I go there with Sławik, for whom she has a weakness. The day before yesterday we played the whole morning and afternoon, then, as it was Christmas Eve and fine clear springlike weather, we left there at night. After parting from Slawik, who was due at the imperial chapel, I strolled along slowly alone, and at midnight went into St. Stephen's. When I entered there was no one there. Not to hear the mass, but just to look at the huge building at that hour, I got into the darkest corner at the foot of a Gothic pillar. I can't describe the greatness, the magnificence of those huge arches. It was quiet; now and then the footsteps of a sacristan lighting candles at the back of the sanctuary, would break in on my lethargy. A coffin behind me, a coffin under me; — only the coffin above me was lacking. A mournful harmony all around — I never felt my loneliness so clearly; I loved to drink in this great sight, till people and lights began to appear. Then, turning up the collar of my cloak, as once — do you remember? — along the Cracow Suburb,[1] I went to hear the music at the imperial chapel. On the way, I passed through the finest streets of Vienna, not alone now, but in the company of a cheerful crowd, and reached the Castle, where I heard three numbers of a not very good mass, sleepily sung, and then, at 1 in the night, went home to bed. I dreamed of you, of all of you, of them, of my dear children. Next morning I was waked by an invitation to

[1] A street in Warsaw.

dinner from Pani Elkan, a Polish lady, wife of a banker. I got up, practised mournfully; then came Nidecki, Leidenfrost, Steinkeller; parting from them, I went to dinner at Malfatti's. Szaniasio [?], a Pole, who has since been killed, ate more zrazy [1] and cabbage, I swear, than any Carmelite. I was not far behind; you must know that this rare man — in the full sense of the word a *man* — Dr. Malfatti, is so considerate of everyone that, if we come to dine with him, he searches out Polish food for us. After dinner came Wild: a famous — perhaps today the most famous — German tenor. I accompanied him from memory in the air from Othello, which he sang like a master. He and Heinefetter support the entire opera here; it is true, it is a miserable one, quite unworthy of Vienna. Fräulein Heinefetter is almost completely lacking in feeling; a voice, such as I do not often hear, everything sung well, every note accurately performed; purity, flexibility, portamenta; — but so cold that I almost got my nose frostbitten while sitting in the front row near the stage. Off the stage she is pretty, especially in masculine dress. In Othello she is better than in the Barber, in which, instead of a lively, innocent young girl in love, she has to represent a thoroughly practised flirt. In Mozart's Titus, as Sextus, she is charming; in The Crusader [2] also. She will soon appear in the Magpie; I am curious to see. Wołków understood the Barber better; if only she had Heinefetter's throat. Certainly she is one of our first women singers, if not the first. I was to have gone to hear Pasta; you know I have letters from the Saxon court to the Milan viceroy's wife. But how am I to go? My parents tell me to please myself, and I don't want to go. To Paris? Here they advise me to wait. Return home? Stay here? — Kill myself? — Not write to you? Give me some advice, what to do. Ask the persons who dominate me, and write me their opinion, and so it shall be. I shall stay here next month. So write, before you leave for the *East* and the *North;* but I hope you will not need to go. So write before you start, *poste-restante,* Vienna; and before you start, go to my parents, to Cons—— While you are there, fill my place with them. Visit them often, let my sisters see you, let them think

[1] A favourite Polish dish.
[2] Meyerbeer: *Il Crociato in Egitto.* 1st performance 1824.

you are coming to me, and I in the next room; sit by them, and let them think I sit behind you. Go to the theatre, and I will come there. I read the papers diligently; I have been promised the Polish dailies. — I'm not thinking of my concert. — There's a certain *Alois Schmidt,* a pianist from Frankfort, known for very good Études, a man of over 40; I met him here, and he promised to call. He thinks of giving a concert; one must give him precedence. He seems to me to know his work, and I hope we shall understand each other in music. As for *Thalberg,* he plays excellently, but he's not my man. Younger than I, pleases the ladies, makes *potpourris* from the Dumb Girl, gets his *piano* by the pedal, not the hand, takes tenths as easily as I octaves, — has diamond shirt-studs, — does not admire Moscheles; so don't be surprised that only the *tutti* of my concerto pleased him. *He also writes a concerto.*

I am finishing your letter 3 days late. I have read over the trash I have written to you; forgive me, Jasio, if you have to pay on it. Today, at dinner in the Italian restaurant I heard: — "*Der liebe Gott hat einen Fehler gemacht, dass er die Polen geschaffen hat*"; [1] so don't wonder if I can't express what I feel. Don't expect to hear any news from a Pole, after hearing another man answer: — "*In Polen ist Nichts zu holen.*" [2] The curs! Meanwhile they are really pleased, though they don't want to show it. A certain French sausage dealer has come here. For a whole month there have been crowds in front of his elegant shop; there's always some new reason for staring in at the Frenchman's. Some think it's a result of the French revolution, and gaze compassionately at the sausage skins laid out on tablecloths; others are angry that a French rebel should be allowed to open a ham shop, when they have pigs enough in their own country. Wherever you go, they talk about the Frenchman; and one is afraid to start anything that does not begin with the Frenchman — I'll stop, Jasio, because I have to stop. I kiss you. I suppose I shall leave off loving you when I leave off loving life, and my parents, and *her*. My dear boy, write to me. You can even show this letter if you think well, for I have no

[1] The good God made a mistake when he created the Poles.
[2] There's nothing to be got out of Poland.

time to read it over, I have to go to an evening at Malfatti's today, and before that to the post. I will write to you again as soon as I have a moment. My parents may know that I have written to you; tell them, but don't show the letter.

I still can't tear myself away from my dear Jasio! Go, you Wretch! If Watson loves you as much as I do, she is probably glad of the revolution. Have they not hanged her mother? But Old Whiskers—you know whiskers—the sniveller; it's a pity that detestable musical papa is not tolling the bell.[1] Would it not be fine, for instance in the finale to the Magpie, such tutelary bell-ringing. Const—— I can't even write the name, my hand is not worthy. Oh, I could tear my hair out, when I think they may forget me. All these Gressers! Bezobrazov! Pisarzewski! That's enough; I'm like Othello today.

I was going to fold this letter and seal it without an envelope; I had forgotten that with you people can read Polish. As I now have some paper to spare, let me describe to you my life here. I am on the 4th floor; it's true it's in the best street, but I should have to look well out of the window to see what is going on there. My room — you'll see it in my new Stammbuch [2] when I return to you; young Hummel is making a drawing of it — is big and comfortable, with three windows; the bed opposite the windows; a splendid pantaleon on the right side, a sofa on the left; mirrors between the windows; in the middle a fine, big, round mahogany table; a polished parquet floor. It's quiet; after dinner His Lordship does not receive; so I can concentrate my thoughts on all of you. In the morning I am called by an insufferably stupid servant; I get up, they bring me coffee; I play, and mostly have a cold breakfast; about 9 comes the *maître* for the German language; after that I usually play; then Hummel has been drawing me, and Nidecki learning my Concerto. All this in a dressing-gown till 12. After that comes a very worthy German, Leidenfrost, a German who works at the prison; and if the weather is fine, we go for a walk on the glacis round the town, after which I go to dinner, if I am invited anywhere. If not, we go together to the place frequented by the entire academic youth;

[1] I do not know to what this refers.
[2] album.

that is: Zur Boemische Köchin. After dinner black coffee is drunk in the best Kaffeehaus; that is the custom here, even Szanasio goes. Then I pay visits, return home at dusk, curl my hair, change my shoes, and go out for the evening; about 10, 11 or sometimes 12, — never later, — I come back, play, weep, read, look, laugh, go to bed, put the light out, and always dream about some of you.

Your letter was to have gone on Wednesday, but it was too late, so it goes on Saturday. Embrace Elsner.

I began to write clearly, and am finishing so that perhaps you won't be able to read it. Embrace Magnus, Alfons, Reinszmitek. If possible, get one of them to add a line to your letter.

My portrait, of which only you and I know, is tiny; if you think it would give you the smallest pleasure, I will send it to you by Schuch, who will perhaps leave with Freyer about the 15th of next month, circumstances permitting.

In Vienna there is a lot of talk about Klopiki,[1] — they were sorry for Potoki,[1] and certain Wolikis [1] talked with the duke. I can't help laughing; what these people do with our names passes all belief.

Don't pass on the note unless it is really necessary. I don't know what I have written. You can read, the 1st and perhaps the last.

CH.

60.

To the Same.

[*Vienna, 1 January 1831.*]

I have received yours of December 22nd. My Best Friend in the world, you have what you wanted. I don't know what I am doing. I love you more than my life. Write to me. You in the army! Is she in Radom? Have you dug trenches? Our poor parents. What are my friends doing? I live with you all. I would die for you, for all of you. Why am I so alone? Is it only you who can be together at so fearful a moment? Your flute will

[1] Nonsense words suggested by German mispronunciation of Polish names.

have something to wail about; but the pantaleon must wail first. You say you are starting. How can you give it up? Don't send; be careful. My parents! Perhaps they would think evil — But indeed it's genuine. Give me a kiss. Perhaps I shall go to Paris in a month, if it's quiet there. Love me always, as now. Freyer is attached to you; he grieves, not to be with you. I'm going to dine at Malfatti's. Tomorrow I go to Steinkeller's. It is not amusements that are lacking, but the desire for them; and I have not gone in for them in Vienna as yet. Today is New Year, —how sadly I begin it! Perhaps I shall not end it. Embrace me. You are going to the war. Come back a colonel. Good luck to you all. Why can't I even beat the drum!

CH.

61.

To JOSEPH ELSNER IN WARSAW.
Vienna, 26 January 1831.

I am ashamed that your kindness, of which I had so many proofs at parting, should again have anticipated my duty; it was for me to write to you directly I arrived in Vienna. But I put it off, being convinced that my parents would not fail to communicate to you the unimportant news about myself; and also because I was waiting till I had something definite to tell you. But from the day when I learned of the events of November the 29th, until this moment, there has been nothing except distressing anxiety and grief; and it is useless for Malfatti to try to persuade me that every artist is a cosmopolitan. Even if that were so, as an artist I am still in the cradle, but as a Pole I have begun my third decade. I hope, therefore, that, knowing me, you will not blame me that my older feelings predominate, and that I have not yet begun to think of arranging my concert. Also, in every respect the difficulties in my way are far greater now. It is not only that a continuous series of bad pianoforte concerts has spoiled that kind of music by disgusting the public; but, apart from that, what has happened in Warsaw has altered my situation, perhaps as much to my disadvantage as in Paris it might have benefited me.

Nevertheless I have some hope that somehow it will be managed; and during the carnival will give my first concerto, Würfel's favourite. The good Würfel is still unwell; I often see him, and he always loves to speak of you. But for the interesting acquaintance with the first talents here; Slawik, Merk, Boklet [?] etc., I should profit little by being here. Certainly the opera is good: Wild and Heinefetter delight the local public; it is a pity, though, that Duport puts on few new things, and cares more for his pocket than for the opera. Abbé Stadler regrets this; he says it is no longer the old Vienna. He is publishing his Psalms with Mechetti: a work which I have seen in manuscript and admired. About your Quartet: Joseph Czerny has solemnly promised me that it shall be ready by St. Joseph's day. He says he could not deal with it before, because he has been issuing Schubert's works, many of which are still waiting for the press. This will probably delay the issue of your second manuscript. So far as I have yet been able to observe, Czerny is not one of the rich publishers here, and therefore cannot boldly spend money on works which cannot be played at Sperl's or Zum Römischen Kaiser. Here, waltzes are called works! And Strauss and Lanner, who play them for dancing, are called *Kapellmeistern.* This does not mean that everyone thinks like that; indeed, nearly everyone laughs about it; but only waltzes get printed. I think Mechetti is more *entreprenant* and it will be easy to negotiate with him about your masses, because he wishes to bring out important scores of church music. His bookkeeper is a courteous and enlightened Saxon; I spoke to him of your fine masses, and he was not at all averse; and he manages everything in the business. Today I dine with Mechetti; I will have a serious talk, and write to you at once. Hasslinger is now bringing out Hummel's last mass. He lives only on Hummel; all the same, the last things, for which he had to pay him highly, are not selling well. That is why he is holding back all manuscripts and printing only Strauss. As every barrel-organ can play Strauss today, perhaps in a few months they will be playing Nidecki; though in another sense. Yesterday I went with him to Steinkeller, who has given him an opera to write. He counts a lot on it. Schuster, the famous comedian, will appear in it and Nidecki may make a name for himself. I hope this will be good news to you. He has received the order from the committee, but not the money. As for what you write to me about my 2nd Concerto, which Nidecki has studied; it was by his own wish. Knowing that before leaving Vienna he ought to be heard in public, he was to give a concert; and having nothing of his own, except some pretty variations, asked for my manuscript; all that is not precluded, and he will appear not as a virtuoso but as a composer. He will doubtless tell you about it himself. I want to have his overture played at my concert. You will be able to be pleased with us; unless we should disgrace you; like Aloys Schmidt, a pianist from Frankfort, who has just come down on his nose here, though he is a man of over 40, and composes as if he were 80.

My dutiful respects to the whole household; please accept the assurance of the reverence with which I remain for ever

Your grateful and affectionate pupil

F. F. CHOPIN

Greetings to friends and colleagues.

62.

To JAN MATUSZYŃSKI IN WARSAW.
[*Vienna, Spring 1831.*]

Dearest Being!

You have what you desired. Did you receive the letter? Did you pass it on? Today I regret what I did. I threw out a gleam of hope, where I see only darkness and despair. Perhaps she will sneer, perhaps she will make a jest of it! Perhaps! — Such thoughts come at the very moment when your old colleagues: Rostkowski, Schuch, Freyer, Kijewski, Hube, etc., are filling my room with gaiety, and I am laughing; I laugh, and in my heart, as I write this, some horrible presentiment torments me.

I keep thinking that it's a dream or hallucination, that I am with all of you, and all this is a dream; the voices I hear, to which my soul is not accustomed, make no other impression on me than the rattling of carriages in the street or any other casual noise. Your voice or that of Tytus would rouse me from this dead state of indifference. To live or to die seems all one to me today; I have no letter from you. Tell my parents I am cheerful and lack nothing; that I'm enjoying myself grandly and am never alone. You can tell her the same if she sneers. If not, then tell her that she need have no fear, I am bored everywhere. I am not well; don't write that to my parents. Everyone asks what is the matter with me. I'm out of temper. Hube looks after my health. I have a cold. Anyhow, you know what is wrong with me.

Wild is a capital singer, not Polkowski. I know him intimately. Slavik is splendid; we often play together; tomorrow we go to a dinner together. Merk has now promised me a visit with his violoncello. I can't send you any song. Embrace the colleagues. Kiss Magnus, Alfons [Brandt], Reinszmitek, Domuś, Wiluś. I will write to Marcel. Write to me, Jasio! When shall we have a chat! I love you; love me, you. I write as if I were tipsy.

Address: to Jasio.

On trust, so I don't even seal it. Children! To all friends, your sister and your father.

63.

To his Family.
Vienna, 14 May 1831.

My dearest Parents and Sisters!

This week I have to observe a strict diet in letters. I tell myself that I shall get them later, and wait patiently, in the hope that you are all well, both in the country and in town. As for me, I am well, which I feel to be a great comfort in trouble. But for my unexpected good health, I don't know what I should do. Perhaps Malfatti's soups have poured some kind of Balsam into my veins, which destroys all tendency to illness? If so, I am sorry that our periodic feasts ended last Saturday: Malfatti has gone to the country with his children.

You can't think what a lovely place he is in; this day week I was there with Hummel. Taking us round his property, he displayed its beauties by degrees; and when we reached the top of the hill, we didn't want to come down. The Court honours him with a visit every year, and the nearest neighbour is the princess of Anhalt, who doubtless envies him his garden. On one side you see Vienna under your feet, looking as if it joined Schönbrunn; on the other side, tall hills, and the villages and monasteries scattered about on them, make one forget the pomp and tumult of the noisy city.

Yesterday I went to the imperial library with Kandler. You must know that I have long wished to acquaint myself with what is perhaps the richest collection of old musical manuscripts; but I never got round to it. I don't know whether the Bologna library is kept in better and more systematic order; but conceive of my astonishment when, among the manuscripts, I see a book in a case, with the name: Chopin. Rather thick, and in a good binding. I think: I never heard of any other Chopin. There was a Champin; so I supposed it might be his name misspelt, or some such thing. I take it up, look; my hand. Haslinger has presented the manuscript of my Variations to the library. — " Geese," I say to myself; — " you have found something to keep! "

Last Sunday there were to be big fireworks, but it fell through on account of rain. It's a queer thing: when there are to be fireworks the weather is nearly always bad. In this connection I will give you an anecdote: A certain gentleman had a fine tan coat; but every time he put it on, it rained. Though he seldom wore it, he scarcely ever came home with it dry. So he goes to the tailor and asks him: why? The tailor puzzles over it, shakes his head; then asks to leave the coat a few days to be experimented on; he is not yet sure whether the trouble may not sometimes be caused by the hat, the boots or the shirt. Not a bit: the tailor puts on the coat, goes out; it rains cats and dogs; the poor fellow had to go home in a cab, having forgotten his umbrella. A more plausible version, according to many persons, is that the tailor's wife had gone to drink coffee with a cousin or friend, and had taken the umbrella. However it happened, the tailor got wet, the coat was damp; there was nothing for it but to wait till it got dry again. After waiting some time, it occurs to the tailor to rip up the coat; there might be an imp inside it that draws the clouds. A grand thought! He rips the sleeves: — nothing. He rips the skirts: — nothing. He rips the breast: inside the lining is a fragment of an announcement of fireworks! All is cleared up; he removes the announcement and the coat gets wet no more!

Forgive my not being able to write you anything cheerful about myself; perhaps later I shall have good news for you. All I want is to carry out your wishes; I have not succeeded in that yet.[1]

64.

To the Same.
Vienna, 28 May 1831.

I am just back from the post, but nothing has come. On Wednesday I had a letter from Pani Jarocka, with a postscript from the dear Papa, who, niggardly as he is, had scribbled a few precious lines. Anyhow, I see from them that the household is well. As for Marcel and Jasio, I exhort them to write to me; they are such villains that I can't get half a dozen words out of them! I am so furious that if they did write, I'd send their letters back unopened. They will make excuses about not having time; and how it flies! It's the end of May, and here I am still in Vienna; June will begin, and I shall still be here, for poor Kumelski has had a relapse, and is in bed again.

I see this looks like being a dull letter; but don't think that means any indisposition; I am quite well, and enjoying myself finely. Today I got up early, and practised till two; then I went out to dine, and met the good Kandler, who, as you know, has

[1] Karasowski suggests that this may refer to the postponed concert.

promised me letters to Cherubini and Paër. After seeing the patient, I am going to the theatre, where there is to be a concert, Herz: that little Jew violinist who nearly got hissed at Sonntag's concert in Warsaw; and Döhler, pianist, playing one of Czerny's compositions. At the end, Herz is to play his own Variations on Polish tunes. Poor Polish tunes! You don't know with what majufasy [1] you are to be interlarded, to entice the public by calling that Polish music. After that, try to defend Polish music, express any opinion about it, and you'll be taken for crazy; all the more as Czerny, Vienna's oracle in the manufacture of musical taste, has never yet used a Polish melody for variations.

After dinner yesterday I went with Thalberg to the Evangelical church, where Hesse, a young organist from Wrocław, distinguished himself before a picked Viennese audience: The tip-top folk were there: beginning with Stadler, Kiesewetter, Mosel, Seyfried, Gyrowetz, etc., and ending with the verger. The boy has talent; he understands the organ. Hesse left with me a leaf from his album; but I don't know what to put in it; nothing comes into my head.

On Wednesday Slavik and I stopped at the Bayers' till 2 in the night. Slavik is one of the few local artists whom I enjoy and with whom I get on. He played like another Paganini, but a rejuvenated Paganini, sometimes surpassing the first one. I would not have believed it if I had not heard him often; I am only sorry, oh, so sorry, that Tytus did not meet him. He strikes his hearers dumb, he makes people weep; more, he makes tigers weep, for prince G. and Iskr. went away moved.

What is happening to you all?! — I dream of you, I dream! Will there be any end to the bloodshed? I know what you will say to me: — " Patience! " I comfort myself with that.

On Thursday Fuchs gave an evening when Limmer, one of the best artists here, distinguished himself with his compositions for 4 cellos. Merk, as usual, makes them sound better than they really are. We stayed till 12, because Merk had a fancy to play his own Variations with me. Merk [2] tells me he likes playing with me, and I like playing with him, so together we must pro-

[1] Jewish ceremonial songs; sung at the Sabbath meal among the pious Jews.

[2] Chopin's Op. 3: Introduction et Polonaise brilliant pour piano et violoncelle is dedicated to Merk. [Op.]

duce something good. He is the first cellist whom I can admire on closer acquaintance; I don't know how I shall like Norblin; only don't forget about the letter to him.

65.

To the Same.
Vienna, 25 June 1831.

I am well, and that's the only comfort, for there's no luck with my journey. I never had such a time. You know how undecided I always am, and here are obstacles at every step. They promise my passport every day, and every day I drag from Anasz to Kaifasz to get the one I left with the police. Today I learn that they have mislaid my passport somewhere; and not only will they not search for it, but they demand that I should petition for a new one. Odd things happen to everybody nowadays; I'm ready to start, and I can't go. I have followed Bayer's advice and asked for a passport to England, but I am going to Paris. Malfatti will give me a letter to his good friend Paër. Kandler has already written about me to the Leipzig musical paper.

Yesterday I got home at midnight; it was St. John's day, therefore Malfatti's name-day. Mechetti arranged a surprise for him; Wild, Cicimara, Fräulein Emmering, Fräulein Lutzer and my noble self performed some important music. I never heard the quartet from Moses better sung; but "*Oh quante lagrime*" was sung incomparably better by Panna Gładkowska at my farewell concert in Warsaw. Wild was in good voice; I acted as conductor. [Footnote by Chopin: Cicimara said that no one in Vienna accompanies so well as I; and I thought: "I know that as well as you." Hush!]

A huge crowd of strangers listened to the music from the terrace.

The moon shone superbly, the fountains played, a delicious smell from the orangery they have put up filled the air; in a word, a glorious night and a most gorgeous place. You can't imagine how beautifully designed is the salon in which they sang; huge windows, thrown wide, from which you can see all Vienna; plenty of mirrors and very few lights. The extra length of the adjoining oblong vestibule on the left gave an enormous spaciousness to the whole room. The genuine amiability of our host, the elegance and comfort, the merry company, the witty conversation that was the order of the day, and the excellent supper kept us sitting late; it was about midnight when we got into the carriages and dispersed for home.

As regards expenses, I manage; I preserve every Kreutzer as carefully as that ring in Warsaw.[1] Unfortunately, I have already been enough expense to you.

Two days ago I went to the Leopoldsberg and Kahlenberg with Kumelski and with Czapski, who is my daily guest and gives me the greatest proofs of friendship; even to the extent of offering me money for my journey if I should need it. It was a lovely day. I never had a more beautiful excursion. From the Leopoldsberg you can see all Vienna, Wagram, Aspern, Presburg, the Neuburg convent, the Castle where Richard Lion Heart was a prisoner, and all the upper reaches of the Danube. After lunch we went to the Kahlenberg, where king Sobieski had his camp; I send a leaf from it for Izabella. There's a church there formerly a Camaldolese monastery, in which he himself said mass, and dubbed his son James a knight, before attacking the Turks. In the evening we went from there to Krapfenwald, a charming little valley, where we saw queer popular customs. The boys dress up in leaves from head to foot, and in that guise of walking and dancing bushes, go round from one guest to another. One such little rascal, entirely covered with leaves and with branches on his head, is called "*Pfingstkönig*."[2] This is supposed to be the Whitsuntide ceremony. Odd absurdity! A few days ago I spent the evening at Fuchs's; he showed me his collection of 400 autographs, among which is my Rondo for 2 pianos, bound. A few persons had come there to meet me. Fuchs gave me a sheet of Beethoven's writing. Your last letter cheered

[1] A ring given him by Tzar Alexander I in 1825 for his performance on the Eolomelodeon. [Op.]

[2] Whitsuntide King: Jack-in-the-Green.

me very much; it was all my dearest ones on one scrap of paper. So in return I kiss your feet and hands, — such hands as all Vienna cannot show.

66.

To the Same.
Vienna, 1831, July, Saturday.

I see from your letter that you have shaken off your troubles; believe me that I also am no longer in fear of any sort of thing happening to me. Hope, beloved hope!

At last I have my passport. But I can't get off on Monday; only on Wednesday we start for Salzburg, and from there to Munich. You must know that I asked to have the passport *visé* for London. The police gave the visa, but the Russian embassy kept the passport two days, and then gave it back with permission to travel, not to London, but to Munich. Never mind, thought I; only let M. Maison, the French ambassador, sign it.

Besides these bothers, we have had still another; starting for Bavaria, I must have a *Gesundheitspass*[1] on account of cholera; otherwise one can't cross the Bavarian frontier. Kumelski and I have been running about over that for half the day; it is to be finished after dinner. I'm glad that at least we had good company on those imposing stairs, if one can judge by a Polish appearance and passport and a cultivated speech. Alexander Fredo[2] himself was trying, at the same time as we, to get the same pass for his servants.

People here are terribly frightened of cholera; you can't help laughing. They are selling printed prayers against cholera, they won't eat fruit; most of them are fleeing from the town. I am leaving the violoncello Polonaise with Mechetti. Ludwika writes that Elsner was pleased with the review; I don't know what he will say to the second one, for it was he who taught me composition. I lack nothing except more life and spirit; I'm tired, but

[1] certificate of health.
[2] His comedies were very successful in Warsaw at that time.

sometimes as cheerful as at home. When I get a melancholy mood, I go to Pani Szaszek; there I usually find several nice Polish women, whose sincere and really hopeful talk always gives me so good an opinion of myself that I begin to imitate the Viennese generals. It's a sort of new *polichinelle*,[1] just invented by me; you have never seen it, but everybody that looks at it bursts out laughing. Then again there are days when you can't get two words out of me, and no understanding why. Then I go for 30 Kreutzers to Hietzing, or some other place just outside Vienna, to get a change.

Zacharkiewicz from Warsaw has called on me; his wife saw me at the Szaszeks', and could not get over my having grown into so fine a man. I have let my moustache grow on the right side, and it's — quite long. (There's no need for it on the left side, because it's the right that faces the public.)

The day before yesterday the kind Würflisko [2] came to me; also Czapek, Kumelski and many others; and we went to St. Veit. It's a pretty place; but I can't say the same about the so-called Tivoli, where there is a sort of *carrousel*, or sliding on vehicles; what they call here a "Rutsch." [3] It's an idiotic thing. However, crowds of people slide down in these things, for no object; I didn't even want to look at them. But afterwards, as there were eight of us (and all good friends), we began racing down to try who could go fastest, helping ourselves with our feet, competing with each other; and from being heartily disgusted with this silly Viennese game, I became an enthusiastic proselyte; till I recovered my senses, and realized that these things are occupying strong and healthy bodies and muddling capable minds; and this at a moment when humanity is calling on such to defend it. The devil take them!

Rossini's Siege of Corinth [4] has been given in the theatre; very good. I am glad I stayed over for this opera. Wild, Heinefetter, Binder, Forti; in a word, all the best that Vienna has took part, and beautifully. I went once to hear it with Czapek; then on to supper at the place where Beethoven always used to

[1] Chopin was very fond of amateur theatricals.
[2] dim. of Würfel.
[3] Toboggan.
[4] 1st performance 1826.

drink. Oh, before I forget; I shall probably need to take a little more money from Peter's bank than Papa intended; I am as careful as possible, but really I can't help it; I should have too light a purse for the journey. Afterwards, God forbid, if I fell ill or anything, you might reproach me for not taking more with me. Forgive me; you see, I have been here through May, June and July on this money, and I pay for more dinners than in winter. I don't do this on my own initiative, but rather on a warning from others. I hate to be obliged to ask you for it now. Papa has already spent so many pennies for me; I know how hard he has to struggle for the pennies, and nowadays even struggling doesn't help; but, hope! I mind asking more than you mind giving; but it's easier for me to take than for you to give. Well, God will be merciful — punktum!

In October it will be a year since I got a passport; probably I shall have to prolong it; how does one do that? Write, if you can, and how to send the new one. Perhaps it can't be done! —

Often in the street I run after someone who looks like Jasio or Tytus. Yesterday I would have sworn a man's back belonged to Tytus; and it was some confounded Prussian. Don't let all these epithets give you a bad impression of my Viennese education; it's true that they have neither such polite manners nor well-chosen turns of speech; except "*Gehorsamer Diener*"[1] at the end; but I don't pick up anything that is essentially Viennese. I don't even know how to dance a waltz properly; that's a sufficient instance! My piano has heard only mazury —

God give you health! If only none of our friends die! I'm sorry about Gucio. Your letters sting, and leave a great stamp of health; I am so frightened, just panicky.

Your most affectionate

FRYDERYK

[1] your obedient servant.

67.

From his notebook.
[*Vienna, Spring 1831.*]

Today it was beautiful on the Prater. Crowds of people with whom I have nothing to do. I admired the foliage; the spring smell and that innocence of nature brought back my childhood's feeling. A storm was threatening, so I went in, but there was no storm. Only I got melancholy; —why? I don't care for even music today; it's late, but I'm not sleepy; I don't know what is wrong with me. And I've started my third decade! — The papers and posters have announced my concert, it's to be in two days' time, and it's as if there were no such thing; it doesn't seem to concern me. I don't listen to the compliments; they seem to me stupider and stupider. I wish I were dead; and yet I should like to see my parents. Her image stands before my eyes: I think I don't love her any more, and yet I can't get her out of my head.[1] Everything I have seen abroad till now seems to me old and hateful, and just makes me sigh for home, for those blessed moments that I didn't know how to value. What used to seem great today seems common; what I used to think common is now incomparable, too great, too high. The people here are not my people; they're kind, but kind from habit; they do everything too respectably, flatly, moderately. I don't want even to think of moderation.

I'm puzzled, I'm melancholy, I don't know what to do with myself; I wish I weren't alone! —

68.

From his notebook; written in Stuttgart after Sep. 8th, 1831.[2]

The suburbs are destroyed, burned. —Jaś, Wiluś probably dead in the trenches. I see Marcel a prisoner! That good fellow

[1] Konstancja Gładkowska.
[2] See Preface.

Sowiński in the hands of those brutes! Paszkiewicz! — Some dog from Mohilov holds the seat of the first monarchs of Europe. Moscow rules the world! Oh God, do You exist? You're there, and You don't avenge it — How many more Russian crimes do You want — or — or are You a Russian too!!? — My poor Father! The dear old man may be starving, my mother not able to buy bread? Perhaps my sisters have succumbed to the ferocity of Muscovite soldiery let loose! Oh Father, what a comfort for your old age! Mother! Poor suffering Mother, have you borne a daughter to see a Russian violate her very bones! — Mockery! Has even her grave [1] been respected? Trampled, thousands of other corpses are over the grave — What has happened to her? [2] — Where is she? — Poor girl, perhaps in some Russian's hands — a Russian strangling her, killing, murdering! Ah, my Life, I'm here alone; come to me, I'll wipe away your tears, I'll heal the wounds of the present, remind you of the past — the days when there were no Russians, the days when the only Russians were a few who were very anxious to please you, and you were laughing at them because I was there — Have you your mother? — Such a cruel mother, and mine is so kind — But perhaps I have no mother, perhaps some Russian has killed her, murdered — My sisters, raving, resist — father in despair, nothing he can do — and I here, useless! And I here with empty hands! — Sometimes I can only groan, and suffer, and pour out my despair at the piano! — God, shake the earth, let it swallow up the men of this age, let the heaviest chastisement fall on France, that would not come to help us —

— The bed I go to — perhaps corpses have lain on it, lain long — yet today that does not sicken me. Is a corpse any worse than I? A corpse knows nothing of father, of mother, or sisters, of Tytus; a corpse has no belovéd, it's tongue can hold no converse with those who surround it — a corpse is as colourless as I, as cold, as I am cold to everything now —

The clocks in the towers of Stuttgart strike the hours of the night. How many new corpses is this minute making in the world? Mothers losing children, children losing mothers — So much

[1] His sister Emilja's.
[2] Evidently a reference to Gładkowska.

grief over the dead, and so much delight! A vile corpse and a decent one — virtues and vice are all one, they are sisters when they are corpses. Evidently, then, death is the best act of man — And what is the worst? Birth; it is direct opposition to the best thing. I am right to be angry that I came into the world — What use is my existence to anyone? I am not fit for human beings, for I have neither snout nor calves to my legs; and does a corpse have them? A corpse also has no calves, so it lacks nothing of a mathematical fraternity with death — Did she love me, or was she only pretending? That's a knotty point to get over — Yes, no, yes, no, no, yes — finger by finger — " Does she love me? " Surely she loves me, let her do what she likes —

Father! Mother! Where are you? Corpses? Perhaps some Russian has played tricks — oh wait — wait — But tears — they have not flowed for so long — oh, so long, so long I could not weep — how glad — how wretched — Glad and wretched — If I'm wretched, I can't be glad — and yet it is sweet — This is a strange state — but that is so with a corpse; it's well and not well with it at the same moment. It is transferred to a happier life, and is glad, it regrets the life it is leaving and is sad. It must feel as I felt when I left off weeping. It was like some momentary death of feeling; for a moment I died in my heart; no, my heart died in me for a moment. Ah, why not for always! — Perhaps it would be more endurable then — Alone! Alone! — There are no words for my misery; how can I bear this feeling —

69.

[A hitherto unknown letter]

To K. Kumelski.
Paris, 18. IX. 1831.

My dear Life!

You tell me that you have been ill; why was I not there! I would not have allowed it; and I am surprised that dancing did not keep a jigger [?] like you from it. For, indeed, it is not worth while to think in this world; if you were here, you would accept that maxim. Every Frenchman dances and shouts, even if his bones are bare. I arrived here fairly comfortably (though expensively), and am glad that I am remaining here; I have the first musicians in the world, and the first opera in the world. I know Rossini, Cherubini, Paër, etc., etc.; and perhaps may stay longer than I intended. Not because I am getting on any too well here, but because, with time, I may get on well. But you have luck. You are approaching your . . . [word illegible]; perhaps I shall never see them. You would not believe how many [?] Poles there are here. Of those [?] who do not live together or seek each other out . . . but you will find many of them in Berlin. Freymanek, whom I got to know, by some queer chance, at the Italian opera, is here, just back from England, which he cannot praise highly enough. His father and family are in Berlin — he asked me to tell you so — you will probably have pleasure in meeting him, if you suffer from that consumption of the purse so prevalent among us. Also Romuald is said to be there; about that you can learn from Alfons Brandt, the son of that doctor from my native town. Alfons is studying medicine, it will be easier to locate him; and when you find him, embrace him; Romuald has spent his life in their house. He will be able to tell you of many other acquaintances who are there. That Benedykt tells me he is sure that Karol (the horse-doctor) is at home; this will doubtless reassure you about your family. I know no more what Seweryn is doing than I know about Anton and Władzio. But I hope to hear some news of the Bayers; every day I dine with Radziwiłł (whom I found here) and with Walenty, the elder brother of the one who has Stecka, at the Komars', with whom I know Bayer was in correspondence. Yesterday I dined at the house of Pani Potocka — Mieczyslaw's pretty young wife; I am gradually launching myself in the world, but I have only one ducat in my pocket! Even so, that's better than you! But I am writing you nothing about the impression produced on me by this big town after Stuttgart and Strasbourg. There is the utmost luxury, the utmost swinishness, the utmost virtue, the utmost ostentation; at every step advertisements of ven . . . disease; shouting, racket, bustle, and more mud than it is possible to imagine: one can perish in this paradise, and it is convenient from this point of view, that nobody asks how anybody lives. You can walk in the streets in winter, dressed in rags, and frequent tip-top society; one day you can eat the most hearty dinner for 32 sous in a restaurant with mirrors, gilding and gas lighting, and the next you can lunch where they will give you enough for a dicky-bird to eat, and charge 3 times as much: that happened to me before I had paid the necessary tax on ignorance.

What a lot of charitable ladies! They just run after people; nevertheless there is no lack whatever of hefty sharks [?]. I am sorry that, in spite of Benedykt's efforts (by the way, he regards my misfortunes as something very trifling) — the memory of Teressa [*sic*] forbids me to taste forbidden fruit. But I already know several lady vocalists, and lady vocalists here are even more anxious for duets than those of the Tyrol. Once, on my 5th floor (I am at Boulevard Poissonière, No. 27 — you wouldn't believe what a delightful lodging; I have a little room beautifully furnished with mahogany, and a balcony over the boulevard, from which I can see from Mont Martre to the Panthéon and the whole length of the fashionable quarter; many persons envy me my view, but none my stairs) — Well, one evening I was looking through my correspondence — or writing in that album, and glancing at some letters — it seemed to me that all these memories were a dream; I cannot believe the things that really happened; and especially incredible seems the excursion to the Schwarzbach — those Americans! — Ah, nothing like it. — When shall we go over those reminiscences together! I expect to stay here three years. I am in very close relations with Kalkbrenner, the 1st pianist of Europe, whom I think you would like. (He is one whose shoe-latchet I am not worthy to untie. Those Herzes, and so on, — I tell you they are just windbags and will never play any better.) So, if I stay here three years, Bezendz [?] may come along; perhaps I may be able to embrace him and play the Stumma. Keep up a good heart; may all go with you as you desire. I hope it will be so; take warning by Newazendzio [?], who lost many friends on the field [of battle?], who has old parents, and, instead of helping them, is on their hands, who loves like peas against a wall,[1] who now is orphaned of friends and must peg out somewhere in Berlin!

Yours for ever FRYC

Filing has gone to London for a month, with Karwowski, the former prosektor of our University. Stańcio borrowed from me while I had anything to lend; he is now hanging about the Palais Royal — that is all his business here — he hopes to get a pension from the government, for his services as a zealous Austrian — there are packs of such [erased] here! If this scrawl is too stupidly written, forgive my haste. But you know that I would rather play than write. Pos . . . is ill [?]; there's your: "Holy cross above all."

Tell Alfons that Kontratowicz came to see me yesterday; he is a lieutenant; also tell him to write to me.

[A piece torn off]

I am glad you told me of the death of Debol [?]; I have explained to several of his friends here who have been wondering why they had no news and no news at all of him.

Do write to me, don't be lazy!

[Last line torn off]

70.

To TYTUS WOJCIECHOWSKI IN POTURZYŃ.
Paris, 12 December 1831.

MY DEAREST LIFE!

I began to live again when I got your letter. Your contusion! — Various rumours have reached me, I have interpreted phrases in letters from home this way and that — and when Kot wrote to me he used such a strange expression that I was afraid of the thoughts that crowded into my head. So we shall really meet again in life! All these changes and troubles, who could have

[1] A Polish idiom.

foreseen them? Do you remember our talk at Vienna, the night before you left? The wind has blown me here; it's good to rest, but perhaps one frets more when things are easy. Paris is whatever you choose: you can amuse yourself, be bored, laugh, cry, do anything you like, and nobody looks at you; because thousands of others are doing the same as you, and everyone goes his own road. I don't know where there can be so many pianists as in Paris, so many asses and so many virtuosi. You must know that I arrived here with very few introductions. Malfatti gave me a letter to Paër; I had two or three letters from the Vienna publishers, and that was all. But in Stuttgart, where the news of the taking of Warsaw reached me, I finally decided to migrate to this other world. Through Paër, who is court conductor here, I have met Rossini, Cherubini, Baillot, etc.—also Kalkbrenner. You would not believe how curious I was about Herz, Liszt, Hiller, etc.—They are all zero beside Kalkbrenner. I confess that I have played like Herz, but would wish to play like Kalkbrenner. If Paganini is perfection, Kalkbrenner is his equal, but in quite another style. It is hard to describe to you his calm, his enchanting touch, his incomparable evenness, and the mastery that is displayed in every note; he is a giant, walking over Herz and Czerny and all,—and over me. What can I do about it? When I was introduced, he asked me to play something. I should have liked to hear him first; but, knowing how Herz plays, I put my pride in my pocket and sat down. I played my E minor, which the Rhinelanders: the Lindpainters, Bergs, Stuntzes, Schunks and all Bavaria had so raved over. I astonished Kalkbrenner, who at once asked me, was I not a pupil of Field, because I have Cramer's method and Field's touch. (That delighted me.) I was still more pleased when Kalkbrenner, sitting down to the piano and wanting to do his best before me, made a mistake and had to break off! But you should have heard it when he started again; I had not dreamed of anything like it. Since then we meet daily; either he comes to me or I to him; and on closer acquaintance he has made me an offer; that I should study with him for three years, and he will make something really—really out of me. I answered that I know how much I lack; but that I cannot exploit him, and

3 years is too much. But he has convinced me that I can play admirably when I am in the mood, and badly when I am not; a thing which never happens to him. After close examination he told me that I have no school; that I am on an excellent road, but can slip off the track. That after his death, or when he finally stops playing, there will be no representative of the great pianoforte school. That even if I wish it, I cannot build up a new school without knowing the old one; in a word: that I am not a perfected machine, and that this hampers the flow of my thoughts. That I have a mark in composition; that it would be a pity not to become what I have the promise of being;— and so on and so on. If you had been here, you would have said: — Learn, my boy, while you have the chance. Many have tried to dissuade me, thinking that I shall manage to play all right without it, that he makes the offer from arrogance, so that afterwards people should call me his pupil, etc., etc. All that is rubbish. You must know that Kalkbrenner's person is as much hated here as his talent is respected by all and sundry; he does not make friends with every fool, and, as I love you, he is superior to everything that I have heard. I have written to my parents about it. They consent, but I think they are jealous for Elsner. Also you must know that I already have a huge reputation among the artists here; I am giving a concert on December 25th. Paganini's famous rival Baillot will play, also Brodt, a famous oboist; I give my F minor, and the B flat major Variations. A few days ago I received from a German in Cassel who is enthusiastic about these Variations, a ten-page review, in which, after an immense preface, he goes on to analyse them, measure by measure; saying that they are not Variations in the usual sense, but some kind of fantastic *tableaux*. About the 2nd *Variation* he says that Don Juan is running with Leporello; that in the 3rd he is embracing Zerlina and Mazetto raging in the left hand; that in the 5th measure of the Adagio Don Juan is kissing Zerlina in D flat major. Yesterday Plater asked me; where is that D flat major? One can die of the imagination of this German, who insists that his brother-in-law should send it to Fétis, for the Revue Musicale; from this the good Hiller rescued me with difficulty, by telling the brother-in-law that the thing is not

clever at all but very stupid. Hiller is an immensely talented fellow (a former pupil of Hummel) whose concerto and Symphony produced a great effect three days ago; he's on the same lines as Beethoven, but a man full of poetry, fire and spirit. But to return to the concerto. I am also to play with Kalkbrenner (on two pianos, with 4 others, accompanying), his Marche suivie d'une Polonaise. It is a crazy notion. One pantaleon is huge, belonging to Kalkbrenner; the other, which belongs to me, is a tiny monochord, but resonant, like little żyrafki [? [1]] bells; and the other four are large, for an orchestra. Hiller, Osborn, Stamaty and Sowiński are to play them. The last-named is not fit to hold a candle to poor Aleks [?] (whose pupil I have met here). He has not much head, but a good figure, and a heart. Norblin,[2] Vidal [3] and the famous Ubran, such an alto as I have never heard, will support me. The tickets are selling. The hardest thing was to get women singers. Rossini would have let me have one from the opera, if he could have arranged it without M. Robert, the assistant conductor, whose feelings he did not want to hurt with 200 or 300 such requests. But I have told you nothing so far about the opera. I had never really heard the Barber till last week with Lablache, Rubini, and Malibran (Garcia). Nor had I heard Othello till I heard it with Rubini, Pasta and Lablache, nor The Italian,[4] till with Rubini, Lablache and Mme Raimbeaux. If ever I had everything at once, it's now, in Paris. You can't conceive what Lablache is like! Pasta is said to have gone off somewhat; but I have seen nothing more exalted. Malibran depends only on her marvellous voice; no one sings like her! Wonderful, wonderful! Rubini is a splendid tenor; takes his notes authentically, not in falsetto, and sometimes sing roulades for 2 hours together (but sometimes embroiders too much and makes his voice tremble purposely; also he continually trills; which, however, brings him more applause than all else). His mezza voce is incomparable. Schröder-Devrient is here; but does not produce such a *furore* as in Germany.

[1] The old tall upright grand pianos were called in Poland *żyrafki* (little giraffes), but whether any of them had small bell attachments I do not know.

[2] Famous Polish cellist, 1781–1854; cello professor at the Paris Conservatoire.

[3] Famous French violinist, 1789–1867; conductor of the Théâtre Italien in Paris, and first violin in Louis Philippe's orchestra.

[4] *L'Italiana in Algeri.* Rossini. 1st performance 1813.

Malibran played Othello, and she Desdemona. Malibran is small, and the German woman is huge; it looked as if Desdemona would smother Othello. It was an expensive performance; only 24 francs, all places; to see Malibran blacked and playing the part none too well. They are to give the Pirate [1] and Sonnambula,[2] etc. Pasta has gone; they say she won't sing any more. The orchestra is splendid, but not in comparison with the real French opera (l'Académie Royale). I don't know whether there has ever been such magnificence in a theatre, whether it has ever before attained to the pomp of the new 5-act opera, " Robert le Diable," [3] by Mayerber [*sic*], who wrote Crociato [4] — It is a masterpiece of the new school, in which devils (huge choirs) sing through speaking-trumpets, and souls rise from graves (but not, as in The Charlatan,[5] just in groups of 50 or 60); in which there is a diorama in the theatre, in which at the end you see the *intérieur* of a church, the whole church, at Christmas or Easter, lighted up, with monks, and all the congregation on the benches, and censors: — even with the organ, the sound of which on the stage is enchanting and amazing, also it nearly drowns the orchestra; nothing of the sort could be put on anywhere else. Meyerbeer has immortalized himself! But he has spent three years in Paris to get it done; it is said he has paid 20,000 francs to the cast. Mme Cinti-Damoreau sings as superbly as possible; I prefer her singing to Malibran's. Malibran amazes, Cinti delights, and her chromatic scales are better than those of Toulon the famous flutist. No voice could be more highly trained; it seems to cost her so little to sing, as if she just blew it at the audience. Nourrit, the French tenor, has wonderful feeling! and Cholet, at the *Opéra Comique,* where they give Fra Diavolo, La Fiancée [6] and Zampa [7] (a fine new opera by Hérold), is the first amant here: *séducteur,* tantalizing, marvellous, a genius with the real voice of romance. He has created his own style. At the *Opéra Comique* they are now giving " Marquise de Brinvillière ": that

[1] *Il Pirata.* Bellini. 1st performance 1827.
[2] Bellini; 1831.
[3] 1831.
[4] *Il Crociato in Egitto*; 1824 (one of Meyerbeer's early compositions).
[5] Opera by Kurpiński.
[6] Opera by Auber. 1st performance 1829.
[7] 1st performance 1831

was a woman who poisoned people at the time of Louis 14th or 15th. Eight persons [1] have written music about her: Cherubini, Paër, Berton, Hérold, Auber, Baton, Blanquini and Caraffa. I think it would be hard to find a finer concert company. Write me what you think. However, you must observe that I have not got struck silly; — I don't want to make a fool of myself. Pixis is very respectful to me; partly because I play, partly because he is jealous of his girl, who likes me better than him!! For heaven's sake do write to me, — or come. Yours till death, and perhaps not long.

F. CHOPIN

Old Potier is excellent! The young one is here with Herwet [*sic*], Evra, Tiery and Files, but I have not seen them. I am lodging at *No. 27 Boulevard Poissonière.* You did not give me your address, I had to find out from Wodziński. Pleyel's pianos are *non plus ultra.* Of the Poles here I see Kunasik, Morawski, Niemoj, Lelewel and Plichta; there are also a huge lot of idiots. I often call on Panna Jawurek, but that's all. She is pretty. Oleszczyński wants to make an etching of me. Two days ago I went with Brykczyński to Pani Tyszkiewicz; but Poniatowski has not come yet; today I go to Montebello. But for Wodziński I should not have your address, Sir Featherhead. The Wodzińskis expect you here; I want you only sometimes, when I go nearly crazy with melancholy, especially if it rains. Panna Gładkowska has married Grabowski, but that does not preclude platonic affections. Baillot has just come; I must seal this letter. Love me.

I can't refrain from telling you my adventure with Pixis. Imagine, he has a very pretty 15-year-old girl living with him, whom it is said he thinks of marrying and whom I met when I visited him in Stuttgart. Pixis, on arriving here, invited me to call, but did not mention that the girl, whom I had forgotten, had arrived with him. (I might have called sooner, had I known.) He asked me to call, so after a week I went. On the stairs I was pleased to see the young pupil; she asked me in, saying Herr Pixis was out, but it did not matter, come in and rest, he will soon be in, etc. We both feel a little tremulous.

[1] in collaboration.

Knowing that the old man is jealous, I excuse myself, I will come again, and so on. Meanwhile, as we stand discussing prettily on the stairs in the innocence of our hearts, up comes the little Pixis, looks (in the manner of Soliwa) through large spectacles, to see who is on the stairs and talking to his belle, and then, hurrying upstairs, poor fellow, stops in front of me, says brusquely: "*Bon jour,*" and to her: — "*Q'est-ce que vous faites ici?*" — and a huge jeremiad of German devils at her, for daring to receive young men during his absence. I also (smiling and ignoring everything) upheld Pixis, scolding her for going out so lightly clad, just in her stuff dress, and so on. At last the old man realized: — swallowed, took me by the arm, conducted me into the salon, didn't know where to put me to sit, he was so afraid I should take offence and play some trick on him in his absence, or else murder the pupil. Afterwards he accompanied me downstairs, and seeing that I was still laughing — (I could not hide my amusement at the joke of anybody supposing me *capable de* that sort of thing) — he then went to the concierge to find out when and how I got on the stairs, and so on. From that day Pixis can't say enough in praise of my talent to all the publishers, and especially to Schlesinger, who has engaged me to write something on themes from Robert, which he has bought from Meyerbeer for 24,000 francs! How do you like it? I, as a *séducteur!*

71.

To Joseph Elsner in Warsaw.
Paris, 14 December 1831.

Dear Pan Elsner!

Your letter gave me fresh proof of the paternal care and real benevolence which you are still good enough to continue towards the most affectionate of your pupils. In 1830, though I knew how much I lack and how far I have to go if I am to approach any standard of yours, I still made bold to think: — "At least I shall get a little nearer to him; and if not a Cubit,[1] at least a Spindleshanks may come out of my brainpan." But today, seeing all such hopes destroyed, I must think of clearing a path for myself in the world as a pianist, putting off till some later time those higher artistic hopes which your letter rightly puts forward. To be a great composer, one must have enormous knowledge, which, as you have taught me, demands not only listening to the work of others, but still more listening to one's own. Over a dozen able young men, pupils of the Paris Conservatoire, are waiting with folded hands for the performance of their operas, symphonies and cantatas, which only Cherubini and Lesueur have seen on paper;—I am not speaking of minor theatres, though even there it is difficult to get in; and when you do get in like Thomas at Leopoldstadt, no artistic result of importance is achieved, even in spite of fine qualities. Meyerbeer, who has had a reputation as an opera composer for 10 years, had waited in Paris for three years, working and paying, when (there being at last too much of Auber) he arrived at producing his Robert le Diable, which has caused a *furore* in Paris. To my mind, in order to appear before the musical world, a man is fortunate if he is at once a composer and an actor. Here and there in Germany I am known as a pianist; certain musical papers have spoken of my concerts, raising hopes that I shall shortly be seen taking rank among the first *virtuosi* of my instrument; which means:—"*disce puer faciam te*," of course, sir. Today only one possibility offers for the fulfilment of this promise; why should I not seize it? In Germany I could not have learned the piano from anyone; for though there were persons who felt that I still lack something, no one knew what; and I also could not see the beam in my own eye which still prevents my looking higher. Three years are a long time; too long; even Kalkbrenner admits that, now that he has examined more closely; which should convince you that a genuine *virtuoso* of proved worth knows no jealousy. But I would be willing to stick to it for three years, if that will only enable me to take a big step forward in what I have undertaken. I understand

[1] A reference to Elsner's opera: *King Cubit*, and possibly to Chopin's own thin legs. "Łokietek" (cubit) and "Laskonogi" (spindleshanks) were nicknames of two old Polish kings. [Op.]

enough not to become a copy of Kalkbrenner; nothing will interfere with my perhaps overbold but at least not ignoble desire to create a new world for myself; and if I work, it is in order to have a firmer standing. Ries found it easier to obtain laurels for *The Bride* in Berlin and Frankfort because he was known as a pianist. How long had Spohr been noted as a violinist before he wrote Jessonda, Faust, and so on? I hope that you will not refuse me your blessing, seeing on what principle I enter upon this undertaking. My parents will doubtless tell you of the postponement of my concert of the 25th. I have very bad luck over the arrangements; and but for Paër, Kalkbrenner, and especially Norblin (who sends you kindest greetings) I should not be able to give it in so short a time; in Paris 2 months count as short. Baillot, very courteous and pleasant, will play the Beethoven Quintet; Kalkbrenner the Duo, with me and a 4-piano accompaniment. Reich I have merely seen; you know how eager I was to meet that man; now I know several of his pupils, who have given me a different impression of him. He does not care for music, does not even attend the Conservatoire concerts, does not wish to talk of music with anyone, during his lessons looks continually at his watch; and so on; Cherubini also just babbles of cholera and revolutions. These people are dried up chrysalises, whom one can only regard with respect, and learn something from their works. Fétis, whom I know, and from whom one can really learn much, lives outside the town and comes in to Paris only for lessons, as otherwise he would long have been in Sainte Pélagie for debts; of which he has more than his Revue Musicale brings in. You must know that, according to the law, debtors in Paris can be arrested only in their domicile; so he does not stay in his domicile but goes out of town where the law cannot reach him till after a certain time. There is an amazing collection here of interesting musical folk of every description: a multitude. Three orchestras: the Academy, the Italian, and Fédau's, are splendid; Rossini is the *Regisseur* of his own opera, which is produced better than any other in Europe. Lablache, Rubini, Pasta (she has now left), Malibran, Devrient, Schröder, Santini and others enchant us three times a week on a grand scale. Nourrit, Levasseur, Derivis, Mme Cinti-

Damoreau, Mlle Dorus sustain grand opera; Cholet, Mlle Casimir, Prevost are admirable in comic opera; in a word, here, for the first time, one can learn what singing is. Certainly today, not Pasta but Malibran (Garcia) is the first singer in Europe —marvellous! Walenty Radziwiłł raves over her, and we often bring you up in this connection, saying how you would admire her! Lesueur thanks you for remembering him, and asks me to send you a million salutes; he always remembers you most kindly and asks me every time:—"*et que fait notre bon monsieur Elsner,*"—"*racontez-moi de ses nouvelles,*"[1]—and at once refers to your Requiem that you sent him. All of us here love and admire you, beginning with me and ending with your godson, Antonij Orłowski, who probably will not very soon get his operetta performed, because the *sujet* is not the best one, and also the theatre is closed till new year. The king is not lavish with money, times are hard for artists altogether; only the English pay. I could go on writing till tomorrow; enough of this dull letter. Accept the assurance of my gratitude and the respect with which I remain till death your most affectionate pupil

F. F. CHOPIN

I kiss the hands of Pani and Panna Elsner, and wish them all good things for the New Year.

72.

To TYTUS WOJCIECHOWSKI IN POTURZYŃ.
Paris, 25 December 1831.

MY DEAREST LIFE!

This is the second year that I have to send your name-day wishes from beyond ten frontiers. One glance might do more to keep you in my heart than ten letters. So I will leave that; I

[1] And what is our good Mr. Elsner doing? Tell me some news of him.

don't want to write *ex abrupto*, and have not bought one of those little books of etiquette, with lists of congratulations, which girls and boys sell in the streets for 2 *sous*. This is a queer people; as soon as evening comes you hear nothing but voices calling out the titles of new chapbooks; sometimes you can buy 3, 4 sheets of rubbish for a sou. It is: — "*L'art de faire les amants, et de les conserver ensuite*," [1] "*Les amours des prêtres*," [2] "*L'archévêque de Paris avec Mme la Duchesse du Barry*," [3] and a thousand other such indecencies, sometimes very wittily written. It is really wonderful to see the methods people hit on here to earn a few pennies. You know that there is great distress here; the exchange is bad, and you can often meet ragged folk with important faces, and sometimes you can hear menacing remarks about the stupid Philippe, who just hangs on by means of his ministers. The lower class is thoroughly exasperated, and would be glad at any moment to change the character of their misery; but unfortunately the government has taken too many precautions in this matter; so soon as the smallest street crowds collect, they are dispersed by mounted gendarmerie. You know that I live on the 4th floor, but in a most charming place, on the boulevard. I have a private iron balcony, very graceful, overlooking the street; and I can see up and down the boulevards a long way to both right and left. Opposite me Ramorino [4] was lodging in the street, in the place called *Cité bergère*, where there is a big courtyard. You doubtless know how the Germans received him everywhere, how in Strasbourg the French harnessed themselves to his carriage; altogether, you know how enthusiastic the masses are about our General. Paris did not want to be behindhand. The School of Medicine, the so-called "*jeune France*," which wears little beards and doubtless has regulations about the fastening of neckties (you must know that here every political party wears them differently — I mean the extremists; the Carlists wear green waistcoats, the Republicans and

[1] The art of having lovers and keeping them.

[2] The love affairs of priests.

[3] The archbishop of Paris with the Duchess du Barry.

[4] Girolamo Ramorino, Italian general; born 1792, court-martialled and shot 1849. Served in the French army; took part in the Piedmontese insurrection of 1821; in 1830 joined the Polish insurgent army, but proved to be more a hindrance than a help.

Napoleonists — that is just "*jeune France,*" the Saint Simonists or new christians, who are creating a separate religion, and are also for equality, and have enormous numbers of followers: these wear blue, and so on, and so on). So about a thousand of such young men, with a non-ministerial tri-colour flag, marched through the whole town to welcome Ramorino. Though he was at home he did not want to risk unpleasantness with the government (he is a fool about this), so, in spite of the cries and shouts of "*Vive les polonais,*" etc., he would not show himself. His adjutant (probably Dzialyński) came out and said that the General invites them to call on him another day. And the next morning he moved out from there. Two or three days later, an enormous crowd, not only young men this time, but a general crowd, collected in front of the Panthéon and crossed Paris to Ramorino. It increased like a snowball as it passed from street to street, till by the bridge (pont neuf) the mounted men began to disperse it. Many were hurt; nevertheless a large crowd collected on the boulevards, under my windows, joining those who arrived from the other side of the town. The police could do nothing with the surging mass; a detachment of infantry arrived; hussars, mounted *adjutants de place*[1] on the pavements; the guard equally zealous, shoving aside the excited and muttering crowd, seizing, arresting free citizens, — nervousness, shops closing, groups of people at all the corners of the boulevards; whistles, galloping messengers, windows crammed with spectators (as at home on Easter Day); and this continued from 11 in the morning till 11 at night. I began to hope that perhaps something would get done; but it all ended with singing of "*Allons enfants de la patrie*" by a huge chorus at 11 at night. You will scarcely realize what an impression these menacing voices of an unsatisfied crowd produced on me. The next morning people expected the beginning of a constitution[2] from this *émeute*, as they call it here, — but the idiots are sitting quiet to this day. Only Grenoble has followed Lyons, and the devil knows what is going to happen next. Today, in the Théâtre Françon where only melodramas and *tableaux* with horses are given, they are to give a review of our contemporary history.

[1] Military police.

[2] Phrase ambiguous.

People are rushing like mad to see all the costumes, and Panna Plater, who plays a part in it, with persons who are given such names as Lodoiska, Faniska, — there is even one called Floreska; [1] there is a general Gigult, supposed to be Plater's brother, and so on. But nothing amused me so much as the announcement in one of the theatres, that during the entr'acte " Dobruski's mazurka *Jeszore Polska mirgineta* " [2] will be played. As I love you, I am not joking; I have witnesses, who shared my amazement that the French can be so stupid! A propos of my concert; it is put off till the 15th on account of the singer, whom M. Veron, the director of the opera, has refused me. Today there is a big concert in the Italian opera house, with Malibran, Rubini, Lablache, Santini, Mme Raimbeaux, Mme Schröder, Mme Cavadory; Herz will play also, and — what is most interesting to me — Beriot, the violinist with whom Malibran is in love. I wish you were here; you can't think how mournful it is to have no one to wag one's tongue with. You know how easily I make acquaintances; how I like to gossip with people about blue almonds; [3] — well, I have no end of such acquaintance; and not one with whom I can be sad. In feeling I am always in a state of syncopation with everyone. It torments me, and you would not believe how I long for a pause, to have no one come near me all day long. When I am writing to you, I cannot bear to hear the doorbell; some person in whiskers, huge, tall, superb, — comes in, sits down to the piano and improvises he doesn't know what, bangs and pounds without any meaning, throws himself about, crosses his hands, clatters on one key for five minutes with an enormous thumb that once belonged in the Ukraïna, holding the reins or wielding a bailiff's cudgel. Here you have the portrait of Sowiński, who possesses no other merit than a good figure and a good heart. If ever I have seen a clear picture of charlatanism or stupidity in art, it is now, in what I often have to listen to while I am walking about or washing in my room. My ears burn; I could fling him out of doors; but I must spare his feelings, even be affectionate on my side. You

[1] Imaginary names, purporting to be Polish.

[2] An attempt at the opening words of the battle hymn of the Polish insurgents: "*Jeszcze Polska nie zginęła*": Poland has not perished yet.

[3] impossible dreams: castles in the air.

can't imagine what it's like; but as people here think a lot of him (they can't see beyond neckties), one has to be chums with him. Most of all he enrages me with his collection of pothouse tunes; senseless, vilely accompanied, put together without the slightest knowledge of harmony or prosody, with contredanse cadences; these he calls a collection of Polish songs. You know how I have longed to feel our national music, and to some extent have succeeded in feeling it;— sometimes he gets hold of something of mine, now here, now there; something the beauty of which often depends on the accompaniment; and starts to play it in a tipsy, cackling, pothouse or parish organ style; and there's nothing you can say, because he won't understand anything beyond what he has picked up. On the other side there's Nowakowski. And he talks! About everything; especially about Warsaw, where he has never been. Of the Poles here I see most of Wodziński and Brykczyński; very nice boys. Wodzyńsio [1] always asks me why you don't come. They expect you because they don't know you. I think I do, and I know when you will come. At the moment when I start to describe to you a certain ball, at which a certain deity with a rose in her black hair enchanted me, I shall get your letter. Everything *moderne* has gone out of my head; I turn all the more to you, take you by the hand, and weep. I have had your letter from Lwów; we shall not meet, then, till later; and perhaps not at all, for, seriously, my health is bad. I am gay on the outside, especially among my own folk (I count Poles my own); but inside something gnaws at me; some presentiment, anxiety, dreams — or sleeplessness, — melancholy, indifference, — desire for life, and the next instant, desire for death: some kind of sweet peace, some kind of numbness, absent-mindedness; and sometimes definite memories worry me. My mind is sour, bitter, salt; some hideous jumble of feelings shakes me! I am stupider than ever. My Life, forgive me. Enough. And now I must dress and go out, or rather drive out, to the dinner that is to be given today for Ramorino and Langerman; there are to be some hundreds in the immense restaurant Au Rocher Cancal. A few days ago Kunacki and the good Biernacki brought me an invitation, so *décidément* Karol is not his

[1] diminutive of Wodziński.

son-in-law. There was a lot of news for me in your today's letter. You favoured me with 4 pages and 37 lines: that has never happened in my life before, never in my life have you granted me such abundance; and I needed something like that, needed it badly. What you write about the journey is really so, according to my belief. Don't think evil about that, dear; I will go in my own carriage, but just engage a driver for the horses. Dear, forgive my letter being such a contrast. I must stop, or I'll never get to the post, and I'm my own valet. Write, please; I embrace you. Yours till death.

FRYC

I send this letter, relying on your mercy.

73.

[Fragment]
[In French]

To FERDINAND HILLER.
Paris, 2 August 1832.

. . . Your Trios, my dear Fellow, have long been finished; and, being a greedy person, I have swallowed your manuscripts into my repertory; your Concerto will be performed this month at the Conservatoire contest by Adam's pupils; Mlle Lyon plays it very well.

La Tentation,[1] an opera-ballet by *Halévy* and *Gide,* has tempted no one of good taste, for it is as little interesting as your Germanic diet is in unison with the spirit of this century.

Maurice, who has returned from London, where he went for the staging of Robert (which had no success), assured us that Moscheles and Field are coming to Paris for the winter; that is all the news I have to give you—Osborne has been in London for 2 months. Pixis is at Boulogne. Kalkbrenner is at

[1] *The Temptation.*

Meudon; Rossini at Bordeaux. All those who know you await you with open arms. Liszt is to write you two lines at the end of this sheet. Goodbye, dear friend.

Most heartily yours,
F. CHOPIN

74.

To DOMINIK DZIEWANOWSKI.
[*Undated, Paris, 1832.*]

DEAR DOMUS'!

If I had a friend (a friend with a big crooked nose; I'm not talking of any other) who killed horse-flies with me at Szafarnia years ago, who always loved me steadily; and if that friend were to go abroad and then not write one word to me, — I should have the worst opinion of him; and even if he afterwards begged with tears for forgiveness, I would not forgive him. Yet I, Fryc, am brazenfaced enough to defend my negligence, and turn up again after all this silence, like an insect that crawls up out of the water when nobody is asking it to do so.

But I won't try for explanations; I would rather admit my guilt, which perhaps seems bigger from the distance than it really is, for I am just torn a dozen ways at once.

I have got into the highest society; I sit with ambassadors, princes, ministers; and even don't know how it came about, because I did not try for it. It is a most necessary thing for me, because good taste is supposed to depend on it. At once you have a bigger talent if you have been heard at the English or Austrian embassy; you play better if princess Vaudemont (the last of the old Montmorency family) was your protector; — I can't say *is,* because the woman died a week ago. She was a lady rather like poor Zielonkowa, or the chatelaine Polanecka; the court used to visit her, she did a lot of good, she hid many aristocrats during the first revolution. She was the first person to present herself at Louis Philippe's court after the July days. She was surrounded by a multitude of little black and white dogs, canaries, parrots; and also possessed the most amusing monkey in the whole of the great world here, which at evening receptions would bite . . . other countesses.[1]

Though this is only my first year among the artists here, I have their friendship and respect. One proof of respect is that even people with huge reputations dedicate their compositions to me before I do so to them: Pixis has inscribed to me his last Variations with a military band; also, people compose variations on my themes. Kalkbrenner has used my mazurka [2] in this way; the pupils of the Conservatoire, Moscheles's pupils, those of Herz and Kalkbrenner, — in a word, finished artists, take lessons from me and couple my name with that of Field. In short, if I were still stupider than I am, I should think myself at the apex of my career; yet I know how much I still lack, to reach perfection; I see it the more clearly now that I live only among first-rank artists and know what each one of them lacks.

But I am ashamed of all this bosh that I have written; I have been boasting like a child; like a man who makes haste to defend himself when his cap is on fire. I would scratch it out, but have no time to write another sheet; anyhow, perhaps you have not forgotten what my character is like; if so, you will remember that I am today what I was yesterday: with this difference, that I have only one whisker; the other refuses and still refuses to grow.

I have five lessons to give today; you think I am making a fortune? Carriages and white gloves cost more, and without them one would not be in good taste.

I love the Carlists, I can't endure the Philippists, myself I am a revolutionist; also I care nothing for money, only for friendship, for which I beg and pray you.

FRYDERYK

[1] Karasowski gives this passage with these omissions.
[2] Mazurka No. 1, Op. 7. [Op.]

75.

To KALASANTY JĘDRZEJEWICZ.

(To be given to Panna Ludwika Chopin, who will doubtless guess to whom to deliver it. In any case information about him can be obtained from Pani Chopin.)

MY VERY DEAR LIFE!

Forgive my sending this scrawl in answer to your nice letter; but you have given me the right to treat you with even more sincerity than before, so I know you won't mind about the paper. You tell me the news I longed for! I have always been fond of you, have always felt as a friend to you, and be assured that you will now find in me the person you ought to find. I would give half my life to be able to embrace you both on your wedding day and see you at the altar; but that cannot be; I can only send you, as you ask, a polonaise and a mazur, so that you can hop about and be really gay and that your souls may rejoice. I will not enlarge upon either your heart or hers, for that is not a brother's part; but you cannot believe how it worried me that this hung fire for so long, or how glad I am that it is to happen at last. May all go well with you. The sight of your happiness will make our whole family happy; it is the beginning of good years after the long chain of misfortunes.

I press your hand and embrace you. Love me.

Your most sincere

FRYC

Paris, 10 September 1832.

My Life, once more, forgive my not writing a long letter. Perhaps I sin in the hope of pardon, but we know each other not from today or yesterday. Once again, love me as I love you.

76.

[In French. A joint letter to Ferdinand Hiller, from Liszt, Chopin and Franchomme.]

Paris, 20 June 1833.

[*The first two paragraphs, omitted, are by Liszt. Chopin continues:*]

He is so right that I, personally, have nothing to add in excuse for my negligence, or laziness, or grippe, or absent-mindedness, or, or, or—You know that I explain myself better in person, and when, this autumn, I escort you back to your mother late at night along the boulevards, I shall try to obtain your forgiveness. I write to you without knowing what my pen is scribbling, because at this moment Liszt is playing my études, and transporting me outside of my respectable thoughts. I should like to steal from him the way to play my own études. As for your friends who remain in Paris, I have often seen the Leo family, and what that entails, during this winter and spring. There have been some evening parties given by certain Ambassadresses; and not one at which people did not speak of someone who stays at Frankfort. Mme Eichthal sends you a thousand kind messages. Plater—all the family—was very sad at your departure, and asks me to assure you of his regret. (Mme d'Appony was much annoyed with me for not bringing you to her before you left; she hopes that when you come back you will be kind enough to remember the promise that you made to me. I can tell you as much about a certain lady who is not an ambassadress.)

[*In alternate phrases.* Do you know Chopin's marvellous Études? *Chopin continues:*] They are admirable—and all the same they will live only till the moment when yours appear. [Author's modesty!!! *Chopin continues:*] A little impertinence on the part of the director—for, to explain to you better, he is correcting my mistakes in spelling, according to M. Marlet's method.

You come back to us in September, isn't it? Try [to let us

know the day, as we intend to give you a Charivari serenade.] The most distinguished company of artists in the Capital: M. Franchomme [present], Mme Petzold and the abbé Bardin, the dancers of the rue d'Amboise [and my neighbours, Maurice Schlesinger, uncles, aunts, nephews, nieces, brothers-in-law, sisters-in-law, etc., etc. —] the third floor, etc.

The responsible editors [F. Liszt,] F. Chopin, [Aug. Franchomme].

By the way; yesterday I met Heine, who told me to "grüssen" you "herzlich und herzlich."[1]

By the way again, grace [*Gruss?*] for all you [incorrect] —please forgive me. If you have a moment to spare, give us news of you, which will be very dear to us: Paris, rue de la Chaussée d'Antin, No. 5. At present I am staying in Franck's lodging. He has left for London and Berlin. I am very happy in the rooms which were so often our meeting-place. Berlioz embraces you.

As for papa Baillot, he is in Switzerland, at Geneva, and so you can guess that I cannot send you the Bach concerto.

77.

[In French]

To M. AUGUSTE FRANCHOMME AT CÔTEAU.
[*Paris, September 1833.*]

Begun Saturday the 14th, finished Wednesday the 18th inst.

DEAR FRIEND!

It would be useless to make excuses for my silence. If my thoughts could post themselves without paper! Anyhow, you know me well enough to know that unfortunately I never do what I ought to do. I arrived very comfortably (except for a small disagreeable episode caused by an excessively odoriferous gentleman who travelled as far as Chartres. He surprised me

[1] greet you heartily and heartily.

in the night). I have found in Paris more occupations than I left, which will doubtless prevent my coming to see you at le Côteau! Côteau! Oh Côteau! My child, tell the whole household at Côteau that I shall never forget my visit in Touraine,—that so much kindness leaves eternal gratitude. People say I have grown fatter and look well, and I feel splendid, thanks to my dinner neighbours who took really maternal care of me. When I think of it, it all seems to me a dream, such a pleasant one that I wish I were still asleep. And the Pornic peasant women! And the flour! Or rather your gracefully formed nose which you were forced to thrust into—

A very interesting visit interrupted this letter, which was begun three days ago and could not get finished till today.

Hiller, Maurice and all the rest embrace you. I delivered your letter to his father, whom I did not find at home. Paër, whom I saw a few days ago, spoke to me of your return.

Come back to us fat and well, like me. Another thousand messages to the estimable Forest family. I have neither words nor possibility to express all that I feel for them. Excuse me. Give me a handgrip, I pat you on the shoulder, I embrace you, I kiss you.

My friend, *au revoir.*

Hoffmann, the corpulent Hoffmann, and the slender Smitkowski also embrace you.

78.

To FELIKS WODZIŃSKI.
Paris, 18 July 1834.

DEAR FELIKS!

You have doubtless been thinking: "Fryc is in the doleful dumps, or he would have answered me." You remember that I always do everything too late. I went to Mlle Fauche too late. So I had to wait till after the good Wolf had gone. If I had not only just come back from the Rhineland, and had not business which I cannot drop now at this moment, I should at once have gone to Geneva to accept with thanks your respected Mother's invitation. But fate is hard, and there is nothing to be done. Your Sister was so kind as to send me her composition. I was more delighted than I can say, and at once, the same evening, I improvised, in one of the *salons* here, on a charming theme by that Maryna with whom I long ago raced about the rooms of the Poznań house — And today! *Je prends la liberté d'envoyer à mon estimable collègue Mlle Marie une petite valse que je viens de publier.*[1] May it give her a hundredth part of the pleasure which I felt on receiving her variations. I end by once more most sincerely thanking your Mother for her kind remembrance of her faithful servant, in whom also flows a little Kujaw[2] blood.

F. CHOPIN

Embrace my dear Antek, and stifle Kazio with *tendresses*, if you can. As for Panna Marja, bow before her very elegantly and respectfully, in wonder, and say to yourself: "Good Lord, how it has grown up!"

79.

To his Family.
Carlsbad, 16 August [*1835*].
(*A postscript to his father's letter.*)

MY DEAR CHILDREN,

This is the first letter you will get with both Papa's and my writing. We are happier than we can describe. We hug each other and hug again; what more can we do; what a pity we are not all together. But, but, it's wonderful! How good God is to us! I'm writing all anyhow; it's better not to try to think today; just to be happy, now happiness has come. That's all I can do today. The same Parents, just the same as ever, only a little older. We walk, I take my Lady Mummy on my arm, we talk

[1] I take the liberty of sending to my estimable colleague Miss Mary a little waltz which I have just published.

[2] Vagabond, scaramouch.

about you, we imitate naughty nephews, we tell how often we have thought about each other. We eat and drink together, we caress each other, we scold each other. I am *au comble de mon bonheur*.[1] The same ways, the same gestures with which I grew up, the same hand that I have not kissed for so long. Well, my children, I embrace you; and forgive me that I can't collect my thoughts and write about anything else but that we are happy at this minute, that I had only hope and now have the realization, and am happy, happy, happy.

I could hug you and my brothers-in-law to death; — my dearest in this world.

CH.

A thousand kisses to P. Żywny for the music, and a million greetings to Pan Wiesołowski, who brought my happiness some dozens of miles nearer to me. *Ditto* to Pan Fryd. Skarbek.

80.

To THE FAMILY OF A. BARCIŃSKI [2] IN WARSAW.
Paris, 14 March 1836.

(In rhyme)

I am well, and flourishing.
   This important news
Goes with a hug
   To the children.

F. F. CHOPIN

(A Postscript by Jan Matuszyński)

Another piece of news
To the respected children,
That Fryc will come
To you next year.

J.

[1] at the height of my happiness.
[2] the husband of his sister Izabela.

81.

To Teresa Wodzińska.

Paris, 1 Nov[ember 1836.]

Most Gracious and Honoured Lady

I send on a letter from Pampeluna, signed by Antoś.[1] I adopted Pani Diller's method, and it has worked. The object of this letter, it seems to me, is to get to the signature, and from Wincenty's postscripts you can see that Antoś is the same as ever, that people love and remember him, that he is as well as he can be, and not alone.

I waited impatiently for this letter; and meanwhile the time for blessings had come to you all, for Feliks is probably already married, and no doubt the wedding was gay and lavish, and everybody danced and drank healths, and calls were paid and returned for some days, and so on. Why, indeed, can't one have one of those mirrors that show everything, one of those rings that transport one where one's thoughts are reaching out to — And my parents who are asking news of me — Pan Byczkowski has not arrived yet; I will do my best for him.

I am glad my letter today is only a cover for that of Antoś; otherwise there would be little for me to tell you, so far as the number of things goes. Today, somehow, news does not flow from my pen. For All Saints' Day, however, the signatures of Antoś and Pani Anatole,[2] put me right. I won't send any others to the Secretary,[3] as I am afraid to make the letter too heavy; before winter I'll write and send some music. Pani Zofia still loves you all and loves to speak of you. Cicholo, my present neighbour, often asks after you.

Why must it be twelve already? At twelve I have to give a lesson and to keep on till six; then dinner, and after that to an evening in society, till 11. As I respect you, that is the truth; I think of nothing but slippers [4] and play for the twilight hour.[5]

[1] Her son, Anton Wodziński. [2] Anatole's wife.

[3] Marja Wodzińska, Pani Teresa's daughter, to whom he was engaged at the time; she signed her letters: "Your faithful secretary."

[4] Pani Teresa had asked whether he wore slippers and woollen socks and went to bed early.

[5] Karlowicz suggests that this may refer to his having become engaged to Panna Marja at dusk.

82.

To the Same.
Paris, 2 April 1837.

I profit by Pani Nakwaska's permission to write a few words. I am hoping to hear directly from Anton and will send it on at once; a detailed letter with a postscript from Wincenty. Please do not be anxious about him. Everybody is still in the town. I have no details, because they all give particulars about themselves. No doubt my letter of this month is in Służew [1] already and has reassured you, so far as that is possible, about that Spaniard, who *must, must* write a few words to me. I will not tell you how grieved I am at the news of the loss of your Mother: not for her, but for you whom I know. (Consistency!) About that, I confess that there was a moment at Marienbad, over Panna Marja's book; in a hundred years I could not have written anything in it. There are days when I can't help myself. Today I would rather be in Służew than write to Służew. I could say more than I can write. My respects to Pan Wodziński, Panna Marja, Kazio, Teresa, and Feliks.

Affectionately
F. CH.

83.

To the Same.
[*Paris*] *14 May 1837.*

MOST GRACIOUS LADY!

Here are a few words from Anton. I haste to forward to you this proof of his good health and spirits. As he asks, I shall answer him at once, without waiting for a reply from Służew. I shall not mention the trouble at home, and shall probably receive a more detailed letter (which also I will forward) telling

[1] The estate of the Wodzińskis.

me what, where and how he thinks of being. I will write no more now, as I do not wish to miss the post; anyhow, everything would be colourless beside Anton's card.

Most affectionately

F. CHOPIN

My respects to Pan Wodziński. Let me remind Panna Marja to write a few words to her brother. I embrace Kazio and Teresa. Greetings to Feliks and his wife.

84.

To ANTON WODZIŃSKI.

[*Undated. Paris, May or June, 1837.*]

MY DEAR LIFE!

You are wounded, and far from us; and at this moment I cannot send you anything — Your family just worries and worries about you — For heaven's sake, do get well and come home. The papers say that your legion is completely destroyed. Don't go into the Spanish war — Remember that your blood can be needed for something better — Tytus writes to ask me to meet him somewhere in Germany. Last winter I was ill again with *grippe*, and was sent to Ems. I am not thinking of it yet; I can't get off to travel. I am writing and preparing a manuscript. I think more about you than you perhaps suppose, and I love you as always.

F. C.

Believe me that I remember you, as I do Tytus — Perhaps I will go for a few days to George Sand; but that will not delay your money, because I will leave instructions with Jasio for those three days —

85.

To Teresa Wodzińska.
Paris 18 June 1837.

Most Gracious Lady!

Antoś is in Saragossa; he is well, and has just written to me, begging that your household should remember him.

Since the skirmish near Huesca, their legion is completely disorganized; many are returning, and now, if ever, is the time when he needs your speedy help. As far as I could I responded to his request last month (immediately after receiving the letter written before Huesca, which I forwarded to you) but that is a drop in the ocean. Wincenty and Maurycy are also in Saragossa; Maurycy's guardians advise them to return; it would be well if he could return with them, as he went.

Meanwhile, when all around is trouble and disturbance, nobody worries here; weddings, balls, and festivities. They are so gay that they end by trampling each other; at the fireworks on the Field of Mars nearby twenty persons paid for their curiosity with their lives in the crush, so that the *hôtel de ville* ball, for which over 15,000 tickets had been distributed, was cancelled. The new princess is universally liked; she is praised not for beauty, but for sense. She is not shy and commits no *gaucheries*, as she has been brought up among such festivities, not on Butterschnitsen[1] in Ludwigsburg. I have been nowhere, not even to Versailles, about the wonders of which not only Philippe's friends but those of the former dynasty enlarge. It has exceeded everyone's expectations. The weather has been propitious for the ceremonies; everything was a success, except the soup at a Versailles dinner for which the *maître d'hôtel* made the king wait. People were afraid the cook would follow in Vatel's footsteps. The Parisians are still to have the Garde Nationale ball at the Opéra, and a fête, which Rothschild is giving to the young prince at Ferière [*sic*], a very beautiful place that he has near Paris.

And is the summer beautiful at Służew? Is there much

[1] Bread and butter.

shade? Can one sit under the trees and paint? Has Teresa still a good place for her cheese-making? Does she not miss Panna Jósefa's or Mlle Malet's help with it? Shan't you see them soon? I could ask a thousand questions. I wonder are there any gaieties? When the Princess arrived I was in the country, near Enghien lake. It is difficult for me to stay in Paris now. The doctor orders me to Ems, but I don't know where or when I shall go.

A few days ago Pani Zofia called on me one evening with Princess Zajączek, and asked affectionately after you. Did your ears burn? Pani Anatole was with the Platers yesterday; she complains a little of her nerves, but is getting fat, and Leosia is growing finely. She cannot forget Teresa's Guermange, and every time she sees my goddaughter (you must know that I have been a godfather here for a long time), every time she hears her, she always ends her ecstasies with *Mademoiselle il.*

Did you like the pianoforte? [1] I do hope so! If not, please beat me, but don't be angry.

Most affectionately
F. CHOPIN

My respects to Pan Wodzyński. To Panna Marja, Kazio, Teresa, the Felikses, in order.

38 rue de la Chaussée d'Antin.

86.

To the Same.
Paris, 14 August 1837.

MOST GRACIOUS LADY!

As I fear that someone else may tell you, wrongly, I prefer to forward to you Antoś's letter of the 3rd inst., so that you may know from his own letter what he is doing. I did not tell you that

[1] At her request he had bought a piano for her in Paris, and sent it to Służew. [Op.]

he had been slightly wounded in the leg at Huesca, as that was about May, and I wished to tell it orally rather than by letter; but as that is now different, and as this midge may reach you as an enormous elephant, I enclose his last letter, in which he writes that the wound is now completely healed. It is also clear from the letter that he intends to return, and that on the three thousand francs which I received on the 9th inst. through the banker Leo, and sent on to Logronio, through Rothschild, on the day when I received Antoś's letter; that is: the 10th. Many of ours are in Logronio, and, in particular, he will find there the good Woroniecki. He will brighten up more if you or Panna Marja would be so good as to send him a few words through me; for, as you will see, in this letter too he complains that no one writes to him from home, though I have always sent on news of you to him whenever I have had it.

Your last letter reached me in London, where I spent last month dawdling about. I had thought of going from there to Germany through Holland — I came back here, as it is getting late, and in my room it will probably be altogether too late for me.

I hope for a less sad letter from you than the last. Perhaps my next one will be only a postscript to one from Antoś.

Most affectionately

F. CHOPIN

I send my respects to Pan Wodziński; and remind Panna Marja of her brother. To the Felikses, Kazio, Panna Józefa, Teresa. — Your acquaintances here are well, and doubtless are thinking neither of illness nor of sorrows. Pani Zofia was to have heard from Geneva of your being expected there.

87.

To JULJAN FONTANA.[1]
[*Undated.*]

[*Containing French words with Polish spelling; a nonsense letter.*]

Monsieur —
Monsieur Fontana
Cité Danton 3 [?] Confound it.

I send you yesterday's ticket
Nat. Comar. [?]

If you like I will wait for you here at 8½; if not, write me a line to say where to wait.

Your
F. CH.

N.B. If you have an *idea* that they may ask you to play, drop it. *Primo,* I doubt that they will want to dance since the day before yesterday (for I have seen them); *secundo:* I shall be there, also Jelowicki and *Potocka* — and you can enjoy yourself, unless you harbour any sort of *spleen* in your head without a *peruke.* After all, they don't fire off *cannon* at people in any drawing-room — also it is too early for you to get the doleful dumps, though you are 10 years *older* than I.

Carry ammunition in your soul, but don't let anyone suspect it from your nose.

88.

To the Same.
Paris, 1837.

Please, if you can, copy out for me the A flat Prelude; I want to give it to Perthuis. He leaves tomorrow; and you when? If you want to see me, today between 8 and 9.

[1] Juljan Fontana, 1810–1870: Polish pianist and composer; Chopin's fellow-pupil in childhood and lifelong friend. He emigrated to France after the failure of the insurrection (1831), and after Chopin's death brought out many of his unpublished compositions, including much immature work.

89.

To the Same.
Paris, 1837.

I send you a *stall* for Musard; but *please* don't sit down; because it has been given me by acquaintances with whom I promised to go, and I can't.

With love
FR. CH.

90.

To the Same.
Paris, 1837.

Come this evening and bring me that *Hungarian* [1] *by force.* Freppa will sing, and we may hop a little.

Catch Sadowski by the —; [2] he has got to come. Go to the club and get General Skarzyński.

91.

To WOJCIECH GRZYMAŁA.[3]
[*Paris; undated.*]

My Dear, I urgently must see you, even if it is 12 or 1 in the night. Don't fear any worries for yourself, Dear. You know how much I always value your affection. It is a question of some advice that I want.

Your
CH.

[1] Liszt.
[2] Word suppressed by Hoesick, through whom this letter is known.
[3] Wojciech Grzymała: Polish journalist; b. 1793; Chopin's intimate friend. Settled in France after the failure of the insurrection, 1831.

92.

To the Same.
[*Paris, 1837.*]

Well, but, when I can't?!!!

I should cut my throat with this McDaniel razor that I brought for you, if I did not want to give it to you first. I have a musical dinner, and can't manage to wriggle out of it, *eel* as I am.

I hug you like a *boa.*

CH.

93.

To the Same.
[*Paris; undated.*]

Something has happened to me (as the ladies say at home); I can't spend the evening with you because of a superboring strange dinner without even truffles.

A hug.

F. CH.

94.

To the Same.
[*Paris; undated.*]

MY LIFE!

I am not taken by surprise, because yesterday I saw Mar,[1] who told me she had arrived. I must sit like a stone till 5 o'clock, giving lessons (just finishing the second one). God knows what will come of it. I am really not well. I've called on you every day, to give you a hug.

Let's dine together somewhere.

CH.

[1] Marliani?

95.

To JULJAN FONTANA IN PARIS.
[*Palma, 19 November 1838.*]

MY DEAR.

I am in Palma, among palms, cedars, cacti, olives, pomegranates, etc. Everything the *Jardin des Plantes* has in its greenhouses. A sky like turquoise, a sea like lapis lazuli, mountains like emerald, air like heaven. Sun all day, and hot; everyone in summer clothing; at night guitars and singing for hours. Huge balconies with grape-vines overhead; Moorish walls. Everything looks towards Africa, as the town does. In short, a glorious life! Love me. Go to Pleyel; the piano has not yet come. How was it sent? You will soon receive some Preludes. I shall probably lodge in a wonderful monastery, the most beautiful situation in the world; sea, mountains, palms, a cemetery, a crusaders' church, ruined mosques, aged trees, thousand-year-old olives. Ah, my dear, I am coming alive a little—I am near to what is most beautiful. I am better — Give my parents letters and anything you have to send me to Grzymała; he knows the safest address. Embrace Jasio. How well he would recover here! Tell Pl[eyel] that he will soon get a manuscript. Don't talk much about me to the people I know. I will write you many things later — Say that I am returning after the winter. The post leaves here once a week. I write through the Consulate here. Send my letter to my parents, just as it is. Post it yourself.

Your

CH.

I'll write to Jasio later.[1]

[1] Note in Fontana's hand: "Received 28 December, 1838."

96.

To the Same.
Palma, 3 December 1838.

My Juljan!

I don't give notice at my lodging. I can't send you the manuscript, for it's not finished. I have been as sick as a dog these last two weeks; I caught cold in spite of 18 degrees of heat, roses, oranges, palms, figs and three most famous doctors of the island. One sniffed at what I spat up, the second tapped where I spat it from, the third poked about and listened how I spat it. One said I had died,[1] the second that I am dying, the 3rd that I shall die. And today I'm the same as ever; only I can't forgive Jasio for not giving me a consultation when I had an attack of *bronchite aigue*, which can always be expected in my case. I could scarcely keep them from bleeding me, and they put no setons or vesicators; but, *gràce* to Providence, I am now as before. But all this has affected the Preludes, and God knows when you will get them. I shall stay for a few days in the loveliest district in the world; sea, mountains, everything you want. I shall lodge in a huge, old, ruined monastery of Carthusians, whom Mend. has expelled, as if specially for me. It is near Palma, could not be lovelier; porches, the most poetic of cemeteries; in a word, I shall be happy there. Only I still have no piano. I wrote to Pleyel; just rue de Rochechouard. Find out. Say that I was very unwell at first, but am all right again. Anyhow don't say much about me, or about the manuscripts. Write to me; I have not had one letter from you yet. Tell Leo that I have not yet sent the Prelude to Albrecht, that I love them very much and will write to them. Post my letter to my Par[ents] yourself at the Bourse, and write. I embrace Jasio.

Don't tell people that I've been ill; or they'll make up a tale.

[1] "*zdechnal*": croaked, kicked the bucket; used of animals.

97.

[No.]

To Wojciech Grzymała in Paris.
[*Palma*] *3 December* [*1838*].

My Dear, send to Fontana the letter for my Parents. I cough and grunt, but I love you. We often speak of you. No letter from you as yet. This is a diabolical country, so far as post, people and comfort are concerned. The sky is as beautiful as your soul; the earth as black as my heart. I love you always.

Ch.

98.

To Juljan Fontana in Paris.
Palma, 14 December 1838.

My Juljan.

Not a word from you yet, and this is my 3rd note, if not the 4th. Perhaps my people have not written? Perhaps some misfortune has happened there? Or are you lazy? No, you're not lazy, you're a good fellow. No doubt you have sent on my two letters to my people (both from Palma), and have written to me, and the post here, the most irregular one on earth, has not sent the letters — I heard only today that the piano was put on to a trading vessel in Marseilles on Dec. 1st. The letter has taken 14 days from Marseilles. So I can hope that the piano will spend the winter in the dock, or at anchor (for here nothing moves but the rain), and that I shall receive it when I am starting back; which will be a great consolation, as, besides 500 francs' duty, I shall have the pleasure of dispatching it back again. Meanwhile my manuscripts sleep, and I can't sleep; only cough and, covered with poultices for a long time past, wait for the spring or for something else — Tomorrow I go to that wonderful monastery of Valdemosa, to write in the cell of some old monk, who perhaps had more fire in his soul than I, and stifled it, stifled and extinguished it, because he had it in vain. I think I shall soon send you my Preludes and a Ballade. Go to Leo. Don't say that I'm ill; they'd get a thousandfold scare. And to Pleyel.

Your

CH.

99.

To the Same.
Palma, 28 Dec[ember] 1838.

— or rather Valdemosa, a few miles away. It's a huge Carthusian monastery, stuck down between rocks and sea, where you may imagine me, without white gloves or haircurling, as pale as ever, in a cell with such doors as Paris never had for gates. The cell is the shape of a tall coffin, with an enormous dusty vaulting, a small window, outside the window orange-trees, palms and cypresses, opposite the window my bed on rollers [?] under a Moorish filigree rosette. Beside the bed is a square *claque nitouchable* for writing, which I can scarcely use, and on it (a great *luxe*[1] here) a leaden candlestick with a candle. Bach, my scrawls and (not my) waste paper — silence — you could scream — there would still be silence. Indeed, I write to you from a strange place.

Three days ago I received your letter of the 9th, and, as it is a holiday, and the post will not leave till next week, I am writing to you at leisure; this I.O.U. which I am sending you will probably reach you in a Russian month.[2] Nature is a beautiful thing, but it's better to have no dealings with human beings. No roads, no post. I have come here many times from Palma, always with the same driver, always by a new way. The torrents make the roads, the avalanches keep them in repair; today you can't pass here, because it's been ploughed, tomorrow only mules can manage; and what vehicles!!! Therefore, my

[1] luxury.

[2] A Polish idiom: "*Mañana*"; "some time, never"; used particularly about the payments of debts.

Juljan, there is not a single Englishman, not even a consul. As for what people are saying about me, it doesn't matter. Leo is a Jew! I can't send you the preludes; they aren't finished; I'm better now, and will make haste; and I'll send the Jew a short open letter of thanks that will go down to his heels (let it go where you like on him). The rascal! And the day before I left I went to him, so that he shouldn't send to me. Schlesinger is still more of a cur, to put my waltzes into an album!! and sell them to Probst, when I gave them to him for his collection for Gyc. But all these lice don't bite me so much now; Leo can be as furious as he pleases. I am only sorry for you; but in a month at the latest you will be free, both from Leo and from my landlord. Use Wessel's money if necessary. What are the servants doing? Give the porter 20 francs from me for New Year, when you get the money, and pay the *fumiste* [1] when he comes. I don't think I have left any important debts. In any case, I promise you, we shall be all clear within a month at most. To-night the moon is glorious; it has never been like this. But! But! You write that you forwarded a letter from my people; I never saw it, never had it. And I do need it so! Did you stamp it? How did you address it? Your letter is the only one that I have had yet; it was very badly addressed. Don't write Junto unless you have forgotten something, and that gentleman (*en parenthèse* a perfect idiot) is called Riotord. I send you the best address [*Crossed out; a postscript inserted:*] No; I would rather you addressed as I did the piano. The piano has been waiting 8 days in the port, according to the *douane*, [2] which wants a mountain of gold pieces for the piggish thing. Nature is benevolent here, but the people are thieves, because they never see strangers, and so don't know how much to demand. Oranges can be had for nothing, but a trouser button costs a fabulous sum. But all that is just a grain of sand, when one has this sky, this poetry that everything breathes here, this colouring of the most exquisite places, colour not yet faded by men's eyes. No one has yet scared away the eagles that soar every day above our heads! For Heaven's sake, write, always stamp your letters and add: "*Palma de Mallorca.*"

[1] chimney-sweeper.
[2] custom-house.

I send you the I.O.U. and a letter for my people. I love Jasio and am sorry that he did not qualify completely for director of charity children somewhere in Nuremberg or Bamberg. Anyhow let him write, that a man —[1]

I think this is the 3rd or 4th letter for my people that I am sending you. Embrace Albrecht, but don't say much.

100.

To the Same.
[*Undated; beginning 1839.*]

My Dear.

I send you the Preludes. Copy them, you and Wolff; I think there are no errors. Give the copy to Probst, and the manuscript to Pleyel. Take Probst's money, for which I enclose a note and *reçu,* at once to Leo; I have no time to write him a letter of thanks; and from the money that Pleyel will give you, that is: fifteen hundred francs, you can pay the rent: 425 fr. to the New Year, and politely give up the lodging. If you can let it for March, do; if not, I shall have to keep it for one more quarter. You can give the remaining thousand to Nougie from me. Find out his address from Jasio, but don't tell him anything about the money, or he'll be ready to burst in on Nougie, and I don't want anyone but you and me to know about this. If the lodging lets, give part of the furniture to Jasio, and part to Grzym. You can tell Pleyel to write through you. Before New Year I sent you an I.O.U. for Wessel. Tell Pleyel that I am quits with Wessel. In a few weeks you shall have a Ballade, a Polonaise and a Scherzo. Tell Pleyel that I have arranged with Probst about the time of publication of the Preludes. I have still not had one letter from my parents!! You must stamp the letters. But don't you know what has become of the first one? I embrace you. I live in a cell; sometimes I have Arab dances, African sun,

[1] Sentence unfinished.

Mediterranean sea. Embrace Albrecht and his wife; I will write to them. Don't say that I am giving up my lodging, except to Grzymała. I don't know, perhaps I won't come back till May or later. *Give Pleyel* the letter and *preludes yourself*.

Write.

Your

F.

101.

To the Same.
Marseilles, 7 March 1839.

My Juljan, you have doubtless heard from Grzymała about my health and my manuscripts. Two months ago I sent you my preludes from Palma. From these (after copying them for Probst) you were to give Leo a thousand; and from the fifteen hundred that Pleyel was to give you for the preludes, I asked you to pay Nougie, and one quarter to the landlord. In the same letter, if I am not mistaken, I asked you to give up the lodging, which, unless it can be let for April, will have to be paid for till the next quarter day (I think till July). You have probably used Wessel's money to pay the New Year quarter; but if not, please use it for this quarter. The other manuscripts must, no doubt, have only now reached you, for they spent a long time at the custom-house, and on the sea, and again at the custom-house. Sending the preludes, I wrote to Pleyel that I will give him the ballade (which the German, Dr. Probst, has) for a thousand; for 2 Polonaises (for France, England and Germany, as the Probst *engagement* ends with the ballade) I have asked fifteen hundred. I think that is not too much. So, after receiving the other manuscripts, you should have two thousand five hundred, and from Probst five hundred for the ballade (or six hundred, I don't quite remember), which, together, makes three thousand. I asked Grzymała to send me at least five hundred at once (which need not interfere with sending the rest on quickly). That's all about business. Now, if — which I doubt — the lodging is let by next month, share the furniture between you three: Grz. Jaś. and you.

Jaś. has more space, — though not more oil in his head,[1] to judge by the childish letter he has written me, thinking I am going to become a Carmelite. Give Jaś the most useful [household?] lumber. Don't bother Grzymała with much [?]; [2] take what you want; I don't know whether I shall come back to Paris in the summer, so you keep it — for [?],[3] we will write to each other, and if my lodging has to be kept on till June, which is likely; please, even if you have another lodging of your own, stay in mine with one foot, for I shall come on you for the payment of the last three months. In the second polonaise you have a sincere and truthful answer to your letter; — it is not my fault that I am like that fungus which looks like a mushroom, but poisons those who pull it up and taste it, mistaking it for something else. I know that I have never been any use to anyone — but also not very much to myself. I told you that in the bureau, in the first drawer from the door, there is a roll, which either you, or Grz. or Jaś might open — now I beg you to take it out and burn it *unread*. Do this, I beg you, for our friendship; that paper is no longer needed. If Antek goes away, and does not return me the money, it will be very Polish; i.e. Polish in the bad sense; all the same, don't mention it to him. See Pleyel; tell him I have not had a single word from him. That his little piano is in safety. Does he agree to the terms I wrote him? All three letters from home reached me at once, together with your letters, just before I boarded the ship. I send you one more. Thanks for the friendly help that you give to a feeble person. Embrace Jaś; tell him that I am — or rather, that they were not allowed to bleed me, that I have vesicators, that I don't cough much, only in the morning; and that I am not yet regarded at all as a consumptive. I drink no coffee, nor wine — only milk; I keep warm and look like a girl. Send the money as soon as you can; communicate with Grzymała.

Your

FR.

I enclose 2 words for Antek. I'll write to Grzymała tomorrow.

[1] A Polish idiom: brains, commonsense.
[2] Word illegible; paper injured in several places.
[3] Illegible.

102.

To the Same.
[*Undated. Marseilles, March 1839.*]

My Dear: If they're such Jews, hold back everything, till I come. The Preludes are sold to Pleyel (I have received 500 francs) — so I suppose he has the right to wipe the other side of his belly with them; but as for the Ballade and Polonaises, don't sell them, either to Schl. or to Probst. I will have nothing to do with any Schönbergers at any time. So, if you have given the Ballade to Probst — take it away, even if he would give a thousand; tell him I asked you to await my return. That when I come, we will see. We have had enough of these fools, both you and I. I beg your pardon, my Life. You have dragged round like a real friend, and now you will also have my house-moving on your shoulders. Ask Grzymała to pay the moving-expenses. About the porter, he is certainly lying; but who is going to prove it — you will have to give it to him, to avoid a row. Embrace Jaś; I'll write when I feel in a good humour; I am better, but I'm furious. — Tell Jaś that no doubt neither he nor I will get either a word or a penny out of Antek.

Adieu; I embrace you.

Yesterday I got your letter, with Pleyel's and Jasia's. If you liked Clara Wieck, you were right; she plays — no one better. If you see her, greet her from me, and her Father too. I embrace you and Jaś.

F. Chopin

103.

To the Same.
[*13 March 1839. From Marseilles.*]

Many thanks, my Life, for your running about. I did not expect that Pleyel would Jew me; but, if so, please give him this letter. I think he won't cause you any trouble about the Ballade and the Polonaise. But, in the opposite event, get 500 for the ballade from Probst, and then take it to Schlesinger. If I have got to deal with Jews, let it at least be Orthodox ones. Probst may swindle me even worse, for he's a sparrow whose tail you can't salt. Schlesinger has always cheated me; but he has made a lot out of me, and won't want to refuse another profit; only be polite to him, because the Jew likes to pass for somebody. So, if Pleyel makes even the smallest difficulties, you will go to Schl., and tell him that I will give him the Ballade for France and England for 800 (he won't give a thousand), and the Polonaises for Germany, England, and France for 1500 (and if he won't give that, then for 1400, or 1300, or even 1200). If he begins to talk about Pleyel and the preludes (for Probst has doubtless told him about them), you will say that they were promised to Pleyel long ago, that he wanted to be their publisher and begged me, before I went away, to let him have them, which is really the case. You see, my Life: I might break with Schlesinger for Pleyel, but not for Probst. What good is it to me if Schlesinger makes Probst pay more for my manuscripts? If Probst pays more to Schlesinger, it is a proof that he has cheated me, paying less. Probst has no shop in Paris; all my things are printed at Schl. The Jew has always paid me, and Probst has often made me wait. You will have to arrange with Schlesinger that you give him the manuscripts on the day when he gives you the money; if he won't give for both at once, then give the ballade separately and the polonaises separately; but not more than 2 weeks between. If Schlesinger won't hear of this, only then go to Probst; but, as he is such an adorer of mine, don't drop on him, as you can on Pleyel. At the slightest difficulty, give Pleyel my letter. If, which I doubt, you have already given him the manuscript of the Ballade and Polonaises, take them away, for Schlesinger or Probst. The scoundrels! — Good Lord, that Pleyel, who is such an adorer of mine! Perhaps he thinks I shan't come back to Paris? I shall come back, and shall pay a visit of thanks to him, and another to Leo. I enclose a card to Schlesinger, giving you authority. Antek's parents must have forgotten themselves strangely for such a thing to happen as has happened between him and me. *Entendons nous;* he did not return the money to me before he left. A brainless and heartless fool! I am better with every day; all the same you had better pay the porter those 50 francs, which I entirely approve, for the doctor will not let me leave the south till the summer. I received the Dziady [1] yesterday. As for the glove man and the little tailor, they can wait, the idiots! What about my papers? You can leave the letters in the bureau, and take the music to Jaś's place or your own. In the table in the vestibule there are also some letters; you need to lock it well. You can seal Schlesinger's letter with a wafer and Schlesinger too.

Write often. Your

CH.

Embrace Jaś.

104.

To the Same.
[*Marseilles*] *17 March 1839, Sunday.*

MY LIFE.

Thanks for all your trouble. Pleyel's a fool and Probst a rascal (he never gave me 1000 fr. for 3 manuscripts). No doubt you have received my long letter about Schlesinger; now I wish, and beg you, give my letter to Pleyel (who finds my manuscripts too dear). If I have to sell them cheap, I would rather let it be to Schlesinger than search for impossible new connections. As Schlesinger can always count on England, and as I am quits with Wessel, let him sell them to whom he likes. The same with the Polonaises in Germany; for Probst is a sly bird: I know him of old. Let Schlesinger sell to whom he likes, not necessarily to Probst. It's nothing to me. He adores me, because he's skinning me. Only have a clear understanding with him about the money, and don't give up the manuscripts except for cash. I will send Pleyel a *reconnaissance*.[2] The fool, can't he trust either me or you? Good Lord, why must one have dealings with scoundrels! That Pleyel, who told me that Schlesinger was underpaying me,

[1] *The Ancestors*; Mickiewicz's great dramatic poem.
[2] receipt.

and now finds 500 fr. too much for a manuscript for all countries! Well, I prefer to do business with a real Jew. And Probst is a rascal to pay me 300 for the mazurkas! Why, the last mazurkas brought me 800 at the first jump: Probst 300, Schl. 400, Wess. 100. I would rather sell my manuscripts for nothing as in the old days, than have to bow and scrape to such fools. And I'd rather be humiliated by one Jew than by 3. So let's go to Schlesinger. I hope you have finished with Pleyel. Don't speak of the Scherzo to anyone. I don't know when I shall finish it, for I am still weak and not fit to write. Scoundrels, scoundrels, they and Mme Migneron! But perhaps Mme Migneron will yet be under your . . . When you come to make shoes for the cobbler,[1] I beg you, make none for Pleyel or Probst: let them go barefoot. I don't know yet when I shall see you. Embrace Grzymała, and give him the furniture; whichever things he wants, and let Jasio take the rest. I don't write to him; I've nothing to say. I still love him; tell him that and embrace him. I'm still amazed at Wodziński — When you get the money from Pleyel, pay the landlady first, and send me 500 at once. Embrace Grzymała and Jaś.

Your
FRYCEK

I received your letter today. No letter from Pleyel. In Pleyel's receipt I left the Op. blank, because I don't know the number.

105.

To the Same.
[*Undated. Marseilles, March or April 1839.*]

MY DEAR.

I am much better. I am beginning to play, eat, walk, and talk, like other folk; you see that I even write easily, since you again receive a few words from me. But about business again. I should very much like to have my preludes dedicated to

[1] a proverb.

Pleyel (there's probably still time, as they are not printed). And the Ballade to Mr. Robert Schuhmann [*sic*]. The Polonaises to you, as they are. To Kessler nothing. If Pleyel does not want to give up the Ballades, then dedicate the preludes to Schuhmann. Gaszyński came to me from Aix yesterday; the only person I have received. My door is shut to all musical and literary amateurs. Tell Probst about the change of dedication, as soon as you arrange with Pleyel. Embrace Jasio. Give Grzymała five hundred from the new money, and let him send me the remaining 2500. Don't go to sleep; love me and write. Forgive me if I burden you too much with commissions, but I honestly believe that you willingly do what I ask of you.

Your

CH.

106.

To WOJCIECH GRZYMAŁA.
Marseilles, 27 March [*1839*].

MY DEAR!

I am much better, and can thank you more vigorously for sending the money. You know, I wonder at your goodwill; but also you have in me a grateful man at heart, though not on the outside. You are so kind as to accept my furniture; please pay for the moving. I venture to ask this last, because I know it won't be a large sum. As for what is happening to my income, the Lord defend me! That idiot Pl[eyel] has made mincemeat [1] of my affairs; but it's difficult; you can't knock a wall down with your head.

We shall meet in the summer, and I will tell you how glad of it I am. My lady has just finished a magnificent article on Goethe, Byron and Mickiewicz. One must read it; it gladdens the heart. I can see you, how pleased you will be. And all so true, so large in perception, on so huge a scale, of necessity, without manipulation or panegyrics. Let me know who translates

[1] *Bigoš*; a Polish national dish.

it. If Mic[kiewicz] himself should care to put his hand to it, she would gladly revise it; and what she has written could be printed as a *discours préliminaire*, together with the translation. Everyone would read it, and one could get rid of many cop[ies]. She will write about it to you or to Mick[iewicz].

And what is yourself doing? May God give you good humour, health and strength; those are such necessary things. What do you say about Nourrit? It astonished us very much. We often take you for a walk. You wouldn't believe how happy we are in your company. Marseilles is ugly: an old, but not ancient place; it bores us rather. Next month we shall probably go to Avignon, and from there to Nohant. There, no doubt, we shall embrace you, not by letter, but whiskers and all, if your whiskers have not gone the way of my *favoris*.

Kiss — not your — hands and feet. To you I sign myself, with undying highest sentiments:

A real Camaldolite

CH.

107.

[In French]

To M. ERNEST CANUT IN PALMA.
Marseilles, 28 March 1839.

DEAR SIR!

More than a month ago I received from Pleyel a letter about the piano. I have put off answering in the hope of hearing some news from you, and have only now replied to him that you have acquired the instrument for twelve hundred francs.

As my health is quite restored, I am leaving Marseilles at once; and, as I do not go directly to Paris, I feel obliged to ask you, in order to avoid delay, to be so kind as to send the payment to Paris, to M. C. Pleyel and Co., rue de Rochechouard, No. 20, who have been notified.

Please accept the assurance of my distinguished regard.

F. CHOPIN

108.

To WOJCIECH GRZYMAŁA.
Marseilles, 12 April 1839.

MY DEAR!

Mar[liani] wrote to us that you are still unwell and that your bloodletting did not help you much. We supposed here that you were quite well again, as it appeared from your yesterday's letter; and today such a disappointment! Mar[liani] writes in the same letter that my mother is said to be coming to Paris, being frightened about me. I can scarcely believe it; however, I am writing a letter to my people (which please be kind enough to send to the post), to reassure them. It will be the third from Marseilles. If you have heard anything of this, write me a line. For my mother to leave my father would need something altogether extraordinary. He is out of health and needs her more than ever, I could not understand such a separation. My Angel is finishing a new novel: Gabriel. Today she is writing in bed all day. You know, you would love her even more if you knew her as I know her today. I can imagine how annoying it must be to you if you are not allowed out. Why can't I be here and with you at the same time! How I would look after you! I have been taught how to look after people! And you would enjoy being looked after by me, for you know my feeling towards you. I have never been of any use to you, but perhaps I should be able to nurse you now. It seems that our Genoa project is now changed. Probably we can meet and embrace about the middle of May, on her estate. May Heaven give you a quick recovery. I kiss the hands of you know whom.

Your

FRYC

[*Postscript by George Sand; then another by Chopin:*] Send my letter by the Bourse post. That always arrives.

109.

To JULJAN FONTANA.
[*Marseilles, 25 April 1839.*]

MY DEAR.

I have received your letter with details about the house-moving. I cannot thank you enough for your really friendly help. The details interested me greatly, but I am angry because you complain and because Jasio is spitting blood. Yesterday I played the organ for Nourrit,[1] so I am better. I also sometimes play for myself, but have not yet begun to sing and dance. The news about my mother would be pleasant enough, but if it comes from Plat[er] it's a lie. The warm weather has really begun here and I shall doubtless leave Marseilles in May. But I shall remain in the south for some time yet, before seeing you all. We shall not hear anything of Antek in a hurry. Why would he write? Only to pay his debts; and that is not the custom in Poland. That is why Raciborski thinks so highly of you, that you have no Polish habits; n.b. you know, not those Polish habits that you know and that I understand. So you live at No. 26. Are you comfortable? On which floor and what do you pay? I am beginning to be interested in places near Paris, for I shall have to think of a lodging; but that is not till I come. Is Grzymała well? I wrote to him lately. From Pleyel I have had only the letter that he wrote through you a month or more ago. Write under the same name, but Rue et Hôtel Beauveau. Perhaps you don't understand about my playing for Nourrit. His body was escorted and goes to Paris. There was a funeral mass, and the family asked me to play, so I played during the elevation. Did Wieck play my étude well? Why could she not choose something better than just the least interesting of the études, — at least for those who do not know that it is on the black keys?[2] She had better have sat quiet. Otherwise I have nothing to write you, except to wish you happiness. Keep my manuscripts so that they may not chance to appear in print before

[1] For the funeral of the French tenor Nourrit.
[2] 5th Étude, in G flat major.

they are given. If the preludes are printed, it's a trick of Probst's. But[1] . . . All that when I come back; then we shan't be pratzi-pratzu.[2] Germans, Jews, rascals, scoundrels, offal, dog-hangers, etc., etc. In short, you can finish the litany, for you know them now as well as I do.

Your

CH.

Thursday, 25 inst. 1839.

Embrace Jasio and Grzymała if you see them.

110.

To WOJCIECH GRZYMAŁA.

[*Nohant*] *2 June 1839.*

MY DEAR!

Here we are after a week's travelling. We arrived very comfortably. The village is beautiful: nightingales, skylarks; you are the only missing Bird. I hope it won't be the same way this year as two years ago. If only for a few minutes! Choose a moment when we are all well, and run down for a few days; take pity on a fellow creature. Let us just embrace you, and in return I'll give you pills and first-class milk. My pianoforte shall be at your service, and you shall lack nothing.

Your

FRYC

Please have my letter posted at the Bourse. Write us a line, and if you have a letter from my folk, send it by Jasio.

[Postscript by George Sand.]

[1] Asterisks substituted for words by Hoesick.

[2] "*bras dessus, bras dessous*": arm in arm; French as pronounced by German Jews. [Op.]

111.

To the Same.
Nohant, Monday [1839].

MY DEAR.

How are you? We here gather from your silence these last days, that nothing has gone wrong with you and that we shall soon embrace you. Please ask to have the letter to my folk posted. It's difficult for you, for I think Jasio is already in the country. Don't forget the thing I asked of you; and besides that, bring the packet with the silver, which Mme Marliani was to entrust to you or to Arago.[1]

Don't curse us, for we bless you; and give me an honest Polish kiss.

Your
F. CH.

[Postscript by George Sand.]

112.

To the Same.
[*Nohant, 8 July 1839.*]

MY LIFE!

So: the post to Chateauroux; you arrive there the following afternoon. From there 2½ hours by the diligence that goes to La Châtre; you get out by this garden, round which the road goes. You give us a hearty hug, sit down at the table etc., etc. I know it's hard for you to leave Paris, and however much I want to see and rejoice in you I don't venture to insist; but the Lady of the House begins to feel sad, and really worries that she can't see you. Promises are pretties; [2] and I wouldn't be surprised [if they are not kept]; all the same, perhaps you will do a kind

[1] Dominique-François Arago: 1786–1853.
[2] *Obiecanka cacanka*; a nursery phrase.

deed, and come to see us. Mme d'Agoult's bed is waiting for you, if you prefer that, as well as two hearts which watch for you and watch, like a kite for rain.

I am not well, and she is ailing; perhaps you will restore us by your presence. The weather is good. Really, come off in the morning, and the next day you will be with us.

I embrace you heartily. Kiss her hands.

Your
F. CH.

Tell Jasio to give you 2 or 3 pairs of my boots from those left in the big wardrobe. Hearty thanks to you.

[Postscript by George Sand,[1] then another postscript in Chopin's hand:]

She won't let me read what she has written to you. C'est une indignité!!!!

113.

To the Same.
[*Undated; Nohant, 1839.*]

MY DEAR.

The end of the month approaches, and so does your visit. We are as happy as children. Don't forget my shoes. Also tell Fontana to give you the Weber booklet of *Pièces faciles* for 4 hands. I strain my ears for your coming. Love us, kiss her hands, and take a kiss for yourself from me.

Your
FRYC

If Fontana can't find it among my music, never mind.

[Postscript by George Sand; then, in Chopin's hand:]

Have the letter to the painter posted, and persuade Arago to come with you.

[1] In this postscript, George Sand tells Grzymała that she is afraid Chopin is bored at Nohant, being unused to solitude and the simple life; that she is prepared to make any sacrifice rather than see him devoured by melancholy. She asks G. to come without fail, and to observe Chopin's real state of mind.

114.

To JULJAN FONTANA.
[*Nohant*] *Thursday* [*August 1839*].

MY DEAR!

Thanks for the letter to Mr. Chopine. It begins: " Wiatrowo, near Węgrowec," and ends: " For you, as for the great master of Music and Composition, Alexander Moszczeński, Starosta [1] of Brzesk." In the middle: " as a music-lover of 80 years old, I send you these two ancient mazurkas which resemble the themes of your variations." The mazurkas, as you may suppose, are respectable: — " ram didiridi, ram didiridi, ram didiridi, rajda "; in a postscript: " My granddaughter Alaxandrina " (as I love you, like that: Alaxandrina) " la ci darem in Gniezno [Gnesen] has played to the satisfaction of the Public at a benefit concert for emigrants. I, my sons, grandsons, granddaughters and particularly Alaxandrina plays on the pianoforte well, with great quickness. Wiatrowo near Węgrowec! " Some good old boy of the old Polish starostas (probably the sort that . . . from the bridge). The best thing in the letter is your address on the envelope, which I had forgotten, and without which I don't know whether I could have answered you so soon; and the worst is the death of Albrecht. You want to know when I am coming back? When the bad weather begins; I need fresh air. Jasio is gone; I don't know whether I asked you, if by any chance a letter from my parents should have come to his address in his absence, to send it on to me. Perhaps you thought of it, perhaps not; in any case, if a letter did come, I don't want it to be lost. But I had a letter from home lately, so they won't be writing just yet, and meanwhile, perhaps, the dear fellow may come home cured. Here I am writing a Sonata in B flat minor, containing the march that you know. There is an allegro, then a Scherzo E flat minor, the march and a short finale, perhaps 3 of my pages; the left hand in unison with the right, gossiping after the march. I have a new nocturne,

[1] Elder or head man of a village community.

G major, which will go together with the G minor, if you remember:

You know that I have 4 new mazurkas: one c minor, from Palma, 3 written here, b major, d flat major and c sharp minor; they seem to me good, as is always the case with younger children, when the parents are growing old. Having nothing to do, I am correcting the Paris edition of Bach; not only the engraver's mistakes, but also the mistakes hallowed by those who are supposed to understand Bach (I have no pretensions to understand better, but I do think that sometimes I can guess). There, you see, I have boasted to you. Now, if Grzym. comes (which has been foretold by the cards), send me the 4-hand Weber. If you have it; and if not, then my last Ballade in manuscript, for I want to look at something. Also your copy of the last mazurkas (if you have them, for I don't know whether my politeness went the length of not forgetting about it). Also tell me whether you took a waltz from me to Mlle Eichthal (if not, it doesn't matter). Pleyel wrote to me that you are very *obligeant*, that you corrected the Preludes. You don't know what Wessel gave him for them (write me what he wrote to you before; it's well to know, for the future); also whether Probst has gone (probably); and when he comes back, if you know. My father writes to me that my old sonata has been issued by Haslinger and that the Germans are praising it. I have now, counting yours, 6 manuscripts; they shall eat the devil before they shall get them for nothing. Pleyel has done me a bad turn with his self-sacrifice, for I have hurt the feelings of the Jew Schlesing[er]. But I hope it will be put right somehow.

I love you always. Write.

Your
FRYC

A propos of what you wrote me about Kalkbrenner, I wrote asking Pleyel to let me know whether he had been paid for the Palma piano; I didn't write about anything else, as you can see; I wrote because the French consul in Majorca, whom I know well, is to be changed, and if he had not been paid, the further negotiations would have been more difficult for me. Luckily he has been well and completely paid, as he wrote to me last week before leaving Belgium. I am not astonished at the various fables; you see, I knew that I was exposing myself to them. But all that will pass, and our tongues will rot, and our souls be unhurt. Don't forget my boots. Send 3 or 4 pairs by Grz[ymała], even if they are old; they will do excellently for morning wear in the country. Write me about yourself, as freely as I write to you. Tell me how you are housed. Do you eat at a club? etc. Wojciechowski writes, asking me to compose an Oratorio. I have answered, in a letter to my parents, why does he start a sugar refinery, instead of a Camaldolite or Dominican monastery? The good Tytus still has the imagination of his school days, which does not prevent my still being as fond of him as at school. He has a boy, the second, who is to be called after me. I'm sorry for him.

115.

To WOJCIECH GRZYMAŁA.
[*Nohant, 20 September 1839.*]

MY DEAR.

Please take a small apartment, or, if it is too late for that, a large one; so long as you get something. As for her apartment, she thinks it is too dear, and cannot be persuaded that it is better to pay more, rather than have a lot of lodgers in the house. Please don't go beyond her instructions; communicate with Bignas, so as not to have sole responsibility.

I embrace you heartily;
Please love me, without fail.

Your
F.C.

I kiss her hands.

[A long postscript from George Sand, with details about lodgings for herself and for Chopin, to whom she refers as: "ton petit." [1] The apartment is to have south windows, and not to be too small, though he is trying to economize.]

116.

To JULJAN FONTANA.
[*Nohant*] *Saturday* [*Postmark: 21 September 1839*].

MY DEAR.

Take the apartment rue Tronchet, 5, only see Grzym[ała]; he may have taken something at the Embassy since my last letter. From your description I like it very much. If it is gone, give the preference to *rue Lafitte*, in spite of the stairs, which do not worry me. I should be sorry if some lodging had been already taken for me at the Embassy, and the Tronchet were free; I would rather lose something than sit in a hole the winter through, with something better available. I would rather have even Lafitte. I embrace you. Do your best. When I see you, I will give you a hug for all your good deeds for me. You're a good fellow, and that's enough. I love you as of old, and I hug Jasio and Grzymała.

Your

C.

More haste and write, my life.

[1] Your little one.

117.

To the Same.
[*On note paper with the initials G.S.*]
Wednesday [*Nohant. Postmark: La Châtre, 26 September 1839.*]

MY LIFE.

Many thanks for your good — not angelic but Polish — soul. Choose a paper like my old *tourterelle*[1] one, for both rooms; but varnished and shiny, with a narrow dark green stripe for a border. For the vestibule something different, but good. If, however, there are any prettier and more fashionable papers, which you like and know that I shall also like, take them. I prefer them smooth, very plain and clean looking, rather than the common *épicier* type. That is why I like pearl colour; it is neither glaring nor common-looking. Thanks for the servant's room; it is very necessary. Now about furniture; it would be a splendid thing if you can manage it. As I love you, I did not dare to bother you about it, but since you are so kind, choose it and put it in. I will ask Grzym. to find the money for the moving; I will write about it myself. As for the bed and bureau, they will have to go to some furniture-polisher to be scoured. You can take the papers out of the bureau, and lock them up somewhere else. I don't need to tell you how to manage. Do whatever you like and think necessary. Whatever you do will be right. You have my fullest confidence. That's one thing; now the second: you ought to write to Wessel. (You did write about the preludes, did you not?) Write to him that I have 6 new manuscripts, for which I ask that he should pay me, now, 300 francs each (how many pounds is that?). Write, and get an answer. (If you think he won't give it, write to me first.) Also write to me, whether Probst is in Paris. Also look round for a manservant. Perhaps you can find some decent, honest Pole? Tell Grzymała about it. Let him find his own food; not more than 80. I shall be in Paris at the end of October, not before.

[1] turtle-dove.

Keep that to yourself. Oh, the spring mattress of my bed needs repairing; not if it would be expensive. Have the chairs and everything well beaten. I don't need to tell you, for you know yourself. Embrace Jasio. My Life, I sometimes worry — I hope God will give him what he needs. But I hope he won't be cheated; though, on the other hand — fiddle faddle, cuckoo. That's the greatest truth in the world! And as long as that is as it is, I shall always love you, as one honest man, and Jasio, as another. I embrace you both. Write soon.

Your
old Ch. with a longer nose than ever.

118.

To Wojciech Grzymała.
Sunday [*Nohant, 29 September 1839*].

My Life!

She is ill in bed; a stomach upset all night. She has just received a second letter; her play is accepted.[1] Buloz writes that he expects her about October 15th. But you write nothing about a lodging for her! She worries about it, and thinks you have so many occupations of your own that you have forgotten about her apartment. If Fontana can be helpful to you, either for the running about or by replacing you, make use of him. He is willing to do anything for me, and a very efficient Englishman at business. He's a good fellow; he has already found me a den. He is attending to my household stuff, and all I need ask of you is to pay the *voiture* for the moving. I'm sorry for your pocket; but it can't be helped, unless you want me to walk the streets, my first days in Paris. She is not writing to you; even an urgent letter to Bignas about the actors was written for her by Rollinat. The infernal tomatoes have made her ill. Your protégé has been here, and the furniture is insured for

[1] The drama: *Cosima*, accepted by the Comédie Française.

30,000. For heaven's sake, a lodging; and for heaven's sake don't curse my importunity. You are probably in the country with your better half. Kiss her hands, from a truly attached *spitz.* Embrace yourself too, and everybody all round.

Yours till death

F. CH.

119.

To JULJAN FONTANA.

Sunday [*Nohant. Postmark: La Châtre. 1 Oct. 1839*].

My Dear, thank you for everything. You have no doubt finished with the superintendent. Have the grey curtains, that were in my study by the piano, hung in the vestibule; and in the bedroom the ones that were in the bedroom before, only underneath them hang the pale muslin ones that were under the grey ones. I should like to have the wardrobe in the bedroom, if there is a good place for it, unless the living-room looks too bare between the windows. If the red sofa that stood in the dining-room can have white covers made of the same stuff as the chairs, it could be put in the drawing-room. But that will doubtless be difficult, as it would mean finding an *ouvrière* [1] or *tapisseur* [2] who would wait till I arrive. Think it over and let me know. I am glad Domeradzki is getting married, for after the wedding he will probably give back my 80 francs. I wish Podczaski would marry too, and that Nakw[aska] would get a husband and Antoś a wife. Let that remain between you and me and this paper. Find me a manservant, and embrace Mme Leo (you will probably prefer the first commission, so if you carry it out, I will release you from the second). Write me about Probst; has he come? Don't forget Wessel. Tell Gutmann that I was glad he asked after me. If Moscheles is in Paris, order him an enema prepared by Cellini [3] from Neukomm's oratorios

[1] workwoman.

[2] upholsterer.

[3] Perhaps a reference to the "Benvenuto Cellini" overture of Berlioz, whose music Chopin disliked. [Op.]

and Doehler's concerto. He will certainly go to the *garderobe* and produce some sort of Valentine! A savage idea, but you will admit its originality! You can give Jasio for lunch, from me, a sphinx's beard and a parrot's kidneys in tomato sauce sprinkled with eggs from the microscopic world. And you yourself can take a bath in an infusion of whales, to restore you after all my commissions; I give them to you because I know that you willingly do for me as much as your time permits; and I'll gladly do the same for you when you marry. About that I suppose I shall soon hear from Jasio. But don't marry Ożarowska, because she's reserved for me. Puff at Pani Plater from me, and sneeze at Panna Pauline.

Your

CH.

See Grzymała and arrange about the moving. I wrote to him that he, poor fellow, will have to pay the *voiture*. Thumb your nose at Osławski, and deafen the muddled young Niemcewicz with Orda.[1]

Don't mention that to anyone; it's a secret. Answer quickly.

120.

To the Same.

[*Nohant. Postmark: La Châtre, 4 Oct. 1839.*]

MY DEAR.

In 5, 6, or 7 days I shall be in Paris; and, for your head, for your neck, let me have paper and a bed, if not the rest. Have pity on me and see that it's done. I must hasten my journey, for George's presence is needed for His art; but this between ourselves. We decided today to travel the day after tomorrow; count two or three days for stopping over on the way; this is Thursday, so on Wednesday or Thursday next we shall meet.

[1] Napoleon Orda, 1807–1883; Polish composer and pianist. In 1838 he brought out in Paris an album of Polish compositions.

Besides the various commissions that I have given you, especially in my last letter (the commission about her lodging, which shall be taken off your shoulders when we arrive, but till then for heaven's sake do your best) —besides all that, I forgot to ask you to order a hat for me from my Dupont in your street. He has my measure, and knows how light I need them. Let him give me this year's fashion, not exaggerated; I don't know how you dress now. Also go in, as you pass, to Dautremont, my tailor on the boulevard, and tell him to make me a pair of grey trousers at once. You can choose the shade of dark grey; winter trousers, good quality, without belt, smooth and stretchy. You're an Englishman, you know what I want. He will be pleased to hear that I am coming. Also a plain black velvet waistcoat, but with a tiny inconspicuous pattern, something very quiet and elegant. If he has nothing suitable, then a black stuff one, good and plain. I rely on you. Not very open; that's all. A manservant, if you can; and if you can, get one cheaper than 80 francs, for I have plunged too far; but if you have already got him, it's all right. I would rather pay 60. My dear Beloved, forgive me once more for bothering you, but I can't help it. In a few days we shall meet, and I shall embrace you for everything. I beg you in God's name, don't mention to Polonia that I am coming so soon, nor to the Jewess (Mme Leo); because for the first few days, perhaps, I shall be in Paris only for you, Grzym[ała] and Jasio. Embrace Jasio and Grzym. I'll write till the last day. I count on finding the apartment.

Your

CH.

Write to me all the time, 3 times a day, if you like, whether you have anything to say or not. I will write again before starting. I await a letter from you. The hat at once, so that it comes in a few days, and order the trousers at once, my Juliś.

121.

To the Same.
[*Nohant*] *4 October* [*1839*].

MY DEAR,

You are a priceless creature. The apartment sounds splendid; only why is it so cheap? Isn't there some very unpleasant *but?* I beg you for God's sake, don't lose time; go to M. Mardelle, *rue de Harpe* No. 89, but at once; find out from him whether he has perhaps found something still better; if not, take him with you (he knows about you), go together, take Grzymała too if you can, and clinch it. N.B. It is essential that it should not face north; weigh *les conditions* that I gave you in my last letter. If the apartment has *la majorité,* take it. Once more, is it all right, does it not smell bad, or is it not dirty, or are there not so many neighbours that you can't go to the privy alone? Is there not a cornet *à piston* in the house, or some such thing? Write by the outgoing courier, even if you accomplish nothing. Make a plan of the apartment. My comrade had a good presentiment that you would find something; and I like what you write of it, but for heaven's sake is it all right? Remember that for her it can't be just anyhow. Think it all over, and make haste. The contract for a year; or, if not, for 3 years at the outside. Arrange it, and God be with you. Love me, and follow your own intuition. Think it over, and decide.

Your

CH.

Is the apartment like anybody's? Has Mardelle not a better one? But don't let him influence your judgment.

122.

To the Same.

[*Undated. Nohant, October 1839.*]

MY DEAR.

From your description and Grzymała's, you must have found such an excellent apartment that we think you have a lucky hand; and therefore the man (he is a great man, for he is the porter of George's house) who will run about to look for an apartment for her, has orders, when he has found several, to go to you, so that you, with your elegant taste (you see how I praise you) can also look at what he has found and give your opinion. What is specially important for her is that it should be as private as possible: a small *hôtel*[1] for instance. Either in a courtyard, or adjoining a garden; or, if there is no garden, a large court. N.B. not many tenants; elegant, not higher than the second floor. If there is a small *corps de logi* [*sic*][2] or something in the style of the Perthuis,[3] but smaller; or, if it's on the street, then not a noisy street. In short, something really good, for her. If it is near to me, so much the better, but if not, that consideration need not deter you. I think there must be such small hôtels, in the new streets near the rue *Clichy, Blanche,* or *Nôtre Dame de Lorette,* etc., towards the *rue des Martyrs.* For the rest, I send you a list of streets, in which M. Mardelle (porter of the *Hôtel de Narbonne, rue de la Harpe,* No. 89, which belongs to George) will search for rooms. If you could look about in our quarter as well, in your leisure hours, it would be excellent. Imagine, we both feel sure, I don't know why, that you will find something splendid, late as it is. Her price is 2000–2500, even a few hundred francs more if necessary, if there were anything *splendid.* Grzym. and Arago have promised to try, but for all Grzymała's efforts nothing good has yet been found. I wrote to Grzym. and asked him to make use of you in this affair for me, my Life. (I say for me, because it is as if for me.) I will write to him again today, telling him to ask your help and that you should employ your

[1] Detached private house of aristocratic family.

[2] *corps de logis:* an auxiliary building, detached from the main structure.

[3] Hôtel of the de Perthuis family.

smell-out-itis[1] for me. She wants: 3 bedrooms, two of them together and the third shut off, for instance by the salon; next to the third one a light study for her. The other two bedrooms can be small; even the third not very large; then a salon, in proportion, and a dining-room. A fairly large kitchen, 2 rooms for servants and a cellar. Parquet floors of course, fresh, and if possible needing no repairs. But a small private house would be the best, or a separate wing in a courtyard, looking on to a garden. It must be quiet, private, no smithy near, no girls, etc., etc. You understand perfectly. Good stairs. Well exposed to sunlight, facing south (almost essential *exposé au midi*). Once more: it must (absolutely) have a 3rd bedroom, with a study, adjoining it and shut off from the other 2 bedrooms. And if possible, that bedroom or the study should have a separate entrance (this is not essential). No bad smells. Fairly high. No smoke; light, as attractive as possible; that is to say: a pleasant outlook, to a garden or a large courtyard; garden by preference. There are many gardens in the faubourg St. G[ermain]; also in the faubourg St. Honoré. Find it like lightning, by inspiration; something splendid, and near to me, in those new streets; and as soon as you have it, let me know at once. Don't dawdle — Or get hold of Grz., take him along with you; look, engage it, *et que celà finisse.*[2] I send you a list of streets and a stupid example of an apartment. If you find anything, and write, draw a plan; only if it's something good. But there won't be time to write, so you had better engage it, rather than lose it by being too late. I am writing to Grz. too, and to M. Mardelle (he's a decent man and not a fool; he wasn't always a porter); he has instructions to come to you if he finds anything. You search, on your side; and let it remain between ourselves. I embrace you. Jasio *ditto.* You will have our genuine gratitude if you find anything.

F. Ch.

So, if you find anything and have to sign the contract, don't take it for more than 3 years, if you can't get it for less. You know, she is quite convinced that you will find it.

[1] *wąchalitis:* a nonsense word, from *wąchać*, to smell out.
[2] and let that finish it.

Tuesday.

[According to Hoesick, Chopin added to this letter a separate card with the "stupid example," on which George Sand wrote in pencil a whole list of streets; among others rue Neuve St. George, rue de Londres, rue St. Lazare, rue de Clichy, rue Blanche, rue Pigalle, rue de la Tour d'Auvergne, rue Labruyère, rue Neuve Bréda et rue Bréda, rue Navarin, etc. — 32 in all. To this list Chopin added: Nôtre Dame de Lorette; under "rue de Clichy" he added and underlined: "On the best side." In the margin, against a list of streets from the rue Tronchet to the rue St. Florentin, he adds: "or faubourg St. Honoré"; against another set of streets, from the rue de l'Université to the rue St. Dominique, he adds: "faubourg St. Germain."

George Sand adds to the first set of streets: "On the best side. Perhaps you may hear of something. N.B. Engage from October, that is from now. I beg you, in God's name, be diligent about it, my dear."
Overleaf:

"All to be small, and if possible a whole house.

2 bedrooms; apart from them:
1 bedroom and study
Salon (small)
Dining-room
Kitchen (fairly large)
2 Servant's rooms
Cellar and Garden

For instance:

Street, or preferably garden.

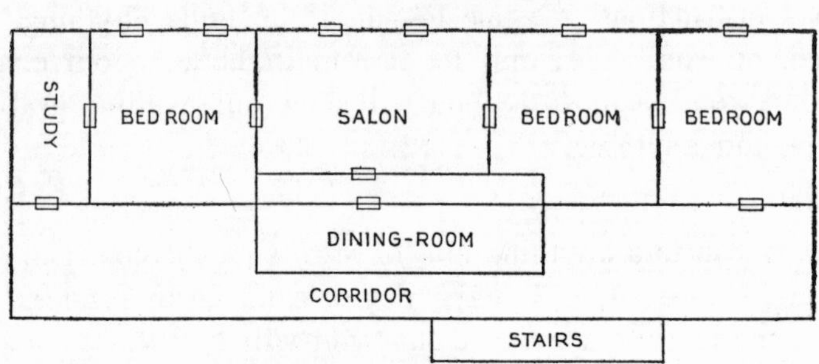

pas de voisinage; surtout[1] no smithy or anything of that sort."]

[1] No neighbours, especially.

123.

To Wojoiech Grzymała.
[*Nohant, 8 October 1839.*]

My Dear!

We leave here Thursday morning without fail. The post horses are engaged, and on Friday about 5 we reach Paris. Go round to the messenger (M. Marliani). I have written to Juljan, dear fellow, that he should wait for me in my lodging. Thank you a million times for your today's letter, which explained things for her and decided her to choose the apartment in the rue Pigalle. She will write you a line.

I embrace you, and kiss her hands.

Your
Ch.

124.

To Juljan Fontana.
Monday [*Nohant. Postmark: 9 Oct. 1839*].

You are priceless!

T A K E Pigalle, both houses, don't stop to ask. Hurry. Bargain if you can (taking both together), but if not, then take them for 2,500, and don't let it go, for it seems to us admirable; just splendid. She regards you as the best and most logical — and I add the most splenetic-angelic-Polish-souled of beloved friends.

Your
F. Ch.

We start for certain in three days. Embrace Jasio and Grzyma.

125.

To the Same.
[*Nohant, apparently Tuesday, 10 October 1839.*]

MY LIFE.

The day after tomorrow, Thursday, we start at 5 in the morning, and at 3, four, or at latest 5, we will be at rue Tronchet No. 5. Please tell the people. I have written to Jasio today, to engage that servant for me and to tell him to wait for me from noon, in the rue Tronchet apartment. If you have time to run in about then, we can have the first embrace. You are a *brick*. Once more, my sincerest thanks and those of my comrade, for Pigalle. Now I beg you, as I am short of trousers, ask the tailor to be sure to have the grey ones that you ordered for me (and the waistcoat if possible) ready on Friday morning, so that I can change as soon as I arrive. Also tell him to bring them to the Tronchet and give them to Tineau (the valet), who no doubt will be already there. (The valet is called Tineau!!) The same with the hat from Dupont; and in return I will alter the second half of the Polonaise for you till I die; [1] perhaps yesterday's version won't please you either, though I cudgelled my brains over it for about 80 seconds. I have my manuscripts in order, properly annotated. There are six of them with your polonaises, not counting the 7th, an Impromptu,[2] which perhaps is poor; I don't know yet, it's too new (yes!). But I hope it's good; not like Orda's [3] or Zimmermann's or Karsko-Koń's, or Sowiński's,[4] or a pig's, or some other animal's; because, by my reckoning, it ought to bring me at least 800 francs. Well, we'll see later. And, my dear, as you are so efficient a person, command that no black thoughts and choking cough shall come to me in the new lodging; wish that I may be kind, and wipe out for me, if you can, any past episodes. It

[1] Fontana had asked to have an alteration made in the middle section of the A major Polonaise, which is dedicated to him. [Op.]

[2] 2nd Impromptu: F sharp minor.

[3] Or: "Orłowski's"?

[4] Puns on names: *Koń:* a horse; *Sowiński,* by elision, becomes *Swiński* piggish, swinish.

would be good if I could still have a few years of big, completed work. You will place me under a big obligation if you can do that, and also if you yourself grow younger; or else if you can bring it about that we are not born.

Your
OLD ONE

126.

To the Same.
[*Nohant*] *Thursday.*

MY DEAR:

I send you 3 letters; 2 from Mme Marliani, the 3rd from Marliani himself. The letter to M. Salucas is very good. There is a daughter there, whom they advise to profit by you. I expected a letter from Aguado [?] to M. Balguerie [?] but it has not come. The latter is a very rich local man. When it comes, I'll send it straight on. May God give you good luck.[1]

Your
CH.

Write.

127.

[In French]

To MESSRS. BREITKOPF AND HÄRTEL IN LEIPSIC.

GENTLEMEN!

I have always had cause to be satisfied in my dealings with you; and feel that before severing our relations I owe you a direct explanation. M. Probst, through whose intermediary my affairs with you have been conducted, has just told me that he has written to you about my last manuscripts, and that, having received no reply, he believes himself authorized to refuse me the price of 500 francs each. It is a price below which I would give

[1] The reference is to Fontana's journey to Bordeaux. [Op.]

up nothing. I have in my portfolio a long Sonata, a Scherzo, a Ballade, two Polonaises, 4 mazurkas, 2 Nocturnes, an Impromptu. Be so kind, Gentlemen, as to reply by return courier how matters stand, in order that I may be able to come to a direct understanding with you.

Yours truly,
F. CHOPIN

rue Tronchet, No. 5, Paris. 14 Dec. 1839.

128.

To JULJAN FONTANA IN BORDEAUX.

I send you a letter from Wessel, doubtless about my old business. Troupenas has bought my 7 compositions, and will conduct business with Wessel direct, so don't you bother. What are you doing? How are you getting on? I cough, and do nothing. Liszt has arrived; he is going to London. Albrecht and Perthuis are well. We had the Easter festival in the club. Wodzyński is still dirty as to the body and clean as to the soul. I love you, but you know that I don't know how to write. Write if you have time. I hope all is well with you.

Your
CH.

Paris 23 inst. [*April 1840.*]

129.

[In French]

To MME OURY [1] IN PARIS.

DEAR MADAM,

How I thank you for your charming letter. You would have received a reply accompanied by a manuscript for Mr. Beale,

[1] Famous French pianist; 1806–1880.

if I had not promised my new compositions to Mr. Wessel. As for the little waltz which I had the pleasure of writing for you, I beg you to keep it for yourself. I do not wish it to be published.

But what I should like is to hear it played by you, dear Madam, and to attend one of your elegant reunions, at which you so marvellously interpret such great authors as Mozart, Beethoven, and Hummel, the masters of all of us. The Hummel Adagio which I heard you play a few years ago in Paris at M. Erard's still sounds in my ears; and I assure you that, in spite of the great concerts here, there is little piano music which could make me forget the pleasure of having heard you that evening.

Accept my respectful homage, dear Madam, and be so kind as to give my friendly greetings to M. Oury.

130.

[In French]

To BREITKOPF AND HÄRTEL IN LEIPSIC.

GENTLEMEN,

As Sig. Paccini is publishing a waltz of mine in the " hundred-and-one " on the 30th inst., I think it best to send you a proof. I hope that the publication will encounter no difficulty; the price remaining in proportion to our last agreement.

Accept, if you please, the expression of my distinguished regard.

FR. CHOPIN

Paris, 18 June 1840.

131.

To Jozef Elsner in Warsaw.
Paris, 24 July, 1840.

Dearest Pan Elsner!

I send you a few words from Schlesinger.[1] I won't make philosophical remarks about Jewry; but I must defend him a little, for it is true that great works, such as your Oratorio, cost a lot to publish, and do not sell, because, except the Conservatoire, no other *établissement* performs such things. And the Conservatoire lives on old symphonies which it knows by heart; and the public is lucky if it sometimes gets a chance to hear a bit of Haendel or Bach. Haendel has only just begun to be appreciated last year, and even then only excerpts, not whole works. Thus, last winter a chorus from Judas Maccabeus was performed several times, also a chorus of Bach, I don't know which; but since I have been here, except Beethoven's Jesus on the Mount of Olives, which I have heard only once, no long great work has been given. Many novelties are tried through at the Conservatoire rehearsals; but there is such a spirit here that no one wants to perform any big works except those of the dead. Therefore we shall not hear at present either Mendelsohn [*sic*] or Schneider, or Spohr, or Neukomm, or you; and if Cherubini were not at the head he too would not be played. The Conservatoire sets the tone for greater music; therefore a publisher can count only on what the Conservatoire will bring in. And the Conservatoire has its own copyists. How I regret that I did not hear, in Petersburg, that work of yours which, I am convinced, stands higher than everything of the kind that has been written. You will doubtless have it printed in Germany; and I am convinced that somewhere in Cologne, Munich, Düsseldorf or Leipsic, where there are musical festivals every year, devoted only to such works, — somewhere on the Rhine I shall hear your masterpiece before long. Another coun-

[1] Schlesinger (the publisher) had explained to Chopin in very courteous terms, that he could not publish such a work as an Oratorio, because there was in France no public which would care to buy music of this kind. [Op.]

try where such oratorios are frequently given and which has the necessary respect for such works, where a thousand singers can easily be got together for such a purpose, where Neukomm and Mendelsohn are better known than Adam or Halévy: England, will doubtless jump at your work. Perhaps, some day, in Birmingam [*sic*], in the hall specially built for such things, where a few years ago Neukomm had an enormous organ put: perhaps some day we may admire and rejoice in what now ravishes me even in thought. I await a few words from you, and embrace you from my heart, from my heart.

CHOPIN

My respects to Pani Elsner and Pani Nidecka.

Orłowski is in Rouen, but if he were here, he would add his name. How many times we have thought of you, just *à propos* of the Conservatoire. How many times have we wished to hear, from that mass of skilful violinists, your Offertory: [1] Joseph (if I am not mistaken), in which the violins rush through the richest harmonies. If you have had it printed, please send it to me. I will take it to Habenek, and feel sure that he will have it tried through, as it is short and effective. Write me a few lines, please, please, please.

132.

[In French]

To BREITKOPF AND HÄRTEL IN LEIPSIC.

GENTLEMEN,

Several months ago I received from you a letter in which you were so kind as to offer me your publications as in the past; but it contained no mention of a waltz, published in Paris by Paccini, which I had thought best to send to you some time before.

As I now have several pieces for publication (among others a Concert Allegro, a Fantasia, etc.), I should be glad if,

[1] Probably a slip of the pen.

before entering into negotiations with regard to these new things, you would have the goodness to answer me in a few words about this waltz, and to send me the price of my last compositions.

Awaiting an answer shortly

Yours truly
CHOPIN

5 rue Tronchet, Paris, 4 May 1841.

133.

To JULJAN FONTANA.
[Nohant] 2 July 1841.

MY DEAR.

I send you a letter to Pleyel for Buchholtz, about whom my father wrote in his last letter. I am also writing to Pleyel that I have asked you to call on him about the *loyer*.[1] If it is December with you, it is no better here; last night the wind uprooted enormous trees. But it is St. Médard: that is 40 days end tomorrow, so there is hope for the weather. Talk of the weather, between us!!! My Dear, my old Brother; perhaps I may yet play in the dark for you again some day, as an apology, if you still want to listen to this kind of justification of me. I embrace you most heartily, my good Juljan. Write.

CH.

Tell Jasio to write me a word, the good fellow.

Sunday, in the night.

[1] rent.

134.

To the Same.
[*Postmark: 23 July 1841. Nohant.*]

My Dear!

Please take this letter to Pleyel, and talk to him, to himself. I am writing about a better pianoforte, for mine is not good. Read his letter, and seal it. You can see from it that I am asking you for an answer. Write to me at once when he can have it ready to send off, so that I can arrange things with the messenger from Châteauroux. I doubt his refusing or delaying. But if he should, don't hit him, only write to me. Once more I beg your pardon for the commission; but it's not the last one, don't be afraid.

Your
Ch.

Write.

Wednesday.

135.

To the Same.
[*Undated.*]

My Dear,

I send you a hundred fr. for various expenses. First of all, repay yourself for the charivari; pay the hire (that light), the house porter, the flower woman, who claims for six [bunches?]. Buy me some *bon soin* soap at *Houbigand Chardin's* in the *faub. St. Honoré,* 2 pairs of Swedish gloves (you'll find an old pair in the drawer for a measure), a bottle of patchouli, a bottle of bouquet de Chantilly. In the Palais Royal, in the gallery, on the theatre side, almost in the middle, is a big shop of *galanterie* (as they call it with us); it has two show windows with various little boxes, ornaments and trifles; shining, elegant and expensive.

Ask there whether they have one of those tiny ivory hands, for scratching your head. You must have seen such a toy more than once; a little hand, usually with bent fingers, white, set on a black rod. I think I saw one there; ask, and they will tell you. So find such a toy and send it to me, if it is not more than, for instance, 10, 15, 20 or even 30. Make Pleyel give you a copy of my Preludes, and take all my études from Schl[esinger]. If Suss has Dantan's little bust of me, buy 2 and have them well packed for travelling; if not, please go to Dantan, who lives at St. Lazare, the same place as Alkan (whom you may embrace if you see him), and ask if it is to be had, and where to get it (profit by the same occasion to remind him about my bronze one, which he was to have had cast). In the drawer you will find, at the top, a flat metal flask, sewn up in flannel, to put on the stomach with hot water, also the air cushion that I bought for the journey. Pack them up, and include *Kastner* (or rather, you have an *emballeur* [1] opposite); have them made into a comparatively large parcel, well packed, and send them to me *par Lafitte et Cayard*, address as on letters. Please make haste. The rest of the money you can keep for other parcels. Don't pay Schlesinger, and don't wait for him if he hasn't got Kastner; but send without fail Cherubini's *traité;* I think it's *du contrepoint* [2] (I don't remember the title well). If he won't give you the Cherubini without the money, pay for it, because perhaps Cherubini may have issued it himself, and he may have it only on commission. In a few days I will write to Troupenas through you. I embrace you; the post is just going. Forgive me; but you will have the letter on Sunday. Send on Monday.

CH.

[1] packer.

[2] Cherubini's *Treatise of Counterpoint and Fugue.*

136.

To the Same.
Sunday [*Undated*].

I send you the tarantella. Be kind and copy it; but first go to Schlesinger, or to Troupenas, and look at the Recueil of Rossini's songs, or rather songs edited by him, in which there is a Tarantella (in *la*); I don't know whether it is written in $\frac{6}{8}$ or in $\frac{12}{8}$. People write both ways; but I should like it to be the way Rossini has it. So *if* it's $\frac{12}{8}$ or however it is, with triplets. In copying, make one measure of two. You understand, dear. It will be

I also beg you, instead of repetition signs, write it all out. Be quick, and give it to Leo with my letter to Schubert. You know that he leaves Hamburg before the 8th of the next month, and I don't want to lose 500 fr. As for *Troupenas,* you have time. And if my manuscript is not metrically right, don't give it to him, but copy it out again, and also make a 3rd copy for Wessel. It's a bore for you to copy the beastly thing, but I do hope that it will be a long time before I write anything worse. So, please, look at the number of the *last work;* that is, the number of the last mazurkas, or perhaps the *waltz,* that Paccini brought out, and give the tarantella the next number. I'm not anxious, for I know that you are both willing and efficient. I hope you will never get another letter from me so crammed with commissions as this. If it weren't for my having been obliged to have only one foot in the house before I left, you would not have this nuisance. It's still not the end. Charles forgot the metal hot-water flask sewn up in flannel, to lay on the stomach. It looks like this.

[a drawing]

If you can find it in the drawer, please send it. Also buy me *Witwicki;*[1] I haven't got it. And go to the Palais Royal, the gallery on the theatre side, No. 37 (I think), and buy me a blouse en toile ceru [*ciré?*] for 14 fr.: *blouse de chasse fermé par devant, forme de chemise.*[2] If it's not 37, then 47 or 27.

The shop is like this:

[a drawing with indications: gallery, entrance, corridor, etc.]

He is the only one who has these blouses. I bought one from him a week ago: small mother-of-pearl buttons, well made, two breast-pockets, etc. Never mind it, Dear — I have thought it over. If I need it I'll write to you. So just attend to the tarantella, and give it to Leo. Tell Leo to keep the money he receives, till my return. I beg your forgiveness once more for my importunity. Today I received the letter from my people, that you forwarded. Tell the porter to give all my letters to you. Don't forget me.

Your

CH.

[The last paragraph is crossed out.]

137.

To the Same.

[*Undated.*]

MY DEAR.

Since you are so kind, be kind to the end. Go to the *roulage;*[3] that is: Messrs. *Hamberg* and *Levistal, successors to M. Corret fils ainé et C-nie: Rue des Marais St. Martin, Nr. 51, à Paris,* and ask them to send at once to Pleyel's for the pianoforte, so that it may be sent off the next day. Tell the roulage people that it must go *par un envoyé acceléré et non* ordinaire.[4] It costs

1 *Evenings of a Pilgrim:* Vol. I. [Hoes.]
2 Of oiled cloth; a hunter's blouse, closed in front, shaped like a shirt.
3 transport.
4 by express, not freight.

more, but will be much quicker. The cost will probably be 5 fr. the centner. I will pay here, and you only ask for a receipt, or bill stating how much it weighs, and when it is to leave, and how soon they undertake that it shall arrive in *Châteauroux*. This roulage goes straight to Toulouse, and only drops things on the way; so the address on the *Pleyel piano* must be not *à la Châtre*, but *Mme Dudevant à Châteauroux* (as above). The corresponding firm in Châteauroux knows about it and will send it on to me at once. I need the *bill* only in order to tie down the roulage people; they don't need to send it to me, because it is only in case of needing it if some complaint should arise. The correspondent here in Châteauroux says that *par acceléré* it should arrive in 4 days from Paris. So make them promise to deliver it in Châteauroux in 4 or 5 days. Tell them to address *à Châteauroux* (and tell Pleyel that I will write to thank him in a few days). Take the *revers* for the *acceléré* from Hamberg and Levistal. Make haste and write me a few good words. Now about our business. If Pleyel does not please you and you think Erard would be better, change; but don't do it lightly; satisfy yourself first that Erard will really be more obliging. I don't see why you should be tied to Pleyel if the other is more serviceable; *selon toutes les probabilités* [1] they ought to be courteous to you there. As for the Tarantella, seal the letter and send it to Hamburg.

I am afraid to make this letter too late, so I will write tomorrow about the other matters, Troupenas and so on; for now, I embrace you.

CH.

Thank Antoś for his good wishes. But I will not trouble him with any commissions. Wish him a pleasant journey. Embrace Jasio and tell him to write.

Tell Pleyel I will write to thank him. Address the piano: *Mme Dudevant, à Châteauroux; bureau restant* chez [2] M. Vollant Patureau.

[1] in all probability.
[2] At the office of.

138.

To the Same.
[*Nohant. Postmark: La Châtre, 11 August 1841.*]

My Dear!

Thanks for all your good commissions. Today, the 9th, I received the pianoforte, and the other things two days ago. Don't send my little bust home; they would be frightened; just leave it in the drawer. Embrace Jasio for his letter. I will write him a few words shortly. Tomorrow I shall probably send away my old manservant, who loses his head here. He is an honest fellow and knows his work, but grumbles and upsets the people here. I shall probably send him off and tell him to wait for me in Paris. So if he turns up in your house, don't be scared; the only way to get rid of him is to tell him to wait for me at home, and then in a week or two write to him, either that I am coming back later than I expected, or some other thing, and cross his palm for the journey. Here we have fairly good weather. The man waited 3 days in Châteauroux for the pianoforte; I recalled him yesterday, on receiving your letter. What sort of voice the pianoforte has, I don't know yet, as it is not unpacked. The great event is to be tomorrow. As for inquiries about the roulage, don't bother; it's not worth quarrelling over. You did the best you could; a few drops of one's blood gone sour and a few days wasted on waiting are worth no more than just to blow one's nose as soon as the business is over. So forget both my commission and your trouble. Next time, God willing, it will go better. I am writing these few lines late at night. I thank you once more for all you have done; but it won't be the end, for now we shall have the Troupenas affair on our shoulders. About that I will write you more fully later, but now I wish you goodnight; and don't dream, as Jasio did, that I have died. Just dream that I'm being born, or something like that — Indeed, I am now becoming as meek as a baby in swaddling-clothes; and if somebody wanted to hold me in leading strings I should be quite pleased; N.B.: with a well wadded cap on my noddle, because — I feel it — I should stumble and fall over every minute. Unfortunately what awaits me seems to be not leading strings but a staff, or crutches, if I reach old age at my present pace. I once dreamed that I had died in a hospital; and it stuck so fast in my head that it seems to me like yesterday. If you outlive me, you will know whether to believe in dreams; a few years ago I dreamed of other things, but my dreams did not come true. And now I dream awake; dream and wake up scorched,[1] as they say; which is why I write you such rubbish. Isn't that so? Send me a letter from home soon, and love your old.

CH.

139.

[From French into Polish]

To CAMILLE PLEYEL.
[*Nohant, 1841?*]

MY VERY DEAR FRIEND,

A few days ago I received your pianoforte, for which I thank you most warmly. The instrument arrived in good tune, almost in chamber-concert tune. But I have not yet played on it much, as the weather is so fine that I am out of doors nearly all the time.

I wish you as good weather for your vacation. Write me a few lines (unless you think you have used your pen often enough during the day). I hope you will all keep in health, and I lay my homage at the feet of your Mother and Sister.

Faithfully yours,
F. CHOPIN

[1] *szałki-opałki;* from the words: *szał:* extasy or exaltation, and *opalić się:* to get scorched.

140.

To Juljan Fontana.
[*Undated.*]

My Dear,

My poor man has *really* gone today. He is starting, and will probably reach home; that is, reach you, together with this letter. If he has any things in the house, give them to him, or let him take them. *He is paid right up*, so he can make no claims. But please, I should not like to risk his living in the house. He is friends with the porter, who perhaps would permit it. And, please, I have nothing more to do with him, and don't you take him for any money, for he will cost you more than he is worth. Yesterday I wrote you a letter in the night, and now am writing this second warning that I have *quite, quite* dismissed him. So don't let him manage to stay in the house.

Your
Ch.

141.

To the Same.
[*Nohant. Postmark: 16 August 1841. La Châtre.*]

My Dear.

Thanks for your kind letter. Open any letters that you consider necessary. Don't give the manuscript to Troupenas till Schubert writes the date of publication. No doubt there will soon be an answer through Leo. It's a pity that the Tarantella went to Berlin; for, as you saw from Schubert's letter, Liszt is involved in these money affairs, and I may have unpleasantness about it. He is a touchy Hungarian and ready to think — as I said the manuscript was not to be given up without the money — ready to think that I don't trust him, or something of that sort. I don't know just what, but I have a presentiment that we shall have a pie.[1] Don't tell Leo anything about it, he's ill; go to him

[1] A Polish idiom: "a pretty kettle of fish."

if you have a chance and remember me to him; thank him (though it is for nothing), and apologize for his trouble; it was, after all, a courtesy on his part to undertake the consignment. Also remember me to Pleyel, whom you will see when Portales sends you the domiciliary paper (as you know, you and Pleyel). Tell him to forgive me for not writing to him (don't tell him that he has sent me a very bad pianoforte). Your milkwoman is the *épicier*[1] in the *rue Castellane,* opposite the market. He sells milk every morning. Please post the letter to my parents *yourself,* but only *yourself,* at the bourse before 4. Forgive me for bothering you so much, but you know how much my letters to my people mean to me. *Escudier* will doubtless send you that fine Album. If you like, you can tell Troupenas to tell Escudier from me that he can send you a copy for me; but if you don't want it, don't bother. One more worry: at your leisure, copy that wretched Tarantella once more, to send to Wessel as soon as we know the day. If I worry you so much with this Tarantella, believe me, it is for the last time. I shall probably not send you any manuscript from here. If there is no communication from Schubert within a week, write to me, please, but don't importune Leo about me. In that case you could give the manuscript to Troupenas. But I will write to him about it. Meanwhile I embrace you heartily.

Your

CH.

Write, whenever you have a free moment.

Wednesday, in the night.

142.

To the Same.
[*Undated*] *Friday, in the night.*

MY DEAR.

Well then, I send you a letter to Bonnot; read, seal, and deliver it; and if, in passing through the streets that (you know

[1] grocer.

of old) are possible for me, you should find something suitable, please let me know. The condition about stairs does not exist any more. I send you a letter to Dessauer, which has come to me here, in a letter of Frau Diller, from Austria. Did you send it on? I did not recognize your hand. It came today. Enough about that. Dessauer must be back in Paris by now. Ask Schl.; he is sure to know. Charles has doubtless returned. Don't give Dessauer many details about me; don't even tell him that you are searching for a lodging; not even to Antoś, because he will tell Mlle de Rozières, and she starts gossip and tales about everything, that even come round to me here in the queerest way — You know how easily things grow out of nothing, when they pass through a mouth that smears them all over and makes something else out of them — I don't want to say much; but some of the most innocent things that I have written to you have come *de retro* to me that way. I am not writing to Jaś. but tell him that I will. What you tell me about Poland seems to me ludicrous; may God grant it, but I don't think so. About that unhappy Tarantella, you have doubtless given it to Troupenas (which means Masset); and, if you think well, send it to Wessel by post. Tell him to let you know at once when he receives it (and if Schubert has not answered, write him a word, so that he should let us know at once, and inform Wessel). You [have] to write a lot of letters, but perhaps it amuses you? Here the weather has been beautiful for several days, but as for my music, that's ugly. Mme Viardot was here for 15 days; we didn't do so much of music as of other things. Please write to me; anything you like, but write. I hope Jasio will get well. But, but! Don't forget to put on Troupenas's copy: — *Hamburg, chez Schubert; London, Wessel;* and the same on Wessel's copy. In a few days I will send you a letter to Mechetti in Vienna, to whom I promised something. If you see Dessauer or Schlesinger, ask whether a letter to Vienna ought to be prepaid. I embrace you. Keep well.

143.

To the Same.
[Undated. Postmark: La Châtre, 25 August 1841.]
Tuesday.

My Dear.

I have received your letter, in which you tell me about Troupenas. Thank you. 300 was owing. Also thank you for Albrecht. No doubt you already have my letter to Bonnot. No doubt you already know whether letters to Vienna should be prepaid. But if Dessauer has arrived, consult him, before posting my letter to Mechetti. It's a money matter, so I should not like the letter to get lost somewhere in Austria; for you know how I love writing. Offer him a new manuscript (a kind of polonaise, but it's more a fantasia). That's one thing. Now the next. Go to Roth with the letter, which you can read and seal. He lives in the rue Neuve des Mathurins (close to you), in one of the new houses *near the rue Montblanc.* You know *on the left,* going from you, the house with the fine gate, where you can drive in *sideways,* No. 6 or 10. Now, Doctor Roth lives in the *entresol,* the first vestibule from the gate. If he says he can procure the Tokay for me, find out *at what price* and let me know at once. I will send you the money, and instructions, how to send the Tokay to Marseilles. You are both practical and kind; that is why I load you with commissions. Up till now you have done everything beautifully for me. There is only one thing, in your today's letter, which is really unpleasant for me (but you could not guess that!!); it is: that you gave my little bust to Antek. Not that I mind his having it; not that I need it, or value it (you don't even need to order another from Dantan); but because, if Antoś took it to Poznań, the gossip will start again, and I have had too much of it already. If I did not charge Antoś with any commissions, it was just on that account; for what better opportunity could one have? But, you see, Antoś *did not understand!!!* Perhaps you will understand! It will seem so strange to my Parents, that not they should be the first to have this plaster. They won't believe that I did not give it to him. In Antek's home I hold another place than that of pianist.[1] Certain persons will see it differently. You know them! All this will come *retro* to me with another colour. These are very delicate matters that are better not touched upon. Well, it has happened. I beg you, Dear, don't mention to anyone what I have written here; let it remain between us. If I have not glossed it over, it is because you will understand. Don't reproach yourself about it. Love me, and write. If Antek has not yet started, please leave the matter as it is; it could only be made worse; he would tell Mlle de Roz[ières] all about it, for he is well meaning, but weak! And she is loose-tongued and loves to display her *intimité* with him and to pry into other people's affairs; she would smear it all up and make an ox out of nothing,[2] not for the first time. She is (between ourselves) an insufferable pig, who has dug her way in some queer fashion into my private garden, and is rooting about for truffles among the roses. She is a person to keep away from. Whatever she touches feels her incredible indiscretion. Ask the good Charles how long ago he came to me, and tell him I will willingly give him a testimonial. Say a kind word to him. I'll write to Jasio. Embrace him. Love me.

Your

CH.

144.

To the Same.

[*Undated.*]

MY DEAR.

Thank you for arranging with Roth; but 200 bottles are too much for me. I am sorry you have had the trouble, and I send a testimonial for *Charles,* whose name is Louis. No doubt you

1 He had formerly been engaged to Anton Wodziński's sister, Marja.

2 A proverb; make a mountain out of a molehill.

already have an answer from Hamburg. If you send to Wessel, ask him, at the same time, whether he wants a new Polonaise; the one that I am sending to Vienna. Write me a line, and let me know what Jasio is doing. I will write to him. Tell him to write to me, too. Embrace Albrecht and Leo if you see them, also Alkan.

Your

CH.

Wednesday.

145.

To the Same.
[*Nohant, 13 September 1841.*]

MY DEAR.

I have received all your letters and Dessauer's parcel. Hasslinger is a scoundrel. He wants to print, or rather he has printed, and wants to publish, the things that I gave him for nothing in Vienna 12 years ago. What do you think of that? I shall not answer him, unless I write a *sharp* letter; and if I do send it, I shall leave it unsealed for you to read. As for Dessauer's illusion about Mechetti, the other Viennese publisher, I have had a letter from Fräulein Miller, who tells me that he did not want to give *Mendelson* anything for a thing for that same Album, for which I offered him the Polonaise. Liszt's article on the concert for *Cologne* cathedral greatly amused me. And 15,000 persons, counted, and the president, and the vice-president, and the secretary of the phil[harmonic] society, and that carriage (you know what the cabs there are like), and that harbour, and that steamboat! He will live to be a deputy or perhaps even a king, in Abyssinia or on the Congo; but as for the themes of his compositions, they will repose in the newspapers, together with those two volumes of German poetry. Schlesinger's medal with the Queen's portrait, I swear, is a guinea. As for Antek, I am convinced that his illness is exaggerated. When he wrote to me, it was too late, because his Dame

Partlett[1] at once wrote an emotional, frantic letter to the Lady of the House; that she is going to him; that she is defying the conventions, — those dear conventions! — that his family are worthless, savage barbarians! — that the only exception is Nakw[aska], in whom she has found a friend, and who is giving her the passport of her governess, so that she may rush to save him; that she has to write so briefly (3 full pages), because she does not know whether he is alive; that she expected this after the terrible parting and the nights that he has spent in tears; etc., etc. She needs a cudgel! A cudgel! The old frump! What makes me most furious is that I love Antek, and not only can't help him, but have the appearance of lending a hand in all this. I perceived it too late; and, not seeing what was going on, and not knowing the lady, I recommended this broomstick to Mme Sand as a pianoforte teacher for her daughter. She has wormed her way in, representing herself as the *victim* of her love; and *knowing my past affairs* through Polonia, which she has seen in various situations, she is forcing herself into the *intimité* of Mme S[and] (and you would not believe how cleverly, how sly she is, and how skilfully she has taken advantage of my relations with Antoś). You may imagine, how nice for me; especially since (as you have perhaps observed) Antek does not care for her, except just as a person who contributes for him and costs him nothing. Antoś, with all his good nature, is apathetic, and allows himself to be led by the nose, especially by such a cunning intriguer, who, you may suppose, has an appetite for him. She makes use of him to defend herself, and, *par ricochet*, of me too (which matters less); and, worst of all, of Mme Sand. She thinks that, because Antek and I have been *intimes* from our childhood, we must — [several words crossed out, and dashes inserted.] That's enough, isn't it?! Now to less unsavoury things. I have lost a bet: a Strassburg pie — I send you 50 francs. Please go to Chevet in the Palais Royal, and buy one for 30 fr. It has to be a big one. They come from Strassburg in round wooden boxes. Address to me, and send it by diligence as quickly as possible. If the 30 [fr.] size is small, then give 35 or 40. But let it be a generous

[1] Mlle de Rozières

one. It annoys me to be obliged to spend so much money on a pie, especially when I need it for other things. Give my letter to the German editor. Embrace Jasio. Send me a description of the apartment on the 1st floor, with the *number* and details: are there stairs? Does one have to enter near the stable? Does one have to get tired going in? Is the *lieu*[1] on the street? Is it high? Does it smoke? Is it dark? etc. I should like to be somewhere in the *Montblanc* or *Mathurins*, or on the boulevard near the *Chaussée d'Antin*. Keep out enough from the 50 fr. to continue the Charivari subscription, which, I think, ends in a few days. Write to me soon. Shall we ever get back to our own land!! Have they gone quite mad?! I'm not afraid about Mick[iewicz] and Sob[ański]; they're solid heads, they can stand exile, they won't lose either their senses or their energy. May God repay you for your good friendship. Write, and love an old man, as he loves you, old Englishman.

CH.

Sunday. Tell Jaś to write to me.

I am not sending you the letter to Leipsic today.

146.

To the Same.
[*La Châtre, 15 September 1841.*]
3 in the night; stars.

MY DEAR.

Send this letter to Germany. Post it at the bourse. This morning I received your letter and Fräulein Müller's. She writes to me about the manuscripts for Mechetti. Please describe to me also the apartment in the Place Vendôme. Stairs? Is it an attic? Embrace Albrecht; I'm very sorry for the good fellow. Also write to me, to whom does the next house belong? To Tamburini? Send a large pie. At the end of this month I will send you my own

[1] place.

pies from my own smoky kitchen. The kitchen needs whitewashing, but lime has disappeared from the district. For any other scullion a white kitchen, for me a smoky one. Love me, if you don't find it too hard. I embrace you, my Old Man.

CH.

Tell Jasio a lot about me. I agree with you *à propos* of the apartment, that I had better take the one next door to me. Write, even if you have not decided.
Monday.

147.

To the Same.
[*Undated.*] *Saturday.*

Please read this letter and send it on at once to that fool. Don't send me any pie if there isn't a Strasbourg one. And about the apartment. As the Mathurin one faces due North, I am undecided, and should like a description of that *1st floor in the Tronchet.* You do not say *which No. in the Tronchet.* Let me know, and be prepared to copy the Polonaise for Mechetti. Wessel is a rogue; I will never send him anything more after the: " *Agréments au Salon.*" Perhaps you don't know that he has given that title to my second Impromptu, or one of the Waltzes. Embrace Jasio. I will write to you more fully tonight. Don't waste time on Wessel. Address to him, and write at the top that in case of the absence of Herr Wessel, Mr. Stapelton, or Stapleton, can open it, if you consider that necessary. I embrace you and Jasio. Clearly, I was not born to make money.

CH.

Mick[iewicz] will come to a bad end, unless he was having a joke with you all.

148.

To the Same.
[*Undated.*]

My Dear.

What you have done is well done. It's a wonderful world! Masset is a scoundrel, and Pelletan another. Masset knew about the Paccini Waltz, and that I had promised it to the Gazette. I did not want to take one step without first referring to him. If he won't accept for 600, with London (his price for my *ordinary* manuscripts was 300), 3 times 5 = 15. But to give so much work for 1500 fr. is impossible. Especially as I told him the things may turn out so that I cannot give them for that price. For instance, he could not demand that I should sell him, say, *12 Etudes,* or *une Méthode de piano* for 300 fr. The same with the Allegro maestoso which I send to you today; I can't give it for 300 fr., only for 600. For the Fantasia,[1] 500. I will let him have the Nocturnes,[2] the Ballade[3] and the Polonaise[4] at 300, like those which he printed before. That is: for Paris, these 5 things for 2,000. If he doesn't care to have them (*entre nous*) I shall be glad, because Schlesinger will be delighted to buy them; but I do not wish him to regard me as a person who does not keep his promises. *Il n'y avait qu'une convention tacite d'honnête homme à honnête homme;*[5] so he need not complain of my terms, which are very moderate, especially as it is long since I have published anything. All I want is to get out of this position with decency. I know that I am not selling myself. But tell him, if I wished to take advantage of him or to cheat him, I could write 15 bad things in a year, which he would buy at 300, and I should have *a larger income.* Would that be more honest? My dear, tell him that I don't write often, and publish little; don't let him think that I am raising my prices;

[1] F minor; Op. 49.
[2] C minor and F sharp minor; Op. 48.
[3] 3rd Ballade, A flat major; Op. 47.
[4] F sharp minor; Op. 44.
[5] There was only an understanding, as between one honest man and another.

but when you see the blots on my manuscript you will see, yourself, that I have a right to ask 600, when he gave me 300 for the Tarantella (for the Bollero [*sic*] 500). I beg you, for God's sake, respect my manuscript; don't crush me, or smear me with pitch, or tear me to pieces (all things of which you are incapable; but I write it because I do so love my laborious writings). Make a copy. *Yours* can remain in Paris. Tomorrow you shall have the Nocturnes, and by the end of the week the Ballade and Fantasia; I can't polish them enough. If it bores you to copy them, do it *for the remission of your great sins,* for I don't want to give this spider's web to any hack copyist. Once more, I rely on you; for if I had to write out those 18 pages once more, I should go mad. But don't crumple them!!!—I send you a letter to Haertel. Try to find me another valet, not the one you have. I expect to be in Paris at the beginning of November. I'll write to you tomorrow. Write.

Yours

CH.

Monday morning.

I have just re-read your letter—I see that he asks about just Paris. So *settle* the question as best you can, but *press* him for 3,000 *pour les 2 pays* (or 2,000 for Paris alone), if he himself should lay stress on that; because *la condition des 2 pays* is easier for him and more advantageous for me: if he does not consent, it may perhaps be in order to have a *pretext for breaking* with me. So we will await his answer from London. Write always openly, and be always very courteous with him, my Dear; be *cold,* but not to me.

CH.

149.

To the Same.
[*Undated.*]

MY DEAR.

Grzym[ała] will tell you about the apartment. About the Polonaise, I promise. I embrace you. Thanks for your letter, and no doubt we shall soon meet. Write to me, if only about the weather. Embrace Jasio; he is probably better. Once more, thank you for the shoes, and music, etc., etc.

150.

[In French]

To MME GEORGE SAND.
[*Paris, 25 September 1841.*]

Here I am in the rue Tronchet, arrived without fatigue. It is eleven in the morning. I am going to the rue Pigalle. I will write to you tomorrow, don't forget me.

I embrace your children.

CH.

Saturday.

151.

To JULJAN FONTANA.
[*Nohant posting station. La Châtre,*
1 October 1841.]

MY DEAR.

Yesterday, Thursday, I came here. I have done the C sharp minor Prelude for *Schlesinger;* it is short, as he wished. As it is to come out at new year, like Mechetti's Beethoven, don't give up my Polonaise *to Leo* (even though you have copied it already) because tomorrow I will send you a letter to Mechetti, in which I will explain to him that if he wants a short thing, I will give him for that Album, instead of the Mazurka that he asked for (which is already old), *today's* Prelude. It is well modulated and I can send it without anxiety. Let him give me 300 for it (that's right?), and *par dessus le marché*[1] let him have the Mazurka, but not print it in the Album. If Troupenas, that is, Masset, should make any difficulties, don't come down a farthing; tell him that perhaps he would prefer not to print everything (he won't want that; I could sell them higher to someone else). Tell him the 600 includes London, and that these manuscripts are far more important than those former ones. That's as far as I am concerned — Now. In the drawer of the bureau, on the right-hand side from the bottom [a drawing of the bureau, with inscription: " This one " on one drawer] you will find a parcel, sealed, and addressed to Mme Sand (in the place where the money is usually kept). Pack it up in oiled cloth, seal it and send it by diligence, addressed to *Mme George Sand.* Sew the address round with packthread, so that it should not tear off. That is what Mme Sand asks. I know you will do it beautifully. I think the key is the second one in the glazed cupboard, on the upper shelf, near the shaving-brush. If it's not there, get a locksmith to open it. I love you as of old. Embrace Jasio.

CH.

Write a line.
Thursday, the 5th.

I reopen this letter, to tell you that this parcel, or pocketbook, should be packed between boards, or in a little box, or however you think, to keep it from getting wet, or torn, or lost.

[1] Into the bargain.

152.

To the Same.
[*Nohant, October 1841.*]

DEAR.

Thanks for sending the pocketbook. I send you the Prelude in large writing for Schl[esinger] and in smaller for Mechetti. You can cut down *similarly* the manuscript in my handwriting of the Polonaise, put it together with *that* Prelude (numbering the pages), add my letter to Mechetti, seal it up in the envelope that I send you, and give it into *Leo's hands*, asking him to *send it by post*, as Mechetti is waiting for it. Post Hasslinger's letter yourself, and if you don't find Schlesinger, leave a letter for him, but not the manuscript, till he lets you know that he accepts the Prelude in settlement of the account. If he does not want the London *propriété* on any terms, tell him to write to me. And you write. Tell him that I do not demand that 100 fr. at once. Also *don't forget* to add the *opus* to the Polonaise, and the *number* to the Prelude that you send to Vienna. I don't know how Mme Czerniszew [1] spells her name; perhaps in the thing under the vase, or somewhere in the drawer of the little table, near that bronze ornament, you can find a card from her, or from the governess, or the daughter. If not I should be glad (if you don't mind) if you would go to her — they already know you as my friend — at the *Hôtel de Londres, Place Vendôme*, if they are still in Paris, and ask, from me, that the young princess should give you her name in writing. You can say why: is it Tscher, or Tcher? Or, still better: ask Mlle *Krauze*, the governess. Say that I want to give a surprise to the young princess, and ask Mlle Krauze (who is very pretty) to write to you whether it is Elisabeth, and whether Tschernischef or ff: how they usually write it. Say that she can tell the princess (the mother), but not the daughter, as I don't want her to know till I send it from here. If you would rather not do it, don't mind saying so to me; just let me know, and I will find out elsewhere.

[1] The name is Russian: written in French: Tchernicheff; or in English: Chernyshev. There is endless confusion about the transliteration of Russian names.

But tell Schlesinger not to print the title yet; tell him I don't know the spelling. But I hope that you will find a card in the house with the name. About the moving, I am glad that you have found an apartment. You can have the drawing-room *sofa*, and give the rest to *Pelletan, 16 rue Pigal*[*le*]. I shall have to take the bed out of the bedroom, because *décidément* I shall live in one of the pavilions [1] of the rue Pigal. Enough; only a little will remain for you. Today I will write you the details. I must stop, for the post is going, and I want my letter to Vienna to go off this week without fail. So in an hour's time I will write you, with details.

Your

CH.

153.

To the Same.

[*Nohant*] *7 October 1841.*

MY DEAR

Then, have the furniture moved; I especially recommend to your care the bit of crockery in the drawing-room. As the drawer of the cabinet where they are does not lock, take them out for safety. As it is decided that I am going to live in one of the pavilions, I shall need the bed. Household stuff, music, anything you come across, you can have sent to the *rue Pigal*. You will need money for that. So if that 50 is too little, let Jasio spare you what he can. As for the price of the lodging, you can go to Pleyel, whom I have notified to give you the money for the rent. Give 20 fr. to the porter, as a tip from me, and tell him to forward all letters to rue Pigal, 16. The Fountain (not you, only the one that stands in the vestibule) may be useful to you; those little sofas are shabby, but there are the covers. I am sorry, my Dear, that I can't offer you these bits of things; but as the proverb says, the fairest maiden can give only what she has. Don't be angry when you are moving.

[1] annexes?

Don't forget my little things by the fireplace. As for the pendule,[1] take it; but I don't know if I can leave it with you; I probably can, though, as perhaps I shall have no room for it. Don't do all the moving on one day, so that you don't completely *lose your temper!* Write to me if there are any difficulties. Pelletan, from the *rue Pigal,* will be notified.

About Wessel; has nothing come? It occurs to me that, if you did not put his address in full on the envelope this time (I never know what it is) the letter probably failed to reach him. We'll wait.

If by any chance you, or Jasio, or Albrecht, or Alkan, or Grzymała, should know of a valet; or if you meet with one:—sometimes one can find them. But not through *Charles,* or there will be *cancans;* and, living in the *rue Pigal,* I shall need someone who won't be quarrelsome and upset Mme Sand's country servants. It's just a chance. Perhaps you can hear of something satisfactory in the *Club.* Tomorrow or the day after I'll send you a letter to my people. My father greets you kindly. Don't forget about Troupenas. Don't be cross; you are at your zenith, as I am at mine; we should have got past worrying. I am over 30. Your Panna Młokosiewicz, I hear from my sister (whom I asked about her) has had bad luck; she has been ill. Some say it is enlargement of the liver, some, that it is a dropsical swelling; but they have pumped out the water, or whatever it was; and she is now well, and slender, and graceful, as before. No one knows the truth. Our Nowakowski, who was to have come here, has reached Warsaw. I am glad. Some young lady from the governesses' Institute fell in love with him and has lost her place. You remember him; he's bald, and much more of a *ninny* than we are; and is still going in for *conquêtes!* A good prognosis for us. Today is the 7th (half past 2 in the night). You will move on the fifteenth; or sooner? You still have a week. I'll write to you if I remember anything urgent. I particularly beg you, don't forget to give the porter instructions, with the 20 francs, that *people and letters should be sent on to the rue Pigal.* I'm sorry for you. I see you in the middle of dust and

[1] clock.

confusion. But if I could be in Paris myself for the moving, I should probably not bother you.

Your old

CH.

Greetings to Leo, and don't forget to tell him to send to Mechetti by *post,* not through anybody. Post Hasslinger's letter yourself; don't give it to Leo.

154.

To the Same.

[*Nohant. Postmark: La Châtre, 10 October 1841.*]

MY DEAR.

You have probably received my letters and compositions. You read the German letters, and sealed them, and did everything as I asked; didn't you? Now about Wessel; he's a windbag and a cheat. Write him what you like; but say that I have *no intention of giving up* my rights over the Tarantella. As he did not *return* it in time — and if he has lost on my compositions, it is doubtless because of the *silly titles* which he has given them without my consent and in spite of the strong objection several times expressed by Mr. Stapleton [*sic*]; and if I were to listen to my feelings, I would never send him anything more after those *titles.* Speak as strongly as you can. About the moving: *M. Pelletan* of the *rue Pigal* has been formally notified today by Mme Sand, who thanks you for the few kind words that you sent with the pocketbook. Have my letters sent to *16 rue Pigal,* and impress it *very earnestly on the porter.* Mme Sand's son will be in Paris about the 16th; I will send you by him the manuscript of the concerto and nocturnes. Write. It's all rain and mud here. Embrace Jasio. As for Antek, I think I told you that his illness is not so terrible, and that there's a good deal else in it. No doubt we shall soon see him;

but he won't even see his people. Love me as of old. Write a line.

Your
FRYC.

Saturday morning.

155.

To the Same.
[*Nohant*] *Wednesday* [*28 October 1841*].

MY DEAR.

We are coming without fail on *Monday*, that is, the 2nd, at 2 in the afternoon, or perhaps at 5 or 6, in case of anything unexpected. You have offered me your help in arranging things in the *rue Pigal.* I don't want it; thank you, but it would be asking too much of your kindness; but what I will ask of you is to come at 2 on Monday to the *rue Pigal.* Also to go there before, and see Pelletan. Things are standing still. *Moreau* is there with his wife; they are *servants* of Mme Sand, whom she sent from here to Paris with permission to stay in the *rue Pigal* till they can find a job or lodging. If they are still there, be sure to see Pelletan, to whom Mme Sand wrote that they must move out without fail *before Monday*, even before Sunday would be better. If Pelletan is very *busy* (he is publishing a new newspaper: — *Le 19 Siècle*), see to it, after communicating with him, that the windows shall be opened (if it is not raining) and the place aired, especially Mme Sand's pavilion. And that fires are made in the fireplaces and stove, for two or three days. If *Moreau,* whom Mme Sand may keep for a few days (that is, to come in, without his wife, *but not to sleep in;* Pelletan knows about it): — if Moreau is *disponible,*[1] he knows Mme Sand's service well, so only see that he opens the windows and lights the fires. But if Moreau is not *disponible* (Pelletan will tell you), then let the *porter*, M. *Armand* and his (very decent) wife attend to it, and you *just see* it's done; of course,

[1] available.

communicating with Pelletan, who, poor fellow, may *perhaps* have lost his head with his new *newspaper* and have no time to attend to material things. Speak to him about his *newspaper;* he is a decent fellow, and learned; and treat him in a friendly way, and *don't be cross,* either with me or with him, or with *yourself,* or with anybody. About a valet, have one to look at, but don't engage him, because I don't know whether he will be liked; and although he would be my servant, still, living so close, there might be *various things. En tout cas,* for our arrival, the porters are decent and willing folk; *menagez* them, or better still tip them, if they are to attend to the apartment, not Moreau. But only if it doesn't worry you. It will get done somehow. My old proverb. Anyhow, time flies, the world passes, death pursues us, and my manuscripts pursue you. *Don't hurry with those,* Dear; I would rather people should wait for them in Leipsic, than that it should be *cold,* or dusty, or smelly, or damp in the *rue Pigal* when we arrive. Don't bother about *my* apartment, or about my bed, or about anything. I'll attend to all that myself the next day, and not worry you. That's measure for measure, whenever you may need any such proofs of friendship. Your old bald head can meet my decrepit and mouldy nose, and we'll sing together: Long live the Cracow Suburb![1] to a tune of Bugusławski's, in Krzysztofowicz's tenor, to an accompaniment by Pan *Lenz.*

Your old

CH.

Write either *today,* that is Friday, or not at all. My Life. Go to my hatmaker, *Dupont,* No 8 *rue de Montblanc,* and tell him to make me a *hat* for Monday. He *always* makes my hats. They know me there and won't want any *measure;* but Monday without fail.

Tell the porter at the *rue Pigal* not to send on *any more* letters here.

[1] A street in Warsaw.

156.

To the Same.
[*Nohant, beginning of November 1841.*]

MY DEAR.

Thanks for Masset's letter. No doubt you have already *told* him, but if not do tell him that you have written to me, and that I am very sorry, but that I cannot, *on any terms.* So let him not be *offended* that I am *forced* to apply to others. As for the Prelude for Schl[esinger's] Album, I told Mme *Masset* last time; but don't start that here. I send you *two* Nocturnes; the rest on Wednesday. My departure from here is delayed, so perhaps I shan't reach Paris till the 6th or 8th. Please copy, for the winter is beginning. You shall have the remainder the day after tomorrow.

Your old one —

Write, Dear.

Embrace Jasio.

Find me a valet. I know Marchand, but he is not for me (and, *entre nous,* he drinks).

Perhaps some sharps and flats may be missing.

157.

[In French]

To M. C. PLEYEL IN PARIS.
Paris [*undated*]

Dear Friend, here is what Mr. Onslow writes to me. I would call to see you and tell you about it, but I feel very weak and am going to bed. I love you more and more if that is possible.

CHOPIN

Don't forget M. Herbault, please. So, till tomorrow. I expect you both.

158.

To Panna Yozefa Turowska in Paris.
[*Paris, undated.*]

I promised to write you a few words yesterday evening; but I have not seen Soliva, and today, the more I think over what you told me, the more I regret that you chose just me to honour with your confidence in a matter of which I see that I cannot judge. At your request I gave you well meant advice; and not lightly, but after thinking the matter well over. And I again repeat that, from what I had the pleasure of hearing (not judging of *timbre,* since you were tired from the journey and had a Parisian catarrh), I consider that you have an exceedingly resonant voice, a very pure intonation, and feeling — the most important element in a big talent — and that more knowledge of the art of singing would do you no harm.

That was why I gave you my *sincere* opinion about Bordogni, that he can teach you nothing more; an opinion to which I still hold, and therefore advised you as I thought best. I was mistaken; it is not a question of knowledge, but of name. I should have thought of that; but it is too late now. Count on me and my willingness to serve you in any other case; but I have recommended you to Soliva, whom I rate above Bordogni, too highly to be able, today, to ask him to refuse me the very thing which I so earnestly desired and worried him over a few days ago. Please forgive me, and believe that I really wish to serve you in any other matter: for instance, by *sincere* speech.

F. Chopin

I await *Lablache's* answer, and will forward it to you at once.
Saturday morning.

159.

[In French]

To MESSRS. BREITKOPF AND HÄRTEL IN LEIPSIC.

GENTLEMEN,

I have just received your letter, with the cheque payable the 13th of Dec., and beg you to accept my thanks for your punctuality. The numbers of [?] on the manuscripts are rightly placed. Mechetti, at Vienna, has a prelude for his Beethoven Album, and a Polonaise.

I have asked Schlesinger to arrange with you about the day of issue. He has begun the engraving, and I hope that you also will wish it to be done promptly.

I do not send you the London address, as I have been forced to leave Wessel and have not yet made any definite arrangement elsewhere; but let that not keep you back. I beg you also to place on the title page of my nocturnes, instead of Mlle Emilie, Mlle Laure Duperré.

Cordially yours,

F. CHOPIN

Paris, 3rd Dec. 1841. No. 16, rue Pigalle.

160.

To WOJCIECH GRZYMAŁA.

[*Undated. Before April 1842.*]

I must stay in bed all day, I have so much pain in my beastly face and glands. You don't know how cross I am that I couldn't go to the Roule[1] yesterday. If *Raciborski* will let me go out tomorrow (Jasio is in bed himself and had bloodletting today), I will come to you at once. I know nothing about the fort [epiano?] But the day before yesterday I told them to

[1] The Czartsryskis lived in the rue du Roule.

follow Paër's advice. Write a line about your health. Are you better? I will pray here.

CH.

161.

To the Same.
[*Paris; undated.*]

MY DEAR LIFE.

I have called on you twice to tell you that I am back; but the wigmakers probably forgot to tell you. We shall meet at Leo's at dinner; and tomorrow, if you like, I will wait in till 2, as I am doing the whole day today. I will go out only to post this letter. I am dining with Frankom [Franchomme?] and shall be home at 10. If you want to come in, even at night on your way back from the opera, I'll embrace you. I would come to you but it would have to be very early, and for me, the morning, — by the time I finish choking, it's 10 o'clock. I embrace you most heartily.

Your old
CH.[1]

Nohant[2] expected on the 9th.

162.

To the Same.
[*Nohant. Postmark: La Châtre, 28 July 1842.*]

MY DEAR.

Tomorrow night we go to Paris to look for lodgings. On Saturday evening we shall be at the rue Pigalle. I shall spend the

[1] Hoesick supposes this letter to have been written "probably during the first days of November 1841." Dr. Opieński regards this as a mistake, as in 1841 Chopin was still at Nohant in early November, as is shown by one of the letters to Fontana, who was to expect him on the 6th or 8th.

[2] George Sand's arrival.

day here. Mlle de Rozières arrived today, and will stay with Solange for the few days. The post is going, so I can't write more. I hope I shall find you well.

Your old
F. CH.

She [Mme Sand] does not add a postscript, because she has guests from town.
Wednesday evening.

163.

To the Same.
[Paris; undated.]

MY DEAREST LIFE.

For God's sake, was it for *tomorrow that you told me to engage your* [?][1] Please, send it to me tomorrow, and run in yourself, for a moment; it will be a kindness.

Your
CHOPIN

Wednesday.

164.

To JÓZEF ELSNER IN WARSAW.
Paris, 8 November 1842.

Dear, always dear Pan Elsner! You can't think how much pleasure every word of your note has given me; and I thank you warmly for the music sent by the Turczynowiczes. They were successful here, were much liked, so they must be pleased, and Pan Damse too. I am not answering his letter, but please be so kind as to tell him how great an impression his children (as he calls them) produced here.

[1] The word does not make sense.

I embrace you heartily. I love you still, as a son, as an old son, as an old friend.

CHOPIN

My respects to Pani Elsner.
Greetings to all around you.

165.

To TOMASZ NIDECKI IN WARSAW.

I have received your letter, dear Tomasz, and at once asked the people I know to inquire for a harpist. So far I have seen no one who would consent to go to you for the price; especially as you do not write whether you will pay for the journey. As for a mechanician, that seems to me easier; and yesterday someone was to ask Pillet, the director here, whether by any chance one of his men may be leaving. You see that I am attending to your commission, so far as I can; but I am sorry to say that, till now, without success. Write whether you will pay the harpist's journey. I think it is absolutely necessary if we are to get it settled. Always count on my old friendship.

F. CHOPIN

Embrace Pan Elsner and my acquaintance.
Paris, 30 November 1842.
Rue St. Lazarre [*sic*], *Place d'Orleans.*

166.

To WOJCIECH GRZYMAŁA.
Nohant, Tuesday [*Undated. 1842?*].

MY LIFE!

I hope this letter will find you more cheerful than the last one did. Here, health is so-so. Weather beautiful. Tomorrow, or the next day, we expect the good Delacroix.[1] He will have your room.

Forgive me for asking you once more to send a letter to the Viennese editor; but I think, for Austria, they have to be stamped. They will tell you at the bourse. I ask this favour of you, because the letter contains manuscripts of mine, laboriously written out; I don't want to entrust them to any uncertain fate.

I won't bother you with any more commissions, for I know how unpleasant they are.

I hope all will go well with you. Be well, and don't fret.

Your old

CH.

167.

[In French]

To MESSRS. BREITKOPF AND HÄRTEL IN LEIPSIC.

GENTLEMEN,

I have to offer to you a Scherzo (for 600 fr.), a Ballade (for 600 fr.), a Polonaise (500 fr.).

Besides these I have written an Impromptu, of several pages, which I do not even offer to you, as I wish to oblige one of my old acquaintances, who for the last two years has been constantly asking me for something for Herr Hofmeister. I mention it in order to explain to you my motive in this matter.

If my Scherzo, Ballade, and Polonaise are acceptable to you, be so kind as to write me a word by the next courier, and to let me know when you would like me to send them to you.

Most faithfully yours,

FR. CHOPIN

15 December 1842.
Paris, Place d'Orléans No. 9 rue St. Lazare

[1] The painter Delacroix spent some time at Nohant in the summer of 1842.

168.

To WOJCIECH GRZYMAŁA
[*Nohant, undated, 1843.*[1]]

MY LIFE!

I told you that I should beg you to send a letter to my parents, and another to Leipsic with manuscripts. I have no one except you, to whom to entrust either of them. Be so kind as to post them at the *bourse* when you are passing. My manuscripts are worth nothing, but it would mean a lot of work for me if they were lost. Here the health of the Lady of the House is no better. I drag along as I can, but I don't know when we shall meet. The weather is still fine here; the children can enjoy games, and there is a notion of returning late, especially as the city is expensive. You have doubtless finished your hotel, or nearly. There is no day that I do not think of you, and of all that ought to give you happiness. I hope I shall find you well, cheerful, and, as far as possible, happy. Several days ago we made an excursion in this neighbourhood to see the banks of the Creuse; the lad [2] made drawings of the views. It was a very successful trip, with friends who are neighbours; but she has been unwell since we returned, and has not been able to work for a few days. That distresses her, so things are not cheerful.

I embrace you most heartily.

Your old
CH.

I respectfully kiss her hands.

169.

To THOMASZ NIDECKI IN WARSAW.

DEAR TOMASZ!

Nobody wants to go to you, even for twice as much; but I am not surprised, for Labarre, whom I asked to help me in this

[1] According to Hoesick.
[2] George Sand's son, Maurice.

matter, assured me that he cannot get anyone to go to Lyons for very good pay; all the artists are so fond of Paris. They would rather suffer want here than live decently abroad or in the provinces. I'm sorry that I could not be of any use to you this time; but we will still love each other as in the old days in the Leopoldstadt.

F. CHOPIN

Paris, 25 January 1843.
9 Place d'Orléans, St. Lazare.

170.

[In French]

To MESSRS. BRIETKOPF AND HÄRTEL IN LEIPSIC.

DEAR HERR HAERTEL:

I send you your leaf with my signature, and — since you talk business to me — should you like me to send you by M. Maho my two Nocturnes and my three Mazurkas, for the price of 600 francs for each of the 2 works? Please tell M. Maho, who will let me know.

I am very sorry to have had so little of the pleasure of meeting you during your stay in Paris this year; I hope to make up for it when you come again.

Till next time, then. Kindly present my respects to your household.

Yours faithfully
FR. CHOPIN

Tuesday morning.

171.

To MAURICE SCHLESINGER IN PARIS.
[*Nohant*] *22 July 1843.*

DEAR FRIEND!

In the *Impromptu* which you have issued in the Gazette [1] of June 9th the pages are wrongly numbered, which renders my composition incomprehensible. Though I am far from the meticulousness which our friend Moscheles shows with regard to his works, I still feel it my duty to your subscribers to ask you to insert in the next number the following *erratum:*

Page 3: read p. 5.

Page 5: read p. 3.

If you are very busy, or too indolent to write me a word, you can answer me in your publication by means of this *erratum;* which will also show me that you, Mme Schlesinger and your children are all enjoying excellent health.

Very sincerely yours,
FR. CHOPIN [2]

172.

To WOJCIECH GRZYMAŁA.
Saturday [*Undated. Nohant, 1843?*].

MY DEAR!

You can't think how this Spanish gossip affects me. Judge of things as they are. I remember, one evening in my [3] Lady's house, she was very severe against *today's Agatha;* it was after that evening that she decided to see the favourite. You took up the defence, and did not share her enthusiasm for the one who is now in London, and who was then, it was said, to be engaged

[1] *Gazette municipale;* Paris, Schlesinger, *éditeur.* [Op.]

[2] This letter, written in French, is given by Hoesick in a Polish translation. The French original appears to be unknown. [Op.]

[3] Chopin refers to Mme Sand as "*moja*": mine. Perhaps a nearer rendering than "my Lady" would be the Irish: "Herself."

for grand opera. That evening my Lady told you that you must be in love with Agatha — I don't know whether you noticed it; but I was upset, and that evening, in her room, I told her not to joke about it, because you really know Mlle Agatha, and nothing would be easier than to make a mess of things and cause unpleasantness for you and others. Now, believe me or not; but, as I love my mother, I never said another thing to her. Yesterday, after your letter, I told her that she must have at some time made a joke about you and Agatha, to the Spaniard,[1] or the Red-head, or somebody: because the Spaniard is saying silly things to you and representing them as coming from me or from her. She then swore to me that really nothing about you and Agatha had ever come into her head; adding that she knows your affections to be engaged elsewhere; also that the Spaniard, when she wants to find out something, has a trick of presenting nonsense of her own invention as established facts, and throwing the blame on those who are most intimate with the persons about whom she is curious. Beyond this, there has not been a word on the subject. You can see from this how much she respects certain things. The weather here is neither fine nor bad. The first day she was very unwell; now she rides on horseback, very well, by day; is cheerful, writes, paints and amuses herself.

Your
Ch.

I have torn off a second sheet, so that she shall have more space to write to you. Please write.

173.

[In French]

To Mme George Sand.
Monday [*Paris 14 August 1843*].

Here I am, arrived at eleven, and here I am at once at Mme Marliani's, both writing to you. You will see Solange[1] at

[1] This may refer to Mme Viardot-Garcia.
[2] George Sand's daughter.

midnight on Thursday. There was not a seat either Friday or Saturday; nothing till next Wednesday, and that would have been too late for everyone. I should like to be back already,—you don't doubt that; and I am very glad that fate has compelled us to start Thursday. Till Thursday, then, and tomorrow, with your permission, I will write again.

Your very humble

CH.

I have to choose the words that I know how to spell.

174.

[In French]

To MME GEORGE SAND.
Friday [*September 1843*].

Here is what Maurice has written to you. We have had your good news, and we are happy that you are pleased. Everything that you do ought to be big and beautiful, and if we don't write to you about what you do, it is not because it does not interest us. Maurice sent you his box yesterday evening. Write to us, write to us! Till tomorrow. Think of your old ones.

CH.

To SOL[ANGE].
Maurice is well, and I too.

175.

[In French]

To MME GEORGE SAND.
[*Paris, 26 November 1843.*]

So you have finished your survey, and your stables have tired you. Take it easily before the journey and bring us your fine weather from Nohant, for we are in the rain. Nevertheless, as I ordered a carriage yesterday after waiting till three for the weather to clear, I have called on Rotschild [*sic*] and Stockhausen, and am none the worse for it. Today, Sunday, I am resting and am not going out; but by preference, not by necessity. Believe that we are both well, that illness is far from me, and that I have only happiness before me. That I have never been more hopeful than for the coming week, and that all will go as you wish —

Four more days. CHOPIN

176.

[In French]

To MESSRS. BREITKOPF AND HÄRTEL IN LEIPSIC.

I, the undersigned, domiciled in Paris at rue St. Lazare No. 34, acknowledge that I have sold to Messrs. Breitkopf and Haertel in Leipsic the rights of the following works composed by me; namely:

Opus 12 Variations on themes by Loudovic
" 15 Three Nocturnes
" 16 Rondo
" 17 4 Mazurkas
" 18 Grand Waltz, *brillante*
" 20 Scherzo [1]
" 21 Second Concerto
" 22 Grand Polonaise
" 23 Ballade
" 24 4 Mazurkas
" 25 12 Études in two numbers
" 26 Two Polonaises
" 27 Two Nocturnes
" 28 24 Preludes
" 29 Impromptu
" 30 4 Mazurkas

[1] See note at end of letter, page 264.

Opus 31 Scherzo
" 33 4 Mazurkas
" 34 Three Waltzes: 1–3
" 35 Sonata
" 36 Second Impromptu
" 37 Two Nocturnes
" 38 Ballade
" 39 Third Scherzo
" 40 Two Polonaises

Opus 41 4 Mazurkas
" 42 Waltz
" 46 Concert Allegro
" 47 Third Ballade
" 48 Two Nocturnes
" 49 Fantasia
" 52 Fourth Ballade
" 53 Polonaise
" 54 Fourth Scherzo

I declare that I have ceded this property to the said firm, without reserve or time limit and for all countries except France and England, and I acknowledge that I have received the price agreed upon, for which a separate receipt has been given.

F. Chopin

Paris, 10 December 1843.

In this First Scherzo (B major) Chopin has used the melody of the beautiful old Christmas Carol: *Lulaj Jezuniu*, which is still sung in Poland.
Here is the version kindly sent to me by Dr. Opieński:

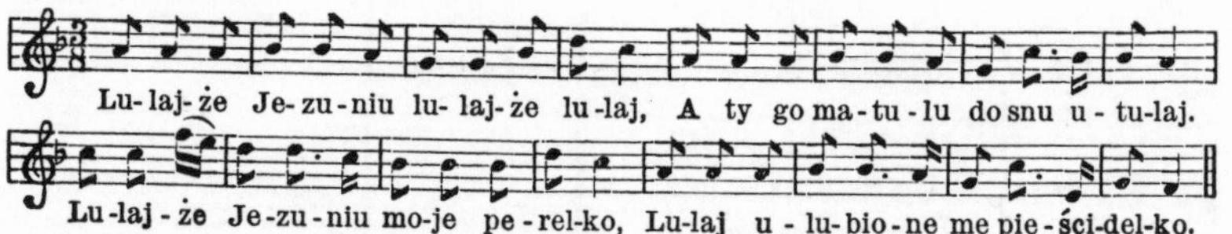

Lully, baby Jesus, lullaby lully;
And thou, dear mother, soothe him to sleep.
Lully, baby Jesus, my little pearl;
Lullaby darling beloved.

As is frequently the case with folk-tunes, there are several variants. Chopin gives:

177.

To MESSRS. BREITKOPF AND HÄRTEL IN LEIPSIC.

I, the undersigned, Frederick Chopin, domiciled in Paris, rue St. Lazare, Place d'Orléans, acknowledge that I have sold to Messrs. Breitkopf and Haertel in Leipsic the rights of the following works composed by me; namely:

(a) Opus 55 Two Nocturnes for piano
(b) " 56 Three Mazurkas " "

I declare that I have ceded this property to them without reserve or time limit, and for all countries except France and England, and I acknowledge that I have received the price agreed upon, for which a separate receipt has been given.

F. CHOPIN

Paris, 16 July 1844.

178.

To WOJCIECH GRZYMAŁA.
[*Nohant. Postmark: La Châtre, 27 July 1844.*]

MY DEAREST LIFE!

Here I am in Nohant. On the way I thought only of your last talk. You are always a dear, and may God give you a better financial fate. The Lady of the House was as much worried over your last affairs as over your *salto mortale*[1] down those stairs. I am writing to you because I forgot to ask you about the Fireworks. Could you not get, through that kammerdiener of Philippe, a seat in a window at the Tuileries for my sister? If you can manage it easily, as your thoughts are freer [than mine], help my good sister to get a sight of the show. Write me a line about what is happening over your affairs. Don't write

[1] head over heels.

much; only whether things are better? Give my respects at Enghien; and if you see my sister, send her here to me.

I embrace you most heartily.

Your old

CH.

[A very affectionate postscript from George Sand. [Op.]]

179.

[In French]

To AUGUSTE FRANCHOMME.

Nohant Castle, near La Châtre (*Indre*) [*1 August 1844*].

DEAR FRIEND.

I send you a letter from Schlesinger and another for him. He wishes to put off publication, and I cannot accept that. If he should persist in his determination, give my manuscripts to Maho, so that he may get M Meissonier to take them for the same price, 600 francs. I think that Schlesinger will engrave them. They should be out for the 20th. But, as you know, all that is necessary is to register the title now. I'm sorry to trouble you; I love you, and turn to you as to a brother. I embrace your children. My greetings to Mme Franchomme.

Your faithful friend

F. CHOPIN

A thousand compliments from Mme Sand.

180.

[In French]

To the Same.
Nohant, 2 August [*1844*].

DEAR FRIEND.

I was in a hurry yesterday when I wrote, asking you to approach Meissonier through Maho if Schlesinger refuses my compositions. I forgot that Henri Lemoine has paid a very high price to Schlesinger for my studies; I would rather have my manuscripts engraved by Lemoine than by Meissonier. I am giving you a lot of trouble, dear friend, but here is a letter which I send you for Lemoine. Read it and arrange with him. He must either publish the compositions or register the titles by the 20th of this month. Ask of him only 300 francs for each piece, which will make 600 francs for the two. Tell him that he need not pay me till I return to Paris. Leave the two works for 500 francs if you think it necessary. I would rather do that than give them to Meissonier for 600 francs, as I suggested yesterday without thinking it over. If, meanwhile, you have already negotiated with M. it is different. If not, do not cede anything for less than 1,000 francs. For Maho, who is the correspondent of Härtel (who pays me well), you can reduce the price for Germany, knowing that I sell my compositions so cheaply in Paris. I give you a lot of bother with my affairs. All this is in case of Schlesinger persisting in his intention of not publishing anything this month. Ask 800 francs from Lemoine for the two works, if you think that he will give it. I am not stating any price to him, so as to leave you full liberty. I have no time to lose before the courier goes. I embrace you, dear brother; write me a line.

Your faithful
CHOPIN

My greetings to Madame and a thousand kisses to your children.

181.

[In French]

To the Same.
Nohant, 4 August [*1844*].

DEAR FRIEND.

I have confidence in your friendship, so the speed with which you have arranged the Schlesinger affair does not surprise me at all. I thank you from the bottom of my heart, and await the moment when I can be of some use to you. I imagine that all is well with you, that Mme Franchomme and your dear children are in good health, and that you love me as I love you.

Your faithful

F. CH.

Mme Sand sends a kiss to your dear babykin, and to you a cordial handshake.

182.

To WOJCIECH GRZYMAŁA.
[*Paris. Undated; autumn, 1844.*]

I arrived the night before last, and am running about all the time with my sister, so every morning passes for nothing. How can I see you? Today I take them to Rachel, so I shall be near you. Perhaps I'll run in at night or tomorrow morning. They will still be here on Monday, and on Tuesday I go to Nohant and then home. Mme S. embraces you heartily.

Your old

CH.

183.

[In French]

To Mlle Marie de Rozières.
[*Paris. Undated; autumn, 1844.*]

If you are lazy, that is bad, and I shall scold you this morning; but at half past 1, by your permission, instead of at 1, and at No 5. I do not think I can go out while it is so slippery. Here they are asleep; otherwise they would send you a thousand kind messages.

Till we meet.

Ch.

184.

[In French]

To the Same.
Nohant, Tuesday [*1844*].

I write to you without a dictionary, to *entrust* to you my letter for my mother. You gave me permission to do so, and I thank you in advance, and beg you to keep well. Here things are not so bad, except for the pianos, of which one does nothing at all, and the other very little. The *very little,* of course, is mine. Suzanne tells me that you have been very kind about my No. 9, and I am so grateful for it that I should like to be able to write you a long and interesting letter in proof of all my gratitude. But I don't know how, so I confine myself to pressing your hand.

Fr. Ch.

Did they send you the Sonata and the Berceuse? Give us some news of you. Don't go into the crowd to see the *petits nautiques.* Take care of yourself; and if by chance there should be a letter from Warsaw, send it to me. I send my own sealed, but you can put in a word for Louise,[1] which will give her great pleasure. Be so kind as to tell Mme Étienne (if you think of it) to give my address to the persons who bring two musical periodicals, so that they can be sent to me here.

185.

[In French]

To the Same.

[*Postmark: Orléans, 3 September 1844.*]

DEAR MLLE DE ROZIÈRES,

So we have dreamed that we have seen Louise. God grant that she return safe and sound to her family. You have been as charming as possible, and I have not thanked you enough for all your kindheartedness. I am sorry that Maurice is not there. I think he is to arrive today, as if to make me regret that I did not wait for him. In any case, I did what I thought best. Remind him of Varennes, and Marquis.[2] Possibly he may have a second key with him; make him tell you, if he comes. If there is a letter for me from Mme Sand (which I cannot reasonably suppose), keep it for me, please. Also, don't forget that case. It ought to be *tarred* and covered with *oiled cloth;* it appears that the packers know this. If M. Frank (who lives above me) does not send the *Encyclopédie* and *l'Humanité* tomorrow, would you please remind him to do so. Write me a word. God will bless you; you love Louise. Pardon me for bringing you into my affairs.

Your devoted

CH.

Orléans. Gaillard was with the same convoy.

[1] Ludwika Jędrzejewicz.
[2] George Sand's dog.

186.

[In French]

To the Same.
[*Nohant. Postmark: La Châtre, September 1844.*]

I have time only to ask you to send this letter to Vienna, stamped if necessary (which is quite possible), for in Austria it is not the same as everywhere else; also to thank you for your excellent letter and to remind you of the case, of M. Frank and M. Duwe; also to place myself at your feet. Very soon you will get a second letter with more scrawls in it.

If my letter is delayed a day, it may miss them. Everyone is well here. Maurice has just written.

Adieu.

CH.

Saturday.

187.

To the Same.

Thanks for the excellent letter of my sister, who, thank God, is standing the journey fairly well. Thanks also for M. Duwe and M. Frank, for whom I send you a line, which you will be so kind as to let him have at once, if he has not yet sent the books. Otherwise keep the letter. I send you by diligence M. Laroux's l'Humanité, which you will put with the other books, and send off the case as soon as possible, for when you receive this letter it will be ten days since they left. Ask M. Duwe to look again at the custom-house receipt; would it not be better, instead of what is there now, to put simply: — "*books for study, periodicals and dictionaries.*" Also let him be so kind as to let me know whether it goes by Danzig or by Stettin, and how it will arrive at Thorn. Perhaps, it would be better to put "by Hamburg" *only*. Perhaps he has good connections at

Danzig or Stettin? I should not like it to get lost on the way. I thank you for all your kindnesses. Solange will write to you. Mme Sand is not very well today. She will only say good morning to you in my letter. It is raining. We have just been having a lesson on the new Beethoven Sonata.

Your colleague

CH.

Nohant, 11 Sept. [1844.]

188.

To HIS SISTER LUDWIKA JĘDRZEJEWICZ.

Nohant, 18 September 1844.

My Dear — I send you the little songs that you heard one evening. Solange, who sends you a kiss (she has reminded me of it twice), wrote out the words for you from memory, and I the music. I hope you have arrived all right, and that you received news from me at Vienna and at Cracow. I sent to Vienna my little song that I promised you: — "Handsome lad, what do you want," and to Cracow a few words for Pani Skarbek. If you did not get either one or the other, which is possible, for the Austrian posts crawl very slowly, have the Cracow letter forwarded to you, as I should be glad to have you give it to Pani Skarbek yourself; the Vienna one doesn't matter, I can write out the song for you again. I addressed: — "*To Prof. Jędrzejewicz, poste restante.*" It's the Cracow one that counts. I dreamed of you both today. Write me a line. I've been a bit inclined to grumble for some days. Maurice has not come yet, but is to return tomorrow, or the next day. You remember my telling you, when leaving here, that I should return by postal service, and that our whole journey will be for the preservation of certain conventionalities.[1] After dinner today we propose to go to Ars. An aunt of the Lady of the House is here with her ward; as I wrote to you to Vienna, she lives with the ward, and, as I wrote to you to Vienna, she lives in your room.

[1] Probably an allusion to some escapade of Mme Sand's son, Maurice. [Op.]

Often, when I come in, I look to see if there is nothing left of you, and I see only the same place by the couch, where we drank our chocolate, and the drawings that Kalasanty copied. More of you has remained in my room; on the table lies your embroidery — that slipper, — folded inside an English blotter, and on the piano a tiny pencil, which was in your pocketbook, and which I find most useful. I must stop, as we are starting. I embrace you most heartily. Embrace Kalasanty. Tell him that Hipolit asks to be remembered to him. Kiss the children too.

Do write.

Your old

CH.

189.

[In French]

To AUGUSTE FRANCHOMME.

Nohant, 20 September 1844.

DEAR FRIEND.

I did not write to you earlier, because I was expecting to see you this week in Paris. As my journey is put off, I send you a line for Schlesinger, so that he may deliver to you the price of my last manuscripts; that is: 600 francs (you will keep out 100 francs for me). I hope that he will pay it to you; if not, ask him (without showing any annoyance) to write a few words in answer, which you will send on to me, and I will write to M. Leo to repay you before the end of the month the 500 francs which you have had the kindness to lend me.

What can I say to you? I often think of the last evening which we spent with my dear sister. How she did enjoy listening to you. Afterwards she wrote to me from Strasbourg, asking me to remember her to you and to Mme Franchomme. I hope that you are well and that I shall again find you so. Write to me, and love me as I love you.

Your old

CH.

A thousand compliments to Madame. I kiss your children. A thousand compliments from Mme Sand.

190.
[In French]

To MME GEORGE SAND
[*Paris, 23 September 1844.*]
Monday, half past 4.

How are you? Here I am in Paris. I gave your parcel to Joly. He was charming. I have seen Mlle de Rozières, who kept me to lunch. I have seen Franchomme and my publisher. I have seen Delacroix, who keeps his room. We talked for two and a half hours; of music, of painting, and especially of you. I have engaged my place for Thursday; Friday I shall be with you. I am going to the post; then to Grzymała, then to Leo. Tomorrow I shall try over some sonatas with Franchomme. Here is a leaf from your little garden. Grzymała has just come. He says good-day to you and is writing you two words. I will say nothing more except that I am well and that I am your most fossilized fossil.

CHOPIN

191.
[In French]

To MLLE DE ROZIÈRES.
Nohant, 22 Oct[*ober 1844*].

Here is another letter for Warsaw. I abuse your kindness. I will tell you all that better *viva voce*. My sister has written to me in great haste; she asks me to tell you how fond she is of you, and that she will write to you. She is sending her son to college. And you, certainly, are sending me to the devil because I bore you with my correspondence. This does not prevent me from begging you, if you see Franchomme, to be so kind as to ask him to let me know whether he has received the manuscripts for Leo (that is to say, a letter). Please keep well. Here it's not so bad, but no exaggerated good health. Next month I shall have the honour to make my bow to you in person; meanwhile, I beg you to deign to accept all that one says at the end of a letter when one is lucky enough to have a volume of epistolary models.

CH.

No one else is writing to you. She sends you kisses and awaits news of you.

192.
[In French]

To the Same.

It is long since I gave you any news of us, because I expected to see you soon. Plans being modified, I again write you two words before leaving for Paris, begging you to be so kind as to take charge of the letter for my mother. I hope that your health is quite restored, and that you are not behaving like Donna Sol[ange],[1] who has been rather unwell for some days. She says she will soon write to you.

Please be so kind as to let the porter at No. 9 know that I shall be in Paris in a few days. Also please ask Perrichet to make at once a pair of curtains of plain muslin for my sitting-room, if those I have are too shabby. Would you be so good as to find out?

Accept all my thanks in advance. Till we meet, I hope soon.

CH.

My sister sends in her letters a thousand affectionate messages for you. Amuse yourself with Bach for me.

Nohant, 31 Oct. 1844.

[1] A pun on "Solange," the name of George Sand's daughter, and "Doña Sol," the heroine of Victor Hugo's *Hernani.*

193.

To his sister Ludwika.
For Ludwika.
Nohant, 31 Oct. 1844.

My belovèd Dear. So you are together. I received both your letters, from Vienna and from Cracow. Fräulein Müller wrote to me that she is happy to have made your acquaintance. She's a good soul, isn't she? And Pani Szaszek too. It's a pity that neither Mme Diller nor Mme Dessauer was there. Fräulein Müller, if she is going to Paris now, will wait a little time for me; I expect to stay here two or three more weeks. The leaves have not all fallen, only turned yellow, and the weather has been fine for a week; the Lady of the House profits by this for various planting and arranging of that courtyard in which, you remember, they danced. There is to be a big grassplot, and flower beds. The idea is to put, opposite the dining-room door, a door leading from the billiard room to the greenhouse (what we call an orangery) which is to be built on. Your Cracow letter came just at the right time. Scypio amused me; but I did not find out whether, in my Cracow letter, you received a few words for Pani Skarbek. Don't forget to write me about that. I suppose your children are well again now. Write to me about Dr. Domus, and also about Tytus's arm. Sol[ange] is not very well today; she is sitting in my room and asks me to send you hearty greetings. Her brother (courtesy is not in his nature, so don't be surprised that he has given me no message for your husband about that little machine for cigars) is leaving here next month to go to his father for a few weeks, and will take his uncle with him, so as not to be bored. That manuscript that I brought has not yet been printed, and there may be an action about it. If it should come to that, it will mean a greater profit here, but of course unpleasantness for the moment. You remember how, when we were driving across the Vic (on the road to Châteauroux) the Lady of the House would sometimes stop, and go in to see a sick woman. They could not cure her; and a few days ago, with many tears from her daughters, she was buried in the cemetery by the garden here. Nor did the one live that Sol used to go to. You remember how I once got out of the carriage in the square by the column, in Paris, and went to the Treasury, about some business, to a very old friend of this household. He called on me the next day. He was a good friend, the oldest friend of the father and mother of the Lady of the House. He was present at her birth, he buried her mother, and really belonged to the family. Well, returning from dining at the house of a certain deputy, a friend of his, he fell downstairs, and died in a few hours. It was a great blow here, for they were devotedly fond of him. De Rozières writes affectionately of you in every letter; my letter of today goes through her hands, and I will give her many compliments from you, for she deserves them. She was very kind, wasn't she? Tell Nowakowski that I love him as of old. I do not yet know his quintet but have ordered it. Let him sometimes write me a line. The good Franchomme has written to me in a very affectionate tone about you; he and his wife. As I expect to be in Paris with Jan a few days before the Lady of the House, you need not worry about any bundles, or pillows, or anything of the sort. Everything in the house will have to be cleaned and put in order, as usually before the winter. Write me the number of your house.

Embrace vour children and husband.

Your

OLD ONE

The Lady of the House embraces you; you know how they love you, for they wrote. The bear is in the ascendant here.[1]

[1] I cannot find out to what this refers.

194.

[In French]

To MLLE DE ROZIÈRES.
[*Nohant. Postmark: La Châtre, 14 November 1844.*]

As you wished me to let you know before I come, I haste to inform you that I shall have the pleasure of greeting you in Paris on Sunday (I believe at half past noon). The diligence which will bring me is that of *Bourges, Laffitte* [*sic*] *and Co. St. Honoré.* I do not know exactly at what hour these vehicles arrive, but it is during the day. Be so kind as to have a fire lit in my lodging, and to ask Mme Durand to make an exception in my favour on *Sunday* and to come to see me after 1. I thank you in advance for all this, and I will say goodbye for the present.

Good day, good day, good day.

CH.

Thursday morning.
Here all is well and the weather is fine.

195.

[In French]

To the Same.
Nohant, Thursday, 20 [*November 1844*].

Monday or Tuesday evening, I will thank you *viva voce* for all your kindness. The letter from Valenciennes was really from my compatriot. I send you in exchange one from Louise, and I keep my compliments for my arrival. *Monday*, then or *Tuesday.*

CH.

All is well here. They will start soon after me. They send you a thousand messages.

196.

[In French]

To MME GEORGE SAND.
Monday, 3 o'clock [*2 December 1844*].

How are things with you? I have just received your excellent letter. It is snowing so hard here that I am very glad you are not travelling, and I reproach myself with having perhaps put into your head the idea of travelling by post in such weather. The Sologne must be in bad condition, for it has been snowing since yesterday morning. Your decision to wait a few days seems to me the best thing, and I shall have more time to get your rooms heated. The essential point is that you should not start on your journey in this weather, with a prospect of suffering. Jan has put your flowers in the kitchen. Your little garden is all snowballs, sugar, swan, ermine, cream cheese, Solange's hands and Maurice's teeth. . . .

Yesterday I dined at Franchomme's; I did not leave till four, on account of the bad weather, and in the evening I went to Mme Marliani. Today I dine at her house, with Leroux, she tells me, if the sitting of the court in his brother's case, which is to be heard today, finishes early. I found the Marlianis fairly well, except for colds. I have not seen either Grzymała or Pleyel; it was Sunday. I hope to go to see them today, if the snow stops a bit. Take care of yourself; don't get overtired with your parcels. Tomorrow a new letter, with your permission. Always yours, older than ever; very, extremely, incredibly old . . . .

CH.

197.

[In French]

To the Same.

Thursday, 3 o'clock [*5 December 1844*].

I have just received your most excellent letter, and I see that you are quite worn out by these delays. But, out of pity for your friends, be patient; for really, we should all be anxious, if we knew you to be travelling in this weather and not in perfect health. I wish you would engage your places for the latest possible date, so that it may be less cold; here it is fabulous; everyone says that the winter is coming too suddenly. " Everybody " means M. Durand and Franchomme, whom I have already seen this morning, and at whose house I dined yesterday, in a corner by the fire and in my thick overcoat, beside his big boy. The boy was pink, fresh, warm and bare legged. I was yellow, faded, cold and with three flannels under my trousers. I promised him some chocolate from you. You and chocolate are now synonyms for him. I think that your hair, which he spoke of as so black, must now, in his memory, have become chocolate colour. He is quite comic and I like him very particularly. I went to bed at half past ten; but I slept much less soundly than the night after the railway. . . . I am going out, as always, to take this letter to the Bourse, and before going to Mlle de Rozières, who expects me to dinner, I shall go to see Mme Marliani, whom I did not see, either yesterday or the day before. . . . My lessons are not yet started. *Primo:* I have only just received a piano. *Secundo:* People here don't know yet that I have arrived, and it is only today that I have had several callers on business. It will come little by little; I am not anxious. . . . I think that morning has dawned, and that you are in your dressing-gown, surrounded by your dear fanfi,[1] whom I beg you to kiss for me, and also to put me at your feet. As for the mistakes in spelling, I am too lazy to look in the Boiste.[2]

Your mummified ancient,

CH.

[1] Probably meant for fanfans: darlings (children).

[2] A dictionary.

198.

To STEFAN WITWICKI.
Paris, Easter, 1845.

MY DEAREST LIFE.

I have missed you very much this year. We could have grieved for many things together. I have often thought of writing to Grafenberg, but it ended with thinking: it became the impossible, the moment I took a pen in my hand, — and now it is more helplessness than laziness that makes Mme Sand's letter go off a week late.

What shall I tell you: that tomorrow, Monday, is the Easter festival at Prince Cz[artoryski's]; that Mick[iewicz] is not lecturing this year; that many of his followers are abandoning him; that it is said they have written apologies to His Majesty. But what is grievous is that 2 (it is said that Pilichowski is one of them) signed documents before a notary, giving themselves into subjection, like property, like slaves, to Towianski: [1] n.b., they don't bind themselves for their children, but for the whole of their own lives. Could anything be more insane? Mick. is not in the same relations with Tow. as before. Tow. declares that they have *overweighted* the thing, that they have gone too far. In a word: disputes; so no doubt it will come to a melancholy end. Apart from this, everything is as of old. I am sorry you cannot be with us and Delacroix this evening at the Conservatoire, to hear Haydn's Creation. It is only the second concert we are attending this year; the first was the day before yesterday, with *Mozart's requiem.* Today Grotkowski will come to sing to you; [2] some new ones that he does not know (not new to you). My dear Ludwyczysko [3] searched for you in Vienna on her way home. They always ask for you. Mother has got

[1] Andrzej Towianski, 1799–1878; Polish religious mystic and founder of the sect of Messianists. His conversion of Mickiewicz caused great offence, both in Polish circles and at the Collège de France, where the poet lost, in 1844, his post as professor of Slavonic literature, through preaching Messianism in his lectures to the students.

[2] Chopin's songs on words by Witwicki.

[3] Ludwika.

through the winter fairly well. She is tired, and has aged. Perhaps we may meet again somewhere. I don't need to remind you what she is like — you know how good she is — ; and you can imagine how much her letters have helped me. I have seen Zaleski once; he was kind enough to call on me. I should be glad to see him oftener. He was looking fairly well. Grzym[ała] is younger than ever; dances like a 20-year-old. Here it is colder than ever; this is the first day without snow in the garden. Spring is forgetting us. Keep well; may this be a blessed year for you. Love me as I do you, although I do not deserve it as much as you.

Your old

CH.

199.

To WOJCIECH GRZYMAŁA.
Nohant, Wednesday [*25 June 1845*].

MY LIFE!

Please post this letter to Solange at the little post office, and the one to my family at the bourse. Do come, if only to stop me bothering you with my commissions. Here there are headaches ever since the railway, which in Orléans sets people down in the mud instead of in the street. I am fairly well, and so is the pistol.

I embrace you most heartily.

CH.

Write.

[An affectionate postscript from Mme Sand.]

200.

To the Same.
[*Undated.*]

My Dear,

Tomorrow, Thursday, at $5\frac{3}{4}$ in my lodging, or at 6 in the gilded Café *de la Cité,* in the inner room. Then we will go to M. Marl[iani]. As for the Dawn,[1] it has had a heavy fog; today I hope for sunshine, and before evening will send you a word.

May the Lord God have you in his keeping.

Your old

Fr.

Wednesday morning.

201.

To the Same.
[*Nohant*] *8 July* [*1845*].

My Life.

I know from Leo's letter — he has written to me about my Berlin publisher, and mentions you — that you are well, and I see that you are always the same, beloved even by those who know you only of late. No doubt your thoughts are still on the Rhine, unless you are up to your ears in business — nevertheless, write me a line about yourself. Are we really to expect you here; and when? The country is beautiful now, not like a few weeks ago. We had great storms and torrents of rain. The rivers, even the little brooks, overflowed extraordinarily. The oldest persons cannot remember such a flood. It destroyed mills and swept away bridges. Viardot, who came here a few weeks ago to fetch his wife, went back to Paris alone on account of the danger, and it was only within the last few days that Susanne escorted her from here. I did not write by them, but asked

[1] A reference to Mme Sand's baptismal name: Aurore.

Susanne to call on you and find out how you are. Please do try to get to manage a vacation for yourself, or, if possible, to find some business in the Château. It would be a good action; you would rejoice, among others, your old, ever attached

CH.

My heartiest respects to the princes. We are all fairly well here. The Lady of the house is writing a new novel.

202.

To his Family.
[*Nohant, 20 July 1845.*]

MY DEAREST ONES,

We have been here for a month already. Mme Viardot came with us and stayed three weeks. We are all in excellent health; but during the winter there was fever in the village. Françoise's husband (perhaps Ludwika remembers) was ill all the winter, but is up now. The weather is good, but when we arrived there were great storms. The Indre rose so high that at Montgioray Chativon (brother of the Lady of the house) had his whole garden flooded and water in his house. Viardot, who came to fetch his wife, could not take her away, for the roads were flooded to Châteauroux, and there, where we often took our drives, where the fine view is, it was impossible to pass. It did not last long; there was much damage in the meadow lands, but it is already forgotten. I was not made for the country, though fresh air is good for me. I don't play much, as my piano is out of tune; I write still less, that is why you have had nothing from me for so long. I think that you must all be in the country; that Bartolosko Antolosko[1] has forgotten about illness; that Ludwika is following the advice of the Marjolaine, not to get tired. Tell her that she heard the manuscript of the novel which we are reading here; that an autograph has been given to me for her;

[1] family diminutives.

that just before leaving, I saw Gutm[ann], and told him to embrace you all; and that at the moment of departure I liked him better. He really is a good fellow. Tell dear Izabelisko [1] to take a little rest after her anxiety over her husband's health, and to give Kalasanty a beating, for he is the strongest and can stand such a present. I feel strange here this year; often in the morning I go into the next room, but there's no one there. Sometimes I seem to fill the place of an acquaintance who comes for a few days; so I do not drink chocolate in the morning, and have moved my piano; it is by the wall where the little sofa and table used to be, where Ludwika often sat embroidering my slippers and the Lady of the house working at something else. The bureau at which I write stands in the middle; on the left lie some of my music papers, M. Thiers and some poetry that would make your whiskers [tumble off] [2] on the right Cherubini; in front of me that repeater you sent me, in its case (it's 4 o'clock); roses and pinks, pens, and a bit of sealing-wax left by Kalasanty. I am always with one foot among you, with the other in the next room, where the Lady of the house works; at this moment I am not with myself, but only as usual in some strange outer space. Granted, it is only those *espaces imaginaires;* [3] but I am not ashamed of that; you know, a proverb has grown up here: — "he went to the coronation by imagination," and I am a real blind Mazur.[4] So, not seeing far, I have written three new mazurkas [5] which will probably come out in Berlin, because a man I know has begged me for them: Stern, a good fellow and a learned musician, whose father is starting a music-shop. Also I have received an invitation from the committee which is to put up a monument to Beethoven (at Bonn on the Rhine), to come for the inauguration. You can guess how likely I am to go. If, however, you were there, perhaps I would take the journey. But that is for next year. I don't know whether I wrote to you that princess Obreskow, who is a great music-lover and has much affection for me, will be passing by you

1 family diminutive.
2 The phrase appears to be imperfect.
3 Imaginary spaces.
4 A proverb; referring to the folk of Mazovia.
5 A minor, A flat major, F sharp minor; Opus 59; published by Stern. [Op.]

that autumn, and on her way back wants to bring Mamma in her carriage; and then, next spring, your daughters and sons-in-law and grandchildren will have to come to fetch her back. Really, I am very fond of this lady, and she is a person of great sincerity; for that matter I must have written to you long ago about her kindnesses to me; but I admit to you that I was amused at her delightful projects. Still, if you do see her, be very good to her on your side, for I have had many proofs of her kindheartedness and am very fond of her. She is extremely devoted to music. Her daughter, princess Soutzo, is my pupil. In a word, she is a very worthy lady (though perhaps a little too lively in appearance). Mme Viardot also, who will be passing through your town, told me that she will call on you. She sang for me here a Spanish song of her own which she composed last year in Vienna; she promised to sing it to you. I like it very much, and doubt whether anything finer of that type could be heard or imagined. This song will unite me with you; I have always listened to it with great enthusiasm.

My sonata and berceuse are already out. About the berceuse, I think of the kind of person that Ludwika would like; these are difficult things, but not impossible; I have several times made inquiries, and perhaps something can be found. What am I to tell you about Paris? Before I left, Mme Hofman was very ill; they were anxious about her. I hope she is better, for Albert wrote nothing about it. He wrote to me only what the newspapers have written without mentioning names, about Victor Hugo, to whom the following adventure happened two weeks ago. M. Billard, a *historical painter*, not specially famous, and an ugly man, had a pretty wife, whom Hugo seduced. M. Billard surprised his wife with the poet, so that Hugo was obliged, as the man wanted to arrest him, to show his medal of a peer of France, in order to gain a moment's respite. M. Billard wanted to bring an action against his wife, but it ended in a private separation. Hugo suddenly started off for a several months' trip. Mme Hugo (who is fine) has taken Mme Billard under her protection; and Juliette (an actress of the Porte St. Martin theatre, who has been famous here for 10 years, and whom Hugo has long been keeping, in spite of Mme Hugo and his children and his poems on family morality) — this Juliette has gone with him. Parisian tongues are glad to have something to wag about; and it is a funny story. Add to it that Hugo is getting on for fifty and always, on every occasion, plays the part of a serious person, superior to everyone. Donizetti has come to Paris, where he expects to spend the summer and write a new opera; Donizetti, who wrote Lucia, Don Pasquale, La Favorite, etc. Lamartine and his wife are here in Neris:[1] the nearest springs, half a day's journey from here; Méry was there, and now is probably still with Priesnitz, from whom I have had no news for a long time. Here in Châteauroux there are big preparations for a ball for the duke of Nemours, who is coming with his wife, on their way to Bordeaux. "*Les sauvages indiens*"[2] (Ioways) [*sic*] have already sailed from Havre on the ship "*Le Versailles*." The wife of one of them, — his name was Shinta-yi-ga: "*little wolf*," and hers Oke-wi-mi in Indian, which means: "*the she bear who walks on the back of another*" — died (poor creature) of homesickness; they are putting a monument to her in the *Montmartre* cemetery (where Jasio is buried). Just before her death she was baptized, and the funeral was at the Madeleine, in her parish; the monument is to be a peculiar one, designed by M. Préault, a fairly well known sculptor, and M. Lassus, an architect. It is to be of stone, with bronze flowers winding up it and broken off at the top by *un fantôme*[3] (supposed to be *mal du pays*), then bronze bas-reliefs with gilded views of their *montagnes rocheuses*,[4] the banks of the Missouri, etc.; their life over there; and some verses by M. Antony Deschamps. I hope I am giving you plenty of news. Tell Barteczek[5] that the electro-magnetic telegraph between Baltimore and Washington gives remarkable results. Often orders given from Baltimore at 1 in the afternoon are carried out, and the goods and parcels ready to leave Washington by 3; and small parcels, asked for at half past 4, arrive by the 5 o'clock convoy, reaching Baltimore at half past 7, from

1 A watering-place near Montluçon.
2 The wild Indians.
3 a phantom.
4 Rocky mountains.
5 Diminutive for Bartolomeusz.

Washington, 75 English or 25 French miles; I think that's quick!! And the year since we saw the Jędrzewiczes has gone as fast as on an electric telegraph wire. If this letter doesn't hang together, it is because I write a phrase a day. Yesterday Sol interrupted me, to play 4-hand duets with her; today, to see a tree cut down; one of those near the pavilion where Chaigne lived, in the garden near the road, where the Jędrzejewiczes alighted. The tree got frozen, so it had to be felled. I have had letters from Paris, from Franchomme, and from Mlle de Rozières, who looks after my lodging. Franchomme writes that Habenek is going to Bonn for that inauguration, that Liszt has written a cantata, which will be sung, with Liszt conducting. Spohr will conduct a big concert, which will be given in the evening; three days' music. Also, *à propos* of monuments, Lesueur (the musician) is also to have a monument in his native town, Abbeville. Lesueur was Napoleon's music-director (a member of the Institute), and a professor in the Conservatoire. Pan Elsner knew him well and gave me a letter to him when I came to Paris. He was a worthy and enlightened man; he died 10 years ago, before Paër and Cherubini; he was not very old. Speaking of monuments, the equestrian statue of the duke of Orléans (who was killed, jumping out of his coach) will be finished in a few days. It stands on the Louvre square, in Algerian bronze, probably with bas-reliefs. It is the work of Marochetti, one of the most famous sculptors here. Marochetti, for all his Italian name, is a Frenchman, and is a man of very great talent; all the most important works are entrusted to him. The statue faces the Tuileries. One bas-relief represents the taking of Antwerp, the other some Algerian episode. A propos of statues: near the government depository of marbles, by the Champ de Mars, where loads of waste marble from various monuments are thrown (*en dernier lieu* from the Madeleine), the heavy rains have washed out some of the heaps, and one of the guardians noticed among them the arm of some statue, raised above the other stones, as if in protest against its fate. They finished what the water had begun, removed the accumulated loads, and found a Greek statue of marble, an antique of very fine workmanship, representing Hercules *arrêtant la chèvre d'Amalthée;* [1] the goat is no longer there, only the horns. A very interesting subject, because known only from a few small *pierres gravées.* [2] A commission, consisting of MM. Letronne, Le Bas (the one who raised the obelisk) etc., etc., decided to have it placed at once in the *Palais des Beaux Arts;* there, where I left the Jędrejewiczes last year, and came back to find them in the room where there is that semi-circular fresco by Delaroche, representing all the famous painters of various periods; do you remember? For the fourth time I sit down, in the hope that this time I shall finish this letter. The weather has had time to change since that page, and today it is raining. I hope Paris will have good weather for this month's celebrations; this year it's not as when the Jędrzejewiczes saw it last year; it is to be illuminated. On the Seine, this summer, the speculators in human whims have hit on a new notion. There are several vessels, very smartly got up, and gondolas in the Venetian style, that ply in the evenings. This novelty delights the boulevard crowds, and it is said (I have not yet seen it myself) that great numbers of persons go on the water. This year the Elysian Fields are to be less brightly illuminated, but on the other hand there is to be a mass of lights on the quay, also fireworks, water-sports, numbers of boats crowded together, etc. etc. There will be no lack of inventiveness, and great precautions, to minimize accidents. Minimize, because there is no way of preventing a few persons from getting drowned; just as, on land, they trample each other from curiosity. For the rest, the Kalasantys must remember what a crush there is on such days; but people are so stupid that, the more they are squeezed, the better they seem to be amused. There is a big storm outside, and another in the kitchen. One can see what is happening outside, but I should not have known what was happening in the kitchen if Susanne had not come to complain of Jan, who had been pouring out varied abuse of her in French, because she had taken his knife off the table. The Jędrzejewiczes know what his French is like, so they can imagine what charming remarks: *Laide comme cochon; bouche comme dèrrière,* [3] or still more attractive. I don't know whether they

1 catching the goat of Amaltheus.

2 carved stones.

3 ugly as a pig, mouth like buttocks.

remember that, if you ask him: "Is there any wood?" he answers: "*Il est sorti*";[1] and to: "Is Susanne in the house?" — "Il n'y a pas."[2] But they often quarrel; as Mme S.'s maid is very skilful, quick and useful, it is possible that I may have to dismiss him for the sake of peace, which I should hate to do, for new faces are small joy. Unfortunately, the children also dislike him, though he does his work well and regularly. Time for dinner. I would still go on writing, but I really want to get this letter off today. It goes to Mlle de Rozières, who will take it to the post herself. I am writing to her to forward to me anything that may come from you. I am not worrying, because I know this is a moment when some are going to the left and others to the right, or if not, you are full of various plans. But please be sure to persuade Mother to go to the country, and let Bartek get a good rest. No doubt the Lord is keeping the children in good health for Ludwika. Tell Kalasanty not to give such lessons as he gave here to Maurice, who to this day utters such words as wziwzina, siuzam,[3] etc. Let Izabela, as the bravest one, keep a watch that the dear Ludwiczysko[4] should not get too tired. Izabela and I are the blond ones; we value the brown-haired one very highly. Embrace our friends, beginning with the neighbours and ending outside the barriers, if you are still in town; Pan Fryder[yk] Skarbek,[5] Elsner, Nowak, Bełz[a], Tytus, and all the womenfolk. Last night I had a pleasant dream about Pani Kozubowska. I often think of Pani Lutyńska, for last year I was told a lot of good things about her.

I embrace my Mummy and all of you most heartily.

CH.

If you see Domuś, or Panna Ludwika, or the Juliusz couple, remember me to them. The Lady of the House is working. I won't interrupt to ask her to write a word to Ludwika; but I know in advance that she would send her hearty greetings. Now, this

[1] He is gone out.
[2] There isn't any.
[3] Attempts at the sounds of Polish.
[4] Diminutive of Ludwika.
[5] Probably count F. Skarbek, a famous economist.

minute she has finished her writing and will send Ludwika a few words. *Adieu,* my dearest ones.

20 July 1845.
St. Ludwika's day next month.

An anecdote about Hugo for Kalasanty. A certain lady, of the type that, speaking of horse-racing, wanted to see "*six petites chaises*[1] (steeple-chase; let Bartek pronounce it in English: what we call here *une course aux clocher;* I don't know whether we have a term for that; it's racing to a goal, straight across ditches, hedges and all similar obstacles): — Well, some such lady, hearing about somebody that he was in the same predicament as Hugo, remarked: *qu'il a été trouvé flagrant dans le lit*[2] (*en flagrant délit*). If he already knows this tale let him forgive me for my good intention and accept the other lady who wanted to know: — *ce que c'est que ce tabac du père Golèze* (Stabat de Pergolèse).[3] But that's a chestnut! A newer one is the lady who, engaging an apartment, asked the landlord: *de lui faire peindre le nombril* (for *lambris*),[4] as it was dirty. *En tout cas,* let him remember that Godfroi [*sic*] de Bouillon was *ainsi nommé, parcequ'il a été le capitaine le plus consommé de son temps.*[5]

203.
[In French]

To Mlle de Rozieres.
[*Nohant*] *Monday* [*1845*].

Dear Mlle de Rozières.

Here is my letter for Warsaw, which I *entrust* to you. As for the letter supposed to be from *my people,* that you thought I had

[1] six little chairs.
[2] flagrant in the bed.
[3] What is this Daddy Golèze's tobacco (Pergolesi's *Stabat*).
[4] To paint her navel (for *wainscot*).
[5] So called because he was the most consummate (*consommé*) captain of his time.

received, it turned out to be — imagine — a *thick* letter from somewhere in *Austria.* It was only to get this other letter which I am sending you, forwarded to a certain M. Mikuli. Mme Etienne knows his address. Ask her to take it to him and to *get a receipt* (the letter may possibly be important). As soon as I have a word from Louise, I will send it to you. All that you do with Mme Bethon will be quite good; but don't make her go back over the music which she has played, unless it is *very* necessary. Thanks in advance for all your kindness.

C.

Would you be so kind as to let me know when Franchomme will leave Paris, because I want to send him my stuff before then if possible.

204.

[In French]

To Auguste Franchomme.
Nohant [*30 August 1845*].

My very dear friend,

Here are three manuscripts for Brandus and three for Maho, who will give you Härtel's price (1,500 fr.). Don't give up the manuscripts till the moment of payment. Send a note for 500 francs in your next letter, and keep the rest for me. I am giving you a lot of trouble that I should like to spare you; but — but —

Ask Maho not to change the manuscripts for Härtel; because, as I do not correct the Leipsic proofs, it is important that my manuscript should be clear. Also, ask Brandus to send me two proofs, so that I can keep one.

And now, how are you? And Mme Franchomme and your dear children? I know that you are in the country (if Saint-Germain can be called so), which must do you all the good in the world, with the beautiful weather we are still having. Look at my erasures! If I once get started in a gossip with you, I shall never end, and I've no time to finish my letter, because Eug. Delacroix, who kindly offers to take charge of my commission to you, is just starting. He is the most admirable artist that one could meet. I have spent delightful hours in his house. He adores Mozart, and knows all his operas by heart. Certainly I do nothing but erasures today. Excuse me. Goodbye, dear friend, I love you always, and think of you every day.

CH.

205.

To his Family.

It's stupid, never to finish on the same day as one begins; this letter has taken five days to get written.

[*Nohant*] *1 October* [*1845*].

MY DEAREST ONES.

Yesterday I had your letter, forwarded from Paris, in which you tell me of Mamma and the Barcińskis having started.

Ten days ago I sent a letter to Paris, to Mlle de Rozières, addressed to Mamma in Nowy Swiat.[1] I hope Zuzia has been told to fetch my letters; if not, take notice that a letter has gone there for you, longer than this one, because I put all my news into it. You will find in it also a few words for Ludwika from my Châtelaine.[2] With this letter I send to Mlle de Rozières, to Paris, Ludwika's letter, which she will doubtless answer, as she likes writing, though she often has nothing to say; but it is a very pleasant fault, and I wish I had it. I am glad you have got half of them off to the country, and that Henryk also is in the fresh air; but it's a pity you could not arrange that you could go too. I feel sure that last year's journey is one of the reasons, and I can't be sufficiently angry with myself. But you also have joyful memories, so we can be glad of what we have had, and hope that we shall meet again before the railway is finished, and that

[1] A street in Warsaw.

[2] George Sand.

Kalasanty will again be bitten by *rougets* [1] and have to scratch. There are fewer of them this year, and the hypothesis is that they overate themselves on Kalasanty last year, and died.

You have hot weather; here also it was very hot a few days ago, but now we have frequent rains, and they are waiting for a change for the grain, which is plentiful this year, but will be late. Last Sunday was the festival of St. Anne, the local patron saint. As the courtyard has been altered, and this year is all borders and flowers, all the dances were on the grass in front of the church. You remember the village festival at Sarzay, so I won't remind you either of bagpipes or of booths, or of various kinds of dancers. We have had over a dozen acquaintances here, including Ler[oux], about whom Ludwika asked me. He is now 8 miles from here, at Boussac, a little town where there is a subprefecture, as at Salliatre, in the depart[ment] of the Creuze. The townlet is very old, and has a castle on the Creuze with ancient associations. Not far off there are Druid stones; the district is famous for its beauty. He has a printing license, and prints there a daily paper, which is edited here and called the *Eclaireur*. This printing press, however, is not yet worked by his new *procédé*, for, as everyone has a *but*, his *but* is that he begins things, but does not quite finish them. When he has thrown off a grand idea, he has had enough. The same with that new machine, which he has not finished, or not properly finished. It works, but not quite perfectly. It has already cost him and his nearest friends (among them especially the owner of M. Coco) some scores of thousands, and it needs double the amount, besides will, and especially perseverance; and the combination of all that does not seem likely at this moment. Nevertheless, the thing exists, and before very long some *exploiteur* will take it up, and show himself to the world, dressed in borrowed plumes. Such persons have already appeared and are still appearing, wanting to buy the invention; but he does not wish that. Besides two volumes on hydr. [aulics?] he has many articles in the Encyclopædia and in the *Revue* where " Consuelo " is. Everything that he has written belongs together. In the *Revue* he has

[1] "Harvester" ticks: *Leptus autumnalis*, common in some parts of France in autumn, and causing extreme irritation of the skin.

several lectures of great value, some unfinished. All these things were on the table in the *Square d'Orléans*. What news can I tell you? That Mme Viardot has already gone to the Rhine (on Meyerbeer's invitation, given in the name of the King of Prussia) together with Liszt, Vieuxtemps, etc. The royal family is to receive the queen of England, who has gone to Germany with her husband, Prince Albert. Mendelssohn is also in Coblenz, engaged in musical preparations for his king, because queen Victoria is to be received in Stolzenfels. Liszt is to call out the hurrahs in Bonn, where the Beethoven monument is to be placed, and where also the crowned heads are expected. In Bonn they are selling cigars: véritables cigarres à la Beethoven,[1] who probably smoked nothing but Viennese pipes; and there has already been such a sale of old bureaus and old desks which belonged to Beethoven, that the poor composer *de la symphonie pastorale*[2] would have had to drive a huge trade in furniture. It reminds one of that *concierge* at Ferney, who sold such endless numbers of Voltaire's walking-sticks. M. Blanqui, a professor, an old acquaintance of Kalasanty, has been decorated by the young queen of Spain on his return from Madrid, where he was sent with M. Salandroure, a manufacturer of fine Aubusson carpets, to visit the industry there. Nobody is interested or inquisitive about that, but I thought of it because Kalasanty knows him. As for mamma's travelling companion [?],[3] she does not need to know anyone, she knows everybody. Where is Lorka going? I am sorry for Antek Wodz[iński]; he will soon have a second posterity. Méry probably knows about that girl friend; that she was ill and is now better; poor Mme Dupont's husband told me about that before I left Paris. Nowak[owski] plays my berceuse, and I am glad to know it; it seems to me that I can hear him from the distance. Embrace him. The Sonata dedicated to Elsn[er] has been published in Vienna by Haslinger; at least, he sent me the printed *épreuve*[4] some years ago to Paris; but, as I did not send them back to him corrected, but merely sent a message that I should prefer to have several things changed, he

[1] real Beethoven cigars.
[2] of the pastoral symphony.
[3] The phrase is ambiguous.
[4] proof sheets.

may have stopped the printing, of which I should be very glad — Oh, how time goes! I don't know how it is, but I can't do anything of any value, and yet I am not idle. I don't wander from corner to corner, as I did with you, I just sit whole days and evenings in my room. Yet I must finish certain manuscripts before leaving here, for I can't compose in winter. Since you left I have composed nothing but that sonata.[1] Now I have nothing ready for the press except some new mazurkas, and I need to have something. I hear the diligences passing the garden; won't one of them stop, and won't one of you get out! Write to me frankly, whether the marjolaine [2] advice did Ludwika any good, also whether Antek Bartolo is perfectly well. Mummy must be enjoying the thought of her excursion. But I will say frankly that, not knowing her present state of health, I do not dare to press her much in winter, with her rheumatism. I leave my joy to your wisdom, but I protest with all my soul against all excursions. However, if Mummy were to fall ill here, and I were ill too, Izabela would come to nurse us, and after Izabela her husband, and after them you two; Zuzia and Pani Lutyńska will keep Louise. *Voilà tout.*[3] Tell Ludwika's husband to write to me sometimes. Short letters; if he only says: " good day "; I miss him in your letters. Tell him always to put the number of the house on every letter. I never remember either your number or Antol's; I have it written down, but in Paris, so from here I always have to address with circumlocution. One must have a wooden head, really, to write so many times and never remember your number. I am just back from a drive with Sol, who took me all over the place in a cabriolet in the company of Jacques. Jacques is an enormous dog of a very fine breed, who has been given to the Lady of the house to replace old Simon, who has aged greatly this year and has a paralysed paw. An inseparable friend of the fat Coco, although he comes of a superb breed. When it rains, he squeezes himself into the cabriolet, and lies down; but however carefully he disposes himself, his head gets wet on one side and his tail on the other; he tries to take shelter, but he is too big for such advantages. At this moment the

[1] In B minor.
[2] Marjoram was used in domestic medicine.
[3] that's all.

Lady of the house is in the village, together with our neighbour, a kind doctor, visiting a sick man, who in his delirium wants to insist on going out, to a woman a few miles from here, who *remet les fourchettes de l'estomac;*[1] it is impossible to persuade him. Someone wrote to me from Paris that Artot, the violinist, is dead. That boy, so strong and healthy, with those big bones and broad shoulders, died of consumption in Ville d'Avray a few weeks ago. When I was in Ville d'Avray before leaving here (we passed through there on our way to Versailles), going to visit my goddaughter, Albrecht's child, I travelled with Mme Damoreau. She was nursing him, and told me then that he was very ill. I am sorry for Mme Damoreau, for she was really attached to him. The year before last they travelled together to America. No one, seeing us two, would guess that he would die first, and of consumption. Jan, according to his custom, has for a quarter of an hour been ringing for dinner. (The Lady of the house once promised him that she will pour cold water over him if he goes on ringing so long.) I must shave, for I have a big beard, so I must once more leave this letter. I have shaved, but it doesn't make me any fatter, though they tell me here that I have put on flesh; anyhow, I am far from rivalling poor Okołow. Embrace his sister-in-law (if I am not mistaken) with whom I often played 4-hand duets in the Miodowa Street, where I used often to see Panna Czajk[owska]. Write to me about my godparents. Embrace the Pruszaks. Shake the hand of my old colleague Polec. Tell Elsner to come here to Néris to get his leg cured. Is Dobrzyński going to Paris? I can believe that he was successful with Meyerbeer. I am glad that you will hear David's symphony.[2] Except for a few genuine Arabian songs, the only merit of the rest is the orchestration. But what surprises me is that with you they are making costumes and decorations for it, whereas here it was performed by people in black frock-coats, sitting on benches with their music in their hands or on the music stands. Such a thing had not occurred to his greatest admirers (who are steadily diminishing in numbers, as usually happens after such an engouement).[3] Notice the song of the

1 puts back one's brisket.
2 *Le Désert*, which had a great vogue in its time
3 Infatuation.

Muezzin (that is what they call the man who sings every hour from the turret of the mosque, according to the Arabian religious custom); at the first concert here, the Arabs from Algiers wagged their heads and smiled for joy at that tune. Very soon I will write again to say that I love you heartily. I should like to write a lot, but I should not know from which end to begin if I were going to talk to you by letter the way we talked sitting over our chocolate side by side in my room in the morning. I embrace you all most heartily.

[In a postscript] The good Franchomme has written to me and asks to be remembered to you. [Next two lines by Mme Sand, in French:] *Good day, my dear; we love you, we kiss you affectionately; may the good God bless you always.* [In Chopin's hand:] She did not want to let this letter go without putting in a word. You are such dear folk (I write in the plural, because you are all so). M. Brunel, the engineer (French by birth) who built the tunnel under the Thames in London, has now invented, among other works, a new locomotive, by means of which it will be possible to go 50 English miles an hour. The machine will run on eight wheels. That will not make railway travelling pleasing. Sol, who has just brought me some chocolate for a snack, tells me to embrace Ludwika. She is very good-hearted. I am not surprised that you do not know Isidore,[1] for it has not yet come out in book form. Teverino [1] is to begin coming out next month as a *feuilleton* in the paper: "La Presse." N. B. *Feuilletons* have no connection *avec le corps* [2] of the paper, which takes a quite opposite view of many things.

[1] novels of Mme Sand.
[2] with the paper itself.

206.

To the Same.
Paris. Friday, 12 December [*1845*].

MY DEAREST ONES,

I have received your last letter, in which you write that you are all well except Barteczek, and that even he is much better; and that Mummy is standing the winter fairly well. Here it is not yet very cold, but dark and damp. Mme S[and] returned on Tuesday with her son and daughter, and I have been here for two weeks. As you may remember, I usually come back first; and this year especially, as I had to get rid of Jan and engage another manservant. [A footnote:] For the last year he has been wanting to go every month, but always protesting with tears that he loves me dearly; and I would not have dismissed him, but that he irritated the others. The children used to make fun of him. Up to the last he was hoping that Susanne would be sent away; every day he used to thank me. [Letter continues:] It's a serious matter for me, because I must have someone really decent; but my friend Albrecht has found me a Frenchman, Pierre, very honest and skilful, and I hope a loyal person, who has been 7 years in the service of the parents of my E flat major waltz.[1] He is very clean, rather slow, but so far has not made me feel impatient. Ludwika, who knows Nohant, may be interested to know that Luce, that little girl, Françoise's daughter, is now with her lady, as well as Susanne; or rather with Solange. A propos of all that Ludwika asks about in her letter, it's all lies and has no resemblance to the truth. Lr. [Leroux] is in excellent health; the children have had measles, and Maurice was to have gone in a few days, but is not going, as it is not a suitable time, to his father, who has not left his estates in Gascony all the summer. [A footnote:] Never believe evil rumours; there are plenty of folk in the world who cannot rest if they see anyone happy. [Letter continues:] Before I arrived here, but after I left Nohant, Mme S. was in Chenonceaux, near Tours, staying with her de Villeneuve cousins. Chenonceaux Castle is renowned

[1] Mr. and Mrs. Horsford.

all over France; it was built in the time of François I by the famous *traitrant* (the bankers of those days) Thomas Boyer, who took a long time to build it; it is built in the middle of the river Cher. In the arcades on which the castle stands, there are huge kitchens, so you can imagine what a structure. François I, inheriting from this banker, lived in it, and many things remain from his time. Later, Catherine de Medicis lived there constantly (here they use this castle in the decorations of the second act of the Huguenots; I think Ludwika saw it); the wife of our Valois also spent her widowhood there. All the rooms are kept with furniture of the period, which probably costs a pretty penny every year to keep up. In the time of Louis XV, or perhaps of the Regency, it fell after Vendôme to M. Dupin (de Francueil), to whom Rousseau was secretary. This M. Dupin was Mme S.'s grandfather, the one whose portrait hangs over the fireplace in the big downstairs room next to the dining-room at Nohant. Mme Dupin, his first wife, was famous for her intellect and beauty; and in her day everything that the last century had of brains foregathered in Chenonceaux; Voltaire, and Mably, and so on, and so on. There are a lot of Montesquieu's manuscripts, too. Rousseau speaks of Mme de Francueil in his *Confessions.* At Chenonceaux there are boxes of his correspondence with her; very interesting, but probably they will never be published. Mme S. had found several manuscripts by Mme Dupin, probably of great interest, especially beautifully written. Also Rousseau's opera (*Le Devin du village*),[1] of which it is said that M. Francueil wrote the overture, was played for the first time in the theatre of the château. You doubtless know that Rousseau wrote poetry and music which had a great success 70 years ago. Certain things in that opera have taken root, and are fairly well known in France. I have told you about Chenonceaux, now about Paris. Gavary sends best greetings to Ludw. and Jędrz. (he sends her Massillon, his own work); so the Franchommes. I dined at both houses before Mme S. arrived, and we talked a lot about you both. I am already starting my treadmill. Today I have given only one lesson, to Mme Rothschild, and have excused myself from two, as I had other work. My

[1] *The Village Soothsayer.*

new mazurkas have come out in Berlin at Stern's, so I don't know whether they will reach you; you, who in Warsaw generally get your music from Leipsic. They are not dedicated to anyone. I should like now to finish my violoncello sonata, barcarole and something else that I don't know how to name;[1] but I doubt whether I shall have time, for the rush is beginning. I have received many inquiries whether I will give a concert, but I doubt it. Liszt has arrived from the provinces, where he has been giving concerts; I found his card in the house. Meyerbeer also is here. I was to have gone today to an evening at Leo's to see him there, but we are going to the opera, to the new ballet (new for Mme S.): *Le diable à quatre,* in which the costumes are ours. I am writing to you now after the ballet, on Saturday morning. Nothing is changed at the opera; it's just as it was when you were there. As yet we have seen nothing else; neither the Italian theatre where they give Verdi's music, nor Mme Dorval in the new drama: *Marie Jeanne,* which is said to be one of her best parts. Today is December 17th. I broke off this letter and could not sit down to it again till today. Here it's a very dark and horrid day. Today is to be the first performance at the Grand Opera of an opera by Balfe, the man who wrote: "The four sons of Aymon" (I think we saw it together at the Opéra Comique). The title of today's one is "The Star of Seville." [A footnote:] The Cid, but not after Corneille, only after Calderon. [Letter continues:] The poem is by M. *Hypolyte* [*sic*] Lucas (an inferior *feuilleton*-writer). People don't expect much of it. Balfe is an Englishman, who has been in Italy and has passed through France. Tomorrow at the Italiens: Gemma di Vergi. But yesterday all of us, including Luce, went to the Porte St. Martin theatre, where they played a new drama by M. Dennery (not very good); in which Mme Dorval plays remarkably. The title is Marie Jeanne. It's a girl of the people, who marries an artisan; through his misconduct she is left in penury with an infant son, and, to save the life of her child, for whom she has no food, in despair, she takes the baby to the *enfants trouvés.*[2] The scene is finely given. Everybody blubbers; you hear nothing but blowing

[1] Karłowicz supposes this reference to be to the Polonaise-Fantasia. [Op.]
[2] Foundling hospital.

of noses all over the hall. From her youth up Mme Dorval has had no such part, anyhow not since: " Ten years of a gambler's life."

Sunday, 21 December. Since I wrote the last line, I have been to Balfe's opera; it is not good at all. They sing most excellently, and I hated to hear such gifts wasted, when Meyerbeer (who sat quietly in a box, reading the libretto) has two operas quite ready: "*Le Prophète*" and "*L'Africaine*." Both are in 5 acts; but he does not want to give them to the opera without a new singer, and Mme Stolz, who governs the director, will allow no better singer than herself. The decorations are fine, the costumes very rich. I have sent through Glücksberg two volumes for Ludwika and Izabela: the Old and New Testaments with English engravings. The engravings have been regarded here as fine; they are from the most famous masters of the old and new schools: Rafael, Rubens, Poussin. Many of the pictures are here in the Louvre; perhaps Ludwika will remember them. For Anton, who has no children, I have sent a little volume of Gavarni's drawings, *des enfants terribles,* and so on, so that he may laugh, and remember the light and silly wit of Paris. For Kalasanty Grandville's drawings illustrating proverbs. Grandville was the first to begin a career of this kind and no one has understood it better than Gavarni. You have probably seen Grandville's Lafontaine.

24 December. You see, there is no keeping one's head on his shoulders here, before New Year. The doorbell never leaves off tinkling. Today the entire household has colds. That I cough insufferably is not surprising; but the Lady of the house has a cold, and her throat hurts, so that she has to keep her room, which makes her very impatient. The better health people usually have, the less patience they have in bodily suffering. There is no remedy for that in the world; even intellect is no help. All Paris is coughing this week. Last night there was a huge *tempête,* thunder and lightning, hail and snow; the Seine is enormous; it is not very cold, but intolerably wet. Klengel, from Dresden, is here, with Pani Niesołowska. He called on me and I have promised to call on her. Perhaps it had better not be mentioned. Liszt also called on me; he has separated from Mme Calergis, and I see, from my questions, that there has been more talk than fact.

Tytus's brother has been here; he is better, and has gone to Italy. He told me a lot about Tytus, and I liked him very much. Embrace Tytus. Gutmann you have doubtless already seen. Łaski, whom I saw at the opera, can also tell you that he saw me in good health. Here the new year is starting badly on account of the weather; the shopkeepers complain that there are fewer *flaneurs*[1] than usual. I have still not ventured into the town for my shopping. I must find something for my goddaughter, and meanwhile my godson will get nothing this year; but that is a long way off! I should like to leave him a grand fortune, but that, somehow, is not in my nature. I'll think about it some time, when I go to bed and can't sleep. I have tried over part of my violoncello sonata with Franchomme, and it goes well. I don't know whether I shall have time to print it this year. Fryderyk's wife's uncle came to see me lately. He is a dear and good soul; has grown younger, plays the fiddle, he tells me, as he did in his youth; and does not cough. He is healthy, kind and witty; bears himself simply and well, wears no wig, only his own grey hair; in a word, is still so handsome, that the young folk of today may well look old beside him. Méry has not written to me for a very long time and I have no news of him. The belovéd being is not well. Today is Christmas Eve (Our Lady of the Star).[2] They don't know that here. They eat dinner at the usual hour: 6, 7, or 8, and only a few foreign families keep up those customs. For instance, yesterday Mme Stockhausen did not come to the dinner at the Perthuis' (of my sonata), because she was busy with preparations for the children, for today. All the protestant families keep Christmas Eve, but most Parisians make no difference between today and yesterday. We have a sad Christmas Eve here, because she is ill and will not have a doctor; her cold is very bad, and she has had to go to bed. Everybody curses the climate of Paris; they forget that in the country in winter it is still worse, and that winter is winter everywhere. These two or three months are hard to get through. I often ask

[1] idlers.
[2] A Polish name for Christmas Eve.

myself how people of impatient temper can live under a sky even more inclement than this one. Sometimes I would give years of my life for a few hours of sunshine. I have outlived so many persons younger and stronger than I, that I think I must be immortal. Vernet's daughter, the wife of Delaroche, who did the hémicycle at the *Palais des Beaux Arts,* died a few days ago. All Paris grieves for her. She was a person of really delicate intelligence, quite young, and pretty, though very thin. All the celebrities here were guests in her house; everyone adored her; she was happy in her domestic life, rich and respected. Her father was at the head of the mourners, and blubbered like a calf; there was a moment when they thought the mother would lose her reason. — *26 December.* Yesterday and today Mme S. has been in bed here, with a sore throat. She is a little better. In a few days she will probably be all right, but meanwhile I have no more time to write to you. Sol also has a cold; and I worst of all. I embrace you all heartily. Don't ever worry about me; the Lord is good to me. I love you. Happy New Year to you and all friends.

F. Ch.

[In a postscript:]

Mme S. embraces Ludwika. I send a note from Mlle de Rozières. I have no time to read over what I have written.

207.

[In French]

To Mlle de Rozières.

Thanks a thousand times for your good letter. Here is mine for my mother. It is hot weather. The glacière will be welcome. Thank you once more. Everyone is well. We expect Maurice soon. My kindest respects.

Ch.

If you are *ever* sending anything here, would you please include my little score of the *Mozart Requiem*, which I left at No. 5 (or No. 9), and which is with the Stabat.

Nohant, Whitsuntide, 1846.

She sends you a thousand loves and will write to you.

208.

[In French]

To the Same.
Nohant, Saturday [*Postmark: La Châtre, 2 September 1846*].

I send you, dear Mlle de Rozières, a very urgent so-called manuscript (you will find in it blank music paper at your service); it is a fraud, to induce Pierre to bring the *touton Havannais.*[1] Give it to Pierre only on the morning of his departure, which should be Wednesday, the 22nd, at half past 7, from Nôtre Dame de Victoire [*sic*]. Be so kind as to do your utmost to make it reach Mme Sand complete. I rely on your affection for her. Louise embraces you. Thanks, thanks in advance for your kindness. Please also examine Pierre's list of commissions, so that he may forget nothing. Goodbye, good day, good evening, good night; I press your hand.

Yours faithfully,

CH.

209.

[On paper with the initials: *G. S.*]

To his Family.

Begun a dozen times; today I will send it. I enclose a line for Ludwika from the Lady of the house.

[1] A mixture of French and Polish: *tytuń* = tobacco.

Sunday, 11 October 1846.
Ch. de Nohant, at the table by the piano.

My dearest Ones.

No doubt you are already back from your holidays. All at home; Mummy back from Panna Józefa; and Ludwika from the Ciech[omskis'], and the Antons from the gardens of the mineral springs, with a new stock of health for the winter. Here we have had such a beautiful summer as I cannot remember for a long time; and, though it is not a very fertile year, and in some districts there is anxiety about the winter, here they do not complain, as the vineyard harvest is particularly good; in Burgundy it is even better than in the year 1811, for *qualité,* but not for *quantité.* Yesterday the Lady of the house made jam here, from the kind of grapes known as Alexandrian. It is a kind with very large clusters of muscat form; but in this climate it does not ripen perfectly, and therefore is excellent for jam. There is not much of any other fruit; but thick foliage, still very green, and abundance of flowers. There is a new gardener. Old Pierre, whom the Jędrzejewiczes saw, has been dismissed, in spite of his 40 years' [service], even from the Grandmother's days; and so has the good Françoise, Luce's mother: the two most old established servants. God grant that they may please the young man and the new cousin better. Sol, who has been very unwell, is now quite strong again; and who knows whether, in a few months, I may not write to tell you that she is to be married to that handsome boy whom I mentioned to you in my last letter. The whole summer has been spent here on various drives and excursions in the unknown district of the *Vallée Noire.* I was not *de la partie,* for these things tire me more than they are worth. I am so weary, so depressed, that it reacts on the mood of the others, and the young folk enjoy things better without me. I did not go to Paris, as I expected to do, but I had a very good opportunity to send my musical manuscripts, so I took advantage of it and did not have to move. But I expect to be in the Square in a month, and hope still to catch Nowak[owski], about whom I know only from Mlle de Rozières, that he left a card in my lodging. I should like to see him. But he is not wanted here. He will remind me of many things. And then, we can talk Polish: Jan is no longer here, and since Lorka left, I have not spoken a word in my own tongue. I write to you about Lorka. Though she was courteously received here, there has been no kindly memory of her since she left. The cousin did not like her, therefore the son did not; so there were jokes, and from jokes it went on to insults, and as I did not like that, we don't mention her at all. It needed so fine a soul as Ludwika to leave a good memory behind her with everyone here. More than once the Lady of the house said to me in Lorka's presence: — "*Votre sœur vaut cent fois mieux que vous*";[1] to which I replied: — "*Je crois bien.*"[2] Let Izabela tell me whether Anton's parents are still alive, and various things of the sort. Jaś has written, after eight years; lamenting that he did not listen to me, but saying that now he is working as best he can, and trying to make use of the knowledge that he acquired long ago in Grignon. He is well, and well-intentioned; he lives in Gascony, and works. I have written to him and hope to write again. Today the sun is shining beautifully and they have gone for a drive; I did not want to go, and am making use of the time to have a chat with you. That little dog, Marquis, has stayed behind with me, and is lying on my sofa. He is a remarkable creature: his coat is like marabou, and pure white; Mme S[and] attends to him herself every day, and he is as clever as you please. He even has originalities which are quite enigmatic. For instance, he will never eat or drink from any gilded vessel; he pushes with his head, and overturns it if he can.

I have read in the Presse, among other names, that of my godfather, as a member of the Frankfort congress of prison workers. If he should come as far as Paris, I should like to see him; I will write to Mlle de Rozières, asking her, if she should find such a card at my concierge's, to let me know at once. Among other news, you have probably already heard of M. Leverrier's new planet. Leverrier, of the Paris observatory, noticing certain irregularities in the planet Uranus, ascribed them to some other planet, still unknown, and described its distance,

[1] Your sister is worth a hundred of you.
[2] I should think so.

direction, size: in a word, everything, just as Galle in Berlin and — [Adam] in London have now observed it. What a triumph for science, to be able to arrive at such a discovery by means of calculation. At the last sitting of the Academy of Science, M. Arago proposed that the new planet should be named Leverrier, but suggested calling it Janus. M. Leverrier would prefer Neptune. But in disagreement with a certain proportion of the Academy of Science, many were in favour of naming the planet after the discoverer who proved the thing purely by force of calculation: a feat unheard of until now in the history of astronomy; and as there are comets called Vico and Hind, and Uranus was called Herschel, why should there not be a planet Leverrier? The king at once made him an officer of the legion of honour. Also you have doubtless heard of the invention of *la poudre de coton* [1] by Herr Schönbein. Here people are curious about it, but have not seen it yet. But in London, experiments made in the presence of Prince Albert (the Queen's husband) confirmed the statement that it is stronger, makes no smoke, is not greasy or dirty, and if soaked with water regains its force after drying. The explosion is much quicker than with ordinary powder; because, when it is placed on the ordinary kind, *l'explosion a lieu,*[2] and the other does not even catch fire. But I am writing scientific things to you, as if you had not Antek, or Bełza. Wish the latter joy in his new status. Lord, how pleased Matusz[yński] would have been about that. There is not a day that I do not think of him. I have not now one of my school friends left in Paris. But *à propos* of inventions, here is one more, which is more *de mon domaine.*[3] Mr. Faber, in London (a professor of mathematics), a mechanician, has exhibited a very ingenious automaton, which he calls Euphonia, and which pronounces fairly clearly not one or two words, but long sentences, and, still more surprising, sings an air of Hayden [*sic*] and *God save the Queen.* If the directors of opera could have many such *androids,* they could do without chorus singers, who cost a lot and give a lot of trouble. It's a strange thing, to get to that by means of levers, bellows, valves, little

[1] guncotton.
[2] the explosion takes place.
[3] in my line.

chains [an undecipherable word], pipes, springs, etc., etc. I once wrote to you about Vaucanson's drake, which digested what it ate; Vaucanson also made an android that played on the flute. But until now no machine has sung *God save the Queen* with the words. Two months ago this Euphonia was exhibited in Egyptian Hall, which, as Bartek knows, is a place given up to various curiosities. A great rival of the Italian opera is being prepared in London for next year. Señor Salamanca, a Spanish banker, a member of the Chamber of [?], has taken a lease of a theatre called *Covent Garden;* one of the largest theatres in London, but one that has never had much success, on account of its site, which is far away from the fashionable world. Mr. Lumley, the general director of the Royal Italian theatre, which is recognized by the whole London world as the elegant one, did not hurry himself over engaging his usual singers for next year; he felt quite sure of having them in his theatre with its silken hangings. Salamanca has got ahead of him, and has engaged, at higher salaries, Grisi, and Mario, and Persiani; in a word, all, except Lablache. So there will be two theatres. Mr. Lumley is said to have engaged, besides Lablache, Miss Lind, and Pischek (of whom Berlioz said that he is the best Don Juan) — [?] So, as fashion and elegance count for more in London than any wonders of art, next *saison* will be interesting. It is said that the old opera (that is Mr. Lumley's) will hold out, for *toutes les chances sont*[1] that the Queen will frequent it as usual. The Parisian opera has not yet given Rossini's operas. Habeneck, the conductor of the orchestra, has had a bad attack of apoplexy, which has compelled him to refrain from conducting for a few months. But he is now well again, and M. Pillet (the conductor) has been waiting partly for him. The Italians have already started in Paris. Coletti, a baritone, who is new to Paris, has appeared in "Semiramide," and is very well spoken of. He is young and good-looking, apart from his talent, and various tales have been going round about him for some time. His father had trained him for the church, but he left Rome, and became an actor in Naples. In Lisbon he spent several years, turning women's heads, it is said; and (if what

[1] all the chances are.

one used to hear about that is true) two ladies fought a duel over him there; if, with all that, he really sings very well, he ought to do. I doubt whether duels will be fought over him in Paris, but they will pay him well, better than in Portugal. He has also sung with success in Madrid, where a great festival is now in preparation for the wedding of the Queen with her cousin, and of the Infanta, her sister, with the last son of King Philippe, the duke of Montpensier. Dumas, M. Maquet (a young author, who writes his *feuilletons* for him under his directions) and Louis Boulanger, a well known painter, have been sent from here together by the minister of education, M. Salvandy, with the mission of describing and painting all the ceremonies and events. There is a great deal of talk about the presents which the duke of Montp[ensier] is to bring for his betrothed. The Queen (who is very fat, though young) is preparing for her bridegroom, besides the throne, a collar of the golden fleece in diamonds, and also a very rich sword with a diamond hilt, *dont la lame a servi à Charles III, et le bâton de capitaine général.*[1] 17 gorgeous carriages are being prepared, to take the bridal party to the Atoch [*sic*] church, where both marriages are to be solemnized together, and for the journey to Madrid from Aranjuez (which is pronounced Aranhuez). It's about like Versailles here. If such descriptions amuse you, you probably have them by Dmuszewski, in your papers. You doubtless know that the Infanta is not yet quite 15 years old, and that she is better looking than the Queen. Next month her husband will bring her back to Paris, where there is to be a ball in the *Hôtel de Ville* and various other festivities. If I see her, I will tell you whether she is as beautiful as the duchess of Joinville (a Brazilian princess), who is the beauty of the family: tall, pale, dark, with large eyes. Mlle Rachel, who is said to have wanted to resign from the French Theatre on account of illness, is better, and they say that she will soon appear again. You know that Walewski has married Signorina Ricci, an Italian, whose mother was a Poniatowska, the sister of that musical amateur who writes operas in Vienna, and who has now been in Paris, where Pillet has given him a poem for a grand opera. The poem is by the Dumas, father and

[1] the blade of which belonged to Charles III, and a fieldmarshal's bâton.

son. For Dumas, though still young, has a son (from before his marriage), who is also a writer. I don't know the title of Poniatowski's new opera, but it is to be performed this winter.

Today we have thunder here, and it's rather hot. The gardener is transplanting flowers. Some additional land has been bought for the *Jardin des Plantes* at a cost of something over 9 thousands, adjoining, among other *terrains,*[1] some which once belonged to Buffon. All the same, it will never be on a hill and above the Wisła [Vistula], like your beautiful situation. The giraffe, which, I think, was still there, for the Jędrzejewiczes to see, is dead. I wish I never had any other sad news to write. This year I have received more notices of weddings than of deaths; except old *count de Sabran,* whom I liked very much; about whom I perhaps wrote to you 8 years ago; who wrote charming fables, or rather invented them orally, for he wrote nothing, or very little; he imitated some of Krasicki's. His was the only funeral invitation I have received. But I have seen one of my girl pupils married in Bordeaux, another in Genoa: in Genoa, where they are only now putting a monument to Christopher Columbus, who was born there. I must have written to you from there about the palace which still bears his name and *écusson.*[2] Mme Viardot is in Berlin with her husband and mother. She has not been here this year. In a month she will be in Paris, where I expect to see her, and will then return to Berlin, where she is engaged for the winter. It is said that, besides Grisi and Persiani, Salamanca has engaged her for next summer in London, but I know nothing about that *directement.* I should like to fill up my letter with good news, but I know none, except that I love you and love you. I play a little, I write a little. Sometimes I am satisfied with my violoncello sonata, sometimes not. I throw it into the corner, then take it up again. I have three new mazurkas,[3] I don't think they have the old [word illegible]; but for that one must have time to judge rightly. When one does a thing, it appears good, otherwise one would not write it. Only later comes reflection, and one discards or accepts the thing. Time is the best censor, and

[1] sites.

[2] coat of arms.

[3] B major, F minor, and C sharp minor; dedicated to Countess Czosnoska; published in 1847. [Op.]

patience a most excellent teacher. I hope soon to have a letter from you; but I am not worrying, and I know that, with your large family, it is difficult for you to get round to writing to me, especially as, between us, the pen is not enough; I don't even know how many years we should have to spend talking, *pour être au bout de notre latin,*[1] as they say here. So don't be surprised, or grieved, if you don't get letters from me, because it will be for the same reason as with you; the pleasure of writing to you is mixed with a certain annoyance: the conviction that there are no words between us, scarcely even things. My greatest happiness is to know about your health and state of mind. Always keep hopeful thoughts; you [2] have children to be a comfort to you (I write in the plural, because I know what the Antons are to their sister's children); and of the Grandmother [illegible] one need not speak! If only you keep you health, all is well. I am fairly well here, as the weather is good. The winter is approaching mildly, and with care should pass harmlessly like last one; thank the Lord that things are no worse. So many folk have a worse time. True, many have a better time, but I don't think about them. I have written to Mlle de Rozières to ask the *tapisseur* [3] to put in the carpets, curtains and doorhangings. It will soon be time to think of the treadmill, that is: the lessons. I shall probably leave here with Arago, and leave the Lady of the house to stay on for some time, as her son and daughter are in no hurry to return to town. Last year there was a question of spending the winter in Italy, but the young ones preferred the country. But in the spring, if Sol or Maurice should get married (both things are in the wind) she may change her plans. This is between ourselves. It will probably end that way this year. The boy is 24, the daughter 18. But let all this remain between us. It is 5 o'clock, and so dark that I can scarcely see. I must end this letter. In a month I will write to you from Paris. Meanwhile I look forward to having a chat about you with Nowak. Embrace Tytus if you see him, and the lodger Karol; and my godfather, when he returns; and if next year he should

[1] at the end of our Latin.

[2] In these family letters, except for messages to one individual or another, the plural pronoun: *Wy* (you) is employed, instead of: *Ty* (thou).

[3] upholsterer.

go to Brussels for a congress like this year's one in Frankfort — that is where it is to be —, I have great hope of seeing him, for the railway has long been finished. Write to me about the Józios too, and about all our good friends.

I embrace you most heartily, and I kiss Mummy's hands and feet.

CH.

[In a postscript:] I am sorry for this empty sheet of paper that goes to you with nothing on it; but if I don't send this now *à la hâte,* I shall begin again tomorrow and never get finished. I am sending it by Mlle de Rozières, who will slip in a card for Ludwika, as usual. I embrace you all most heartily.

210.

[In French]

To MESSRS. BREITKOPF AND HÄRTEL IN LEIPSIC.

I, the undersigned, Fred. Chopin, domiciled in Paris at 34 rue St. Lazare, acknowledge that I have sold to Messrs. Breitkopf and Haertel in Leipsic the rights of the following works composed by me; namely:

Op. 60 Barcarole for Piano
Op. 61 Polonaise for Piano
Op. 62 Two Nocturnes for Piano

I declare that I have ceded this property to the said firm for all time and all countries including Russia and excepting France and England and I acknowledge that I have received the price agreed upon, for which a separate receipt has been given. Paris, 19th November 1846.

FR. CHOPIN

211.

[In French]

To MME GEORGE SAND.
Wednesday, 3 o'clock [*25 November 1846*].

I trust that your headache is over and that you are now better than ever. I am very glad that all your company has returned, and I wish you fine weather. Here it is dark and damp, and one cannot avoid colds. Grzym. is better. He had an hour's sleep yesterday for the first time in seventeen days. I have seen Delacroix, who sends a thousand kind messages to all of you. He is suffering, but he goes to his work at the Luxembourg. Yesterday evening I went to Mme Marliani. She was just going out with Mme Scheppard, M. Aubertin (who has had the audacity to read your: "Mare au diable"[1] aloud in college as an example of style), and M. Arpentigny. They were going to hear a new prophet. He is not an apostle. His new religion is that of the Fusionists;[2] their prophet had a *révélation* in the Meudon wood, and *saw* God. He promises, as the highest happiness in a certain eternity, that there shall be no more sex. This idea does not greatly please Mme M[arliani], but the captain is *for* it, and declares that the baroness *en ribotte*,[3] every time that she makes fun of his *fusionism*. Tomorrow I will send you the fur and the other things you want. The price of your piano is nine hundred francs. I have not seen Arago, but he must be well, because he was out when Pierre took him your letter. Please thank Marquis for his laments at my door. Be happy and well. Write when you need anything.

Your devoted

CH.

[1] *The Devil's Pool;* one of G. Sand's stories of Berrichon life.
[2] The name Fusionists, applied to a political coalition, was not used till after the revolution of 1848.
[3] raves over it.

To your dear children.

I have your letter, which has come six hours late. It is good, good and perfect. Well then, I will not send your things to-morrow, I will wait. Won't you send me your cloak to have it attended to here? Have you any workwomen who could do it? Then, I await your instructions. I am very glad the sweets were a success. I am lacking in steel and flint but I do not know whether I have enough tinder. I will take this letter to the big post office before going to see Grzym.

212.

[In French]

To the Same.

Paris, 12 December 1846. Saturday, half past two.

How nice of your salon it is to be warm, and of the snow at Nohant to be charming, and of the young people to hold a carnival! Have you a sufficient choice of quadrilles for the orchestra? Borie has been to see me; I will send him the piece of cloth that you mention. Grzym. has almost recovered, but now Pleyel has a relapse of fever. He has become invisible. I am very glad that our bad weather here has not made itself felt with you. Be happy and well, you and yours.

CH.

To your dear children. I am well.

213.

[In French]

To the Same.

Tuesday, half past two. Paris, 15 December 1846.

Mlle de Rozières has found the piece of cloth in question (it was in Mlle Aug[ustine]'s coat box), and I sent it on yesterday evening to Borie, who, according to what he told Pierre, is not starting today. Here we have just a gleam of sunshine, and Russian snow. I am very glad of this weather for you, and I imagine you walking a lot. Did Dib dance at yesterday's pantomime? Keep well, you and yours.

Always devotedly yours.

To your dear children.

I am well, but I have not the courage to leave my fireplace for a moment.

214.

To WOJCIECH GRZYMAŁA.
[*End of December 1846.*]

I saw the Princess at 5, and she asked me to tell you that she could not carry out your commission today between 5 and 6, but hopes to do so tomorrow!

I could not come to you, because *Wład. Plater* [1] platerized me right up to this moment about the Mazurkas *that were to be played at a ball.* Dinner now, and then several evenings of great grief await me.

Till next year, then;
May it be better than this.

CH.

215.

To the Same.
[*Undated.*]

I had just addressed and sealed my letter, when yours came, before I had put your name. About Plichcina: she is to come to

[1] Count Władisław Plater 1806–1869. Emigrated after the failure of the insurrection of 1830, and founded the Polish national museum at Rapperswyl, Switzerland.

me (and I to her, if I can) — but you know that I can't count on myself at all now. And, besides, she will surely spend her remaining moments in Paris otherwise than on such visits as mine. Anyhow, it is possible that we may not meet, so it will be best if you write *clearly,* not to her son through her, but to her, telling her what she is to say to her son; or, if you like, write to *me clearly* (from your last letter I should not have known what to say to Plichcina). So write to me *clearly,* calling a spade a spade, without mincing matters, what Plichcina is to say and do, and I will *at once* write to her if I am unable to leave here. Only make haste.

Your

CH.

216.

To the Same.
[*Undated.*]

I'm as sick as a dog; that is why I didn't come to you. I know you are always on the island now, for the ball.[1] Tomorrow morning before 10 I will send you the remaining tickets that are not disposed of. And if I can, I'll go to the ball. They are coming from Nohant *on Saturday evening,* probably for dinner. So, if not tomorrow, I shall see you the day after.

Ask your kind *garde* [2] to return my dressing-gown if she has mended it.

I embrace you heartily.

CH.

Thursday evening.

217.

[*Without date or address; probably to Krystyn Ostrowski. The date 1846 has been added in another hand. Original in Rapperswil Museum Library.*]

1 The Czartoryski family frequently gave balls at the Hôtel Lambert on the Isle St. Louis in Paris.
2 *garde-malade:* sick-nurse.

I return with many thanks the letters which you kindly entrusted to me, and if you will be writing shortly to Pan Hanka, please thank him for his kind remembrance and for the music that he has sent to me.

I regret that the bad weather forbids me to thank you personally.

F. Chopin

218.

To Wojciech Grzymała.
[*Undated.*]

My Life

H. Lucas has sent by Louis Blanc a box for today for Mme Sand. So, as she wishes to take her cousin with her to the box, let me come to you for the 3rd act.

During the first two I shall sit by the fire.

I embrace you most heartily.

Ever yours,

Ch.

The number of her box is 6, the first tier.

219.

To the Same.
[*Undated.*]

My Life.

I remind you about a ticket for the Chamber of Deputies for my kind Gutman [Ignace Gutmann]. If you pass along my street, don't neglect my number.

Yours till death.

Ch.

Friday.

I send you a word to Princess Galitzyn, and a copy for yourself.

220.

To the Same.

[*Undated.*]

I thought this was from Pillet, and opened it, and it's I don't know what. They brought it this minute.

CH.

I'm waiting for the doctor, and he doesn't come.

221.

[In French]

To MME GEORGE SAND.

Wednesday, half past 3 [*30 December 1846*].

Your letters made me *very happy* yesterday. This one should reach you on New Year's day, with the usual sweets, the *stracchino* [1] and the *coald-* [*sic*] *cream of Mme de Bonne Chose.*[2]

Yesterday I dined at Mme Marliani's and took her to the Odéon to see " Agnès." Delacroix sent me a good box, and I placed it at Mme Marliani's service. To tell you the truth, I did not much enjoy it, and I greatly prefer " Lucrèce "; but I am no judge of these things. Arago came to see me; he is rather thin and hoarse, but always friendly and charming. The weather is cold, but pleasant for those who can walk, and I hope that your headache is gone, and that you walk, as before, in your garden. Be happy, be happy all of you, in the coming year, and when you can, write to me, please, that you are well.

Yours with all devotion

CH.

1 A kind of cheese.

2 Mrs. Good Thing: possibly the trade name of some dealer in cosmetics.

To your dear children.

I am well. Grzym. is steadily better; I shall go with him today to the Hôtel Lambert, with as many wraps as possible.

222.

[In French]

To the Same.

Tuesday, 3 o'clock [*12 January 1847*].

Your letter ammused me. I have known many bad days, but as for Bonjours,[1] I have never met any except the everlasting candidate for the Academy, M. Casimir Bonjour. My improvised *friend* makes me think of the *megalomaniac* gentleman at Châteauroux, whose name I don't know, and who told M. de Préaux how well he knows me. If this continues, I shall end by regarding myself as an important personage. So you are now quite absorbed in dramatic art. I am sure that your prologue will be a masterpiece, and that the rehearsals will give you much amusement; only don't ever forget your *wilchura*,[2] or your muse. Here it is cold. I have seen the Veyrets, who send you their respects. I won't forget your flowers or your gardener's bill. Take care of yourself, amuse yourself, be well, all of you.

Your devoted

CH.

To your dear children.

[1] *Bonjour:* Good day, is found in France as a family name.
[2] for *wilczura:* in Polish, a garment of wolf fur.

223.

[In French]

To the Same.
Sunday, half past 1 [*17 January 1847*].

I have received your kind letter of Thursday. So you are really rivalling the Porte St. Martin [theatre]. The " Cave of Crime "! — But it's more than interesting. Your *Funambules,*[1] turned into Frenchmen, or even the Opéra with *Don Juan;* it is becoming to the last extent romantic. I can imagine the emotions of Marquis and of Dib. Happy spectators, naïve and not over instructed! I am sure that the portraits in the salon must also regard you with astonished eyes. [?] Amuse yourself as thoroughly as possible. Here, as I told you, there is nothing but illness on illness. Be well, all of you, and be happy.

Yours with all devotion

CH.

To your dear children.
I rub along as I can.

224.

To JÓZEF NOWAKOWSKI IN PARIS.
[*Undated*] *Wednesday evening* [*1847*].

What is happening to you? I have not seen you since Friday. Come to me at No. 9 between 12 and 1. You know that it is difficult for me to leave the house, and if you have not much pleasure in seeing me, I have much in seeing you, and that for no other reason than just because you are the same person as in the old days at home, and such an original as no other under the sun. When once you leave here, even if you were to pay for

[1] tightrope dancers.

it we shan't see each other any more. Afterwards you'll be sorry that you didn't give me a sight of your whiskers again.

CH.

225.

To WOJCIECH GRZYMAŁA.
[*Paris, 17 February 1847.*]

MY DEAREST LIFE!

I beg you, come *without fail* this evening about eight. Besides the household you will find Arago and Delacroix. I will play a duet with Franchomme. But *come*, my Life, if only for a moment. Today is Ash Wednesday. Come, if only for a penance, for having spent carnival sadly.

Your old

CH.

Wednesday.

226.

[In French]

To MME GEORGE SAND.
Saturday [*10 April 1847*].

Thanks for your good news. I passed it on to Maurice, who will have to write to you. He is well; I too. Everything here is as you left it. No violets, no jonquils, no narcissus in the little garden. They have removed your flowers, they have taken down your curtains; that is all. Be happy, be in a good humour, take care of yourself; and just a word about all that when you can!

Your devoted

CH.

227.

To his Family.

[Paris. *The year is not given, but the contents show it to have been written in 1847.*]

Begun in the week before Easter, and I am finishing it on April 19th.

MY BELOVED DEARS.

When I don't answer at once, afterwards I can't get started, and my conscience drives me away from the paper instead of to it. Mme Sand has been here for 2 months, but leaves for Nohant directly after Easter. Sol is not going to be married yet; after they had arrived here for the contract, she changed her mind; I am sorry about it and sorry for the boy, who is a good fellow and in love; but it is better that it should happen before the wedding than after. It is supposed to be just put off, but I know what is behind. You ask what I shall do this summer; just the same as always: I shall go to Nohant as soon as it is warm, and meanwhile I shall stay here and give a lot of lessons, not fatiguing ones, in my own place, as before. If Tytus comes abroad, as he intended, I should like to spend a little time with him here. About you Barcińskis, it seems as if you are not decided; but if you do come I should be able to meet you somewhere, because I have time in the summer, and can spend a little of the money earned during the winter if I have any luck with health. This year my attacks (*crises* — not to write it in the manner of the nurse that Albert had when he was ill: "*La cerise de Monsieur*"[1]) — well, my attacks have not been frequent, in spite of the extreme cold. I have not yet seen Pani Ryszczewska. Pani Delfina Potocka (for whom I have a real affection) was to have called on me with her, but went to Nice a few days ago. Before she left I played her my violoncello sonata with Franchomme in my lodging. That evening, besides her, I had the prince and princess of Württemberg and their daughter, and Mme Sand; and it was nice and warm.

[1] *Crise:* attack (of illness); *cerise:* cherry.

Franch[omme] has this minute brought my box for tomorrow's Conservatoire, and sends greetings to the Jędrzejewiczes. Poor fellow, all his three children are seriously ill with measles. A trouble from which I am safe. Nowak (whom Franch. often saw at my place, but regarded him as stupid, ever since he was once present when Nowak would not go with me to an evening at Legouvé's, where he would have met a whole crowd of the learnéd world, and would have seen and heard, for instance, Lablache) — Nowak is perhaps already with you. He is a good fellow, but so empty-headed, that may the Lord have mercy on him. For example: he had a letter to Janin. Two or three weeks before he left, he told me about it. I said that it was too late; but the same day I took him for the evening to Gavard, and Janin was there; so I wanted to introduce him, but he did not wish it. A few days later, he came and told me that he had given the letter to Janin, and that Janin is going to write an article about him; but asked me to write and tell Janin what to say about his compositions, and that my letter must be sent off by 4 that afternoon. I could not understand this. I asked: with whom did he go to Janin. He replied: with the editor of the Courier, an *intimate* friend of Janin. I know the editor *en chef* of the Courier, Durieu; I ask: is it he? No; some other name, which I had never heard in my life. But I thought it might be some household friend of Janin; so I told Nowak to come to me the next morning, and we would go to Janin together, so that he could tell me himself what he wanted to know. The next morning I announce myself at Janin's; he and his wife received me most charmingly, and I explained that I had come to thank him for his kind reception of my countryman. To which he replied that he had told Nowak, a few words from me (*un petit mot de Chopin*) would be all the introduction he needed: — *et imaginez-vous, he added, qu'il s'est fait presenter par un imbécile dont je ne sais même pas le nom;* [1] so the *ami intime* was a person whose very name Janin does not know. We both laughed over the good Nowak, and he regarded the few words from me as an article; poor Nowak understands no French at all, except

[1] And imagine that he had himself introduced by an idiot whose name I don't even know.

garçon, café, bougie, cocher, doner [*sic*], *jolie mademoiselle, bon* [*sic*] *musique*.[1] Like Cichocki with the little stove, he spent his time here over some bit of furniture, and finally I was obliged to send for him in order to see him. His studies are being published here through my mediation, and with a dedication to me. This publication seems to be all the world to him. It makes him happy to be in print. He is too old to learn anything new, or to get any sense into his head. He is kind, and what he bites off he will eat, so I am fond of him as he is, we have known each other so long; but I had forgotten that there are still so many persons with us, who live without knowing how, why, or to what end. As far as he can, he loves us all; and as far as I could, I helped him here; but I often knocked at the door of his soul, and there was no one at home.[2] His wig (which Durand made for him) covers a big hole; but he understands and knows that himself, for where and how was he educated? On my side, I expected too much of him, but I could not dissociate him from memories of you. He gave me Kolberg's [3] songs; good intentions, but too narrow shoulders [for the job]. Often when I see such things, I think it would be better to have nothing; this laborious stuff only distorts things and renders harder the work of the genius who will one day disentangle the truth. Till that time, all these beautiful things remain, rouged, with their noses straightened and their feet cut down, or stuck on stilts; a laughing-stock for those who look upon them without respect.

I have written too useless things to you, but a week ago. Today I am again alone in Paris; Mme S. has left with Solange, the cousin (that one) and *Luce*, and three more days have passed. Yesterday I had a letter from the country; they are well and cheerful, only they have had rain, as we have here. This year's exhibition of painting and sculpture began some weeks ago; there is nothing very important by masters already known, but some new real talents have been discovered. There is a sculptor named Clésinger, who is exhibiting only the second

1 Waiter, café, candle, cabman, give, pretty young lady, good music.

2 A Polish and Russian idiom: "Rat-tat-tat; no one at home": no brains.

3 Oskar Kolberg: "*Pieśni ludu polskiego*": *Songs of the Polish Folk;* a collection of folk songs with piano accompaniments written by Kolberg.

year, and a painter, Couture, whose enormous canvas, representing a conversation in Rome at the time of the Roman decadence, attracts everyone's attention. Remember the sculptor's name, for I shall often write to you about him; he has been introduced to Mme S. Before she left he made a bust of her, and one of Solange; everyone admires them greatly, and they will probably be exhibited next year. I start this letter for the 4th time today, 16th of April, and don't know whether I shall even now get it finished, for I must go today to Scheffer, to pose for my portrait, and must give 5 lessons. I have written to you about the exhibition; now about music. David's: " Christopher Columbus " has almost as great a success as The Desert. I have not yet heard it, though it has been performed three times, and I don't feel impatient to hear it. One young unbroken colt said: " *On a crié bis, on a crié ter* (terre means earth, land). The 4th part, in which there are Indian songs, is said to be very good. Yesterday Vieuxtemps gave his second concert; I could not go, but Franchomme told me today that his playing was great, and that his new concerto is very beautiful. He came to see me the day before yesterday, with his wife; I played to him for the first time. But that yesterday, at Leo's they sat me down at a table after dinner, to look at the album of a certain painter who has travelled about America for 16 years, and I could not put it down (wonderful things! But too many to see at one time) — but for that, I should have gone to Vieuxtemps's concert. Tomorrow they promise a Spanish theatre (at the Italian opera). A Spanish troupe has arrived, and they are to play at court today. The queen mother of Spain is here now (Christina). Today, before the Spaniards, Mlle Rachel is to play Athalie at court; she is said to be marvellous in the part; I have not yet seen it. Athalie is given with Gossec's choruses. Gossec was a well known and respected French composer at the end of last century. In the choruses to Athalie (which are fairly dull) it has been customary of late to play at the end a very beautiful chorus from Haydn's " Creation." When Gossec was very old (about 35 years ago), hearing this, he remarked quite naïvely: — " *Je n'ai aucun souvenir d'avoir écrit celà.*" [1] People found it very easy to believe him. I

[1] I have no recollection of having written that.

send Ludwika a note from Mlle de Rozières, but not from Mme S., for they were in a hurry to start. Today I have again had news from Nohant; they are well, and again rearranging the house — they like altering arrangements — and Luce, who left here with them, has also been dismissed on arriving, so they tell me. So, of the old servants whom the Jędrzejewiczes saw, not one is left. The old gardener, who had been 40 years there, then *Françoise,* who had served for 18 years, now Luce, who was born there and was carried to her christening in the same cradle with Solange: — all since the arrival of that cousin, who is calculating on getting Maurice, and he is taking advantage of her. This between ourselves.

11 o'clock. Mlle de Rozières has come, and is warming herself by the fire; she is surprised that my letter has not gone yet, grieves about the age of her own letter and wants to write another. Again an interruption of this letter; the day is gone. Well then, yesterday I went to Scheffer, then visited Delacroix; but that meant that I gave fewer lessons; I did not want to dress for dinner, so I spent the evening at home, humming over tunes from the Wisła [Vistula]. Today I woke at 7; my pupil Gutmann came to ask me not to forget his evening. Durand came, and brought some chocolate; my chocolate is sent to me from Bordeaux, where they make it specially, without any flavouring, in a private house belonging to the cousins of one of my kind pupils, who keeps me going with chocolate. Today we again had a little frost in the morning, but fortunately it was very slight, and probably did no harm to the crops, which are expected to be good this year. Grain is extremely dear here, as you know, and there is much distress, notwithstanding a great deal of *charité.* Mme S. gives a great deal of help in her village and in the district, as you may suppose, and this is one of a dozen reasons why she left here so early this winter, quite apart from the adjourning of her daughter's marriage. Her latest work to come out is: "Lucrezia Floriani," but for the last 4 months the Presse has had her new novel, entitled (for the present) "*Piccinino*" (which means: little one). The scene is laid in Sicily. It has many beauties; I have no doubt that Ludwika will like it better than Lucrezia, which here also has aroused less enthusiasm than

the others. Piccinino is the *sobriquet* [1] given to one of the local bandits, on account of his small size. There are fine characters, both women and men; it is natural and poetic, and I remember how much I enjoyed hearing it read. Now she is again beginning to write something, but in Paris she had not a moment to think quietly. Three more days have passed; this is the 18th. Yesterday I had to give 7 lessons, to pupils who are going away. In the evening, instead of dressing and going out to the *Faubourg St. Germain,* I went with Alkan to see Arnal at the Vaudeville in a new piece by M. Duvert, called: "*Ce que femme veut*" [2] — Arnal is as funny as usual, and informs the public how he wanted *psipsi* [3] in the *chemin de fer* and how he could not get out anywhere, all the way to Orléans. There is not an indecent word, but everybody understands and roars with laughter. Once, he says, the train stopped and he wanted to get out; but they told him it had stopped: "*pour prendre de l'eau pour la machine et celà n'était pas son affaire du tout,*" [4] and so on. Today is the 19th. Yesterday a letter from Nohant interrupted me. Mme S. writes me that she will be here at the end of next month, and to wait for them. Probably it is about Sol's wedding (but not with the man about whom I told you). May God grant them good things. In the last letter they were all cheerful, so I have good hopes. If anyone deserves happiness, Mme S. does. At this moment Turczynowicz brings me Stefan's religious songs, but I can't read them before he leaves, for he says he is starting today. I gave him a word of thanks, for he demanded it in writing. If you meet Stefan anywhere there, thank him, and Kolberg too for his laborious work. I will stop, for I have to give a lesson to young Mme Rothschild, then to a lady from Marseilles, then to an Englishwoman, then to a Swedish one, and at 5 to receive a family from New Orleans who have an introduction from Pleyel. Then dinner at Leo's, an evening at the Perthuis', and to sleep if I can. I embrace you. Nowak is doubtless already with you. Wernik is well; we are beginning to learn a little. Embrace Tytus, and write me about him, also about

[1] nickname.
[2] *What woman wills.*
[3] To pass water.
[4] To take in water for the locomotive, and that was not a bit what he wanted.

Dresden. Lorka is not here; the good soul wrote to me from Dresden. Méry has written from Rome; he is going to Hyères, where Zofia Roseng[art] is; she is fairly well and happy; she has written to me. I embrace Mummy most heartily, and all of you.

[In a postscript:] Jasio writes to me that he is well; but, but! — that he thinks of getting seriously to work, that he counts only on his own powers. I forget many interesting things that I could write to you, and write dull ones instead; but forgive me, my head is not always equally clear; today I have decided to send off this everlasting letter, so be satisfied with the news that I am well and that today there is sunshine for the first time in a week.

228.

[In French]

To MME GEORGE SAND.

[*Undated.*]

Maurice left yesterday morning, well, and in fine weather. Your letter arrived after his departure. I hope to have another letter from you, determining the date of your arrival, so as to have fires in your rooms. So, have good weather, fine ideas and all the happiness in the world.

Yours with all devotion.

CH.

To the young folk.

Wednesday.

229.

[In French]

To the Same.
Thursday, 29th [April 1847].

You perform prodigies of industry, and I am not surprised. May God assist you. You are well, and you will be well. Your curtains are still here. Tomorrow is the 30th. But I am not expecting you, as I have had no definite news. The weather is fine, and the leaves are beginning to try to sprout. You will have a comfortable journey, without having to cut off your sleep. Send me a line before starting, please, because there must be fires in your rooms. Take care of yourself. Be happy and at rest.

Yours with all devotion

CH.

To the young folk.

230.

[In French]

To the Same.
Saturday [15 May 1847].

How can I tell you how much pleasure your good letter that I have just received has given me, and how much interested I am in the excellent details concerning all that is now occupying you. You know well that among your friends, no one more sincerely desires the happiness of your child than I do. Tell her so from me, please. I am well again. God uphold you always in your strength and activity. Be happy and at peace.

Yours with all devotion

CH.

231.

[In French]

To Solange Clésinger.
[*Paris, May 1847.*]

I have already asked your Mother, a few days ago, to convey to you my sincerest wishes for your future; and now I cannot refrain from telling you of all the pleasure that I have derived from your charming little letter, from which you appear to me to be so happy. You are at the summit of joy, and I hope that you will always remain there. With all my soul I desire your unchanging prosperity.

Ch.

232.

[In French]

To Messrs. Breitkopf and Härtel in Leipsic.

I the undersigned Fr. Chopin domiciled in Paris rue St. Lazare No. 34 acknowledge that I have sold to Messrs. Breitkopf and Haertel, Leipsic, the works hereinafter specified and composed by me; namely:
Op. 63 Three Mazurkas for the piano
" 64. Three Waltzes " " "
" 65. Sonata for Piano and Violoncello

I declare that I have ceded this property to them without any reserve or limit for all time and for all countries except France and England, and I acknowledge that I have received the price agreed upon, for which a separate receipt has been given.

F. Chopin

Paris, 30 June 1847.

233.

[In French]

To Solange Clésinger.
[*Undated.*]

I am much grieved to know that you are ill. I hasten to place my carriage at your service.

I have written to this effect to your Mother.

Take care of yourself.

Your old friend
Ch.

Wednesday [1]

234.

To Wojciech Grzymała.
[*Paris*] *17 September 1847. Wednesday.*

Princess Marcellina has come for a few weeks. That is, they are still in Dieppe. I am too ill to find rooms for them; if you can, will you come? I hope you are well. Here the bad weather is starting already.

Write me a line if you can't come.

Yours till death
Ch.

[1] This letter, doubtless written in the summer of 1847, appears to have been the immediate cause of the rupture between George Sand and Chopin. She had quarrelled with her daughter and son-in-law, had turned them out of the house, and had expressed a wish that he should cut them. [Op.]

235.

[In French]

To SOLANGE CLÉSINGER.
Paris, Saturday, 18 Sept. 1847.

I thank you sincerely for your good news. I already have the sachet, and have mentioned to Mlle R.[1] that you will write to her. The other day I entered Lafitte and Co.'s courtyard by one door just as you were leaving by the other; it was quite simple: I had a No. 7 on my cab. That is why I did not answer you yesterday, the 17th for my letter to catch you still at Besançon. So you are to travel about the beautiful Franche-Comté; and I beg you not to forget me in your wanderings, so that I may know where to write to you. My Swede [2] has deserted me, and I cannot follow him to Stockholm. Still no news. And you, keep well.

Allow me to give you a warm handshake, with all my wishes for happiness, to you and to your husband.

CH.

236.

[In French]

To the Same.

I was just writing to thank you for the visit of M. Bouzemond's clerk, and to ask for news of you, when your good letter was brought to me. It has done me more good than a bottle of Molin, and now I feel quite ready to let myself be carried off by M. de Rothschild to spend a few days on his estate at Ferrières. Poor Enrico was snuffed out three days ago in an asylum (Mme Marl[iani] has let the apartment and has been living in a *hôtel*

[1] Mlle de Rozières.

[2] A Swedish masseur, who had been treating Chopin. See Delacroix's Journal. Vol. I, p. 252. [Op.]

garni). She begins to miss the good Enrico badly. She came to see me yesterday and told me that she was astonished to have received from Nohant no answer to her last letter. (Apparently she had asked some question, according to her custom.) No one has any news; neither Grzym., nor Delacroix, who sincerely regrets not having seen you, nor Mlle de R[ozières], whom I will notify of your next letter. She expects soon to begin her lessons at Chaillot. I have already begun my lessons; and there is a pupil waiting now for the end of this sheet, which I should have liked to fill with all sorts of good news; but I have none to give you, and I relinquish my pen, wishing both of you all possible happiness, and thanking you with all my soul for your kind words. My old friendship, always and always.

CH.

Press your husband's hand for me, please; and correct my French as of old.
[*Paris*] *Saturday, 2 October* [*1847*].

237.

[In French]

To the Same.
[*Paris*] *Tuesday* [*1847*].

I received your letter with pleasure, and read it with grief. What are all these slanders about! Your husband has never borrowed any *large sum* from me *to pay for your furniture*. You returned me the 500 fr. as soon as you reached Besançon. Also I found the 5 louis in my purse, and always forgot to thank you for the delicate way in which you repaid your creditor for *large sums*.

Your devoted

CH.

To your husband.

238.

[In French]

To the Same.
[*Paris*] *Wednesday, 24* [*November 1847*].

Every morning for the last fifteen days I begin to write, to tell you how sad I am at the outcome of your two visits to Nohant. But the first step is made; you have shown affection, and there is a certain drawing together, since you have been asked to write. Time will do the rest. Also, you know that one must not take too literally everything that people say; and, even if, for example, she will not any longer *know* a foreigner like me, it can scarcely be the same with your husband, who has become a member of the family. Yesterday I saw Mlle de Rozières, who told me that Mme Bascans has had news of you, but still no news from Nohant. Mme Bascans is in bed with a feverish chill. All Paris is ill; the weather is frightful, and you do well to be under a clear sky. Stay there and keep well and in a good humour. I will try to give you some news that will be better than our climate; but for that, this *hateful year* must *end*. Besides all else, it has taken away from Grzym. *all his fortune.* He has just lost everything in an unfortunate commercial affair. Delacroix has been to see me, and asked me to express to you all his regrets that he could not manage to meet you. Bignat has not come. Mme Marliani is having a *legal* separation. Here is news of all sorts. Also, in the *Siècle,* there is an article by your Mother on the history of Louis Blanc. That is all. I choke; I have a headache, and I beg your pardon for my erasures and for my French. Give me a good handshake, you and your husband too. May God keep you.

Your devoted
CHOPIN

[*Paris*] *Wednesday, 24* [*November 1847*].

Give me a sign of life. Next time I will write more and better.

239.

To HIS SISTER, LUDWIKA JĘDRZEJEWICZ.

One of my old letters, begun, and not burned.
[*Paris*] *Christmas, 1847.*

MY VERY DEAREST CHILDREN!

I did not answer at once, because I am terribly busy. For the rest, Mlle de Rozières probably answered Ludwika at once, and told her that I am well and up to my ears in work. Thank you very much for the little bust of my godson. He has a physiognomy of genius; but the person who modelled it is doubtless a mediocrity and involuntarily left his mark on it. I send you by chamberlain Walewski a tiny Lady's Companion for Ludwika from my kind Scottish lady, and have now sent off the New Year engravings by the usual route. Gavard has given me for Ludwika his drawings, half of which I have had for a long time lying here, waiting for an opportunity to send them. Some day I'll bring them myself. Ludwika can thank him if she likes. Besides that there is Bosphore's History of Paris, for Ludwika; "Ireland," "*Rome,*" and "*France*" for Izabela; "*Paul and Virginia*" for little Ludka. For Kalasanty: "*The Gentlemen,*" and: "*The Magdalens,*" and for Bartek: "*The Professors*"; comic. The day before yesterday — Christmas Eve, I spent in the most prosaic manner, but I thought of you. I send you my most earnest wishes, as every year. Lorka is here; I often see her. She has aged; you would like her better now. She leaves this week for Dresden. It is a pleasure to talk with her of you; she loves you sincerely. I have met prince Michael's daughter, and her husband also. I am teaching Mme Calergis; she really plays very well, and in all respects has a huge success in the Parisian great world. Sol is with her father in Gascony. She saw her Mother before leaving. She was in Nohant with the Duvernets; but her Mother received her coldly, and told her that if she will leave her husband she can come back to Nohant. She saw her bridal bedroom converted into a theatre, her boudoir into a dressing-room for actors, and writes that her

Mother spoke to her only of money affairs. Her brother played with her dog; and all he found to say to her was: — "*Veux-tu manger quelque chose?*"[1] Neither the cousin nor those other people were visible; in a word, her two visits were failures. Before leaving next day she went back there; but was received even more coldly than the first time. Still, her Mother did ask her to write, and say what she intends to do. The Mother appears to be more bitter against her son-in-law than against her daughter; yet in the famous letter to me she wrote that her son-in-law is not bad; it is only her daughter who makes him so. It seems as if she wanted, at one stroke, to get rid of her daughter and of me, because we were inconvenient; she will correspond with her daughter; so her maternal heart, which cannot do without some news of her child, will be quieted, and with that she can stifle her conscience. She will believe that she is just, and will pronounce me an enemy for having taken the side of her son-in-law (whom she cannot endure only because he has married her daughter; and I did all I could to prevent the marriage). A strange creature, with all her intellect! Some kind of frenzy has come upon her; she harrows up her own life, she harrows up her Daughter's life; with her Son too it will end badly; I predict it and could swear to it. For her own justification she longs to find something against those who care for her, who have never done her any discourtesy, but whom she cannot bear to see about her, because they are the mirrors of her conscience. Thus, to me she has not written one word more, she will not come to Paris this winter, nor has she mentioned me at all to her daughter. I do not regret that I helped her through the eight most difficult years of her life: the years when her Daughter was growing up and her Son living with his Mother; I do not regret what I have suffered; but I am sorry that the Daughter, that carefully overcultivated plant, sheltered from so many storms, has been broken in her Mother's hand by a carelessness and levity pardonable perhaps in a woman in her twenties, but not in one in her forties. What has been and no longer is, leaves no trace in the register. When, some day, Mme S. thinks the matter over she can have only kind memories of me in her soul. Meanwhile she is now in

[1] Will you have something to eat?

the strangest paroxysm of motherhood, playing the part of a juster and better mother than she really is; and that is a fever for which there is no remedy in the case of heads with such an imagination, when they have entered into such a quagmire. For the rest: — "even cypresses have their caprices." [1] Meanwhile the winter here is not very good. There is a great deal of *grippe*, but I have enough with my usual cough, and am no more afraid of *grippe* than you of cholera. I smell my homeopathic flasks from time to time, give many lessons in the house, and manage as I can. I want to write to you every day; and this letter, begun in the old year, is being finished on January the 6th, 1848. Lorka left for Dresden yesterday. Her step-sister is going to marry Olizar. Before she went to her train we dined together at the house of Pani Ryszczewska, whom I like very much. They are all older, and better than when they were too young. I don't know whether I wrote to you that the good Wojciech-father (Grzymała) has suffered heavy financial losses, and has had — and still will have — grave annoyances. A man who had his fullest confidence, whose *habilité* [2] was known and valued by all bank advisers and persons *du métier*, [3] has swindled him and absconded. The thing is gradually being cleaned up; he comes out as clear as crystal, and is the first to suffer, and those who had shares in the enterprise will lose less than was at first supposed. The enterprise is an *entrepôt* [4] in connection with the *Nord* railway. The goods are housed there, to be then dispatched to right and left. The business is a good and straightforward one, but this gentleman of his, who was the chief manager there, signed for illegal sums to which he had no right; could not pay when they were protested and had to bolt, leaving the whole mess on the shoulders of our good Wojciech, who has succeeded in partially extricating himself, but not entirely yet. I tell you this in case any ugly stories should reach you; there are plenty of charitable folk in the world. A new story by Mme S. is coming out in the Débats: a Berrichon village tale, like the *Mare*. [5] It begins

[1] A quotation from the old Polonaise: "From high Parnassus."
[2] skill.
[3] of that occupation.
[4] storehouse.
[5] *La Mare au Diable.*

well; it is called: "*François le Champi.*" "Champi" is the rural term for the bastard children who are usually given to poor women to bring up, the hospital paying for them. There are also rumours about her memoirs; but Mme S. herself wrote to Mme Marliani that there will be more of her thoughts on art, on literature, etc. than of what is usually understood as memoirs. And, indeed, it would be too early for that; for dear Mme S. will yet pass through strange things in life, before she grows old; many beautiful and many ugly things will befall her. Mme Obreskow is here, and talks a lot to me about Mummy, whenever we meet, and I have promised to dine with her once a week.

240.

[In French]

To SOLANGE CLÉSINGER.
[*Paris*] *31 December 1847.*

I thank you sincerely for your kind remembrance. I do not need to tell you how much happiness I wish you in the year now beginning. I at once took your letter to your husband, who will leave tomorrow, as he tells me, to rejoin you. He has been working hard at his marbles for the exhibition, which has prevented him from leaving Paris earlier. M. de Larac has received notice for the apartment at No 3, as well as for that of Maurice, which makes me inclined to believe in the good idea of my compatriot, if there is a compatriot. So long as everybody is satisfied. I have faith in things coming right little by little; I think that soon you will receive 90 lines instead of 9, and that the grandmother's joy will be the joy of the young mother. You will adore together the little angel that is coming into the world to restore both your hearts to their normal condition. Here is the programme for 1848. There is a new novel, with the title: *François le Champi,* which should begin to appear in a few days in the Débats. Hetzel also makes vague announcements in the newspapers of some kind of *Memoirs.* Mme Marliani has had some news about that, and tells me that the book is to treat of the arts and of literary matters. A certain capitalist, M. Latouche (I believe), will furnish the money for Hetzel, who is merely to publish. I delivered your compliments to Mlle de Rozières, who will write to you if she has not already done so. I cough, and I am entirely taken up with my lessons. It is cold, I do not get out much, for it is too cold. Take care of yourself, and come back in good health, both of you. This year is fairly lively; the national guards have given their habitual serenade in the Square. I have bought some things for my goddaughter at the hôtel Lambert; the sale, up to yesterday, had brought in 20 thousand fr. There were some very fine things. Your husband sent a little water-colour which was very welcome. Delacroix did a little Christ which was much admired. Gudin, Lehman and others also gave some of their drawings. I can't see any more; it is snowing, and getting dark. Mme Adelaïde is dead; there will be deep mourning for 2 months. I choke, and I wish you all possible happiness.

Your devoted

CH.

241.

To LUDWIKA JĘDRZEJEWICZ.
[*Paris*] *Thursday, 10 February 1848.*

MY LIFE!

About your books: the *Gallery of Versailles* is a gift from *Gavard to Ludwika.* The beginning of it was to have gone 6 months ago when there was an opportunity; but it came back to me, and has been lying here. What I am sending now is what has come out since; I don't know how much. One must not look a gift horse in the mouth. *Gavard* gave it to me packed up, so I did not see it, and just sent it through my usual book-seller, and therefore have not sent the beginning, which was not packed, and has got a little dirty from lying in the drawer. Never again will I send you books through that *idiot,* now that Spies is dead. All the *rest* is *correct*. I had no time to sign the *Bosphore* for you, Ludwika. I have no time to ask Gavard what is missing, and *Frank*, through whom it went, cannot know, as I gave it to him packed up, as Gavard sent it. One would have to ask Gavard, and he would have to find out from his employee, and so on; It's not worth while, especially as it was a gift. If, however, it is really necessary, then in next letter. [The words from: "One would have . . ." to "next letter" are crossed out, and a footnote is added with an asterisk:] * Gavard has just come, and has made a note of it. [Letter continues:] As for me, I am as well as I know how to be. Pleyel, Perthuis, Leo and Albrecht have persuaded me to give a concert. All places have been sold out for a week. I shall give it in the Pleyel salon on the 16th of this month. Only 300 tickets, at 20 fr. I shall have the fashionable world of Paris. The King has taken 10, the queen 10, the duchess of Orleans 10, the duke of Montpensier 10, though the court is in mourning and none of them will come. They want to attend a second concert, which I probably shall not give, for even this one bores me. Mme S. is still in the country, with Borie, with her son, with Lambert and Augustine; whom, apparently, she is giving in marriage to some teacher of drawing from a little town called Tulle, a friend of Borie. She has not written one word to me any more, and I don't write either. She has told the landlord to let her apartment here. Sol is with her father, Dudevant, in Gascony; she writes to me. Her husband is here, finishing his marbles for the exhibition, which is to be in March. Sol has been ill at her father's house. They have no money, so it is better for Sol to spend the winter in a good climate. But the poor thing is bored. She has a cheerful lune de miel! [1] Meanwhile her Mother is writing a very fine feuilleton in the Débats. She is putting on a comedy in the village in her daughter's bride-room; she has forgotten herself, is doing crazy things, and will not come to her senses till her heart begins to ache badly; at present it is dominated by her head. I have had my cross to carry. May God pity her, if she can't distinguish between genuine affection and flattery. And yet perhaps it only appears to me that others are flatterers, and perhaps her happiness is really

[1] honeymoon.

there, where I can't see it. Her friends, her neighbours have long understood nothing of what was happening there of late; but now perhaps they are accustomed. For the rest, no one will ever be able to steer through the caprices of such a mind. Eight years of any settled arrangement was too much. God willed just those to be the years in which her children were growing up, and if I had not been there, I don't know how long ago the children would have been with their father, not with her. Maurice, too, will run away to his father at the first opportunity. But perhaps, after all, those are the conditions of her life, of her literary talent, of her happiness? Don't let it worry you, for it's all long over. Time is a great physician. I have not managed to get over it yet. That is why I don't write to you, for what I begin, I burn. There's no use in writing! Or better nothing; only that we have not met for a long time, without any quarrels or scenes, and that I could not go there, on the terms of keeping silence about her Daughter. The Daughter, on the way to her father, saw her mother, but was coldly received by her; her Son-in-law she did not choose to see at all, but is in correspondence with the Daughter, however coldly; which is a comfort to me, for at least something will remain between Mother and Daughter.

[Postscript:] I send this letter so that you may know that I am well, and have the truth about the books.

I will send the letter to de Rozières.

242.

To his family.
[*Paris*] *Friday, 11 February 1848.*

To all my Dear ones.
My Dearest ones.

I have not written to you for a long time, for it's this way: the more behindhand I get, the more things accumulate to write about — and so many — and so many that the sheer mass of them ends in nothing at all. That's how it is that today I am writing you only a few words, so that you may know I am well and have had your letter. I have had *grippe*, like everyone here, and if I write shortly today, it is because my thoughts are occupied with my concert, which is to be on the 16th of this month. My friends came one morning and told me that I must give a concert, that I need not worry over anything, only sit down and play. All tickets have been sold out for a week, and all are at 20 fr. The public is putting down names for a second concert (of which I am not thinking). The court has ordered 40 tickets; and though the newspapers have merely said that perhaps I will give a concert, people have written to my publisher from Brest and from Nantes, to reserve places. I am astonished at such *empressement*,[1] and today I must play, if only for conscience' sake, for I believe I am playing worse now than ever before. I shall play (for the interest of it) Mozart's Trio with Franchomme and Alard. There will be no posters and no free tickets. The hall is conveniently arranged, and has room for 300. Pleyel always jokes about my stupidity, and will decorate the steps with flowers to make me more willing to play. I shall be as if at home, and my eyes will meet scarcely any but familiar faces. I have a piano here already, and play on it. Yesterday I signed for a very fine Pleyel piano and had it packed up to go to Cracow for Pani Adam Potocka (née Branicka). Through someone, I don't know whom, I have received your blanket, which is admired by those who have seen it. I thank you, my Dearest ones. It is cold with you; here the frost is over, but there was a time when the Seine froze over. Wernik is working very well, tell his mother. Nowakowski has written to me, but I have nothing to write about to him. I am giving many lessons. I am very busy, on all sides, and yet get nothing done. Jasio has written me a nice letter; he asks after Antek Bartolo. He has been through a good school of misfortune, has passed through that necessary alembic, and has come out of it a man; I should like to see him here. If you are going to travel, I will do the same, for I doubt whether I shall spend next summer, like this one, in Paris. If

[1] eagerness.

God gives us health, we will meet, and embrace, and talk. More after the concert. Méry is no longer here to write to you for me.

I embrace you most heartily,

CH.

To all.

243.

[In French]

To SOLANGE CLÉSINGER.
[*Paris*] *Thursday, 17 February* [*1848*].

Since your letter came, I have been in bed for several days with a frightful *grippe,* and have given a concert at Pleyel's. Between while, I have started some thirty scribbles to you, and had even finished a letter, when your husband came last week to see me and give me news of you. So my letter needed rewriting, to tell you that I had found your husband well and satisfied with his marbles, and to tell you also how sorry I am about your horrid *jaundice.* Soon now you will have your husband with you, which will complete your convalescence. He will give you the news from here better than I could ever write it. Leroux is in Paris. I met him at Mme Marliani's. He asked me to let him come and see me again; he was very tactful and did not talk about the country [Nohant]. M. de Bonnechose is here. Grzym. is in bed. Paris is ill, and you do well to stay at Guillery. Write me a word in pencil, please, in one of your spare moments; I shall not be so slow in answering now that my *grippe* and my concert are over. Maurice is in Paris. He is not living here. He came to see De Larac without coming upstairs to me. Poor boy, he tricked the people of the house needlessly. Mlle de Rozières is sure to have written to you. I must finish my epistle, for my lessons are to begin. It is needless to tell you how unhappy I am about not being able to write to you always and easily.

Your very devoted

CH.

244.

[In French]

To the Same.
[*Paris*] *Friday, 3 March* [*1848*].

I cannot refrain from writing at once to tell you how happy I am to know that you are a mother and are well. The arrival of your little daughter has given me, as you may suppose, more joy than the arrival of the Republic. Thank God, your suffering is over and a new world begins for you. Be happy and take care of yourselves, all of you. I badly needed your good news. I was in bed during the events; I have had neuralgia all last week. Paris is quiet, from fear. Everyone is enrolled. Everyone is in the national guard. The shops are open, but no buyers. The foreigners are waiting with their passports for the ruined railways to be repaired. The clubs are beginning to form. But I should never end, if I began to write to you about things here.

Thanks again for your good letter.

Your most devoted

CH.

Mallefille is governor of Versailles. That Louis Blanc should be at the Medici Palace as president of the commission for labour organization (the really big question of the day) is quite natural. Barbes is governor of the same Luxembourg Palace. Forgive my erasures and muddles. Mlle de Rozières will write to you.

245.

[In French]

To the Same.
Paris, 5 March, Sunday [*1848*].

Yesterday I went to Mme Marliani, and as I left, I met your Mother in the doorway of the vestibule; she was entering with Lambert. I said good day to your Mother, and my second phrase was: had she had any news of you lately. — " A week ago," she replied. — " You have heard nothing yesterday, or the day before? " — " No." — " Then I can tell you that you are a grandmother; Solange has a daughter, and I am very glad that I am able to be the first to give you this news." I bowed and went downstairs. Combes the Abyssinian (who has tumbled right into the Revolution on arriving from Morocco) was with me, and as I had forgotten to say that you are doing well, an important thing, especially for a mother (now you will easily understand that, Mother Solange), I asked Combes to go up again, as I could not manage the stairs, and tell her that you are *going on well,* and the child too. I was waiting for the Abyssinian at the bottom of the stairs when your Mother came down with him and put to me, with much interest, some questions about your health. I answered that you had written me a few words, *yourself, in pencil,* the day after the birth of your child, that you have suffered much, but that the sight of your little daughter has made you forget everything. She asked me whether your husband was with you, and I replied that the address of your letter appeared to me to be in his handwriting. She asked me how I am; I replied that I am well, and asked the *concierge* to open the door. I bowed, and found myself in the Square d'Orléans on foot, escorted by the Abyssinian.

Your Mother has been here for some days, according to what Boccage told Grzym. She is lodging with Maurice at rue Condé, No. 8, near the Luxembourg. She dines at Pinson's (the restaurant where we once went with Delatouche); that is where she receives, and it was there that she yesterday told Combes to call on her, saying that she is soon leaving for Nohant. I presume that a letter from you awaits her at Nohant. I thought her looking well. I suppose that she is happy in the triumph of republican ideas, and that the news which I gave her yesterday still further increases her joy.

Take care of yourself, take care of all three of you.

Your devoted

CH.

Things continue calm. Mallefille is no longer at Versailles; he was in the government for only three days.

246.

[In French]

To the Same.
[*Paris*] *Saturday, 11 March* [*1848*].

Courage, and be calm. Take care of yourself for those who are left.[1] I have just seen your husband. He is well, he has courage and hope. Yesterday and the day before, I saw him working at his bust of liberty; the bust is finished today, and is considered superb by all the Thorès of Paris. Tomorrow it is to be moved to the hôtel de ville. Marrast is mayor of Paris (M. Bascans will be useful). Your husband knows M. Caussidière, who is at the head of the police and who will have the bust escorted by the national guard. He asked me to tell you that he has too much running about today to be able to write to you, and he will write tomorrow after the bust has been moved, which is to be at 7. So have no anxiety about his health. You see that he does what he can, and that he has courage; take care of yourself in convalescence, so that your separation may be more endurable to both of you. Try to be *calm*, then, for pity's sake *try to be calm;* with the good care you will have from your Father and

[1] Solange's baby had died a few days after birth.

Luce (whom I have always thought of as your kind and attached Luce) your health will return and a new happiness will begin.

I am told that your Mother has left Paris. I have not seen her again since that moment on leaving Mme Marliani's. She has received your letters at Nohant. She is much to be pitied; I feel sure that it is a great blow to her, and I have no doubt that she will do all she can for you. *Courage*, then, and *calmness*. I leave all condolences aside, they seem poor things in the presence of the great sorrows.

Your devoted

CH.

I will write to you often. Don't be anxious about your husband.

247.

[In French]

To the Same.

[*Paris*] *Wednesday, 22 March* [*1848*].

I have just received your letter and have this moment sent to your husband's studio, to know whether he has already started. If he left Paris the day before yesterday, he should now be with you, and he will tell you all you wished to know about the state of affairs here. Everyone is waiting calmly, and things are being quietly disorganized. I am very glad about the kind letters that your mother has written to you. Take care of your health now, and all will go as well as possible. Take advantage of a few rays of sunshine in the south, for here the weather is atrocious.

Your devoted

CH.

To your husband.

248.

To Juljan Fontana.
Paris, 4 April 1848.

My Dear.

Receive as if he were my father, or my elder and therefore better brother, my dear Herbaut, who was my first acquaintance in Paris, when I came here from home. I charge you by the Lyceum,[1] be as kind as possible to him, for he deserves it. He is good, and worthy, and enlightened, and everything, and he will grow fond of you in spite of your bald head. You are a sulky beast, you have never given me a decent word in any of your letters; but it makes no difference; somewhere in your heart you love me just as much as I love you. And perhaps that is even more now, since we have lost Wodziński, and Witwicki, and the Platers, and Sobański, and are both left orphaned Poles.

You are my good old Juljan, and that is enough.

I embrace you heartily, my Dear.

Ch.

If you want to do something good, just sit quiet, and go back only when something really certain begins at home. Our folk are assembling in Poznań [Posen]. Czartoryski has gone first, but God knows how all that will turn out, so that there may be Poland again — What the newspapers write here is all lies. There is no republic in Cracow, nor has the Austrian emperor called himself king of Poland, and in the Lwów [Lemberg] papers, in the address to the Stadion, no one asks him to do so, as quoted here. The King of Prussia also has no particular thought of getting rid of Poznań. He made himself a laughing-stock at home; but in spite of that, the Poznań Germans write him addresses, saying that: — " as this land was won by the blood of their fathers, and as they do not even know Polish, they declare that they do not wish to be under any other government

1 Where Chopin and Fontana had been schoolfellows.

than the Prussian." All this, you see, smells of war, and where it will start, no one can tell. But when it does begin, *all Germany* will be in it; the Italians have already begun. Milan has driven out the Austrians, but they are still sticking in the provinces, and will fight. France will doubtless help, for in order to do things well they must kick out a certain mob — The Russians will doubtless have trouble on their own hand if they molest the Prussians. The Galician peasants have given an example to those of Wolynia and Podolia; there will be no lack of *frightful* things; but at the end of it all is Poland, splendid, great; in a word, Poland. Therefore, however impatient we may be, let us wait till the cards have been well shuffled, that we may not waste our strength, which will be so needed at the right moment. That moment is near, but it is not today. Perhaps in a month, perhaps in a year. All here are convinced that our affairs will be decided before autumn.

YOUR OLD ONE

[A postscript by Teofil Kwiatkowski.]

249.

To WOJCIECH GRZYMAŁA IN PARIS.
[*Paris, undated.*]

I will do as you like, but you are making a mistake if you are really throwing away what is necessary. I will make a special effort to be with you at a quarter before 6, but don't be surprised if I am half a minute late. *In any case I will be with you before 6.*

Your most affectionate

CH.

250.

To the Same.
London, Good Friday [21 April 1848].

I crossed the water without much seasickness. But not by the Courier, and not with my new travelling acquaintances, for they had to search, by boat, for the vessel on the sea. So I preferred the ordinary way of travelling, and yesterday arrived here at 6, as I had been obliged to rest for a few hours at Folkstone. I had a sleep, and now am writing to you.

The good Erskines have thought of everything, even of chocolate, not only of a lodging — which last, however, I shall change, as since yesterday there is a better one in their very street for 4 guineas a week. I am at 10 *Bentinck Street, Cavendish Square,* but in a few days I shall move, so write to their address: 44 *Welbeck Street.* They asked me a lot after you. You would not believe how kind they are; I have only just noticed that the paper on which I am writing has my monogram, and I have met with many such little delicate attentions. Today, as it is Good Friday and one can't do anything here, I am going to the intimates of the ex-king,[1] who lives outside the town. How did you get home? Did you witness any fighting on the way? Did you have any success yesterday with the army? Please write, and may God bless you.

Your old

CH.

251.

[Polish translation from French]

To AUGUSTE FRANCHOMME IN PARIS.
London, 1 May 1848.

DEAR FRIEND!

I am here, but was nearly drowned on the way. At last I have a large and fine room, in which I can breathe and play, and

[1] Hoesick suggests that this may refer to the Perthuis family, who accompanied Louis Philippe into exile. Chopin writes cautiously, avoiding names.

where today, for the first time, the sun has paid me a visit. This morning I am breathing a little better, but the whole of this last week I have not felt too well.

How are things with you, and what are your wife and children doing? I presume that you are definitely beginning to look out for the former tranquillity, is that so? Here I have had several dull callers. I have not yet delivered my letters of introduction. I am just wasting my time, and am glad of it. I love you, and am glad of that too.

Yours with all my heart,

CH.

The very best greetings to Mme Franchomme.
48 Dover Street. Write to me and I will also write to you.

252.

To ADOLF GUTMAN IN PARIS.
London, 48 Dover Street 48, Piccadilly. Saturday, 6 May 1848.

DEAR FRIEND!

Well, at last I am installed in the abyss that is called London. I am breathing better just these last days, because it is only these days that the sun has shown its face. I have called on M. d'Orsay, and though my letter was badly delayed, he received me very well. Please thank the princess [1] in my name and his. I have not yet paid all my calls, because many of those to whom I have letters have not yet arrived. Erard was very courteous, and placed a piano at my disposal. I have one instrument of Broadwood and one of Pleyel: three in all; but what is the use, when I have not the time to play on them. I have innumerable visits to pay, and my days flash past like lightning. Today I have not had one free moment of time to write to Pleyel. Tell me about yourself; what are you thinking about now? How are your people getting on? With us it's bad. I hear of many griev-

[1] Czartoryska.

ous things from over there. Nevertheless, I have got to be heard; I have been asked to play in the Philharmonic; I would rather not. At the end, no doubt, if I play before the queen, I shall have to give a morning recital in a private house with admission limited to a certain number of persons. That, at least, is what I should like. But all this is just projects, nothing but projects. Write fully about yourself. I am always yours, my good Guciu.

CH.

One evening lately I heard Miss Lind in the *Sonnambula*. It was very beautiful. I met her personally. Mme Viardot has called on me. She also will appear in *Sonnambula*. All the Parisian pianists come here. Prudent's concert at the Philharmonic was not very successful; they want classical things there. Thalberg has been engaged for 12 concerts in the same theatre where Lind appears. Hallé is going to play Mendelssohn.

253.

To WOJCIECH GRZYMAŁA.
[*London*] *Thursday, 11th* [*May 1848*].

DEAREST LIFE

I am just back from the Italian theatre. Jenny Lind sang for the first time this year, and the Queen showed herself for the first time since the chartists. Both produced a great effect, — and, on me, so did old Wellington, who sat underneath the Queen's box, like an old monarchical dog in his kennel, under his crowned Lady. I have met J. Lind, and she very graciously sent me a most excellent stall with her card. As I had a good place, I heard well. She is a typical Swede; not in an ordinary light, but in some sort of Polar dawn. She is enormously effective in Sonnambula. She sings with extreme purity and certainty, and her piano notes are steady, and as even as a hair.

A stall costs 2½ guineas.

254.

To the Same.
London, Saturday, 13 May [*1848*].

My Dear!

It's not even laziness that has kept you from hearing anything from me, but just time thrown away on nothing. I can't get out of bed before eight. My Italian, who is concerned with himself and his accounts, wastes my time in the morning; after 10 begin tribulations which bring in no money, and, about 1, a few lessons. I can neither walk, nor be very active, so I can't get about over my affairs; but I see that they are going somehow, and if the *season* were to last 6 months, I might get a little done. Up to now, I know nothing. The day after tomorrow the duchess of Sutherland is to present me to the Queen, who will visit her *in gratiam* for a christening. If the Queen and prince Albert, who know about me, should be pleased, it will be good, for I shall begin from the top. I have been offered the Philharmonic, but don't want to play there because it would be with the orchestra. I have been there, to observe. Prudent played his concerto, and it was a fiasco. There one must play Beethoven, Mozart or Mendelsohn [*sic*], and although the directors and others tell me that my concertos have already been played there, and with success, I prefer not to try, for it may come to nothing. The orchestra is like their roast beef or their turtle soup; excellent, strong, but nothing more. All that I have written is needless as an excuse; there is one impossible thing: they never rehearse, for everyone's time is dear nowadays; there is only one rehearsal, and that is public.

I have not yet been able to deliver all my letters; everybody has to be caught at the same hour, between 1 and 2.

People are writing fine articles about me in the papers. And yesterday at a Covent Garden concert Mme Viardot sang my mazurkas and had to repeat them. She came to a reception of mine with her husband. I returned the call, but did not find them in. She behaves quite differently from the way she did in Paris, and sang my things without my asking it. She has appeared in Sonnambula at the same theatre as Grisi, Persiani, Alboni, Mario, etc. This theatre (Covent Gard.) rivals the Queen's theatre (*Hay Market*), where are Jenny Lind and La Blache. Miss Lind also made her first appearance in Sonnambula. I send you a trashy thing, written two weeks ago. Mme Viardot has not been so successful; the Queen did not come, and she was hampered by having only Flavio instead of Mario to sing with her. She called on me when I was out, and I am to see them on Sunday. Yesterday I was at dinner with J. Lind, who afterwards sang me Swedish things till midnight. They are as distinctive in character as our things. We have something Slavonic, they something Scandinavian, which are totally different; and yet we are nearer to each other than the Italian to the Spaniard.

Here I know all the worst news about the Duchy of Poznań [Posen] from Koźmian Stan[isław] and Szulczewski, to whom Zaleski gave me a note. Misfortune and misfortune; I have lost all desire in my soul. I have 3 pianofortes; one Broadwood and one Erard besides the Pleyel one, but up till now I can play only on my own. At last I have a good lodging, but have scarcely got used to it when the landlord demands that I shall pay double the price or take another room (as it is I am paying 26 guineas a month). It is true that I have a large and splendid drawing-room, and can give lessons (up to now I have 5 persons), but I don't yet know what to do: probably I shall stay here, for the other room is both smaller and less good. I don't want to change an address I have already given. The pretext for the change is that nothing was in writing, so he is free to raise his price.

About Sol, my heart aches. They are to be pitied, for things can never turn out well there. That B[orie] should weep, surprises me. If only the Mother and the children do not weep.

I have not written to Pleyel yet. I don't know when. I embrace you heartily,

Your

CH.

The English newspapers here write bad things about Mme S. For instance, that in some garden (probably the Luxembourg) Ledru R[ollin] was seen lying down, and Mme S. standing beside him, carrying on a conversation.

255.

To the Same.
[*London*] *48 Dover Street, Piccadilly.*
Friday, 2 June 1848.

To all Friends.
MY LIFE.

Here we have had bad weather for a week, and it does not agree with me. Besides that I have to go into society every evening till late. I am not strong enough for such a life. If it only brought in money; but till now I have had only two paid evenings at 20 guineas. I give a few lessons in the house at a guinea, and still have no notion of a decent concert. I have played before the Queen, and the Prussian prince Albert, and Wellington, and all the most elegant persons, at the Duchess of Sutherland's. Everything apparently went very well, but up to the 23rd the Court is in mourning for some aunt, so nothing is going on, and I doubt that I shall be invited there. I don't want to play at the Philharmonic, for it will not give me a penny, only enormous fatigue: one rehearsal, and that in public; and to have any success you must play Mendelsohn [*sic*]. The great world usually gives only balls or vocal concerts; the Queen has not yet given a concert, nor has Devonshire; only balls. I give one lesson a week to Sutherland's daughter. The Duchess of Sommerset [*sic*] also is very amiable to me; invites me to evenings, which the son of Don Carlos usually frequents; also the Westminsters, and everybody that the Lady Duchess (who at the coronation has to follow immediately behind the queen!!) can receive. But the Duke is close-fisted, so they don't pay. So I shall not go there today, in spite of the Spanish prince, as I have to dine at eight at Lady Gainsborough's (she has been very amiable to me). She gave a matinée and presented me to the first ladies. If I could run about all day long from Anasz to Kaifasz, if I could have a few days without blood-spitting, if I were younger, if I were not prostrate under my affections as I am, I might be able to start life again. Add a good servant who would look after me and not waste money and things. My lodging and carriage make it impossible to put things off; then my man wastes my time. My kind Scottish ladies show me a great deal of friendliness here; I always dine there when I'm not dining out in society. But they are used to jigging about and to dragging round London all day long with visiting-cards, and I'm only half alive. After three or four hours of jolting in a carriage, it's as if I had travelled from Paris to Boulogne. And the distances here! — There was a Polish ball here, and it was a great success. I did not go though I had a ticket, for I did not feel up to it, and before it I had a dinner at Lady Kinlogh's [*sic*] with a big company of lords, chancellors and beribboned-shirted devils. I am introduced, and don't know to whom, and am not in London at all. 20 years in Poland, 17 in Paris; no wonder I'm not brilliant here, especially as I don't know the language. They don't talk when I play, and they speak well of my music everywhere; but my little colleagues, whom they are used to shoving aside here; [1] it is that they consider me some sort of amateur, and that I shall soon be a *grand seigneur*, because I wear clean shoes and don't carry visiting cards stating that I *give home lessons, play at evening parties*, etc. Old Lady Rothschild asked me how much I *charge*, because some lady who had heard me had asked her about it. As Lady Sutherland had given me 20 guineas, and as Broadwood, on whose piano I play, had suggested that price, I answered: 20 guineas. The good lady, obviously kind, thereupon told me that it is true I play very well, but that she advises me to take less, as moderation is necessary this season.

So I see that people are not so open-handed here, and that difficulties over money exist everywhere. For the bourgeois class one must do something startling, mechanical, of which I am not

[1] Sentence ungrammatical in original.

capable. The upper world, which travels, is proud, but cultivated, and just, when they are minded to examine anything; but so much distracted by thousands of things, so surrounded by the boredom of conventionalities, that it is all one to them whether music is good or bad, since they have to hear it from morning till night. For here they have flower-shows with music, dinners with music, sales with music: Savoyards, Bohemians, swarms of my colleagues, and all mixed up.

I write to you as if you did not know London! I should like to give a concert in some private great house; if I succeed, I shall have about 150 guineas. That is rare here, for an opera brings in a little over 1000, and before the curtain can go up, over 900 goes in expenses! I don't know about both operas, or what they earn. Yesterday I again saw Jenny Lind in Lucy of Lammermoor. Very good; everyone was enthusiastic. But Gutman, poor fellow; how could he venture to play tricks with his hands! Tell him to be careful and not tire his hands too soon. Mme Viardot has not had much success here, because there are Grisi and Alboni; you know what favourites they are. Viardot called on me two days ago. She told me nothing about Grzegorz, except that she had heard news of him. It seems to have cooled off a little. Poor Sol. If her husband comes here, what is she to do? I am not far from thinking that the Mother is on good terms with her son-in-law, and now, if she has seen him and started to protect him again, may have forgiven him altogether; especially as he is hail-fellow-well-met with Thore, in whose paper she writes, and who is said to have told that Rousseau about Augustine. What has become of that puppet? And Arago; my God, what an ambassador! He doesn't know a word of German. If it were to Bavaria, that would be different; he's a friend of Lola Montes! Liszt would be better as a diplomatist. By the way, last week I was at a dinner here with Guizot; it made me sad to see. It's gilded over, but he suffers morally, though not without hope!

I made a mistake; I've doubled this sheet of paper. Everything is quiet here; no one bothers over the Irish and Chartist questions. They are not such huge affairs as they seem from the distance; and people here are more concerned with the state of things in Paris, Italy and Poland, about which the *Times* recounts such fantastic things that even the English are amazed at its ill will. Chojecki has a bee in his bonnet about the Bohemians interfering. Let these fools mess things up if they like, so long as it's easy later to wash off the pitch. If the trouble gets any worse, they'll have a heavy account to settle with God.

I embrace you heartily.

Your old

CH.

256.

To IGNACY KRZYŻANOWSKI IN LONDON.

May the Lord God help you in your work.

CHOPIN

London, 6 July 1848.

257.

To WOJCIECH GRZYMAŁA

[*London, 8–17 July 1848.*]

Forgive my sending an old beginning (8th July); but I will finish it today.

MY DEAREST LIFE!

God has preserved you these last days, which have been the real beginning of the (apparently motivated) obstinacy of two parties. Up till now it was in people's heads, in their imaginations, in books; in the name of culture, of justice, of solidarity, and so on; but now this mud and misery will call for revenge. And to revenge there is no end! A civil war of principles; then, inevitably, the fall of civilization as the minds of today conceive of it. Your great-great-great-grandchildren will travel, in a few hundred years, from a free Poland to a regenerated France, or to something else in France's place.

Yesterday (July 7th) I gave a second matinée in Lord Falmuth's [*sic*] house. Mme Viardot sang me my mazurkas among other things. It was very beautiful; but I don't know whether I made 100 guineas. I shan't know till Monday. The season here is finishing. I don't know how my plans will turn out. I have not much savings in my pocket, and don't know what I shall do. I may go to Scotland. My Scottish ladies are kind and lovable, but sometimes they bore me horribly. I have sent away the stupid Italian. I am keeping the same lodging, for, with three pianofortes, I must have a large drawing-room. I have a better servant. My health varies from hour to hour; but often in the mornings it seems as if I must cough my life out. I'm depressed in spirit, but my head gets muddled; I even avoid solitude, so as not to think, for I must not be ill long here, and want to avoid getting feverish.

What is Sol doing? Rozières has written me a nice letter. She's a good soul. But write to me about the Mother. Is Clés[inger] going to Russia? There's cholera there now! — The fool! — Write me a line about them. Is the Princess safe? Has Cichocki good news? Gut[man] has written to me, the good fellow; I'm glad he did not break off. Here they are not afraid of any disturbances, and if your papers write anything, there's not much truth in it. Everyone who has even a little property is enrolled as a constable, and among them there are many Chartists, who don't want any violence.

At this moment I have received a letter from Rosièr[es]; she says she saw you going to the wounded Dubose. Please wish him good health. I am going to Viardot, to thank her. I will confess to you that I did not want to ask her to sing for me; but her brother was with me when Broadwood offered me Lord Falmuth's [*sic*] drawing-room, and I went at once to the sister, who most willingly promised to sing. Among other things she sang my mazurkas. Tell that to de Rozières: that Mme V. was *kind*, for it will get about here. Mme S., I know, wrote to V. to inquire *anxiously* about me! ! ! What a part she must be playing there; the just *mother*.

15 July.

I can't finish your letter; My nerves are all on the jump. I suffer from some kind of silly depression, and, with all my resignation — I don't know — I worry about what to do with myself. After deducting lodging and carriage, all I shall have been able to scrape together will perhaps not come to more than 200 guineas (about 5000 francs). In Italy you can live a year on that, but here, not half a year. The *season* is almost finished. I have not played at the Queen's palace, though I have played before the Queen (at the Sutherlands'). The Duchess of Suth[erland] has left London. So perhaps the Queen's director has dug a pit for me because I did not return his call, or because I would not play at the Philharmonic. If the season here lasted six months, I could gradually get known after my fashion; but as it is, there is no time. Everything here is in such a rush.

Every evening I am out. Last week, at Lady Combermere's alone, I met the Duke and Duchess of Cambridge, one of the Weimars (an old lady), and the [Duke] of Hess; all of them very polite. Here and there I am beginning to get a reputation, but it needs time and the *season* is coming to an end. Some newspapers have made a fuss of me, and people say that counts for a lot here. But what are not so plentiful as they say, are guineas. There's a great deal of lying; directly they don't want anything, they have gone into the country. One lady pupil of mine has gone into the country without paying for nine lessons; and others, who are supposed to take two lessons a week, usually miss both; so there is more pretence than fact. I'm not surprised, because they are trying to do too much all round. One pupil came here from Liverpool for a week! I gave her five lessons, as they don't play on Sunday, and she is satisfied. Lady Peel, for instance, wants me to give lessons to her daughter, who has a great deal of ability, but, as she has had a teacher who took half a guinea twice a week, she wants me to give only one lesson a week, so that the effect on her purse shall be the same. This is to be able to say that she is having lessons from me; and she will probably leave town in two weeks.

Monday, July 17.

I have just had a letter from you, and hasten to answer. First of all, my Life, I had to *reject* the newspapers that you sent me, for the post office demanded one pound and fifteen shillings for them, which comes to 45 francs. As I had your letter, I was less grieved at having to refuse newspapers at such a price; you had written on the envelope, and therefore the package was charged at letter rate. I forgot to tell you that the *Charivari* which you sent me once, cost me 5 shillings and something, also because you had written something on the envelope and it was therefore counted as a letter. From 5 shillings to 1 pound and 15 is a big difference; so I asked them to explain, and got my landlord to translate for me. It was the weight, at the postal rate. I rejected the parcel, and think it cannot be returned to you, as your address is probably not on it. If, by ill luck, it comes back to you and you have to pay, you had better return it again to me. But anyhow, don't do that again; because these things are carefully examined here, stamped with post office marks, and, as you see, heavily charged.

My Scottish ladies are kind, and I gave them your letter; but they bore me so that I don't know what to do. They want to insist that I should go to their homes in Scotland; that's all right, but nowadays I have no heart for anything. Here, whatever is not boring is not English.

What is Sol doing? And her mother? And de Rozières? *A propos* of the letter that you enclosed in yours: it's a fool, whom I helped to leave Paris (his name is Wieman) and who now writes for money, so that he can come back to Paris. He's an ass! A year ago I was almost maintaining him; he was determined to go; he went with the first section, and now he's in trouble again. May the Lord keep and preserve us; — the things that happen to our folk!

I embrace you heartily.

Your most affectionate

CH.

258.

To the Same.
[*London*] *July 1848.*

My Life. Thanks for all your kind words and for the forwarded letter from home. Thank God, they are well; but they worry needlessly about me. I am depressed nowadays; I can't find any comfort, I have worn out all feeling — I only vegetate and wait for it to end soon. — Next week I go to Scotland, to a certain Lord *Torphiken* [*sic*], brother-in-law of my Scottish ladies, who are already in his house, near Edinburgh. He has sent me a letter of invitation; so has Lady Murray, a well-known great lady there, who is very fond of music. I will not enumerate a crowd of other oral invitations, with their addresses, for I cannot drag from place to place; that kind of life has disgusted me — and I see no end to it before me. — I shall stay in Scotland till the 29th of August; for the 29th I have accepted an engagement in Manchester, where there will be a big concert. I am to play twice, without the orchestra, and they are giving me 60 pounds. Alboni is coming — but I don't care about that — I shall just sit down and play. I shall stay there two or three days, where Neukomm lives with rich local manufacturers. What I shall do with myself after that, I don't know; if only I could be sure that I shan't be laid up here in winter by illness!

259.

[Polish translation from French]

To Auguste Franchomme.
Edinburgh, 6 August [1848].
Calder House, 11 August.

Very Dear Friend

I don't know how I ought to write to you, but I think it would be almost better not even to try to console you for the loss of your father.

I understand your grief; even time does not always heal this kind of pain.

I left London a few days ago, and made the journey to Edinburgh (407 English miles) in twelve hours. After a day's rest in Edinburgh, I arrived at Calder House (twelve English miles from Edinburgh), the castle of Lord Torpichen, Mrs. Erskine's brother-in-law, where I expect to stay till the end of the month and rest after my London labours.

I have given two musical matinées, which people apparently enjoyed; this does not prevent my having been equally bored. But without them I don't know how I could have managed the three months in expensive London, keeping up a large apartment, as I was forced to do there, a carriage and a manservant. My health might be worse, but I am weaker all the time, and still unable to bear this climate. Miss Stirling wanted to write to you from London, and asks me to explain to you. The reason was that these ladies had a lot of travel preparations to make before starting for Scotland, where they expect to spend many months. One of your pupils, named Drechsler, if I am not mistaken, is living in Edinburgh. He called on me in London, and impressed me as a nice young fellow, much attached to you. He goes in for music a good deal with one of the great ladies here, Lady Murray, one of my 60-year-old London pupils, whose castle also I have promised to visit. But I don't know how I shall manage it, for I have promised to be in Manchester by the 28th of August, to play at a concert for 60 pounds.

Neukomm is living there; but I hope he won't want to improvise on the same day; I am counting on earning the 60 pounds — What to do with myself next, I don't know. But I do earnestly wish that somebody would give me to the end of my life an annual pension for not composing, for never having invented a tune *à la* Osborne or Sowiński (both of whom are my excellent friends, one Irish, the other my countryman), — of which I am prouder than of my perfidious proxy, Antony Kontski, that northern Frenchman and southern scoundrel.

After these parenthetic remarks, I must frankly admit to you that I don't yet know what I shall do in the autumn. But, whatever should happen, don't blame me if you hear nothing from me, for I often think about writing to you. If you see Mlle de Rozières, or Grzymała, one or the other will have news of me; if not directly from me, in any case from some one of our common friends.

There is a very beautiful park here, and the owner of the castle must also be called a very charming person; so I feel as happy here as is permitted to me at all. Of musical ideas there can be no question; I am utterly out of the running, and make on myself the impression of an ass at a masquerade, or rather a fiddle's E string on a bass viol: astonished, tricked, knocked off my balance, as completely as if I were listening to some tuneful phrase of Rodiot (before the 24th of February) or the bow-scraping of M. Cap (after the days of June). But I suppose they must be blessed with the best of health, since I can't manage to avoid them in writing.

But the next serious question is whether you, as I hope, after all these dreadful events, have not to mourn the loss of some friend? And how are your wife and children? Write me a line to London, at Broadwood's address, 33 *Great Pulteney Street, Golden Square*. Here I have the utmost (material) peace, and spend my time on the beautiful Scottish songs; I should like to compose a little, and even could do so, if only to give pleasure to these kind ladies, Mrs. Erskine and Miss Stirling. I have a Broadwood pianoforte in my room, and in the drawing-room is Miss Stirling's Pleyel; pens and paper also are not lacking. I hope that you also are composing something now; and may

I soon be able to hear the new-born work. I have friends in London who advise me to spend the winter there; but I shall follow only the advice of my *je ne sais quoi;* or rather, of whoever advises me last, for I see it makes no practical difference, how long I think about it.

Adieu, dear and loved Friend. Give Mme Franchomme my best wishes for her children. I hope that René amuses himself with his violoncello, that Cécile works hard, and that her little sister constantly reads her books. Please greet Mme Lasserve for me, and correct my spelling and my French.

The population here is ugly, but apparently good-natured. On the other hand the cows are magnificent, but apparently inclined to gore people. The milk, butter and eggs are irreproachable, and so are their usual companions the cheeses and chickens.

260.

To JULJAN FONTANA.

Calder House, Mid-Calder.

Scotland (12 miles from Edinburgh, if that is any pleasure to you).

18 August 1848.

MY LIFE.

If I were well, I would go to London tomorrow to embrace you. It may be some time before we meet. You are my old cembalo on which time and circumstance have played their dismal tremolo. Yes; *two old cembali,* — though you will object to such companionship. That is without prejudice to either beauty or virtue; *la table d'harmonie* is excellent, but the strings have snapped and some of the pegs are missing. The worst is that we are the work of a fine instrument-maker: some Stradivarius *sui generis,* who is no longer here to repair us. We can't give out new notes under clumsy hands, and we choke down in ourselves all that which, for the want of an expert, no one can get out of us. For me, I scarcely breathe; *je suis tout prêt à crever;*[1] and you are doubtless growing bald, and will remain above my gravestone, like our willow trees, do you remember? that show bare tops — I don't know why poor Jasio and Antek come into my thoughts now, and Witwicki, and Sobański! Those with whom I was in the closest harmony have also died for me; even Ennike, our best tuner, has drowned himself. So now I have not left in the world even a pianoforte tuned as I am used to having it. Moos has died, and nobody makes such comfortable shoes for me now. If another 4 or 5 desert me for St. Peter's gates, all the comforts of my life will be gone *ad patres.* My good fellows [brothers-in-law?] and my Mother and Sisters are alive, by God's grace; but there is cholera! And the good Tytus! As you see, you still count among my oldest memories, and I among yours, though you are doubtless younger (what a lot of difference it makes nowadays, which of us is two hours older!). I assure you that I would gladly consent to be even *much* younger than you, if I could embrace you on my journey. That yellow fever has not carried you off, and jaundice me, is incomprehensible, — for both of us have been exposed to yellowness. I'm writing you rubbish because there's no sense in my head. I'm vegetating, and waiting patiently for winter. I dream now of home, now of Rome; now of joy, now of grief. Nobody plays as I like nowadays, and I have grown so *forbearing,* that I could listen with pleasure to Sowiński's Oratorio, and not die. I remember *Norblin,* the painter, saying that a certain painter in Rome had seen the work of another one, and found it so *unpleasant* that he — *died.* What I have left is just a big nose and an *undeveloped* 4th finger. You are a worthless person if you don't write me a line in answer to this present *epistre.* You have chosen a bad time for your journey. But may the God of our Fathers guide you. Be happy! — I think you have done well, to settle in New York instead of in Havana. If you see *Emmerson* [*sic*], your famous philosopher, remember me to him. Embrace Herbet, and kiss yourself, and don't be cross.

Your old

CH.

[1] I am ready to peg out (die).

261.

To his Family.

[This letter is written on three sheets of paper with views of Edinburgh.]

19 August 1848.

MY DEAREST ONES.

Thanks for your good letter, which reached me a week ago, forwarded from London. I spent 3 months in London, and kept fairly well. I gave two morning concerts, one at Mrs. Sartoris's, the other at Lord Falmouth's, with great success but without much fuss. [In a footnote:] Mrs. Sartoris, by birth Fanny Kemble, is the young daughter of a famous English actor; and herself a fine English singer; she was only 2 years on the stage, and then married Mr. Sartoris, a rich man of the world. She has been adopted by the whole of London's high society, goes everywhere, and everyone visits her. Our acquaintance dates from Paris. Lord Falmouth is a great musical amateur; rich, unmarried, *grand seigneur;* he offered me his mansion in St. James's Square for a concert. He has been very amiable. In the street you would offer him threepence, but in the house he keeps a crowd of servants, better dressed than himself. I knew his niece in Paris, but met him first at a concert in London. [Letter continues:] At one [concert] Mario sang for me 3 times, and I played 4 times; at the other Viardot sang 3 times and I played 4, which they much liked, for such short and concise concerts were new to them; they have only long, 20-number concerts with huge announcements. [In a footnote:] I send you a few words from the *Athenæum,* a paper respected by artists. I have no others; for that matter, what do you want with others, — just somebody saying it's good! Let Antek translate for you. [Letter continues:] I limited the audience to 200 at Lord Falm[outh]'s, and to 150 at Mrs. Sartoris's, which, at a guinea a ticket (deducting various expenses) brought in just on 300 guineas. London is frightfully dear during the season; my lodging alone, without anything (it's true I had a very large and high drawing-room, in which 3 pianofortes stood: one sent me by Pleyel, another from Erard, a third that Broadwood put in) — just my lodging, because it has a large and fine staircase and a splendid entrance and is in Dover Street near Piccadilly, cost 80 pounds. Now carriage, manservant, everything is enormously dear; so thát if I had not had home lessons at a guinea, and several daily, I don't know what would have become of me. I had several grand evenings directly after I arrived, and I don't know whether I wrote to you from London — the Duchess of Sutherland had the Queen to dinner one day, and in the evening only 80 persons belonging to the most exclusive London society. Besides the Prince of Prussia (who was shortly leaving London) and the royal family, there were only such persons as old Wellington, and so on (though it is hard to find a parallel). The Duchess presented me to the Queen, who was amiable and talked with me twice. Prince Albert came up to the pianoforte. Everyone told me that both these things are rare. The Italians who sang that same evening were Mario, Lablache and Tamburini. No woman singer. I should like to describe to you the Duchess of Suth[erland]'s palace, but I can't. All those who know say that the Queen of England has no such house. All the royal palaces and castles are old; splendid, but neither so tasteful nor so elegant as Stafford House (as the Duke of Sutherland's palace is called); it is as close to the London palace of St. James as Blacha. For instance, the staircases are famous for their magnificence. They are neither in the entrance nor in the vestibule; but in the middle of the rooms, as if in some huge hall with most gorgeous paintings, statues, galleries, hangings, carpets; of the loveliest design with the loveliest perspective. On these stairs one could see the Queen, under a brilliant light, surrounded by all sorts of bediamonded and beribboned people with the garter, and all descending with the utmost elegance, carrying on conversations, lingering on various levels, where at every point there is some fresh thing to admire. It is true one regrets that some Paul Veronese could not see such a spectacle, so that he could have painted one more masterpiece. After that evening at the Duchess of Suth[erland]'s, I was told that I was to play in the

Queen's palace; but I did not play, I don't know why. Probably because I did not apply for it, and here you have to apply for everything, there is such a congestion of things. Not only did I not apply, but I did not call on the court's *Kapellmeister*, or rather, the man who gets up concerts for the Queen, and conducts the Philharmonic Society's orchestra (which gives the best concerts here, answering to the Conservatoire in Paris). The Philharmonic Society invited me to play for them: a great favour, or rather honour; everyone who comes here tries for it, and this year neither Kalkb[renner] nor Hallé played, in spite of much effort. But I refused, and this produced a bad impression among musicians, and especially among conductors. I refused once because I was not well; that was the reason I gave; but the real one was that I should only have had to play one of my concertos with the orchestra, and these gentlemen give only one rehearsal, and that in public, with entrance by free tickets. How can you rehearse, and repeat! So we should have played badly (although, apparently, they know my concertos, and Mrs. Dulcken, a famous — hm! — pianist here, played one there last year); so I sent regrets to the Philharmonic Society. One newspaper took offence at this; but that does not matter. After my matinées many papers had good criticisms, excepting the *Times*, in which a certain Davison writes (a creature of poor Mendelssohn's); he does not know me, and imagines, I am told, that I am an antagonist of Mendelssohn. It does not matter to me. Only, you see, everywhere in the world people are actuated by something else than truth. But to come back to the London world. Well, my *prix* for an evening in London was 20 pounds, but I have had only 3 such evenings. The second was at the Marquis of Douglas's; he is a son of the duchess of Hamilton, whom I knew long ago in Paris. The young marchioness is a Baden princess. She presented me to the duchess of Cambridge, the queen's aunt (who always talked a lot with me every time I met her afterwards) and to the (not reigning) princess of Weimar. The duke of Hess was there also and the *élite* of London ladies: — lady Jocelyn, one of the famous beauties; lady Lincoln, a sister of the Marq. Douglas, lady Granville (young), lady Cadogan (my former pupil, now *dame de compagnie* to the duchess of Cambridge), and some diplomatists, among whom are several Germans, who are in London and whom I knew long ago in Paris. My third paid appearance, or rather the first in order, was at Lady Gainsborough's. She was formerly maid of honour to the Queen, and has also collected round her the cream of the aristocratic world here. As you know, people here live by names and personages. Lady Dover, a niece of the duchess of Sutherl[and], the duchess of Argyll [*sic*], lady Stanley, whose daughter, my pupil in Paris, is now a maid of honour to the Queen. Why should I enumerate all these names! I have got to know very many of the great world,* among them for instance, the duchess of Somerset; the duke is the premier duke of England, and on great occasions, for instance at the coronation, she follows directly behind the Queen. [* Footnote:] Lady Ailesbury [*sic*], lady Peel, lady Gordon, lady Parke; among the literary men Carlisle [*sic*], Rogers, an old, very famous poet and an honoured friend of Byron; Dickens, Hogarth; an intimate friend of Walter Scott, etc., etc., who wrote a fine article about my second concert in the Delinjus.[1] [Letter continues:] Among the notabilities is lady Byron, with whom I am on very friendly terms. We converse, like the goose with the sucking pig, she in English, I in French. I understand why she bored Byron. Her daughter, lady Lovelace (considered a beauty), is another interesting person. But a person I was glad to meet here was lady Shelburne, formerly Mlle de Flahautt [*sic*], my pupil, and now daughter-in-law to lord Landsdowne (Lansdaun), the president of the council of ministers, who is himself very fond of music and every season gives big vocal concerts in his house. Lady Combermere is also a lady who has been very pleasant to me. Before leaving London I spent an evening at her house. The duke and duchess of Cambridge were there; also Wellington, and the Spanish pretender, Don Carlos's son, prince, or rather count Montemolin. Among the interesting persons I met were, for instance, lady [*sic*] Norton, famous for her beauty (and for her legal fight with her husband) [Footnote:] Barciński may know of her. [Letter continues:] she is a daughter of Sheridan and a great favourite; lady

[1] *Daily News.*

Blessington, whose daughter has married that *count d'Orsay* who is a leader of fashion here, and whose wife has left him. *Count d'Orsay* was very amiable to me. I brought him a letter from his sister, the duchesse de Gramont. Besides that, he is himself an artist, does very good carving and sculpture, paints and draws. Among his fine busts is one of the marchioness of Douro, the wife of Wellington's son, (to whom also I had a letter). *La marquise de Douro* is one of the beauties here. Among the persons I liked was an excellent lady, Mrs. Milner Gibson, whose husband was in the Cabinet a few years ago; and lady Molesworth, who was also very amiable to me. [Footnote:] I can't leave out lady Agasta [*sic*] Bruce, daughter of lady Elgin, and a maid of honour to the Queen's mother, the duchess of Kent. She is very kind and amiable, and good; she also is an old acquaintance from Paris. [Letter continues:] It is difficult to enumerate them all, but I must remember Mrs. Grote, whom I met in Paris (at the Marlianis'). She is the wife of a member of Parliament, a very cultivated woman, enthusiastic protector of Jenny Lind. She met us at the same time.* — Once she invited only us two, and we did not leave the piano from 9 till 1 in the night. [* Footnote:] The Queen, who has come back to town after some hostile demonstrations by the opposition, was to have attended grand opera for a first public appearance, and the occasion chosen was the first appearance of Jenny Lind, who also had just arrived (Sonnambula), so there was an enormous rush for tickets; on the last evening, stalls were sold at 3 guineas. I did not know about it, having just arrived; and on the very day, someone told me that if I knew Mrs. Grote, she could help me, as, apart from her own box, she has so many connections. I called on her, and she at once invited me to her own box. I was very glad, as I had seen neither the Queen, nor Jenny Lind, nor that gorgeous theatre (*Keen's*).[1] But Mrs. Grote's box was on the first floor, and I lose my breath on stairs; so on reaching home I found a ticket for one of the best stalls, from Lumley, the conductor, with the compliments of Miss Lind and Mrs. Grote. The performance was most magnificent; the Queen received more applause than Jenny Lind; they

[1] "Queen's"? Jenny Lind, on returning to London, appeared in *Sonnambula* at Her Majesty's Theatre, on May 4th, 1848.

sang *God save,* with the whole audience standing, and *Wellington* and all the local notabilities. It was an imposing sight, that real respect and reverence for the throne, for law and order; they could not contain their enthusiasm. [Letter continues:] Miss Lind came to my concert!!! which meant a lot for the fools; she cannot show herself anywhere without people turning their opera glasses on her. But that she never sings anywhere except in the opera, not even at great functions, she would have sung for me, so Mrs. Grote said. But I had never dreamed of asking her to do so, although she is a kind girl and we are on excellent terms. It's not the same as with others. One can call it the Scandinavian streak; it's a totally different nature from southerners such as Pauline Viardot. She is not pretty, but pleasant-looking at home; on the stage I don't always like her, but in Sonnambula, from the middle of the second act, she is perfectly beautiful in every and all respects as an actress and as a singer. People say that she will marry Mrs. Grote's brother, but I know for certain that it is not true (they even say that she is secretly married; but her betrothed is waiting for her in Sweden). Mrs. Grote is a very kind woman, though eccentric and a good deal of a radical. She receives a great many interesting visitors; dukes, and lords, and scholars; in a word, the celebrities of the great world. She talks in a bass voice, and does not wrap the truth in cottonwool. Someone who does not agree with her views, on being asked:—"*Comment trouvez-vous Mme Grote?*" replied:—"*Je la trouve grotesque.*" Nevertheless, she has a kind heart, and has given me proofs of it: she invited me to visit her in the country with Miss Lind and Mrs. Sartoris; but I could not. Another person whom I like very much is Mrs. Sartoris (Fanny Kemble). She already knew me from old days, and at evening receptions in London society has never asked me to play if she saw I did not like it. She herself sings very well, and has a lovely voice. She has two children, as beautiful as angels. She herself was very pretty, but has grown fat now, so only the head remains, like a cameo. I feel at home with her; she is natural, she knows my little weaknesses through our common friends, such as Dessauer and Liszt. In talking with her I have often felt as if I were with someone who knows you; but all she knows are the rooms in which we stayed at the Thun's in Tetschen, where she also has spent some pleasant hours. She tells me that they very often speak of us there. That is enough about London. I will not count up other persons to you, but among others I found here some old acquaintances who have been amiable to me; for instance, Bulwer, formerly ambassador to Madrid; Lord Dudley Stewart; Comming [*sic*] Bruce, lady Elgin's father; Moneton Milner [Monckton Milnes?], etc. Broadwood, who is a real Pleyel here, has been the kindest and most genuine of friends. As you know, he is a very rich and highly cultivated man, whose father left the estate and the factory to him and himself settled down in the country. He has the very best connections; he had Guizot and all his family staying with him; and is beloved everywhere. I met lord Falmouth through him. To give you an idea of his English courtesy: one morning he called on me; I was tired, and told him I had slept badly. At night I came back from lady Somerset's, and found a new spring mattress and pillows on my bed. After much questioning, my good Daniel (that is the name of my present excellent valet) told me that Mr. Broadwood had sent it and said he was not to tell me. Now, leaving London 10 days ago, I was met at the train for Edinburgh by a gentleman who introduced himself as coming from Broadwood and gave me, instead of one seat, two (the second opposite so that no one should crowd me); also, in the same coach he had put a certain Mr. Wood, an acquaintance of Broadwood, who knew me too (he had seen me at Lipiński's at Frankfort in 1836), and who has his own music firm in Edinburgh and Glasgow. Broadwood has also arranged that my Daniel (who is a better person than many gentlefolk, and handsomer than many Englishmen) should travel in the same coach; and I made the 407 English miles from London to Edinburgh, by Birmingham and Carlisle, in 12 hours by *express train* (the class of train that stops least often). I stopped at Edinburgh, where a lodging had been engaged for me in the best hotel (*Douglas's*), for one and a half days, to rest. I went to look at the exquisite city, of which I send some very poor views on this paper (I could not get any better ones). [Footnote:] People who constantly have beautiful things in front of their noses, always admire what is less fine, but unfamiliar; because they are not used to it. [Letter continues:] I met there some courteous friends of my friends, who took me about in their carriage to see the town. (Everybody is going to Scotland now, for the opening of the shooting season.) After a rest in Edinburgh, where, passing a music-shop, I heard some blind man playing a mazurka of mine, I got into a carriage, harnessed in the English style, with a led horse, which lord Torpichen had sent, and came here, 12 miles from Edinburgh. Lord Torpichen is an old Scotchman, seventy years old, a brother-in-law of Mrs. Erskine and Miss Stirling, my excellent Scottish ladies, whom I have long known in Paris and who take so much trouble for me. I constantly visited them in London, and to them I could not refuse to come here; especially as I have nothing more to do in London, as I need a rest, and as lord Torpichen gave me a very hearty invitation. The place is called Calder House (pronounce Kolderhaus). It is an old manor surrounded by an enormous park with ancient trees; you can see only lawns, trees, mountains and sky. The walls are 8 feet thick; there are galleries on all sides, dark corridors with endless numbers of ancestral portraits, of various colours, in various costumes, some Scotch, some in armour, some in robes; nothing lacking for the imagination. There is even some kind of red cap [ghost], which appears, but which I have not yet seen. Yesterday I looked at all the portraits, but I have not yet seen which one it is that wanders about the castle. The room which I inhabit has the most beautiful view imaginable. [Footnote:] Though this is not the most beautiful part of Scotland. Towards Stirling, beyond Glasgow, and in the north part is the fine scenery. I have promised to go in two or three weeks to lady Murray, my first London pupil, who usually stays in Edinburgh and is a leader in musical matters. Lord Murray lives in one of the most picturesque parts, by the sea; one has even to go by sea. Also I must go later to Keir, near Stirling (a district famous for its beauty, near the Lady of the Lake), to Miss Stirling's cousin. These kind Scotch ladies here! There is nothing I can think of that does not at once appear; even the Parisian newspapers are brought to me every day. It is quiet, peaceful and comfortable; only I must leave in a week. Lord [Torpichen] has asked me to come for the whole summer next year; they would let me stay for the rest of my life; but what's the use? [Letter continues:] They have put me far from everyone else, so that I can play and do what I like freely; for with these people, as Bartek will tell you, the first thing to do for a guest is, not to interfere with him. I found a Broadwood piano in my room; in the drawing-room there is a Pleyel, which Miss Stirling brought with her. In England *la vie de château*[1] is very pleasant. Every day someone arrives to stay for a few days. The arrangements are most luxurious: libraries, horses, carriages at your disposal, personal servants, etc. Here they usually meet for *lunch* (according to Pan Dmuszewski's spelling: *loncz*), at 2 o'clock (everybody eats breakfast in his own room, when and how he pleases), and for dinner at 7. At evening they sit up as long as, and how, they choose. In the evenings I play Scotch songs for the old lord, who hums the tune with me, poor fellow, and expresses his feelings to me in French, as best he can. Although everyone in high society speaks French, especially the ladies, the general conversation is mostly in English, and I then regret that I don't know the language; but I have neither the time nor the desire for it. However, I understand simple things; I can't starve or come to grief; but that is not enough. This letter has been 10 days or more in getting written; but I am determined to finish it today; I am sorry that you have had nothing from me for so long. The good de Rozierka writes to me that she intends to write you a line without waiting for me. She has gone to her friends in the country, to rest after all the emotions and scares that they have had there. Sol has written to me; she is with her husband's parents in Besançon, and is well. In Paris she saw her Mother; her Mother has been advised to leave Paris. When she arrived at the country house, the peasants received her very badly (she has been mixed up in all the bad things); she was even obliged to leave Nohant, and is at Tours. She has got into deep mud of late, and has brought trouble on many. Illicit proclamations, that have kindled civil war, are attributed to her. Her second newspaper, which also was quite a failure, as it was *ultra*, and merely inflamed the shortsighted, was forbidden; but, like the first one, it was already dying for

[1] life in castles.

lack of readers. Who would have guessed this a few years ago! Her biography has been printed and sold in the streets; written and signed by Augustine's father, who complains that she demoralized his only daughter and made her into Maurice's mistress; that she gave her in marriage, against the will of her parents, to the first comer, after having promised to marry her to her son. He quotes her own letters. In short, a hideous business, that is known, today, to all the scum of Paris. It is vile of the father, but the thing is true. This is what has come of the kind action which she thought she was doing, and which I opposed from the first day that girl entered the house. She should have left her to her parents, not filled her head with thoughts of her son; who will never marry without money (and even then only if he is coaxed into it, for he will have enough money himself). But he was pleased to have a pretty cousin in the house. He made his mother put her on an equality with Sol. She was dressed the same; and better served, because Maurice wished it so. Every time the father wanted to take her away, it was refused, because Maurice wished it so. Her mother was regarded as insane, because she saw things clearly; finally the father began to see. So then Mme S. made " une victime " of the girl, who was supposed to be persecuted by her own parents. Solange saw everything, and therefore was in the way. Maurice needed that Lambert for a screen for him before Solange and the servants. Maurice needed Borie, so that it could appear, in the town, as if Borie were courting Augustine. The mother found her daughter inconvenient, because she, unfortunately, saw everything that was going on. Hence lies, shame, embarrassment and all the rest. — But let us come back to Scotland. I am due in Manchester on August 28th, to play at a concert at which the Italians from London will sing: Alboni, and so on. They are to pay me 60 guineas for it, and as that is a sum not to be refused, I have accepted, and leave here in a week. 200 and something English miles, 8 hours, railway journey. There good acquaintances await me, very rich manufacturers, with whom Neukomm lives (that best pupil of Hayden's [*sic*], formerly *Kapellmeister* to the emperor of Brazil; you know him by name). There is also Mrs. Rich (a daughter of Mr. Mackintosh, a greatly respected former member of Parliament, orator and writer), and my great friend; also these ladies Ersk[ine] and Stirling. After the concert I return to Glasgow, to the sister-in-law of this lord here; from there to lady Murray, then to Stirling, and at the very beginning of October they want me to play in Edinburgh. If it will bring in something, and I am strong enough, I shall gladly do it, for I don't know how to turn round this winter. I have my lodging in Paris, as usual, but don't know how to make ends meet. Many persons want me to stay in London for the winter, in spite of the climate. I want something else, but don't myself know what. I will see, in October, according to my health and my purse, for an extra hundred guineas in my pocket would do no harm. If only London were not so dark, and the people so heavy, and if there were no fogs or smells of soot, I would have learned English by now. But these English are so different from the French, to whom I have grown attached as to my own; they think only in terms of pounds; they like art because it is a luxury; kind-hearted, but so eccentric that I understand how one can himself grow stiff here, or turn into a machine. If I were younger, perhaps I would go in for a mechanical life, give concerts all over the place and succeed in a not unpleasant career (anything for money!); but now it is hard to start turning oneself into a machine. It is fine weather here today, so nothing dry can enter my head. The park has a wonderful light on it — it is morning —, and I forget everything; I am with you, I am happy, and I shan't think about the winter till it is imperative to do so. Now I embrace you heartily.

CH.

[In a postscript:] How good that Ludwika is in the country! And Mummy and Izabelisko ought to go too, in spite of the garden, in which I see all kinds of flowers, fruits and fences. I send kisses and kisses to Bartek, and to Kalasanty too.

I won't send Ludwika wishes for her name-day, for there is no need to say them. May the Lord God keep and bless you, preserve and give you health, and let your children grow and be your comfort. Write to me to Paris, at the usual address, for your letters will be forwarded to me from there, wherever I may be. I will be sure to let you know where I am going to spend the winter.

262.

To Wojciech Grzymała.

[On letter paper with a large steel engraving at the top, showing the Walter Scott memorial with a background of Waverley bridge and the principal buildings of Edinburgh. Hoesick.]

[*Calder House*] *19 August 1848.*

My dearest Life!

I am in Calder-House, near Edinburgh (12 English miles), staying with lord Torpichen, the 78-year-old brother-in-law of the Erskine and Stirling ladies. I have been here for two weeks. The climate does not agree with me very well; yesterday and today I have been spitting blood; but, as you know, with me that does not mean much. I made the railway journey from London to Edinburgh by the *Express train,* 407 miles in twelve hours, and it may have been a little too much for me. Anyhow, it's of no consequence.

I am here to rest after the London season and keep quiet till the 28th of this month, when I am due in Manchester. I have promised to come and play at a concert which Alboni, etc. are giving, and they will give me 60 pounds for it. One can't reject that in these days. After the 28th I don't know what I shall do. *Schwab* (a rich manufacturer whom you may have seen at Leo's) awaits me in Manchester. They live not right in the town, but a few miles outside, and Neukomm lives there with them. Mrs. Rich, that kind old English lady that you met as my guest, is also coming, with Miss Stirling, so I shall not be alone and it will be less dull for me.

In September I have other invitations to Scotland, where September is said to be very beautiful; but not here; near Glasgow, to lady Murray, and *Keir,* near Sterling [*sic*], to Mr. Stirling (Miss Sterling's cousin). I don't count a lot of other invitations, which I can't accept because I can't drag round from place to place. So I shall stay 15 days with one (my lady pupil) and another 15 with the other, who is a rich and clever bachelor.

In Edinburgh people want me to play on the 2nd or 3rd of October. If it is not yet cold (they say the weather is still good then, and it will bring in about a hundred pounds) I am ready to go back to Scotland from Manchester; not quite 8 hours' railway journey. My present valet is excellent, and a good fellow, so life is easier for me. What to do with myself next, I am afraid to think. Yet I must return to Paris, to make some decision about the apartment. If you should happen to see *Larac,* my house-superintendent, ask him *not to be anxious* about his rent. He has not written to me, but that makes no difference. And also say a friendly word to Mme Etienne and ask her to air the place, as I shall no doubt be coming soon.

And you, Dear, would have had a line from me long ago, but for all this travelling; I have begun letters to you a thousand times, and torn or burned them. At the same time I wanted to answer my Mother, who has had no letter for three months; but my time slips away over the stupidest things. I wanted to compose a little here; it's impossible, one always has to do something else.

I read that the Princess is at home. God grant that nothing has happened to Witold [1] in Italy. Greet him from me, as from a faithful dog, and thank him for his letter to lord St[uart]. May God not forget you. Embrace our friends. Write me a line yourself; address *at Mr. Broadwood's, 33 Great Pulteney Street, Golden Square.* I entrust to you a letter to my people, as [if it were] my greatest work. Perhaps I shan't so soon write them another. Mlle Derozières [*sic*] intended to go to the country, as I see from her letter, so I don't write anything to her. Sol is in Besançon, and her mother is in Tours, so Viardot told me. The things that have happened to her! And where is Augustine? May God keep and guard you, that I may find you well. I will write to you soon; now I must stop, for it is three English miles

[1] Czartoryski.

from the castle to the post, and it is time, and tomorrow is Sunday.

Your most attached

CH.

[On another sheet of the same paper, with a steel engraving showing a beautiful view: *Edinburgh from the Calton Hill.*]

Just as I was sealing this, your letter arrived. My dearest Life. Don't ever doubt me; but, as I love you, I could not finish a letter to you, begun every day.

Tell de *Larac* about the apartment; that I will write, and will either send money or come myself. If I knew that I shall have anything to eat in Paris during the winter! I will write to you from Manchester. May God keep you. Here they take excellent care of me; I am better off than at home, for such a home would be difficult. There is even some kind of red cap, or little red hat here, which makes its appearance, as in all the Scottish ballads, but I have not seen it yet. And in the corridors I can't find out which of the numberless and smoke-blackened ancestors it was. I will write to Sol. I don't like that Petersburg. I will write to de Rozières too.

I embrace you most heartily.

CH.

263.

To the Same.
Johnston Castel [*sic*]; *11 miles from Glasgow.*
4 Sep[*tembre 1848*].

MY DEAREST LIFE!

Since I wrote to you, I have been in Manchester. They received me very well; I had to sit down to the pianoforte 3 times. The hall is fine; 1200 persons. I stayed in the country (there is too much smoke in the town); all the rich people live outside. I stayed at the kind Schwabe's; perhaps you have seen him some time at Leo's. He is one of the first manufacturers, owns the biggest chimney in Manchester, which cost 5,000 pounds. He is a friend of Cobden, and himself a great free trader. He is a Jew, but a protestant, like Leo. His wife is particularly kind. They wanted to insist on my staying on, because J. Lind is to come there this week, and also will stay with them (they are great friends). While I was there, that kind Mrs. Rich was there too, whom you saw with Miss Stirling at my place. At the Schwabe's I also saw Leo's brother, who also trades in Manchester. This Schwabe knows Albrecht from Havre, so I at once sent a message through him to our Albrecht, that he must pay the rent and the perceptor [1] in the Square d'Orléans. My life, tell de Larac that. Thanks for your good letter and for Nossarz — I should not think of the wild cat, for even my cashmere is too heavy for me. Embrace him, and say that I will try it at once, if I am able to lift it. But really, perhaps I will try it, when the cold begins! That was a good letter you forwarded to me from princess Marcellina. She asks me whether I am still in London, and to let her know at Ostend, *poste restante*. If I were stronger, I would at once go there myself to answer her. The other letter was from Chrystian Ostrowski, who wants to know about Mickiewicz's drama, which Mme Sand once had in her hands, and which she gave to the *Revue Indépendante* office. There was a big quarrel over it. Pernet, one of the successors, died, and François, the other one, put the blame on Pernet, because he does not know what has become of it. So Ostrowski, queer fellow, asks me, when did it happen? And are there any copies? And where is Mme Sand now, so that he can apply to her!!! I know that they had one search for the drama [2] and could not find it. I shall not answer such letters as Ostrowski's and, as I am telling you about it, you had better, please, *open* them and forward only what is necessary.

Here I am staying with the Houstons. She is a sister of my Scottish ladies. The castle is very fine and luxurious, kept up on a grand scale. I shall stay here for a week, and then go to lady Murray, to a still more beautiful district, where I shall

[1] tax collector.

[2] The subject was the Confederation of Bar. (Hoesick.)

spend another week. Perhaps I may play in Edinburgh, and therefore shall stay in Scotland till October. Please address my letters from now:

To Dr. Lishinski
Warrington Crescent
Edinburgh, Scotland.

Lyszczyński, a Polish homeopathic doctor in Edinburgh, who has married well, lives in tranquillity and has become quite English. He will know where to send my letters.

This letter was begun yesterday, to be finished today; but the weather has changed: it is bad outside, and I am cross and depressed, and people bore me with their excessive attentions. I can't breathe, I can't work. I feel alone, alone, alone, though I am surrounded . . . [1]

Why should I bore you with my jeremiads! You have troubles of your own, up to your ears. I ought to cheer you up with my letter. If I were in a good humour, I would describe to you one Scottish lady, a 13th cousin of Mary Stuart (*sic!!* Her husband, who bears a different name from his wife, really told me that.) Here it's nothing but cousins of great families and great names that no one on the continent has ever heard of. Conversation is always entirely genealogical, like the Gospels; who begat whom, and he begat, and he begat, and he begat, and so on for two pages till you come to Jesus.

They are arranging a concert for me in Glasgow. I don't know what will come of it. They are dear people, kind, and very considerate to me. There are a whole lot of Ladies, 70- to 80-year-old lords, but no young folk; they are all out shooting. One can't get out of doors, because it has been raining and blowing for several days. I don't know what to do about my visit to Strachur (to lady Murray); one has to cross Loch Long (one of the most beautiful of the lakes) and go round the east coast of Scotland, but it is only 4 hours from here.

Today is the 9th. I send you my old letter of Sept. 4. Forgive this scrawl; you know what an effort writing sometimes is for

[1] The next 7 lines are so much crossed out that it is impossible to read through the erasures. (Hoesick.)

me; the pen burns under my fingers, my hair falls out, and I can't write what I want to say, only a thousand futile things.

I have not written to Sol, nor to Derozierka [Mlle de Rozières]. I will write when I am less peevish. I embrace you.

Yours till death —

Write and may God guard you. Say a friendly word to Mme Étienne and tell her I will not forget her.

I forgot to tell you that since my last letter I have had a queer adventure, which luckily ended in nothing, but might have cost my life. We were driving in the neighbourhood, above the sea. The carriage we were in was a coupé, with two very fine young thoroughbred English horses. One horse began to prance, caught its leg and started to kick; the other did the same; as they bolted *sur une pente*[1] in the park, the reins dragged, the coachman fell from his box (he was badly knocked about). The carriage was smashed with banging from tree to tree; we were just tumbling over the precipice, when a tree stopped the carriage. One horse broke loose and bolted frantically, the other fell under the carriage. The windows were broken by branches. Luckily nothing happened to me, except a few bruises on my legs from the jolting. The footman jumped out cleverly; so only the carriage was smashed and the horses injured. The persons who saw it from the distance screamed that two persons were killed, as they saw one flung out and the other falling on the ground. Before the horse moved, I was able to get out of the carriage, and am all right; but no one who saw it, and no one of us who were there, can understand how we were not smashed to pulp. I was reminded of the Berlin ambassador (Emanuel) in the Pyrenees; he was dashed about that way.

I confess to you that I contemplated my last hour with composure; but the thought of broken arms and legs disconcerts me. To be crippled would be the last straw.

[1] on a slope.

264.

To the Same.
1 October, Keir [*1848*].
Perthshire. Sunday. No post, no railway, no carriage (even for a drive); not a boat, not even a dog to whistle to.

My dearest Life.

Just when I had begun to write to you on another sheet of paper, they brought me your letter with the letter from my sister. At least they have escaped the cholera so far. But why don't you send me a word about yourself? You have an easier pen than I, and I write to you every day for the last week, ever since I came back from north Scotland (Strachur on Loch fine [*sic*]). And I know that you have someone ill at Versailles, for de Rozières wrote me that you came to see her, and hurried away to a sick person at Versailles. Was it the grandfather? I don't want to think it was the grandchildren, or your kind Rohan neighbours. In any case I hope it is someone who does not mean much to you. Here we hear nothing of the cholera yet, but in London it is beginning. In Johnston Castel, together with your letter (in which you wrote to me about Sol, that you were in the Gymnase [1] with her), came another letter from Edinburgh, with the news that Prince and Princess Alexander [2] had arrived, and would like to see me. Tired as I was, I took the train and found them still in Edinburgh. Princess Marcellina is as kindhearted as last year. I came to life a little under their Polish spirit; it gave me strength to play in Glasgow, where some dozens of the nobility assembled to hear me. The weather was fine, and the Prince and Princess also came by train from Edinburgh. Little Marcelek,[3] who is growing finely, can sing my compositions, and hums the tune when they don't play correctly. That was on Wednesday, the 3rd; and afterwards the Prince and Princess were so kind as to accept an invitation to dine at *Johnston-Castel* (12 Engl. miles from Glasgow). So we spent the whole

1 The Gymnase Theatre in Paris.
2 Czartoryski.
3 Prince Marcel Czartoryski.

day together. Lord and Lady Murray, old Torpichen (they had come 100 miles), — all of them could not say enough in praise of Princess Marcellina. The Prince and Princess return to Glasgow; from there, after seeing Loch Lomond, they were to return to London, and then on to the *continent.* The Princess talked to me of you, as a close friend — most affectionately — and understands what your fine nature can suffer. You can believe how that day revived me. But today I am depressed; there's a fog, and though from the window at which I am writing, there is the most beautiful view: *Sterling Castel* [*sic*] (that same castle, by the town of Sterling, that you have in *Robert Bruce,* in the night, on the rock; do you remember?) and mountains, and the lake, and an exquisite park — in short, one of the famous beautiful views of Scotland — all the same, I *can't see* a bit of it; only, every now and then, when the fog is pleased to give way to a few minutes of sunshine that can't fight it much here. The owner of this house is called Sterling, a cousin's cousin of our Scottish ladies, and the head of that clan. I met him in London; a rich bachelor, who owns a fine collection here: many Murillos and other Spanish masters. He has just brought out an expensive work (you know, they know how to do that) on the Spanish school. He has travelled everywhere, and in the East; he has brains. All English society, when it travels in Scotland, comes to him. He keeps open house, usually 30 persons to dinner. At this moment there are several famous beauties here: Mrs. Boston left a few days ago; dukes, lords, this year even more than usual, because the Queen has been in Scotland, and yesterday unexpectedly drove past near the railway because she has to be in London on a certain day, and the fog was so thick when she was to sail that she did not return by sea, as she came, and as her sailors and the usual procession expected; — just prosaically by railway from Aberdeen, in the night. People say that must have greatly pleased Prince Albert, who gets seasick, whereas the queen, like a real maritime sovereign, does not mind the sea at all. Very soon I shall forget my Polish, talking only a mixture of French and English — and it is Scottish English I am learning, so I shall be taken for old Jaworka, who talked 5 languages at once. If I don't write you jeremiads, it's not because it would not console me, for you are the only person who knows all about me; but because, if I once start, there will be no end to it, and always the same. I am wrong to say *the same,* because for me the future grows always worse. I am weaker, I can't compose anything, less from lack of desire than from physical hindrances; every week I knock up against a new tree-branch. And what can I do? Still, it saves a few pennies, towards the winter. I have many invitations, and can't accept them if I wanted to: for instance, to the Duchess of Argyl [*sic*] or lady Belhaven, because it is already too late for my health. The whole morning, till 2 o'clock, I am fit for nothing now; and then, when I dress, everything strains me, and I gasp that way till dinner time. Afterwards one has to sit two hours at table with the men, look at them talking and *listen* to them drinking. I am bored to death (I am thinking of one thing and they of another, in spite of all their courtesy and French remarks at table). Then I go to the drawing-room, where it takes all my efforts to be a little animated — because then they usually want to hear me — ; then my good Daniel carries me up to my bedroom (as you know that is usually upstairs here), undresses me, gets me to bed, leaves the light; and I am free to breathe and dream till it is time to begin all over again. And when I get a little bit used to it, then it is time to go somewhere else; for my Scottish ladies give me no peace; either they come to fetch me, or take me the round of their families (*nota bene,* they make their folk invite them constantly). They are stifling me out of *courtesy,* and out of the same *courtesy* I don't refuse them.

265.

To the Same.
[*Edinburgh, 3 October 1848.*]

I began my letter in Keir, and am finishing it only in Edin-[burgh], on the 3rd of October. The weather is fine today, even warm, and I am better. Tomorrow evening I have to play, but have not yet seen the hall or arranged the programme. Jenny Lind and Mrs. Grote, whom I met at the station, have been here and have gone on to Glasgow for a performance. Grisi, Mario, Alboni and all have been here. Jenny Lind goes from here to Dublin. Nothing has been as successful here this year as last year; it is no longer a novelty. Roger was the tenor in Sonnambula; but — between ourselves — he is, as he always was, a *wigmaker's apprentice.*

It's time to stop.

I embrace you from my heart —

Yours till death

CH.

Write to me. If you see Delacroix, embrace him. I am also sending a letter to de Rozières. Go on addressing to me at Lysczyński's.

266.

To ADOLF GUTMANN IN HEIDELBERG.
Calder House, 16 Oct[*ober*] *1848* (*12 miles from Edinburgh*).

DEAR FRIEND,

What are you doing? How are your folk getting on? What news of your country, and of your art? You are unjust to be annoyed with me, since you know how bad I am at correspondence. I have often thought of you, and when I lately read of the disturbances at Heidelberg, I began a lot of letters to you, and ended by burning them all. This note will probably reach you, and will find you at your good Mother's side. Ever since you last wrote to me, I have been in Scotland, Walter Scott's beautiful country, among all the memories and reminders of Mary Stuart, of the Charleses, etc. I visit one lord after another. Everywhere I meet, together with the heartiest goodwill and boundless hospitality, superb pianofortes, magnificent paintings, famous collections of books; there are also hunting, dogs, dinners without end, cellars, for which I have less use. It is difficult to conceive of the refinement of luxury and comfort that one meets in English castles. As the Queen has been spending several weeks in Scotland, all England has followed after her, partly because the court etiquette and usage demand it, partly because it is not possible to settle down in the country at this moment, while there is so much disturbance and rioting. Everything here is doubly brilliant, except the sun, which is the same now as always; the winter is already approaching, and what will happen to me I don't yet know. I am writing at lord Torpichen's. In this castle, just underneath the room in which I write, J. Knox, the Scottish reformer, administered the first communion. Everything here speaks to the imagination: the park with secular trees, the precipices, the ruins of ancient keeps, endless corridors with countless likenesses of ancestors; they even speak of a certain red-capped ghost, which walks about the corridors at midnight. And I walk about in them with my doubts.

The cholera approaches; London is full of fogs and spleen, and in Paris there's no president, no president. But wherever I may betake my cough and my suffocation, my affection for you will remain the same. My respects to your worthy Mother, and heartiest wishes for happiness to all of you. Write a few words to the above address.

With all my heart yours
CHOPIN

I have played in Edinburgh; all the distinguished folk of the region assembled. They say it went off well. There was a little success and a little money. This year everyone has been in Scotland: Lind, Grisi, Alboni, Mario, Salvi.

267.

To WOJCIECH GRZYMAŁA.
London, 17–18 Oct[*ober 1848*].

MY LIFE!

I have been ill the last 18 days; ever since I reached London. I have not left the house at all, I have had such a cold and such headaches, short breath and all my bad symptoms. The doctor visits me every day (Dr. Mallan, a homeopath, well known here, and an acquaintance of my Scottish ladies; Lady Gainsborough is his sister-in-law. He stiffened me up so that I could play yesterday at that Polish concert and ball, which was very splendid); but though I left immediately after playing, I could not sleep all night. My head is very painful, apart from cough and suffocation. Up to now the thick fogs have not begun, but already, in spite of the cold, I am obliged to have the windows opened in the morning in order to breathe a little air. I am at 4 St. James's Place, where I have been laid up for 2½ weeks. I see the kind Szulcz[ewski], Broadwood, Mrs. Erskine (who followed me here with Miss Stirl[ing], as I wrote to you from Edinburgh), and especially Prince and Princess Alexander. Princess Marcellina also is so kind that she calls almost every day, as if at a hospital. Go on addressing to me at Szulczewski's. So now I can't get back to Paris, but I am considering how to manage it, so as to be there. I can't stay here, in this lodging, though it is all right for any ordinary, healthy bachelor or member of Parliament, and though it is in a fine situation, and not dear: 4½ guineas a week with heating, linen, etc., and close to lord Stuart. He has just left me; the good fellow called to know how I was after playing last night. Probably I shall move to another lodging near here, with larger rooms, in which I can breathe better. En tout cas.[1] Find out, please, whether there is anything on the boulevards, beginning from the *Rue de la Paix,* or Rue Royale; — somewhere on the first floor facing south towards the Madeleine, or in the *Rue des Mathurins.* Only not Godot, nor any dismal cramped place; and a little room for the valet. If it were in the *Square,* at No. 9 (where the good Mme Étienne is; for instance Frank's apartment, which was to let, above mine). The one I have now is impossible to [keep] for the winter; I know that already, from experience. If, at least, there can be a little room for the valet on the same floor. I would keep Mme Étienne just the same. But I should not like to give up my present man; if I wanted, or found it possible to return to England, he already knows his way about. Why, why am I bothering you with all this: — I don't know, for

[1] Any how.

I don't care about anything. But I suppose I have to think of my health, so help me out about it, and write me your view of the matter. I have never cursed anyone; but now my life is so unbearable that it seems to me it would give me relief if I could curse Lucrezia — But no doubt she also suffers, — suffers all the more because she will doubtless grow old in anger. I am endlessly sorry for Sol. The world is in a godless way now. Arago wearing an eagle! Representing France!!! Louis Blanc is not respected here at all. Causidier has been turned out by *national guards* from the *table d'hôte* of the hotel la Sablonnière (*Leicester Square*), when he approached it; they told him: *Vous n'êtes pas Français,* and drove him out with their fists. The landlord of the hotel was obliged to escort him across the Square, to prevent his getting knocked about, for the London rabble had begun to clench their fists. Thank Mlle de Rozières, but I won't write, I am too weak, and I haven't the strength to search; there's a letter from my sister (but I'm not sure, I think I sent it on long ago). If I could have a room somewhere upstairs for the valet, let me know, because it may be necessary to begin lighting fires at once. — But what am I going back for! Why should God kill me this way, not at once, but little by little and through the fever of indecision. Apart from all else, my kind Scottish ladies are boring me again. Mrs. Erskine, who is a very religious protestant, good soul, would perhaps like to make a protestant of me; she brings me the bible, talks about the soul, quotes the psalms to me; she is religious, poor thing, but she is greatly concerned about my soul. She is always telling me that the other world is better than this one; and I know all that by heart, and answer with quotations from Scripture, and explain that I understand and know about it. I embrace you heartily. Write, and forgive my being cross and impatient; I'm ill.

Yours till death

CH.

If I were well, with 2 lessons a day I should have enough to live comfortably here; but I'm weak; in 3 months, or 4 at outside, I shall eat up what I have.

If you should find any lodging, don't engage it without writing, or give notice at the old one —

268.

[In French]

To MLLE DE ROZIÈRES.

Keir, 20 Oct[*ober*] *1848. Perthshire.*

I thank you very much for your good letters, and am very sorry not to be able to give you as much pleasure with mine. You know my infirmity, that I can't put 2 words together without real suffering; so I count on your memory and believe myself pardoned. I have just had a word from Ludwika, who speaks tenderly of you. She writes to me that they are well in health; the cholera has spared them. The other parts of the letter are less consolatory. Did I not send to you from London a letter from Ludwika for you? I had one, I am sure, and (unless it has remained with my papers well locked up in London) it seems to me that I forwarded it to you. My Italian that was, did he, on leaving [? French incorrect], keep back out of curiosity the letter that I gave him to post? Anyhow, it will clear itself up. In any case, don't accuse Ludwika, because I know that I still have a word for you in London. I have had only 2 letters in all from Poland: one from Warsaw, and then this last one, written in the country, not far from Thorn, where Ludwika spent the summer with the children. What you tell me about Sol troubles me. I am really grieved about Luce. If Sol should ever go to Russia, with whom could she talk of France? And to whom could she say a word *en berrichon?* [1] That does not sound important. Well then, it is the greatest consolation in a strange land, to have someone who takes you back into your own country every time you look at them, whether you talk to them or they to you. And your travelling; why are you missing it? Unless perhaps you are not yet strong enough for your winter: that winter which I don't know

[1] In the dialect of Berry.

where to spend. I want to do the best, and I am sure I shall do the worst. But that is my fate. No one can escape his destiny. I suffocate better than I did a month ago in this beautiful land of Walter Scott. The Queen left Aberdeenshire yesterday. This year all England came to Scotland, as much to pay court to her Majesty as because there is no place on the continent that is left in peace. The place where I am staying at this moment is called *Keir*, in Perthshire, near Stirling. Tomorrow I go to Edinburgh, where I shall stay a few days; perhaps I may even be heard there. But don't suppose that this will give — apart from the occupation — anything except impatience and exhaustion; still, I find many persons here who appear to care for music; they torment me to play, and, out of politeness, I play, always with a fresh regret, swearing that no one will catch me again — If the weather were fine I would stay through October here, for I have invitations which I have not been able to answer, and life in the castles of the great here is really very curious. It is a thing unknown on the continent. If the weather is fine, I shall go to stay with the Duchess of Argyl [*sic*] at Inverary on Lake Line [*sic*], and also at Lady Belhaven's, one of the greatest houses in this country. She is here now, one of about thirty persons; some very handsome, some very witty, some very original, some very deaf; there is even an illustrious name (Sir Walpool) [*sic*], blind. Dresses, diamonds, pimples on the nose; the most beautiful hair, the most marvellous get-ups, the "beauty of the devil"[1] and the devil without beauty. The last category is the least rare everywhere. All this crowd is going to Edinburgh today for the *Caledonian Raut* [*sic*]. There will be races, amusements, balls, etc., all the week. It is the local fashionables, the sportsmen's club, which gives annual festivals. All the nobility of the land attends. Now I hope that is gossip enough. But indeed I don't know when I shall write you any more of it. I have to write to my folk now, and to Sol, to whom I have written 50 scraps. I scratch out more letters than I write, so it is not laziness. I hope to see you soon (here comes a ray of sunshine and makes me say that; it has only to hide and I shall be convinced of the contrary). Now, give me a good handshake, and write to me at the same address

[1] beauté du diable.

in Edinburgh; wherever I may be, the letter will find me. And Franchomme! I have not answered him, but it is impossible to write all I wish to write to my friends. All this is very stupid; I must finish, for if I tore up my letter the scratching out would continue.

Good day, and a thousand sincere good wishes.

Always yours faithfully,

CH.

I will write to Grzym.

269.

[A fragment]

To WOJCIECH GRZYMAŁA.
[*Hamilton Palace 21 Oct*[*ober 1848*].

. . . Art, here, means painting, sculpture and architecture. Music is not art and is not called art; and if you say an artist, an Englishman understands that as meaning a painter, architect or sculptor. Music is a profession, not an art, and no one speaks or writes of any musician as an artist, for in their language and customs it is something else than art; it is a *profession.* Ask any Englishman, and he will tell you so; and Neukomm assured me of it too. No doubt it is the fault of the musicians; but try to correct such things! These queer folk play for the sake of beauty, but to teach them decent things is a joke. Lady ——, one of the first great ladies here, in whose castle I spent a few days, is regarded here as a great musician. One day, after my piano, and after various songs by other Scottish ladies, they brought a kind of accordion, and she began with the utmost gravity to play on it the most atrocious tunes. What would you have? Every creature here seems to me to have a screw loose. Another lady, showing me her album, said to me: — "*La reine a regardé dedans et j'ai été à côté d'elle.*"[1] A third that she is — "*la 13me cousine*

[1] The queen looked in it, and I was beside her.

de Marie Stuart."[1] Another sang, standing up for the sake of originality, and accompanying herself on the piano, a French-English romance:—"*j'aie aiiemaiie* (*j'ai aimé*), *żej ajmej*"!!![2] The Princess of Parma told me that one lady whistled for her with a guitar accompaniment. Those who know my compositions ask me:—"*Jouez-moi votre second Soupir—j'aime beaucoup vos cloches.*"[3] And every observation ends with:—"*leik* [*sic*] *water*," meaning that it flows like water. I have not yet played to any Englishwoman without her saying to me:—*Leik water!!!* They all look at their hands, and play the wrong notes with much feeling. Eccentric folk, God help them.

[Here a caricature]

This is a certain lord in a *collar* and gaiters, stuttering.

[Here another caricature]

This one is a duke in high boots with spurs, deerskin breeches and a sort of dressing-gown over them.

270.

To the Same.
Edinburgh, 30 October [*1848*].

MY DEAREST LIFE!

Have you forgotten me, that you read into my letters—in which I wrote to you that I am progressively weaker, duller, without any hope, without a home:—to read in this, that I am going to get married? On the day on which I received your dear and good letter, I wrote a sort of instructions for the disposal of my bits of things if I should peg out here.

I have dragged about Scotland, but now it's too cold, and to-morrow I return to London, so lord Stuart writes to me, to play on the 16th at a concert which is to be given for the Poles, before the opening of the ball. On the way back from Hamilton

1 Mary Stuart's 13th cousin.
2 Polish spelling of English pronunciation of: "*J'ai aimé*": I have loved.
3 Play me your second Sigh—I love your bells.

Pallace [*sic*] (60 miles from here), where I stayed a few days at the duke of Hamilton's, I took a chill, and for five days have not been out. I am staying with Dr. Lyszcziński, who is treating me homeopathically, and I don't want to pay any more visits, for the cholera is just round the corner; and then, if I collapse, it will be for the whole winter. If the weather should improve, I should like to go back to Hamilton Pallace, and from there to the island of Ayran [*sic*] (which belongs entirely to them), to the princess of Baden, who has married their son, the Marquis of Duglas [*sic*]; but nothing will come of it. While I was there, they had, besides the great aristocrats of their own family and country, the duke and duchess of Parma; he is prince Luca; she is a sister of the duke of Bordeaux (a very gay young couple). They invited me to stay with them, at Kingston, when I return to London; for now they will live in England, since they were driven out of Italy. That is all right, but I am not fit for it now; and if I made haste to leave Hamilton, it was just because I can't sit at table from 8 till 10½ without pains such as Gutmann had (do you remember?); and in the morning, though I breakfasted in my room and came down late, and was carried on the stairs, all the same, it was too much for me. From Wishaw, from lady Belhaven's, where I stayed before going to Hamilton, I wrote to you before your letter arrived; but it was such a black, sulky letter that I did not send it to you.

After November 16th, if there is any improvement in your affairs, or —

[Remainder missing]

271.

[A fragment.]

To the Same.

[*London, November 1848.*]

. . . the London *fogs* are driving me out, so I am returning to Paris, if it is not too late for the journey.

My Scotswomen are kind; I have not seen them for two or three weeks, but they are coming today. They want me to stay, and go on dragging round the Scottish palaces, here and there and everywhere, as I am invited. They are kind, but so boring that the Lord preserve them! — Every day I get letters, and answer none of them; and wherever I go, they come after me if they can. Perhaps that has given someone the notion that I am getting married; but there really has to be some kind of physical *attrait*,[1] and the unmarried one [2] is too much like me. How could you kiss yourself —

Friendship is all very well, but gives no right to anything further. I have made that clear —

Even if I could fall in love with someone, as I should be glad to do, still I would not marry, for we should have nothing to eat and nowhere to live. And a rich woman expects a rich man, or if a poor man, at least not a sickly one, but one who is young and handsome. It's bad enough to go to pieces alone, but two together, that is the greatest misfortune. I may peg out in a hospital, but I won't leave a starving wife behind me.

Anyhow, I don't need to write you all this, for you know how I think — [crossed out]. So I don't think at all of a wife, but of home, of my Mother, my Sisters. May God keep them in His good thoughts. Meanwhile, what has become of my art? And my heart, where have I wasted it? [crossed out.] I scarcely remember any more, how they sing at home. That world slips away from me somehow; I forget, I have no more strength [crossed out]; if I rise a little, I fall again, lower than ever.

I am not complaining to you, but since you have asked, I explain to you that I am nearer to a coffin than to a marriage bed. My mind is fairly calm [crossed out].

Write me a line. Address: *Szulczewski, Esq., 10 Duke Street, St. James's.* Stuart's Polish literary society is there. I am not sending the fourth letter I have written to you, only a fragment of another, written in an impatient mood, so that you may know how cross I am sometimes.

Yours till death

CH.

[1] attraction.
[2] Miss Jane Stirling.

272.

To DR. LYSZCZYŃSKI IN EDINBURGH.
London, 3 November 1848.

Yesterday I received your kind letter, with a letter from Heidelberg. Here I am as incapable as I was with you, and also have the same affection for you as I had. My compliments to your Wife and your Neighbours. God bless you! I embrace you heartily. I have seen the Princess; they asked after you most affectionately.

At present I am staying at James Place, No. 4. If anything should come for me (by post), kindly send it to that address. Would you please forward the enclosed letter to Miss Stirling, who doubtless is still at Barnton.

273.

[In French]

To MLLE DE ROZIÈRES.
London, Monday, 19 Nov[*ember 1848*].

It is possible that I may be well enough to be able to travel this week and arrive in Paris *Thursday*, *Friday* or *Saturday* (travelling by express), for the English climate at this time of year is quite impossible for me, even according to the doctor, who is not your M. Curie. Since Nov. 1st I have been in my room, in my dressing-gown, and have been out only on the 16th, to play for my compatriots! Please be so kind as to give a look to No. 9, in case I arrive one of those days. Thanks in advance.

CH.

I have written to Grzym.; but as he may be travelling, and may receive my letter too late, I beg you to buy a *cord* of wood from Mme Étienne, and have hot fires made in my rooms, also have furniture and curtains well dusted, especially the bed curtains, for I think I shall have to handle them often. Also have the little alcoves of the bedroom well swept out at the corners. I am in rather a hurry to breathe better, to be able to understand people, and to see the faces of a few friends again.

CH.

274.

[In French]

To SOLANGE CLÉSINGER.
London, Wednesday, 22 [*November 1848*].

You accuse me very unjustly; there has not been a day when I have not tried to write to you. Even before the letter which I have just received, I thought of inquiring whether your husband could not find some work here; and I have taken particulars from persons who know London and its art, and this is what they tell me. Society (except employees, magistrates and lawyers) does not remain in town during the winter. The class which can be useful to your husband is here only in *March* and *April;* so there is nothing to do before the beginning of next season; though that is risky, it *is not impossible,* with certain good introductions; and in the course of one month's visit here, which need not be very expensive, your husband could see what to count on. I know several influential persons, who have promised me to be genuinely useful, but who could do nothing just now.

As for what is happening to you in Paris, it is possible that your Mother is doing her best for you, but that she has no money; that she will return to you the small objects bought apparently in view of this action; and that, once the house is sold, she will arrange your affairs on a fresh basis. She is, after all, your mother, and she knows her duty towards you. She may forget herself, but she cannot forget you.

Tomorrow I go to Paris, scarcely dragging myself, and weaker than you have ever seen me. The doctors are driving me away from here. I am swollen up with neuralgia, can neither breathe nor sleep, and have not left my room since November 1st (except the 16th, to play for an hour in the evening at the concert for the Poles). After that I relapsed; I cannot possibly breathe here; it is an inconceivable climate for persons like me, but only during these few winter months. They light up at 2 o'clock. I have promised to come back here next season!!! Sir J. Clark, the queen's doctor, came once to see me and to give me his *benediction.* So I shall groan in the Place d'Orléans till things get better. I advise you seriously to be very glad, having the good air of Guillery for your lungs, and your husband with you. He will come to you for the remainder of the good weather. As for Russia, the very influential persons who have given me letters for your husband for St. Petersburg, told me that it is very difficult for a Frenchman to penetrate there now without great protection. So don't be in a hurry to accuse Mme Obresk[off], and if England can provide him with work, I think he would make more money there and find it more comfortable. He will not have to fight against the climate, for he has lungs; and if he settles in London, he can prepare work in winter for the season. A little patience. It is possible that the permit for St. Petersburg will arrive. London now is *nothing* for the arts. It is the dead season. Everyone who is free lives outside, and what remains has little initiative for the success of a talent. For your husband's statue, fine as it may be, will need to be much praised to be considered fine at first sight. Afterwards people will say it is his, and everyone will admire it. Above all it is necessary that the royal Dukes and peers of England should think it good, and they are all in their castles, out of London.

Forgive the confusion of this letter; I am suffering much today. Don't ever misjudge my old and tried friendship.

CH.

275.

To WOJCIECH GRZYMAŁA.
[*London*] *Tuesday* [*November*[1] *1848*].

MY LIFE!

Today I have been in bed nearly all day, but on Thursday at this hour I leave this beastly London. I shall spend the night of Thursday to Friday at Boulogne, and on Friday, during the day, shall arrive at the *Place d'Orléans* and go to bed. Besides the usual things, I have neuralgia, and am all swollen up. Please ask that the sheets and pillows may be *dry*. Have some *pine-cones* got in. Ask Mme Étienne to spare nothing, so that I may get warm on arriving. I have written to Derozierka. Have the carpets and curtains in place. I will at once *pay* the upholsterer, Perrichet; even tell Pleyel to send me some kind of piano by Thursday evening, and have it covered over. Have a bunch of violets bought on Friday, so that the sitting-room may smell sweet. I want to meet with a little poetry on my return, — passing through the sitting-room to the bedroom, where I shall doubtless be laid up for long. So, Friday, in the middle of the day, I reach Paris. One more day here, and I should, not die, but *go mad*. My Scottish ladies are so boring, — may the hand of the Lord preserve them! They have fastened on to me, — there's no getting away! It's only Princess Marcellina, and her family, and the good Szulczewski, that keep me alive. If only there were a little room for the valet, even on another staircase; — but if not, never mind. I embrace you. Tell them to make fires, warm and dust the rooms, — perhaps I shall still come to myself. Yours till death.

CH.

[1] Princess Marcellina Czartoryska marked this letter as dating from March; an obvious mistake.

276.

[In French]

To SOLANGE CLÉSINGER.
Paris, Tuesday, 30 January [*18*]*49.*

I have been too ill all these last days to write to you and tell you that I have seen your husband. He came to see me Friday, and I found him well and preparing to work on a statue of *Truth.* Yesterday he wrote me a little line to tell me that he was already starting work. He gave me good news of you; told me that you have all the courage possible in your new state of figure. Here we have March weather, and I have to lie down ten times a day. Molin knew the secret of how to liven me up. Since then I have seen M. Louis, Dr. Roth, during two months; and now M. Simon, a great reputation among the homeopaths; but they just sound me and give no relief. They all agree about climate, peaceful life, rest. Rest, — I shall get it one day without them. The calm of Paris has not been disturbed for one moment during these last days, — though some disorder was expected, — thanks to the *gardes mobiles,* for whom regulations have been made, or on account of the ministerial project for the suppression of the clubs. Yesterday, Monday, there were soldiers and cannon everywhere, and this firm attitude has greatly impressed those who would have liked to cause disorder. Even I am writing about politics to you, instead of telling you more amusing things. But I am becoming stupider than ever, and I attribute it to the *cacao* which I take every morning instead of my *coffee.* Don't ever take cacao, and prevent your friends from taking it, especially if you are in correspondence with them. I will try to make my next letter very intelligent, after the *sulphate* of something which M. Simon will give me to sniff. Meanwhile, read this scribble, as it gives you news of the health and courage of your husband. Mme Obreskoff came to see me yesterday but I had B—on Stockhausen, Legouvé, and others, before whom I did not wish to speak of Petersburg — you know how kind she is, and how talkative. If you write me a line about your health, it will not be waste of time.

Happiness, health, health —

CH.

277.

To the Same.
Paris, Thursday, 5 Apr[*il 1849*].

I have seen Mme Obreskoff, who has no message to send you. I think the political horizon is clouding over more and more on that side, and what was difficult a month ago will be more so now. I learn from Mlle de Rozières that you are well. God keep you in this good health. There, now I'm at the end of my Latin.[1] I have got to my 4th doctor. They charge me 10 fr. a visit, come sometimes twice a day, and all that gives me very little help.

Saturday.

Your husband has just come to see me, before I had time to finish my letter. He looks well, and greatly pleased me by giving me good news of your health. One can't have everything in this world; be content with the greatest of joys: health. Your husband expects to go to London, and I think he is right. It is not impossible that he may have a great success there.

I shall not fail to be of as much use as I can in the matter of information and letters for London. Have no doubts.

278.

To the Same.
[*Paris*] *Friday, 13 April* [*1849*].

I send you all this scribble to let you see that it is not laziness, but weakness, or something of the sort, which keeps me from

[1] at the end of my resources.

writing to you. Your husband is well, he came to see me again yesterday, and told me that he is to be introduced to the president on Monday; he has courage, plenty of it; he has also been to see Delacroix (who has spoken to me of a bust which someone wanted your husband to make). Luck is *never the same* in this world, as M. de la Palisse would say; I have no conversation left any more, except axioms of this kind, so forgive me if I tell them to you. Thus, for inst., I hope that the *spring sunshine* will be my best doctor. One has to add *spring*, because at the opera, in the Prophet, they are preparing a sun which is said to be more marvellous than any in the tropics. It only rises, and does not last long, but it is so powerful that it puts everything in the shade except the music. It is made of sheaves of electric light. I was too ill to attend the rehearsal the day before yesterday, but am counting on the first performance, which is to be next Monday. There is a great deal of talk about a skating-match (skaters on rollers); wonders are related about a fire, about the fine scene-painting, and about Mme Viardot, who, in the mother's part, is to make everybody weep. Now I'm beginning to scratch out again. Please give me news of you when you can. Profit by your climate. Paris is frightful. 36 kinds of weather, plenty of mud, draughts in the room. Nothing goes; for the moment, everything is disgusting.

Your affectionate

CH.

279.

To the Same.
[*Paris, May 1849.*]

An unhappy friend blesses you and blesses your child. We must hope that the future [holds] for you the promise of other favours and consolations. Youth is an obligation; that is to say, you have an absolute duty to be happy and to preserve a good memory of yourself for one who loves you.

CH.

280.

To Wojciech Grzymała.
Monday, 18 [June 1849.]

How are you? I suppose the country is at least physically benefiting you. I do not go out, except sometimes to the Bois de Boulogne. I am stronger, for I have been eating and have dropped the medicaments; but I gasp and cough just the same, only I bear it better. I have not yet begun to play, I can't compose, — I don't know what hay I shall be eating [1] before long. Everyone is leaving; some from fear of cholera, some from fear of revolution. Mlle de Rozières was also frightened away to Versailles, but has come back. The Englishwomen are at St. Germain, Obreskoff at St. Germain. Pot[ocki] is at Versailles; I have not seen him for a long time. I have even been without a nurse for over a week. Princess Czar[toryska] came to see me; and, not wishing me to be alone at night, is sending me Pani Matuszewska, who was Princess Róża's nursemaid. The Prince also called and asked after you. I don't know whether you told anyone to say that you were at the waters; but, not knowing that, I told him you had gone to the country, and he said he had been told you were taking the waters. Kalkbrenner is dead. De la Roche's elder son has died in Versailles. Franchomme's very good maidservant has died. There have been no end of deaths in the *Cours d'Orléans,* only little Étienne was dangerously ill. The Scottish ladies have just come. Among other news they told me Noalek [2] is better, and I replied that King Ch. Albert has died in Lisbon. They stifle me with boredom. I shall leave my lodging at the end of the month and return to the Square, because it is not possible otherwise. Cochet has come back. I can't find out from my Dr. Frenkel, whether to go to some watering-place, or to go south. He has again withdrawn his *tisane,*[3] and given me another medicament, and again, I don't want it. When I ask him about *hygiene,* he answers that a regular régime is not

1 A Polish idiom.
2 The Duke of Noailles: an affectionate Polish diminutive.
3 infusion.

necessary for me. In short, an empty pate. Joking apart, he may be a very good consultant; as good as, for instance, Koreff — but he has no sequence in his mind as Koreff has. Miss Lind came, she sang one evening at my place; Pani Pot[ocka] was there, Beauv[eau], Rotsch[ild]; she has already left for Sweden by way of Hamb[urg]. Mme Catalani, whom I met here on the eve of her departure, has died of cholera. I have seen Cichowski only once, as I wrote to you — It is a long way to town; only those who love me very much, as, for inst., Franch[omme], or those who have close friends near by, as, for inst., the Prince and Princess, occasionally call. Today Pleyel came too; — he's a good fellow! Gutman, for all his good intentions, has not been seen for 10 days; I began to fear he must be ill, — but he writes that he is well. The disease is already abating in the city. Delacroix has been in the country for a week. Let me have a line about yourself. I embrace you heartily.

Your

CH.

Monday, 18 [*June*].

281.

To the Same.

[*Chaillot*] *Friday, 22 June* [*1849*].

How are you? Write me a line. I wrote to you a few days ago through Ludw[ika?]. Probably they have not yet sent on the letter to you. Today I saw Cichowski and Princess Sapieha. She did not ask after you. At the door, Cichowski told me that he knows about your misfortunes (of which I had not spoken to him). He had nothing to say to me about you, nor I to him. But from Zaleski I learn that Pani Plichcina is going to Warsaw in 10 days' time; perhaps she could be useful to you in some way. Find out about it. Cochet, who came today with Lumirski [Lubomirski?], could tell me nothing about your son, as he has not been in Warsaw. So (of course!!!) he has not seen him. Everyone is leaving here. I have not seen either Pani Potocka or Princess Beauveau for 10 days. They are in Versailles. I have had two hæmorrhages during this last night. But I have done nothing about it; I just spit blood, but already much less. That was what brought Princess Sap[ieha] to me, for the Polish woman who looks after me at night told her about it. My Jew, Frenkel, has not come for a week; at the end he even left off putting *papers* into the *urine*, only talked to me about some Englishman whom he saved from cholera by means of some medicine which the *reactionary* French government (Fauchet) will not have him asked to introduce. So I am left to myself, and perhaps may crawl out all the quicker. I shall doubtless return to the Square next month.

Virg [?] came to tell me that she is going with her Deputy to Brit[tany]. She asked for news of you; I had nothing to say. Don't come back if you can get through the hot weather there in tolerable health and comfort. No doubt your Adone and Cich[owski] will arrange your affairs all right for you, so that when you come back you will be less worried.

I must stop; it's misery for me to write, even to you. So many things don't get over the pen.

Your old one.

Mme Obreskow [*sic*], who came here yesterday from St. Germain, asked about the General, and is angry that he is remaining so long in that country place and so far away. I told her that you had returned and had been obliged to go again.

282.

To LUDWIKA JÉDRZEJEWICZ.
[*Paris*] *Monday, 25 June 1849.*

MY LIFE.

If you can, do come [plural]. I am ill, and no doctor will help me as much as some of you. If you are short of money, borrow some; if I get better, I can easily earn and repay the lender; but just now I am stripped too bare to send you any. My lodging here in Chaillot is fairly big, and could accommodate you, with 2 children. Little Ludka would profit by it in every way. Kalasanty the father could run about all day — the exhibition of produce is close by — in short, he would have more free time for himself than he had before, for I am weaker and shall sit at home with Ludwika.

My friends and well-wishers think the best medicine for me will be Ludwika's presence here, as Ludwika will doubtless see from Mme Ob[reskoff's] letter. So try for a passport. I heard today from two persons, one from the north, the other from the south, that people who don't know Ludwika have said that it would be good not only for me, but for my sister too. So, mother Ludwika and daughter Ludwika, bring your thimbles and knitting-needles, and I will give you handkerchiefs to mark and stockings to knit, and you can spend two or three months in the fresh air with your old brother and uncle. The journey is easier now. You don't need much luggage. Here we will manage as cheaply as we can. Even if it is sometimes far for Kalasanty from the Champs d'Élysées to the city, he can stay in my lodging in the Square d'Orléans. The omnibuses go from the square, right to this very door. I don't myself know why I want Ludwika so much, but it's as if it would give me hope. I guarantee that it will be good for her too. I hope the family council will send her to me; who knows whether I won't return with her, if I recover. We should then all embrace each other, as I wrote to you, only still with teeth in our heads and no wigs. Wives ought always to obey their husbands, so the husband must be asked to bring his wife. So I beg him to do it; and if he considers, he can give no greater pleasure and benefit to her, or to me, or even to the children, if he brings any of them (I have no doubt about the daughterkin). It will cost money, that is true, but that could not be better spent, nor could one travel more cheaply. Once here, we can find a shelter. Write me a line soon. Mme Ob., who was so kind as to offer to write (I have given her Ludwika's address), may be better able to convince you. Mlle de Rozières also will add a letter, and Cochet also has probably done so, for he certainly did not find me recovered. His Esculapius has not called for 10 days; he has probably guessed, at last, that there is something beyond his science here. All the same, praise him up well to your lodger and to others who know him, and say that he did me a lot of good, but that I am the sort of person who is satisfied the moment he gets a little better; that everyone regards him as having cured many persons here of cholera. The cholera is abating fast; it is almost gone. Today the weather is fine, so I sit in the sitting-room and admire my view over all Paris: the towers, the Tuileries, the Chamber of Deputies, St. Germ[ain] l'Aux[errois], St. Étienne du Mont, Notre Dame, the Panthéon, St. Sulpice, Val de Grace, the Invalides; from 5 windows, and nothing but gardens between. You will see when you come. Now about passport and money; begin soon, as it takes time. Write me a line at once. You know, " even cypresses have their caprices "; my caprice now is to see you. Perhaps God will allow things to come right; and if God doesn't, then at least act as if He would allow it. I have good hope of it, for I seldom demand much, and would refrain from asking this if I were not pressed by everyone who wishes me well. Hurry, Mr. Kalasanty, and I will give you a large and excellent cigar for it; I know a person who loves to smoke; but in the garden. I hope my letter for Mummy's name-day came in time, so that she did not miss me. I don't want to think about all this or I shall have fever; I am not feverish, thank the Lord; which confuses and annoys all ordinary doctors.

Your affectionate, but sick brother

CH.

26 June.

283.

To WOJCIECH GRZYMAŁA.
Chaillot, 74. [*1849*].

MY LIFE

Yesterday Cich[owski] came to me, the second time since you left (because I wrote to him about the watch); he said that he had given the letter to Orda, and that if possible, he will hurry matters. The tailor has consented to an agreement. He also told me that Pani *Plichcina* is going home — that he wrote to you about it, and also that my *sister* is coming; *which is quite untrue,* for it was only today that I decided to write home about it. But you *know* his news. Pani Pot. is still in Versailles, and goes to Dieppe, to Mme Beauveau. Delacroix is in the country. Gutm. is in London (incognito), as if he had money to throw away; the Englishwomen are at St. Germain, Mme Obresk. also. It is good that you have had news of your son, for Cochet did not see him. Frenkel has not been here for two weeks. I have not spat blood since the day before yesterday, — my legs are swollen, — but I'm still weak and lazy, I can't go upstairs, I suffocate. And your staircase!! I am sorry not to see you, but I would rather you were in the country now than here, when it is so dull and everyone is away.

I am writing to you at Pani Ludw.'s for the 3rd time since I have lost your *garde malade.*[1] I don't know what to do with her, how to thank her. I don't want to send to her there, for there is a guardian, or some such person. She came here to say that she is going away; but someone came in, and before I had a chance to talk to her, she had slipped out. She sent me her visiting-card. She is good and kind, but I don't understand that card. I hope she will call again before she leaves for Brittany. I should not like to send there, because the Deput [?] knows nothing about me, and I fear to cause her unintentional unpleasantness. Keep well, look after yourself and don't give up. I also defend myself, as I can; but probably I shall not be strong enough. Pani Matuszewska, who was with Princess Róża (and whom Princess Anna sent to me so that I should not be alone at night), says that " the Lord Jesus will put it right, you know "; and perhaps a *plaster with honey* and starch might help.

[*Paris*] *2 July, Monday* [*1849*].

[1] sicknurse.

284.

[In French]

To Solange Clésinger.
Paris, Wednesday, 4 July 1849.

Thanks for your good letter. I have received a line from M. Bouscinat at your order, for my carriage, but a recent blood-spitting changes my travelling plans for the moment. It is possible that the Emperor, who is at Warsaw now, may give my sister permission to come to see me; only then, after a thorough examination, shall I know whether I must leave Paris, or whether I can no longer endure long journeys and must stay here. Don't let us talk any more about me. I was glad to see that you reached Bordeaux without fatigue; but this does not prove that you need not take care of yourself. I imagine your little girl with a big head, laughing, crying, noisy, slobbering, biting, and all the rest. You two must be very amusing together. When shall you make her begin to ride on horseback? I hope that now you have enough to do all the time, and that you wish there were twice as many hours in the day and night, even though the little Gascon girl wakes you so often. I start to scratch out again. I have nothing more to write to you, except that, as you have long known, I wish you all possible happiness. The cholera is abating, but, according to what I am told, Paris is becoming more and more deserted. It is hot here, and dusty. There is *poverty,* and *dirt,* and one sees faces that belong to the other world. They are all like Crémieux; even Bignat is said to be growing ugly. D'Arpentigny, however, is blond, and grows handsomer. The exhibition is not well spoken of. Delacroix was in the country for some weeks; he is not very well, perhaps he will go to Aix-la-Chapelle. I am delighted to know that you are in your beautiful district. This is no time to be in a city. Be good enough to write me a few words when your daughter gives you a moment's peace, to keep me informed of the health of *all* of you, now that the family has increased by so large a unit.

Be happy, all of you.

Ch.

285.

To Wojciech Grzymała.
[*Chaillot*] *Tuesday, 10 July* [*18*]*49.*

I am very weak, my Life. I have some sort of diarrhœa. Yesterday I consulted Cruveille, who advises me to take almost nothing, and just keep still. He said that if homeopathy had done me good in Molin's time, that was because it did not overload me with medicaments and left much to nature. But I see that he also regards me as consumptive, for he ordered a teaspoonful of something with *lichen* in it. So, as I can't travel, I have written to Plichcina; in any case he was to come to me. I have also written to Orda. He has not yet answered. I also send on to you a letter which has come here for you from Germany. Pani Brzozowska (born Zamoyska) has taken the lodging above mine. The Zamoyskis have gone to Billancourt. This way I shall probably see the Prince and Princess oftener, till they leave for Trouville, where they are going. Princess Marcellina is in London, for she was ordered to leave Vienna, or at least given to understand so. I have not seen Cichowski for two weeks. Pani Potocka is in Versailles; later she will probably go to Spa. It is hot here. I have no news yet from my sister. I shall stay here this month, but if my sister does not come, I shall go, for everything is too dear here. I play less and less; I can't write anything.

Keep well. Work at your pamphlet; don't give way either to grief or to boredom. You have lived through so much. God grant you strength for the rest.

Your
Ch.

286.

To the Same.
Chaillot, Saturday, 28 July [1849].

After your answer and her letter I just gave up. I didn't know whether to suspect her of hallucinations, or her messenger of theft, or whether to condemn Mme Étienne, or to regard myself as forgetful or crazy; in short, my head went round.

She came to me with a confession, and told everything so stupidly, and her sister apparently knew nothing about it. I was finally obliged to tell her the truth, that I could not understand such munificent gifts from anyone, unless perhaps the Queen of England or Miss Coutt [Coutts?]. But that's how it is. The personage to whom such a sum was entrusted without his knowledge, and who took no receipt from Mme Étienne for the letter (or parcel), went to Alexis Somnambul.[1] Here the drama begins:

Alexis tells him that on a Thursday in March (the 8th) he took some very important papers, addressed — (he wrote down my address); that the packet never arrived *à sa destination;* [2] that he has not got it, that he gave it up, in some kind of small dark room, to which one goes down 2 steps, to some woman (there were two of them, and the *taller* one took it); that she had in her hand a letter, which the postman had given to her; that, taking the letter in question from this person, she told him that she would at once deliver it; but, Alexis added, she carried it downstairs, without even showing it to me, and I never saw the letter. When he was asked whether he could not see what had been done with the letter, he answered that he could not see, but that if anyone would bring him some hair, or a handkerchief, or gloves, belonging to the person who received the letter, he could tell. Mrs. Erskine was present at the séance at Alexis's, and came yesterday to tell me about it, and to ask me how to get hold of something belonging to Mme Étienne, so as to give it to Alexis. I got Mme Étienne to come to me, on a pretext of bringing me Boist and some handkerchiefs; and when she came I said — as if I

[1] A clairvoyant.
[2] at its destination.

wanted to get rid of Mrs. Erskine, who was supposed to be asking for a lock of my hair for a clairvoyante who cures sick people in St. Germain (where the Scottish ladies are now living) — I said, as if I were trying to get out of it, that I would send her some of Mme Étienne's hair, and if she could tell whose it was, I would believe in her and send my own, but that I was convinced she would take the well person's hair for the invalid's. So, at my request, Mme Étienne cut off a lock of her hair and wrapped it up, and Mrs. Erskine took it away.

This morning the messenger came to me with Mrs. Erskine, from Alexis. Alexis had recognized the hair of the person to whom the packet was given. He said that she had put the sealed packet into a small piece of furniture beside her bed, that the packet was still there and not lost, or delivered, or opened. That if the man goes about it tactfully, she will give it up to him, but that care is necessary. So then this man went straight from me, at noon, to the *Square d'Orléans,* found Mme Étienne alone, reminded her that in March he had called and given her a packet for me, which he had told her was very important. She recognized him, and gave him back the packet, which he had given to her all those months back. It had not been *unsealed,* and inside were 25 thousands, *untouched.* At my lodging Mrs. Erskine opened it in his and my presence. What do you think of it? That *clairvoyant!!!* The packet lying so long untouched!! Such queer occurrences make my head swim. You may take notice that I did not accept the *donation;* and that is enough about the matter, in writing. Some day I will tell you more.

Now, believe in magnetism.

It's by God's grace that it was found. There are many details that I don't write to you, for my pen burns.

And now about something else — Princess Sapieha, Izia and Władzio went to Dieppe today. The Princess of Wirtemb. remains. Plichcina is doubtless already in Warsaw.

I begin to doubt about my sister. I am no worse, and no better. I love you, and I wish I could see you.

I embrace you.

Yours.

Write.
Nothing new about Orda.

287.

To the Same.
[*Chaillot*] *Friday, 3 August* [*1849*].

You would not believe how I long to see you for just one hour; but I can't ask you to crawl out of your hole, for, although it is not 200, but only about a score of the Democratic Society who have been ordered to leave (and not one whom I have even known), still, it is a delicate matter, if you are afraid.

As for my personal affair, there are many details which I cannot make fit in, either with magnetism, or with lying or *hallucinations* (Miss St.), or with the honesty of Mme Étienne. It is even possible *que la chose a été faite après coup.*[1] About that there is a lot to tell; among other things, that another anonymous letter was sent to me, which I gave into the writer's hands. I have not spoken a word about the whole matter with Mme Étienne, and shall not do so, though it is a week ago tomorrow. The letter may have been given to her 3 days before; as I was not in the house, and she was here, I could have had it just as well without as with a clairvoyant. All the more, as various conversations coincide!! There is kindheartedness there, — but what showing off! I wish I could see you.

Clésinger brought Solange here, without money, and after a 10-day journey in the heat with the *baby and wetnurse,* at a moment when everyone is fleeing from here to the country! Where his brains are, I don't know!! No head; or rather, a very nasty head! De Rozières is not here; she is at the waters in Belgium with Mme Grille. Sol, therefore, goes about looking for a lodging. He wants to find something near Chaillot; it's amazing, what a fool he is!

Except Franch. and Herbeault, everyone is out of town. Mme Obreskow is in St. Germain, she always comes to see me on Mondays. I drink Bonnes water. My sister still has no permit. Later it will be useless, for his vacation will be over. I gasp, cough

[1] that the thing was got up afterwards.

and am drowsy; I do nothing, I want nothing. That Alexis sticks in my head.

Your
Ch.

I have not seen Cichota [Cichowski?] for two weeks. Of Virg. I know nothing. Orda has not sold the watch. He gave it to Cich. Those to whom he finally offered it, disputed its authenticity. They looked in the books at Breget's; it is not mentioned. Your other affairs are doubtless patched up since then.

Princess Sapieha and the old Prince came to me yesterday evening. The Princess, Izia and Władzio are at Dieppe, and well.

288.

[In French]

To Mlle de Rozières.
Paris, 14 August 1849.

My sister and Jędrz[iejewicz] and my niece have been with me for 5 days now. I am very tired. They too. I wish you as much happiness as I have at this moment, with a little more health, for I am weaker than ever.

Your sincere friend
Ch.

My respects to M. Gr — de Baulin.

289.

[Polish translation from French]

To AUGUSTE FRANCHOMME IN PARIS.
[*Chaillot, August 1849.*]

MY DEAR.

Send me a little of your Bordeaux. I have to drink a little wine nowadays, and I have none. But wrap up the bottle, and put your own seal on it, for these messengers!! And I don't know to whom to entrust this message. How suspicious I have grown!

Wholly yours,

C.

290.

To TYTUS WOJCIECHOWSKI IN CARLSBAD.
Paris, 20 August 1849. Square d'Orléans. Rue St. Lazare 9.

MY DEAREST ONE!

It just needs for me to be as weak as this, and not able to move from Paris, when you are coming to Ostend. But I hope the Lord will allow you to come nearer to me. The doctors do not allow me to travel at all. I drink Pyrenean waters in my room, and your presence would do more for me than all physic.

Yours till death

FRYDERYK.

291.

To NAPOLEON ORDA.
Grande Rue Chaillot, 74 [*undated*].

MY DEAR!

Grzymała is in such haste over his business about the watch of which Cichowski spoke to you, that he has written to me, asking me to adjure you, by all the sharps and flats that ever existed or could exist between us, to hurry about it. As you know, it cost 900 fr. He does not want to wait, so he is not trying to get more; he even writes that you can sell it cheaper, if only you can get the matter settled quickly. My Dear, do your utmost, for our old friendship's sake. In return for that, the Lord will take excellent care of a good Lithuanian, and give Pani Orda a hundred years of health. Meanwhile, please, give her my respects.

I embrace you more feebly than of old, but from the same heart as of old.

Your
CH.

292.

To TYTUS WOJCIECHOWSKI IN OSTEND.
Paris, 12 September 1849.

There has not been time enough to try for a permit for you to come here; I can't go out to see to it myself, as I spend half the day in bed, so I asked an influential friend to help me out. I shan't know anything for certain till Saturday. I wanted to go abroad, to Valenciennes, by train, to embrace you; but a few days ago I was not able to get as far as Ville d'Avraye, near Versailles, to my goddaughter, and the doctors will not let me leave Paris. It's my fault, for being ill; — otherwise I would have met you somewhere in Belgium.

Perhaps you will manage to get here. I am not selfish enough to demand that you should come here for me; I am so weak that you would have only a few hours of boredom and disappointment, alternating with a few hours of pleasure and good memories; and I should like the time that we spend together to be only a time of complete happiness.

Yours always
FRYDERYK.

293.

[Polish translation from French]

To Auguste Franchomme in Paris.

[*Chaillot*] *Sunday, after your departure, 17 September 1849.*

Dear Friend!

I am very sorry that you were not well at Le Mans. But now you are in Touraine, where the sunshine will doubtless improve your health. As for me, I am rather worse than better. MM. Cruveille, Louis and Blache have had a consultation, and have pronounced that I am not to travel, but to take a lodging with south windows and stay in Paris. After much searching, one has been found for me at last, very expensive, it is true, but satisfactory in every respect: *Place Vendôme*, No. 12. Albrecht has his office there at this moment, Meara has been very helpful about finding the place. In short, during the coming winter I shall see you all from under excellent conditions. My sister will remain with me, unless she should be urgently sent for to go home. I love you, and for this time that is all I can tell you, for I am ready to faint from fatigue and weakness. My sister is glad that she will see Mme Franchomme again; and I too am equally glad. May the will of heaven be done — My best greetings to Mr. and Mrs. Forest. How I should like to spend a few days with you all. Is Mme de Lauvergeat also staying by the sea? Don't forget to greet her from me when you see her, and her husband too. Embrace your babes, and write me a line.

Always yours

Ch.

My sister sends a kiss to Mme Franchomme.

294.

[In French]

[The last words which Chopin wrote, in pencil, on a sheet of letter paper.]

As this cough will choke me, I implore you to have my body opened, so that I may not be buried alive.

INDEX